Marilyn Waring
The Political Years

BRIDGET WILLIAMS BOOKS

First published in 2019 by Bridget Williams Books Ltd, PO Box 12474, Wellington 6144, New Zealand

ISBN 9781988545936 (Paperback), ISBN 9781988545905 (EPUB)
ISBN 9781988545912 (Kindle), ISBN 9781988545929 (PDF)
DOI https://doi.org/10.7810/9781988545936

Acknowledgements
The publishers would like to acknowledge the ongoing support of the BWB Publishing Trust, which enables all BWB publications. The commitment of Creative New Zealand to good New Zealand publishing is also acknowledged, and its support for this publication is appreciated.

Front cover image
The National Party caucus in 1979, standing on steps inside the Beehive, Parliament Buildings. The front row is Prime Minister Robert Muldoon (left) and Deputy Prime Minister Brian Talboys (right); Marilyn Waring stands behind them (second from left) – the only woman. Photograph by Ray Pigney, Stuff Ltd/ Alexander Turnbull Library, EP-Politics-National Party, from 1973-01

A catalogue record for this book is available from the National Library of New Zealand. Kei te pātengi raraunga o Te Puna Mātauranga o Aotearoa te whakarārangi o tēnei pukapuka.

Edited by Jane Parkin
Cover and internal design by Jo Bailey
Typesetting by Tina Delceg
Printed by Printlink, Wellington

Marilyn Waring The Political Years

For all those who wrote or said a kind word of support, care or encouragement in these nine years – thank you. This story is for you.

Contents

Preface

I was a Member of the New Zealand Parliament from 1975 to 1984. Every day my office was awash with documents. Fortunately for this account of those years, Jim Traue, from the Alexander Turnbull Library, asked if the library could collect my papers. 'We do not collect MPs' archives as a matter of course,' he told me, but he judged that my collection would be different from the mainstream. I agreed, and at the end of each year filled the cartons and file boxes that arrived from the library.

After I left Parliament, I didn't return to its buildings for more than 25 years. I didn't forget about the boxes. And I collected and read a good number of autobiographies by former women politicians. When I visited in 2010 to assess what was in the archive, there were close to 400 cartons and file boxes containing the papers that had crossed my desk between 1975 and 1984.

It was then I began testing the idea that I was not angry any more, and could think about writing about my experience of that decade using those archives. Autobiography would be the vehicle to tell this story – but how, precisely? I had been embedded in an all-consuming relationship with power in a complex male world with its rules, language, architecture and practices. I had another way of being and seeing in the dominant culture of the environment. This was a challenge I would accept for my writing.

Obviously I am a different woman from my younger self. The woman telling the story is not the young woman who lived it. Just as I changed in those years in Parliament, I have also kept moving over the nine years of research and writing. The older woman has selected what to tell of the young woman's life.

I decided I would let the chronological, multi-layered archive drive the story. Mine was not a simple, uni-dimensional life, and this would not be a tidy narrative ride. The reader would have to travel on my shoulder, to experience how it was 'being' in that environment and trying to survive. To sustain authenticity, the style and pace of the writing had to mirror the real-world content.

Parliamentary debates and proceedings are in the public record. There is an extraordinarily rich texture of material in the thousands of letters and submissions I received in those nine years in Parliament, and in what I preserved on the key issues. In the boxes were all select and caucus committee papers, National Party electorate material from Raglan and Waipā, and some photos. I also accessed the Parliamentary Library's 'vertical file' of press clippings held on me from those years. A National MP is entitled to access the Party's Dominion Council and Dominion Executive minutes for the years they were in office, and I used this privilege, too.

At every caucus meeting from 1975 to 1984 I handwrote extensive notes. This was 'out of order' but I did it anyway. The quotes in the text that do not carry endnotes are from this source. To avoid any accusation that I have attributed comments or behaviours based solely on my notes, I have checked these against the caucus minutes for the relevant years. For the six meetings where I was not present I have relied solely on these minutes.

I had retained my diaries from 1975 to 1984. Their focus was limited to where I had to be and when, outside of parliamentary and select committee attendance. These diaries have been augmented by detailed records generated by my electorate campaign committees in 1978 and 1981.

My own letters to my electorate, especially when travelling, as well as transcripts of media interviews, contribute to descriptions about how I was 'feeling' in those years – a focus of writers on feminist autobiography. Reading the evidence of my actions and reflections I realise I have forgotten much of what I was feeling from moment to moment in a hyper-vigilant environment. But for the most traumatic moments, I retain visceral memories.

I do remember Parliament was a constant place of battle to remain true to myself. All of this experience altered me. Holding the office equalled complicity, not just in the decisions that were made by the government but also in the processes of Parliament. Every morning on waking it was still all there: my self-contempt, others' expectations, the need to stay there, and trying to be stoic. I have exercised a good dose of self-forgiveness as I worked through the archive. In the context of New Zealand in the late 1970s and early 1980s, mine was an extreme and dramatic experience. The incidents speak for themselves.

A key question the feminist academic commentators on autobiography have is: what functions will this autobiography serve? I could say that it challenges the dominant 'history' of that period; it breaks a silence and challenges patriarchal amnesia; that I have tried to make it not about me, but about us. But after 400 boxes of evidence, when I read Grace Paley's description of Christa Wolf's *Cassandra*, I recognised my young self, and what we were doing here: 'She can't do much, but she can *see*. That is her task on earth, to see, to teach seeing, to tell.'[1]

Marilyn Waring, 2019

1975

In 1974, it was my habit to go to the library at Victoria University of Wellington, in New Zealand's capital, to read each morning's newspaper. On 9 July the *Dominion* front page covered Labour Prime Minister Norman Kirk's reaction to Opposition National Party MP Venn Young's plan to bring to parliament a Private Member's Bill to decriminalise homosexuality.[1] Kirk said he would not vote for any legislation that treated homosexuality as 'normal behaviour'. I got up from that table, walked downtown to the Wellington headquarters of the New Zealand National Party, and paid to join the Young Nationals.

That year, I had joined the Women's Electoral Lobby (WEL). In Wellington, this was a very energetic, innovative organisation, with a cross-section of women activists whom I found inspirational and wise. I was a quiet, attentive attender of meetings, and each time learned more about the issues of concern. It was a good environment for this. The first ever parliamentary Select Committee on Women's Rights had reported in 1974.[2] 1975 was declared the first United Nations International Women's Year (IWY). And there was to be a national parliamentary election in late 1975. At one evening meeting early that year, replies to correspondence addressed to three political parties – Labour, National and Social Credit – were read to those attending. Each party had been asked what it was doing to increase the number of women candidates for the 1975 election. All had answered that women had an equal opportunity to be candidates, and that parties would love to have more of them, but women simply did not offer themselves for selection in high enough numbers. I didn't believe this for a moment. It seemed to me that if enough women sought election, even if they lost, this was one line that could be removed from the catalogue of excuses.

Labour Prime Minister Norman Kirk died on 31 August 1974, and the state funeral took place in early September, the week I took up a part-time position in the Opposition Research Unit in New Zealand's Parliament, working on housing, fishing and women. I was fortunate to be assigned to George Gair, National's spokesman on housing.

The 1972–75 National Opposition had not had a woman in their caucus.[3] George understood this was not a good situation, especially given the range of views needed for developing election policies. Others in the Party also saw that the absence of women would be a public relations disaster in an election campaign in IWY. In early 1975 National had not even selected a woman candidate for a safe seat in the upcoming election. There was one chance left to do this – in the constituency of Raglan, held by former Minister of Agriculture Doug Carter, who was retiring. My family home was in the town of Huntly, in the Raglan constituency. The day after the WEL meeting, I reported the details to George, and then suggested quietly that I should contest Raglan to demonstrate the vacuity of those letters from political parties.

Within an hour, Sir Keith Holyoake, a former long-standing prime minister and senior statesman of the parliamentary party, arrived at my Research Unit desk. He was in earnest: 'George tells me you can stand? Do you come from there? Do you have a nomination form?'

'No.'

'Here's one – please fill it in. Do you have Party members up there who would sign?'

'I have no idea. My dad might know.'

'What is your father's telephone number?'

The Party nomination form did not take long. The first page asked for my name, age (22), address – and then for my full pedigree: details of my parents, Bill and Audrey Waring (including my mother's maiden name), perhaps to determine if there was a family history in the Party. Next, it asked for details of my war service, and of my local government experience. Over the page, the form asked what awards and honours I had won. So I left significant blank sections. My work experience, too, was not what the Party was used to: a butchery assistant, a cleaner, a barmaid, a student vacation worker for the Ministry of Foreign Affairs, a telephone technician, a musician, a student – and then a parliamentary research officer. But my generation had enjoyed unprecedented educational opportunities, so there was one question I could answer at some length. My postgraduate majors were political science and international politics, which looked appropriate. I signed the form and posted it to my father, who found 10 Party members to sign the nomination, and submitted it.

I told few people I had done this. I expected nothing to come of it. It was a quiet feminist gesture of my own. Yet I found myself in the parliamentary library in the evenings, reading three months of back issues of the *Huntly Press*, the *Te Awamutu Courier* and the *Cambridge Independent*, the bi-weekly newspapers that covered the Raglan constituency boundaries. I also read three months of the *Waikato Times*, the region's daily newspaper. I would lose the nomination, but it wouldn't be because I wasn't informed about what was of concern to the people of Raglan.

The National Party's selection system in 1975 allowed for a pre-selection cutting down of numbers when there were more than five applicants. The pre-selection committee representation comprised a majority of five from the constituency, with two nominees each from the divisional chairman and the Party president. They were to cull the number of applicants from 11 to five or fewer. I flew to Hamilton to meet these 11 men and to answer their questions. I finished after an hour and went back to the airport to return to Wellington, only to hear my name being called on the public address system: would I come to the desk for an urgent telephone call. Peter Hamilton, the National Party chairman of the Raglan constituency, was on the phone. He wanted to advise me I had made the final five and to catch me in case I wanted to remain in the area and start the campaign to be the Party's nominee. I hadn't given any of this a thought. Making the cut-off was not a possibility I had considered. I flew to Wellington, where I knew I could get briefings from my colleagues in the Research Unit, and could catch my breath.

Back in Wellington, I learned what would happen next. The other candidates, all men – a County Council chair, a Meat and Wool Section chair of Federated Farmers, a National Party divisional councillor, and a popular local farmer who had stood as an independent in the 1972 election – would now be attempting to visit 130 voting delegates, 26 of whom were women.[4] I would need to do the same. There would be three evening meetings at the northern, central and southern ends of the constituency, each of them open to voting delegates and Party members. Delegates could attend all three meetings. Candidates would make a short five- to ten-minute presentation, and then mingle with, and be asked questions by, the attendees.

I suspected the other candidates would make a similar speech at each evening meeting, pressing their case about why they should be selected. I never went near that as a subject. I wrote a different address for each meeting about key issues which would affect Raglan: the proposals on price stabilisation in agriculture, the coal/gas-fired power station being built in Huntly, employment opportunities for young people.[5] I listened hard and picked up threads of concerns from one meeting and responded to them in my address at the next.

George Gair advised me, and then others in Raglan did too (it dawned on me that some were actually backing me), to make some house calls on delegates. I went back north. I borrowed my mother's car and some of her clothes. I began in my home town of Huntly, where three members of one household were delegates. The tea and conversation were going very well until they asked about New Zealand's sporting links with South Africa under the apartheid government. I had demonstrated against these as a student. I joined the silent marches in Wellington to remember the Sharpeville massacre. I was completely opposed to sporting (and other) contacts with South Africa. The National Party policy was to allow these links and not to interfere. I disagreed with this, and said so. We were polite to each other, but I drove away laughing at how hopeless I would be if this were ever real. The next visit was to an older local who thought I was too young: we had a very energetic conversation about what a 'House of Representatives' might mean if there were no women and no young people included. I drove in to see delegate Katherine O'Regan, and played with her children while she finished a chore. 'I've never been a voting delegate before,' she said. 'I don't know what to ask you.'

'I've never been a candidate before,' I replied, 'so I can't help you.'

Peter Hamilton advised that the candidate selection for the neighbouring electorate of Hamilton West would be held a few days before mine if I wanted to watch the process. It was all over pretty quickly: Michael Minogue won on the first ballot. Mike had been a lawyer and teacher, and was well known as mayor of Hamilton since 1968. I was interested to note that among his competition was Valerie Forbes, from Te Awamutu, who had also tried for the Hamilton East candidacy. She was very strong in her advocacy for voluntary unionism. I wondered why she hadn't tried for Raglan.

Selection night arrived on Monday 24 March 1975. Presentation and wardrobe were a challenge. I had my hair 'done'. I certainly couldn't afford an 'outfit'. In the absence of any recent women candidates, there was no established dress code. My mother convinced me that I could wear a long teal smocked satin frock I had worn as a bridesmaid a year earlier.

My father seemed to be more excited about selection night than anyone else. He arrived home early and cooked dinner. 'If you had a choice,' he asked me, 'where would you like to be in the speaking order, and who would you like to follow?'

'I'd like to be last, and to follow Michael Loughnan,' I said. I thought he was the candidate with the most support.

The selection meeting was held in the Ngāruawāhia High School assembly hall. I knew it well. It had been a hub for local primary-school events in my childhood, and I had attended Ngāruawāhia High for the first two years of my secondary schooling. The hall was packed to overflowing on a very humid night. The voting delegates were in the front rows, separated from the rest of the audience by a rope across the seats. There were some family blocks in the voting delegates – the Mackys from Pāterangi, the Fishers from Monavale, the Kays from Kihikihi, the Johnstones of Whatawhata. With luck, I thought, I might have the support of at least two of those.

The candidates were all introduced to the crowd. Then we drew ballots to determine our speaking order. I was last, with Michael Loughnan just before me. We were shown to the staffroom, where we were to wait our turn. I'd taken a pack of cards to pass the time and played Patience. The men paced up and down and didn't speak. We couldn't hear any oratory from the hall, but we could hear applause, and I noted as each of the other candidates came and went that there had not been any laughter.

Finally, it was my turn to deliver a speech I knew by heart:

> The last time I addressed a public gathering in this Hall, I was ten years old. I was in the finals of the Lower Waikato Primary Schools Oratory Competition, and I spoke about the Gardens at Kew.
>
> In his summing up, the adjudicator said two things of me: the first was that you must never say thank you after you've made a speech – you've given something to your audience, and they must thank you for it. The second was that he predicted that I would be 'the second Dame Hilda Ross'.[6] [Delegates laughed loudly.]
>
> I've worked towards fulfilling that prediction since then – majoring in history, liberal studies and languages at secondary school, studying at University for four years for a post-graduate honours degree in political science. I travelled in Britain and Europe and studied the General Elections in Britain and Italy, and the Presidential Elections in Austria and France. In the past year, I have been a Research Officer for the Parliamentary National Party.
>
> So I come to you tonight with some years of useful political background, and I believe I do not overstate the case when I say I could walk into Parliament tomorrow and become a full-time MP without needing to be especially helped and guided through the first two or three years.
>
> In those five years, I've concluded that the nature of our political system is such that it is no longer good enough, efficient enough or effective enough, to have just another good honest hard working man as a parliamentarian. It may have been so 15 or even ten years ago, but the pressures of that 24 hours, seven days a week position have become such that all the goodwill and honest toil in the world will not make for efficient and effective government. What is needed is an understanding of the principles of logic and analysis that must be applied with alacrity over a wide range of subjects in a short space of time.
>
> Our politicians don't just need professional training. They need flexible, adaptable minds – minds that can accommodate or even

anticipate new points of view, minds that are free of the biases and prejudices which so often come with age or with a life led without variety and diversity of interests and employment.

And they need to be physically strong, energetic and healthy, assets which are dominant in youth.

Politicians need to be honest, forthright, trusting and trusted, confident but not over so – I have often thought – they need to be the sort of person that Kipling paints in his poem: 'If you can trust yourself when all men doubt you, But make allowance for their doubting too' – I've reminded myself of that line quite often in the past fortnight.

Politicians are first and foremost representatives of their electorates. They must present and keep before their party caucus, Parliament and the nation, the problems, hopes and wishes of their electorate. Raglan can be spotlighted not by sending a farmer to join a group of farmers, not by sending a man to join a team of middle-aged men, but by sending a representative so different from all the others, so that the interests of Raglan can always be on the front-page of the national newspapers.

Raglan is an incredibly diverse electorate and such a changing one. Twelve years ago it was a majority rural electorate. In 1972, 40 per cent of the voters were farmers, but with four and a half thousand new voters in Raglan in this election – 3,000 of them aged 18–23, 900 of them in Huntly and another 600 in Ngaruawahia, Te Rapa and Te Awamutu, the rural vote is down to 30 per cent.

The National Party candidate must be able to shake hands with and talk to over 20,000 very different people from all walks of life, of all ages and all political leanings. My education in the state and private systems, my employment experiences ranging from the Ministry of Foreign Affairs to a barmaid, my sporting and cultural interests and loves ranging from opera to rugby, have provided me with opportunities to live and work with this broad spectrum of people.

I've grown up as a member of a family in its fourth generation in the Raglan electorate, this is my home, this is the place I want to represent, and these are the people for whom I would cross the floor of the House if it were so vitally in their interests.

But a local representative is also a National Party representative, and a national figure. Cabinet potential must be borne in mind, and the place of the candidate on the National Party platform must be considered. Farmers are well represented in the party: sure my farming knowledge

> is book learning, but there's not much time for getting back to grass-roots once you're in Wellington. The National Party campaign has other platforms for 1975, not the least of which are youth and women.
>
> There will be a quarter of a million new voters in November, aged between 18 and 23: these people don't vote according to stabilisation measures or housing loans or even Springbok tours, they vote by identifying with someone in the party. National has no one to offer them, and Raglan is the Party's last hope.
>
> For the first time this year, National will have a policy on women, but what sort of credibility does a party policy have for 52 per cent of the voting population when that party can't put a woman candidate in a safe seat. None at all and Raglan is the Party's last chance.
>
> I'm a determined woman, and I'm a fighter. I'm going to fight for the electorate, but principally fight for the basic principle of our Party, the freedom of the individual. And I'll fight not with words, but with deeds.
>
> My being here shows my concern for deeds, not words. In the last month, many of you have said how much you have admired my courage in standing. Now, will you show the same courage, and make me the candidate for Raglan?

There were two remaining tests. Each candidate was handed two sealed envelopes containing the same questions: one from the Party president, George Chapman; one from the leader of the Opposition, Robert Muldoon. Chapman's question was on agricultural incomes. I did my best, but this was not my strong suit. Then I opened Muldoon's question. It read: 'What should be the key elements of National's housing policy for the coming election?'

I was momentarily stunned. Asking this question was the only way in which Muldoon could influence the selection. He knew I was working with George Gair on housing policy. We'd had appointments with the Building Industry Advisory Council, the Master Builders Federation, the Concrete and Timber Merchants and bank economists. We monitored apprenticeships and Reserve Bank ratios, and local-authority building permits for new starts and additions and alterations. We followed state-house waiting lists and migration data. I'd learned a great deal from George, and I was pretty certain none of the other candidates would be as strong in this area. I was, however, hardly the person to begin releasing policy. So I stepped forward and said, 'Some of you know that I am working with George Gair in the development of this policy. I cannot tell you what is in it, but I can outline the key challenges it must address.'

All five candidates sat on the stage for the first three ballots. Delegates knew who was dropped after each ballot, and passed the news behind them to others. I had no idea who remained. But delegates I scarcely knew kept giving me huge smiles. I figured I'd probably last for two. I hadn't made a fool of myself; I'd done my best; I'd kept my integrity intact. At last, the chair of the meeting stepped forward: 'The final ballot will be between Michael Loughnan and Marilyn Waring.'

It was nearing midnight. The auditorium buzzed; no one left. The final ballot papers were collected. Then: 'The National candidate for Raglan for the 1975 election will be Marilyn Waring.'

As my name was announced, my every instinct was to step forward and say, 'I think there's been a dreadful mistake.' But it was too late for that. The place rose. Conservative middle-class men and women stood on the school benches, cheering me – and themselves for what they had done. A scrutineer told me later I was ahead from the first ballot and stayed ahead, slowly climbing to over 50 per cent. Much later I was told about a horse one candidate had sold to a family with five voting delegates. The horse had a saddle sore under the blanket, so the family showed their displeasure and block voted for me. Jim Bolger, MP in neighbouring King Country, raced to the stage to embrace me. The family of three from Huntly came up: they wanted to say they had all voted for me from the first ballot. 'If you didn't lie or play politics in the situation you were in when we discussed apartheid and sport,' they said, 'you were who we thought would be the best representative of the people of this electorate: we could trust you.'

The decision might have been overturned. Someone who had been paying attention from the beginning questioned local officials as to whether I was a current member of the Party. I had not renewed my Wellington Central membership. I had been a member for less than one year but subscriptions were for calendar years. Chairman Peter

Hamilton met with my father, and advised that my father had paid 'a family subscription' when he joined and had signed my nomination form.

The result was the lead story in the *Waikato Times* the following day. Political reporter Barry Colman wrote of the two-hour balloting marathon. He described my presentation as 'composed, witty, authoritative and commanding'; sitting MP Doug Carter, he wrote, said it was 'revolutionary. Her winning in a field of that calibre is a great credit to her. I'm just worried that she may work too hard – Raglan is a big electorate to cover by yourself. It is a surprise for a girl to get a country seat, but I don't believe people will take her lightly – I've been talking to some hard-bitten farmers here and they've told me they voted for her.'

I was on the early flight to Wellington the next day to get back to work. The National Party caucus minutes of 25 March record Doug saying I had given a magnificent speech that made the crowd sit up, that I had touched on women and youth, and that I gave 'frankly astonishing replies to the questions on housing and agricultural costs'. Muldoon remarked that I was a 'good worker'. At that point I was called in from the Research Unit and handed a large bouquet of flowers. Muldoon told me how pleased he was that I had made it: 'We are going to win. I wanted a woman, and I will help all I can.' After I left, he turned to former PM Holyoake and said, 'I haven't seen anything like it in 40 years, have you?' Sir Keith agreed.

Editorials reflected the same sentiment. The *Waikato Times* editor wrote: 'Nothing anywhere in a long time has matched the real sensation that 22-year-old Marilyn Waring caused when she won the Raglan candidacy and with it an almost guaranteed seat in parliament ... Perhaps politics are more alive and well than we all believed.' The editorial in the Wellington daily, the *Evening Post*, described the selection as 'a practical expression of an electorate organisation's willingness to disregard the traditional criteria for selecting political candidates – age, sex, and occupational background – and instead attach primary importance to the ability to do the job'.

My life had to change. I gave myself six weeks to earn some money and access all I could from the Research Unit before I left my job. I would spend the weekends in Raglan until I relocated to campaign full time.

The Raglan electorate fell inside the Waikato Māori Tribal Confederation, descended from the *Tainui* canoe. The Waikato people established the Kīngitanga movement in 1858, centred on the Tūrangawaewae Marae at Ngāruawāhia, in an attempt to halt land sales to Pākehā settlers and to have an equal Māori authority to negotiate with the Crown.[7] The burial site for the Tainui people was Taupiri Mountain, on the banks of the Waikato River. I was born in Ngāruawāhia. I spent my childhood in Taupiri, under this mountain, and I had attended high school just down the road from Tūrangawaewae. Just inside the southern boundary of the Raglan electorate was a monument to commemorate the Battle of Ōrākau. The Kīngitanga had not been successful in halting land acquisitions, and on that site in 1864, 'in an unfinished pa about 300 Maoris, with some women and children, poorly armed and with little food and no water, held at bay 1500 better equipped British and colonial troops'.[8] Refusing to surrender, and after 150 were killed, on the third day the Māori escaped southward into exile in the King Country.

While parts of the electorate in the mining areas to the west of Huntly were ugly, barren dump sites from the underground and open-cast coal mines, there were some magically beautiful places too. Both the Hākarimata Scenic Reserve and Mt Pirongia were entirely covered in dense native forest. The glistening black sands of the rugged west coast from Port Waikato to Kāwhia were particularly dramatic, with Raglan beach and harbour a popular holiday resort.

You reached many of the western coastal farms on narrow gravel roads, winding through hilly terrain, often through spectacular native bush, sometimes in view of the Tasman Sea – but always on alert for a school bus, a laden truck or tractor, a flock of sheep or a herd of cattle around any bend. These farms were weathered by the prevailing south-west winds which brought rain but also dried out the earth, assisted by the salt spray whipped over the beaches, rusting roofs and wire fencing. Some of these valleys still relied on shared party telephone lines – differentiated by the Morse code in their ring. Many of the families living here had magnificent gardens of flowers, vegetables, fruit trees. Some caught whitebait in fresh streams, flounder in the tidal mudflats, or snapper off the rocks below their land. The dairy farms of Cambridge and Te Awamutu were different, and on some of the most productive pasture in New Zealand. In the years to come, it was this topography and environment that would sustain me when I had run out of energy.

I needed a campaign committee, and instinctively I knew its members had to be a different group of people from the Party electorate committee. I wanted a good number of Waring supporters, not officials who had supported another candidate. Peter Hamilton would be the chair. Katherine O'Regan became the secretary. Meantime, Raglan was stuck with an unprecedented challenge: its candidate had no car, no savings, and no appropriate clothing. A motor dealer in Huntly lent me a small car to drive. Some farmers with petrol-driven farm vehicles and their own supply offered fuel. Clothes were another issue altogether. With great discretion, MP Doug Carter's wife, Sunny Carter, asked Women's Section branches of the Party organisation in Te Awamutu and Huntly to donate money to help. When I was in Wellington, she recruited a young woman National Party officeholder with excellent fashion sense to take me shopping for some smart new outfits. I was very grateful.

The people of Raglan knew they had to educate me, and for several weeks there was a well-orchestrated round of pass the parcel as I was brought up to speed on pests and parasites and the Huntly Power Project, along with visits to schools, marae, agriculture research stations and coal mines. From Whangape to Kihikihi to Raglan, I was moved through the constituency, attending morning and afternoon teas and evening events hosted by Party members or supporters. The novelty value helped bring out far more people than the Party faithful. In the Puahue hall, the rain belted down on the corrugated-iron roof so loudly we could scarcely hear each other.

One night in Te Ākau was particularly memorable. I'd been there some days, we'd had another evening event, and I was staying with a couple whom I could hear having a small dispute as I went off to sleep. I was awake and bolt upright a few hours later when a gun went off in the next room. Good grief, I thought, he's shot her – but then I heard both hosts talking and an animal shrieking. In the morning, the man said at

Above: The frame on this map indicates the location of the Raglan and Waipā electorates.

Opposite, above: The Raglan electorate that I contested in 1975 included the Labour-voting towns of Huntly and Ngāruawāhia (home of the Kīngitanga movement) in the north, Raglan and the wild West Coast, and rich dairy farming country around Te Awamutu in the south.

After Representation Commission map, March 1972, ATL MapColl 830fbe 1972 12016

Opposite, below: The Waipā electorate that I represented from 1978 to 1984 was very different. Huntly and Ngāruawāhia were now in the Rangiriri electorate, and Raglan was in Waikato. The wealthy rural town of Cambridge and parts of the King Country were inside the new boundaries, making Waipā one of the safest National Party seats in the country.

After Representation Commission map, March 1977, ATL MapColl 830fbe 1976-77 14714

Electorate boundaries – 1975

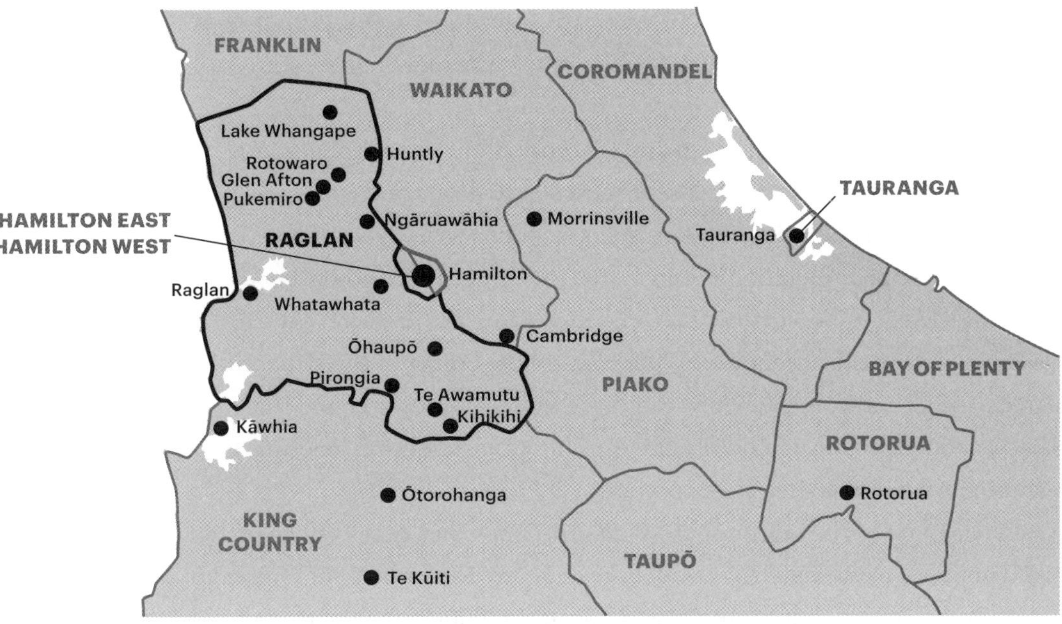

Electorate boundaries – 1978

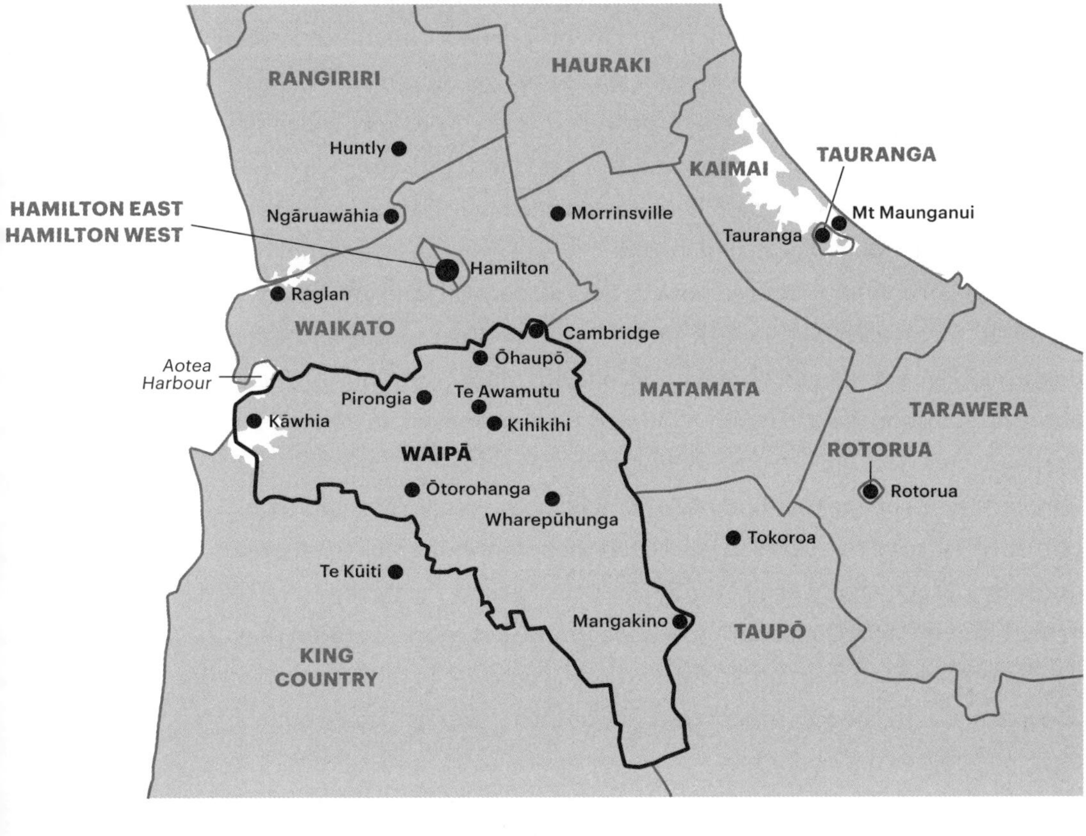

breakfast, 'Hope I didn't disturb you too much last night – a possum came down the chimney.'

In early April Peter Hamilton and I attended the Party's candidate training school in Wellington. There were suggestions and rules and many pamphlets. Candidates were advised not to write newspaper columns or appear in joint meetings with the opposing candidates. We ignored both of these suggestions, and it was too late anyway. Within days of winning the nomination, I had visited the editor of the *Waikato Times* and the editors of each of the three bi-weekly newspapers that I had used to brief myself before the very first pre-selection meeting. I went to find out how they liked to work.

Bruce Martin, the editor of the *Waikato Times*, was quick to the point. 'I am not here to educate the people,' he said, 'so don't make that mistake. I am here to sell a product with a 30-minute shelf life before it becomes tomorrow's fish and chip wrapping paper. If you understand that, we'll work well together.' I asked for their copy deadlines and their advertising rates, had a look around the offices and met reporters. I also accepted an offer made to all candidates to write a short weekly column for the small-town publications. I drew on lots of the information my former colleagues in the Research Unit were sending me, but I also wrote about issues that were of special interest to me. There was one on basic rights, for instance. The Labour MP Mike Moore had introduced a Private Member's Bill to give the government unlimited powers over all coastal land one kilometre above the mean high-water mark, and over all lakes over eight-and-a-half hectares. There had been no consultation with Māori, or even with local authorities. Moore's colleague, Dr Gerard Wall, proposed an amendment to the Crimes Act, which would mean that a claim made to anyone under 20 years of age that homosexual behaviour was normal could be punished by up to two years in jail. I used these two examples to answer questions about why I wasn't standing for the Labour Party, but Rule 242 of the Labour Party Constitution was in fact the key issue. It stated that if you were selected as a candidate, and won, you must at all times vote in accordance with the majority of the Labour Party caucus. That would be an impossible situation for me.

By early May, I had begun spending more time on the road in the electorate, and had a volunteer driver, farmer Jim Shaw. He didn't just drive; he took notes at each meeting so I could follow up or respond to queries. Could Nancy be sent a copy of the Historic Trust Antiquities Bill; what was the current state of a sharemilker's taxation exemption when purchasing their farm?[9] He and I also had a signal to indicate when he could interrupt me and move me on from someone taking up too much of my time. I could rest and think about particular areas of the constituency as he drove. This meant I could arrive at a destination with my own questions: what's going on down in those earthworks? How often is the vegetation so bad on those blind corners? How long are the children on the school bus in any day? Sometimes there was an issue requiring an MP intervention, and we would collect all the details and send them on to Doug Carter. I liked requests that required a follow-up: people inevitably told their neighbours I was as good as my word when the material arrived in the mail. On Monday 26 May, after a meeting at Te Pahu, I stayed with George and Margaret Clark, who had been voting delegates. George chaired the local branch of the National Party. Their daughter, Helen, was active in the Labour Party in Auckland. I met local historians who generously gave me copies of their books, and I read them quickly to glean information about local families and areas.

By June I had left my work in the Parliamentary Research Unit to campaign full time. We met millionaire racehorse stud owners; door-knocked businesses in Huntly, Te Awamutu and Ngāruawāhia; had a beer at the Workingmen's and Cosmopolitan clubs. Brickworks and timber yards were a favourite, as I could always talk housing demand and its effects. I went to race meetings and rugby matches and local repertory productions. I liked these events because I didn't have to talk to anyone, make a speech or answer questions. It was a little down time while still on duty. I spoke at church groups, high schools, Rotary, Jaycees, Business and Professional Women's clubs, Plunket and YWCA committees, and met with officers of the Māori Women's Welfare League. I spoke at the Hamilton Organisation of Women on 27 May. I told them it had seeped through to men in high places that women may have something useful to say, and that it gave an appearance of democracy to have at least one woman on official bodies. I said there was an urgent need for pre-school facilities and the availability of abortions. At the Rotary Youth Leadership seminar, I was reflective: 'Many people believe politics is an all or nothing business. You either support or oppose a party 100 per cent. This intimidates people who feel their integrity is challenged when asked to support or condone a policy they don't agree with.'

When sitting MP Doug Carter was going to the opening of a new building or a farmers' forum, or visiting the Huntly Power Project site and the Huntly Power Planning Forum, I went too. The miners of the Huntly region did not want a woman down the mines, but I went anyway. At the Ruakura Agricultural Research Station field-day, which attracted 10,000 visitors, Katherine O'Regan dreamed up a trick that would be useful on many other occasions. Katherine called the office and advised that I had an urgent message to contact her. The only way to get that message to me was to broadcast it over the loudspeaker, so everyone knew I was there. We were to do this for selected major events for the next eight years.

I sat in the public seats to observe local-authority council meetings. The harbour at Raglan was effectively governed by the Auckland Harbour Board, and one day the Raglan representative on the board, Angus MacDonald, drove me to Auckland for a specially convened briefing meeting. It was thorough, reviewing statistics, labour issues, volumes handled and matters of port maintenance, including of the straddle-carriers in the container terminal.[10] Following this, Harry Julian, chair of the board and a close friend of Muldoon's, took us sailing on Auckland Harbour.

The campaign committee worked hard. We tried to have some fun. When we could, we 'did it ourselves' to save money. We used a stencil to make advertising billboards, and locals helped to put them up. A local farmer carted white planks to the top of a peak that was visible to all from the road to Raglan and used them to spell out WARING. In the very Labour town of Huntly, where we had the family home, we got rid of any reference to National from the billboards, and just had 'Vote for Marilyn, your local girl'. Other supporters took their own initiatives. They wrote letters to the editor, attended the election meetings of my opposition, asked difficult questions of them and reported back. Many branch officials went from house to house door-knocking, and carrying a small card with my name and contact details. I handwrote 'Sorry to miss you, Marilyn' on many hundreds of them so they could be left when there was no one at home. We were modest in our expenditure because we were getting plenty of free media coverage.

I was a curiosity and entertainment. Branches that had been dormant were reignited. New branches of the women's section of the Party formed. Some days there were six different meetings in private homes as we covered the rural areas. I played rounds of golf at different courses on a Sunday. I visited every rural primary school in the constituency and spoke to children about what Parliament was and what MPs did: I was always of the opinion that this news went home.

On 30 June Robert Muldoon spoke to over 1,400 people in Te Awamutu.[11] This event was typical of the Muldoon campaign in 1975. He had a collection of large charts that would be carried on stage and displayed in turn in an early kind of manual PowerPoint. The Labour government's Budget of 22 May had given him plenty to talk about: a trebling of the deficit before borrowing, the continuing high rate of inflation at about 13 per cent, a savage rise in the petrol tax (while exempting commercial users), and increased taxation for those on the maximum tax rates – not something which worried Muldoon, but he could make the most of a broken promise.[12] 'You can't trust them. They said they wouldn't increase taxation,' was all he needed to say. There was a deepening global recession. Savings and private fixed investment were forecast by the OECD to fall sharply.[13] Muldoon played to New Zealanders' expectations. The presentations assumed people were educated; they could understand inflation, trade figures, deficits, migration and the balance of payments. He also played to ignorance and prejudice – about Māori, immigrants, unions, apartheid – and often bagged feminists and political scientists.

In a well-reported speech, Muldoon addressed a WEL luncheon in Wellington on 30 July. He said he had asked a considerable number of women members of the National Party to stand for election. 'An ideal candidate would be 30 to 40, intelligent, articulate, and with some background of experience that would enable her to play a worthwhile role as a representative of the people in her electorate,' he said. But they had refused because of family commitments. He went on:

> If International Women's Year turns out finally to be simply a jolt to the consciousness of the participating nations and ends in a realisation that there are such things as problems in society and government that are particular to women, then that is an achievement and probably about all that will be accomplished. Crusading and banner waving in the cause of nebulous feminism may be stimulating to those who take part, but it is frankly boring to those upon whom it is inflicted, and will be totally non-productive in the parliamentary or government sense.[14]

In answer to a question, he said National would have at least one woman in their caucus following the election. 'She happens to be a very bright young woman who in years to come is likely to be an outstanding political figure in the life of this country.'

There were still National Party conferences at divisional and national level to attend, and I was an early choice for television, radio and print journalists for comment. The feedback from the annual national conference helped: the *Dominion*'s TV critic, for example, wrote that 'Marilyn Waring did much better by being frank and open about shortcomings as well as strengths. She seemed more of a politician and less of a parrot.'[15] I began to be asked to speak at National Party events in other constituencies. I accepted one to assist Tony Friedlander in New Plymouth. It sold out. He was delighted – he saw hundreds of women he had never seen in his campaigning.

I was sending many signals about how I was going to behave. In July, I told Judy Zavos in an interview for *Thursday* magazine that politicians 'shouldn't be denied emotional responses, the right to be wrong, and the right to change their minds'.[16] She asked what the public can fairly expect from an elected representative. 'He or she must be able to adapt to new facts,' I said. 'This is a crucial requirement given the enormous diversity of legislative business that comes before the House. Two other qualities needed are the ability to listen, and the ability to take a stand without trying to toady to anyone.' I felt I had some advantages. 'About half the population is under 35, so it makes more sense that there should be more young politicians to represent them. As well as having health and energy, I feel a younger person has more chance of being open-minded than an older person. Young people tend to look more to the future. They know they can't change the past.'

This was a theme. I spoke to the Huntly Rotary Club: 'The parties count on a short-term response from the voter and the trend is to think in three-year cycles. What has been possible in the past is not necessarily a guide to the future. The year 2000 must not be lost beyond consideration in the mists of time – two out of three New Zealanders now living will be alive in 2001.'

I stayed on the road, visiting pine-forest nurseries, plastics factories, electric-fence manufacturers, retirement villages, rest homes, and the Church of Latter Day Saints school and village at Tuhikaramea. I went to Geoff Chitty's annual bull sale in the Waikāretu Valley. As women's groups did around New Zealand, the local Women's Division of Federated Farmers did the catering for the day, typically raising money to help women and children in hospitals in the city, though Waikāretu's closest doctor was more than an hour away.

The campaign team strategy targeted the largest sites with the highest employment figures. The Auckland Farmers Freezing Company (AFFCO) was a vast meat-processing complex in Horotiu, employing 1,500 workers. There was a smaller export abattoir, the Aotearoa Meatworks, on the outskirts of Cambridge. Having spent many holidays working in my father's butcher shops, I was relaxed in this environment. So too at Tokanui Psychiatric Hospital, the largest employer in the south of the electorate. My father had the meat contract for the hospital, and that delivery had often been part of my holiday work.

Our final month of campaigning was a major logistics exercise. Daily spreadsheets showed the date, driver, campaign hall, meetings and visits, where and with whom I would have breakfast, lunch and dinner, where I would sleep, and who was in charge of the banner that was raised at each evening meeting. Jim Shaw drove me, moved me on, made phone calls, protected me, worried about pamphlets, and took down the names and addresses of those I promised to come back to.

One of the more memorable evenings was in Ōhaupō on 13 November. I had spent the day with Brian Talboys, deputy leader of the Opposition. We had visited the Huntly Brickworks and the power project, and been to a stock sale at Waingaro. The Ōhaupō hall was full. There were people standing along the sides. Brian was introduced and began with a fulsome endorsement of the wonderful candidate, Marilyn Monroe. Once we had all recovered from this, he gave a very sound policy speech and took questions. One of these was a clichéd stereotype about the unions and, in particular, the appalling delays in the movement of produce at the Auckland Harbour container terminal. Brian did not join the easy blaming routine but had a seasoned, reasonable political response. When he had finished, I asked if I might add to his reply. He looked surprised and nodded that I should go ahead. I then outlined the problems the Harbour Board had had with maintenance and spare parts for its straddle carriers, how only three had been in full-time operation for some months, when the others were likely to be fixed, and when normal production might resume. 'How on earth did you know all that?' Brian whispered. 'I went to see them,' I said. At about 9.30 p.m. some of those in the hall started to leave. 'Where are they going?' he wanted to know. There was no public transport to catch. 'To the pub over the road,' I said. 'Well, let's close up here and get there too,' he said, and we did.

On Saturday 29 November, election day, the National Party was elected to government with 55 seats to Labour's 32, an exact reversal of the 1972 result.[17] National took 47.6 per cent of the total vote and Labour 39.6 per cent; the election turnout was 82.11 per cent of enrolled voters. In the final result for Raglan, I took 54 per cent of the vote: that is, 9,895 of 18,187 votes cast. I lost all the booths in mining towns – Glen Afton, the four Huntly booths, Pukemiro and Rotowaro. I lost the three booths in Ngāruawāhia, where I had been to school. I hadn't expected to win in any of these but felt confident of representing them well. Huntly and Ngāruawāhia were the poorer communities of Raglan, and I was determined to make it clear that I could be approached in safety when they had problems.

I received many congratulatory messages from my constituents, from old friends of my parents and grandparents, former teachers, and telegrams from most of the 1972–75 National Party caucus members. I had letters from women's organisations, and from well-known New Zealanders I knew of but had never met.

On Monday afternoon, I was immediately at work attending the Huntly Power Planning Forum.[18] The Huntly project would be the first power station in New Zealand to be built in a residential area; farmland, Māori land, and the air, land and water environments of the Waikato River would all be affected. The forum had been established as a monthly opportunity for many interested parties to meet and update and ask questions. Tangata whenua from Waahi Marae, local-government representatives, unions, Federated Farmers, staff from the Mines Department, the Ministry of Works, the Ministry of Electricity and the Waikato Valley Authority, researchers from the University of Waikato, environmentalists, and journalists from the *Huntly Press* and *Waikato Times* were regularly in attendance at these meetings. Environmental, social and cultural issues were all debated. When I joined the Forum, there was an attitude of deep suspicion of government bureaucrats, largely because the first environmental impact report had been withheld by the Labour government. In addition, Māori were being treated as if they were just another group to be consulted. Huntly had a population of about 5,000. Many of its local coal mines had closed in the 1960s. The Labour and National governments were correct in assuming that there would be little protest at an expansion of employment opportunities. But those attending the Power Planning Forum were keen to ensure that this good news did not come at any price, and that there would be changes from the way things had been done in the past.

The following day my predecessor Doug Carter met me in Hamilton, and walked me to each key government agency in the town: the Rural Bank, Post Office, Housing Corporation, the police station, Transport Department, the Ministry of Agriculture and Fisheries, the South

Auckland Education Board. He introduced me to their managers and staff, and advised me always to try to come to a local office first to resolve problems. 'Ministers and ministerial submissions are a last resort,' he said. 'Try to fix it here, and if you don't feel it can be resolved in Hamilton, then take it to Wellington. Often you'll find there is no discretion to make the decision in Hamilton, and often you will find that the Hamilton office wants to help, and will help you couch your ministerial submissions in such a way that the precedent would fit the policy.' This was fabulous advice. And he finished the day with the following: 'You are younger than everyone there. You will have to live with the consequences of what you do for longer than any of them. Make sure whatever you do, you can lie straight in your bed at night.'

The first caucus meeting of the Third National Government was held in Wellington on Thursday 4 December 1975. I entered the room and headed for a corner seat in the back row. George Gair came and took my arm and led me to a seat beside him in the front row, immediately in front of the leader's chair. 'You need to sit here, dear,' he said. 'That way he won't be able to ignore you.'

The newly elected Prime Minister, Robert Muldoon, spoke first: 'I was aiming at an ordinary bloke and wife who usually voted Labour because of their parents or because he thought he was a "worker". My aim was to move him.' The discourse of the next nine years of male pronouns was already in place. He said he aimed to 'have an open style of government. People must know the good bits and the bad bits.' He promised caucus, 'You will be consulted on all decisions.' He spoke about the Parliament Buildings staff. 'They serve either side,' he said. 'I urge you to treat them kindly – the worst thing is any touch of arrogance.'

He advised us to look after our electorates: we must be seen as concerned responsible MPs. There would be floods of paper and more reading than many of us had ever done before. As for work from the electorate, his advice was to write to ministers. I thought I would stick with Doug Carter's suggestion. Muldoon urged us to reply to mail quickly. 'It pays. People appreciate it. These things add up to a reputation of a bloke on the job.' None of us, he said, would be able to be across all the issues. In parliamentary work, an MP must specialise. He warned that the parliamentary life had some occupational hazards and that increased alcohol consumption was one of these.

Then there was an introduction on how to work with the parliamentary press gallery. They were, he warned, experts at getting information to which they not entitled. It was better to say nothing than to get into difficulties. Muldoon had favourites and enemies, and let us know who they were. We should also keep close to the editors of the local newspapers, especially the free throwaways delivered into every letterbox in the towns.

Caucus secrecy was very important. 'You don't tell your wives or anyone else. It is absolute. This is the most important thing. We are up against the lot – including the Party. We have to stand apart – the burden is ours in the House.' The rule was that you could be absent from caucus only when the most important engagements demanded it, and you must seek leave for that absence from the Party Whips.[19] There were no formal minutes of caucus, although Hugh Templeton was caucus secretary and would make notes.

We then had a briefing on the economy. Muldoon advised that this was 'in much worse shape than I realised. Every forecast is worse. The position is very bad.' Treasury papers described the worst terms of trade for a generation. We had inherited a record and growing inflation at 15.7 per cent, a massive and increasing government deficit of $1,002 million, a very high level of seasonal unemployment, and a massive external account deficit.[20] Private consumption needed to reduce. The oil price was a major issue. 'We will have to make some unpopular decisions before Christmas. Unemployment will be up next year.'

We held a straw poll of which MPs caucus would like to see in Cabinet, and in what roles. It was an empty gesture in the Muldoon era – the appointments were entirely in his hands – but he could always say caucus had been consulted. In 1975 there wasn't a great deal of choice. He had to appoint a Cabinet of 19, two Whips, a Speaker, a chairman of committees and four under-secretaries from 30 Pākehā men.[21] Twenty-seven out of 30 placed him in a non-choice situation. He had to balance North and

South Island membership, and to put some men where they could do the least damage. He also had a limited range of experience and skills to choose from: there were 13 farmers, four accountants, four managers, two lawyers, two from the retail trade, two journalists, a civil servant, a surveyor and a member of the armed forces. More than half of the appointed Cabinet had been members of the armed services, and only four were in their forties.

Then the president of the Party, George Chapman, was invited into the room. The parliamentary National Party did not usually invite Party officials to the caucus room, but this was an historic occasion: National had won with its largest ever majority and the largest number of MPs. He told us that membership was at the highest in the Party's history and the organisation was in great shape. However, there would be boundary changes after the 1976 Census, and by 1978 some of us might have a very different electorate.

The new PM left the meeting, and Brian Talboys, the deputy PM, led us through the logistics of working in Parliament: the appointment of secretaries, travel, the library, the Bills Office, Bills before select committees, and the parliamentary restaurant known as Bellamy's. The selection of caucus Whips would wait until after the appointment of Cabinet members.

I had joined a parliament of 87 members in a unicameral system.[22] Women had been 15 per cent of candidates in the election. Four were successful: Whetu Tirikatene-Sullivan and Mary Batchelor in the Labour Opposition, and Colleen Dewe and I in government. Colleen was a first-term MP and an accountant. She had won the traditionally Labour seat of Lyttelton, a predominantly urban electorate in Christchurch. Whetu had been elected in 1967. She was a social worker and had been Minister of Tourism, Associate Minister of Social Welfare and Minister of the Environment in the previous Labour government. Her Māori constituency covered the entirety of the South Island. Mary Batchelor had been a trade union representative; her seat was Avon, an urban area of high Labour support in Christchurch. I was the only woman MP in the North Island. We joined 83 men: 21 farmers, 14 managers or company directors, nine lawyers and eight other accountants, seven men from the building industry and allied trades, six trade unionists and six teachers. The rest were a cross-section of experience. Three MPs were under 30 – I was the youngest. A further 15 were under 40. These 18 'represented' 46 per cent of New Zealand's adult population at the time.

Counting newcomers Colleen Dewe and me, there had been only 15 women members of Parliament since New Zealand women gained suffrage in 1893.[23] Three women had risen to Cabinet rank: Mabel Howard, in 1947–49 and 1957–60 as Minister of Social Security; Dame Hilda Ross, 1949–57, Minister without portfolio for most of this period until Minister of Social Security in 1957; and Whetu Tirikatene-Sullivan. There were not, and never had been, any women judges of the Supreme Court or the Court of Appeal, and there was one woman magistrate out of 52. There were no women heads of government departments and no women among the 43 principal private secretaries to ministers. In the 1974 local government elections the number of women elected to borough and city councils was a record 170 out of 1,429 positions (11 per cent). In the county councils (the more rural local authorities), the result was a dismal 16 out of 968 (1.7 per cent). Only three of the 26 major city councils had women mayors. Very few women were appointed to statutory boards and commissions.

Men and women had different minimum hourly wage rates. In 1976 this was $1.63 for men over 20 and $1.48 for women, equivalent to $65.20 and $59.20 respectively for a 40-hour week. An unemployment benefit was available to a married man whose wife was in employment, but not to a married woman in similar circumstances. There was no provision in the private sector for maternity leave, no provision in the public or private sector for paternity leave, and no protection for job re-entry to the public or private sectors for women who had recently had children. International Labour Organisation (ILO) Convention 89 prohibited women from working at night. The Labour Department's Immigration 303 forms implied that the applicant was always male.

We four women would have a huge job ahead of us in such an environment. Colleen advised me she wasn't a feminist and had never been the subject of discrimination. I asked her when she began attending the national conference held for accountants, and if she had always been able to attend the annual conference dinner. I knew women had been excluded for years. She grinned and nodded: That's right, she said – we couldn't go. She never claimed a non-discrimination position again. There was no question about the commitment of Mary and Whetu to the achievement of equal rights for women.

My secretary was Olga Hoy. She had been Sir Keith's secretary in Opposition. At the meeting of secretarial staff to allocate positions, most didn't want to work for a much younger woman. Olga had met me and seen me often in the Opposition Research Unit. She thought it would be interesting and fun. Indeed, she was in boots and all, and immediately taught me a great deal about process and procedure. We discussed what the MPs she had worked for in the past had done, and I made it clear what I would or wouldn't do. I wouldn't monitor death notices in the newspapers. I would write to anyone in my constituency, and most women, who were named in the New Year and Queen's Birthday Honours lists. The letters and invitations began their eight-year deluge. In many cases, I advised Olga what the reply was, and she took care of the tone and language, and any particular form – for example, responding to Governor-General or diplomatic invitations. When I didn't know what to do, I'd ask her what Sir Keith might have done, and she would advise me. Olga had a great sense of humour. It was the start of a long and supportive working relationship.

I had an issue, however, with the Speaker's Office. I could not be called 'Ms' Waring in the House, they advised. It wasn't a 'real' or 'appropriate' term for Parliament. I could be Miss Waring or M. Waring. But I knew that if male MPs shared a surname, they could be called by their first and second names. There were three 'Youngs' returned in 1975, and they could choose to be called Trevor or Venn or Bill Young. So it was decided: I would be addressed as Marilyn Waring in the House and the parliamentary record.

1976

It was a man's world. Thirty-one men and eight women members of the parliamentary press gallery fed their views and reports to 37 major metropolitan and provincial daily newspapers, all edited by men. In the National Party hierarchy of the president, and five divisional chairs and two deputies from the Auckland, Waikato, Wellington, Canterbury and Otago regions, Dorothy McNab was the only woman. There were no women on the Party Policy Committee. Each division had one designated woman representative on the full Dominion Council : the woman from the Waikato was Valerie Forbes.

In the first caucus of the year on 21 January I observed how narrow the networks were for appointments to government boards, tribunals and commissions: a mirror image of invisibility in the world. There was a need for a new member of the Tourist Hotel Corporation Board. David Thomson suggested a woman; Duncan MacIntyre suggested a Māori man. Muldoon responded that he needed 'first-class business brains': apparently women and Māori didn't have these. I was mostly sitting quietly. I wanted to watch this collective dynamic and see how different people operated. I figured everyone in the room had a longer party record and more experience than I did. I already knew there was a list of issues on which I would not be falling into line, and the age and gender of those in the room was a formidable barrier. I could sense this was not a room in which we came to an 'understanding': you 'won' or 'lost' here.

One of the key issues on the agenda that day was the proposed visits of nuclear-powered or nuclear-armed vessels from the US Navy to New Zealand ports. If you were growing up in New Zealand and Australia post-1945, there's a chance you knew about the United States using the Marshall Islands as a nuclear-testing site from 1947 until 1962, conducting 105 atmospheric tests. You might have known that mining of 31 per cent of the world's uranium reserves began in Australia's Northern Territory in 1954, and that the British conducted seven atmospheric atomic tests between 1956 and 1963 on traditional Aboriginal land in Maralinga, Australia. Like me, you might have read Nevil Shute's 1957 novel *On the Beach*, in which people in Melbourne wait for the deadly radiation to spread from a Northern Hemisphere nuclear war. My father had been very distressed by the Cuban missile crisis in 1962 and had bought me Bertrand Russell's *Common Sense and Nuclear Warfare* (1959). He collected me from school to see Peter Watkins' *The War Game*, a BBC documentary drama about nuclear war and the consequences in an English city: it was given an R16 rating in New Zealand unless the 14- or 15-year-old was accompanied by an adult.[1] France began its series of more than 175 nuclear tests at Mururoa, in the South Pacific, in 1966. At least 140 of these tests were atmospheric. In 1973, the New Zealand and Australian governments took France to the World Court for its continued atmospheric testing, and forced the last tests before 1976 underground.

New Zealand was a member of the ANZUS alliance with Australia and the USA, and it was argued that a basic principle of this alliance was access to ports.[2] The US had a policy of neither confirming nor denying that nuclear weapons were on board its fleet. Muldoon was at pains to make a distinction between nuclear-powered and nuclear-armed ships, and often claimed that cargo fleets would move to nuclear propulsion in the future. The Labour government had called for a South Pacific Nuclear Free Zone (NFZ) in 1974, and the United Nations General Assembly had endorsed this idea in late 1975. Muldoon claimed that the US and the Australians disliked the idea of the NFZ, it was not realistic, and that Norman Kirk had tried and failed to have it mentioned in an ANZUS communiqué.

Muldoon announced to the caucus: 'We will have nuclear visits. The Americans have told us they have to be able to use their Navy if ANZUS is to work. And [former Labour PM] Rowling knew it. Safety is not an important matter – it is in the hands of the Atomic Energy Committee.'

I was quiet. I couldn't battle on too many fronts at once and so soon.

But I was grateful that two of my newbie colleagues, Aussie Malcolm and Richard Walls, were concerned about issues of safety and general community disquiet at the use of nuclear fuels and weapons. I had company.

I was very happy to be appointed to the Public Expenditure Committee (PEC) and the Parliamentary Library Committee.[3] My caucus committee selections were in part dictated by the issues of the Raglan constituency – Agriculture, Housing, Energy Resources, Environment – and my choices of Education, Justice, Social Welfare and Arts. I couldn't be across every issue. I was also aware my two Waikato MP neighbours, Mike Minogue and Ian Shearer, had strength, commitment and experience across other areas – local government, transport, constitutional issues, conservation, environment, science and technology research, and disability issues – and I would look to them to lead on these. We had shared platforms several times during the campaign, so I could already see they did their research. They would not sit quietly in the background.

A two-day seminar for new MPs was held in early February. We were lectured on image and the media, on how to be a good electorate MP, how select committees worked, how to use the parliamentary library, and how to behave in the House. This was followed on the second day with lectures on the workings of the Privileges Select Committee and the Parliamentary Government Research Unit, and a presentation by the National Party on the organisation and expectations of MPs.[4] It concluded with advice for all the 'new boys' from Sir Keith Holyoake. I took notes of his key points. 'You can't work too hard. No problem is insurmountable or not worthy of consideration. Think of your days in 24-hour segments. Attack is the best means of defence. Ignore all criticism – if you start to defend yourself, you will be caught. Use a variety of tactics. You are going to win.' Hmmm – win what? I wondered. For whom, against whom?

In the afternoon of 8 February I received a call from Mike Minogue. The Minister of Works had advised Huntly Power Project officials to oppose an application from the Huntly Borough Council for a Trust tavern. The story was in the afternoon newspaper and on the radio. I knew nothing about Trust taverns and nothing about the application. Mike took me through it quickly. What this meant was that profits from the tavern were administered by a Trust Board and reinvested in the community. The Minister preferred that a brewery control the tavern because a Trust would take too long to provide facilities. Wow! The power project would have consequences for a great many businesses and facilities in Huntly, but the matter the Minister wanted to be advanced as a matter of priority was a tavern. The Labourers Union told me they had a copy of a memo from the former Labour government Minister, Mick Connelly, advocating the same position. I called the Minister's office staff, who said this position had been advised by officials. Mike urged me to get on to the *Waikato Times*, and I did – so that my first public opposition of a minister in the government was taken for and on behalf of my constituents. We won the right to a poll, and the Huntly community selected the Trust tavern option.

In the 1970s, under the First Past the Post (FPP) voting system, the traditional Parliament meeting dates were still aligned with the late-autumn slowdown in the farming year.[5] In 1976 the Opening of Parliament would be on 23 June, but already there was so much to be done. Select committees and caucus committees were meeting, and caucus met for two full days every fortnight. Although many of the 1975 intake of new MPs were fathers with school-aged children, there was no thought given to work sessions around school holidays. On Tuesday mornings I left home for the early flight to Wellington; I returned to the electorate on Friday afternoons.

With Doug Carter's advice in mind, in February I wrote to every minister, asking for the names and positions of senior departmental officers in Hamilton. I got lists of all education institutions in my constituency, and of all Justices of the Peace (JPs). (It would be my job to nominate those for my electorate.) I arranged to receive the monthly agenda and minutes of the Huntly, Ngāruawāhia and Te Awamutu Borough Councils, and of the Raglan and Waipā County Councils – as well as the South Auckland Education Board and the Auckland Harbour

Board. Many issues which came my way were local government concerns, and there was often not a great appreciation of who was responsible for what. I also negotiated the use of council facilities for meeting constituents. Katherine O'Regan was now my electorate 'agent' and arranged these appointments at least once a month. Friday nights were in Ngāruawāhia, Saturday mornings in Huntly, and Monday mornings in Te Awamutu. Inevitably the council clerk or mayor booked 30 minutes of my time to lobby or update me on local issues.

The annual round of National Party branch meetings in the electorate was held in March and April. Some urban MPs knocked those off in a week. In a large rural electorate this took two months. I would nominate the days I was available, and Katherine worked with branch officials to set up the meetings. In most cases I spent a whole or half day in an area, talking with people who had problems, complaints or views they wanted to share, visiting businesses or schools, or treating myself by calling in on a local weaver, potter or artist. I was eager to go anywhere where I would learn: at 23 I had little experience of anything, and I was a willing sponge for stories.

Electorate chairman Peter Hamilton also had to attend branch meetings. Each year a new branch executive would be elected, and usually there was some discussion of a fundraising venture. Already, I was growing to love these people. They spent many hours going door to door for subscriptions – no mean feat in rural areas. They drove many miles for meetings of the electorate organisation. They thought deeply about many issues. None of them was brash or loud, none of them dripped with jewellery or went in for other forms of conspicuous consumption. All of them worked hard.

By March, there were major economic issues for the government. The Budget forecast deficit of $1,400 million was untenable. George Gair was leading the Cabinet sub-committee effort to cut $300 million from existing programmes, even before new programme proposals from the 1975 policy could be considered. Inflation was running at 16 per cent. Interest rates were rising. I discussed these issues with constituents. I always tried to play a straight bat with them. I reported. I didn't blame, excuse or obfuscate. I thought the more I shared with people, the more we could come up with suggestions or questions that I could take back to Wellington. Once it became clear that I was an active representative, many queries came from outside Raglan. Some were simply throwing a wide net; others were targeted. A key issue for me was to convince women they should not hesitate to contact my colleagues when important issues arose: this way, the men could neither dismiss the issue nor say they had never heard from a constituent about it.

My constituents' concerns drove a great deal of my learning. One of New Zealand's spectacular botanical artists, Audrey Eagle, and a young student, Simon Upton, both from Ngāruawāhia, were opposed to the path of the gas pipeline to the Huntly station that was to cut an ugly swath through the beautiful native forest of the Hākarimata Range. Yes, alternatives had been proposed, but budgetary considerations had ruled them all out. Audrey's and Simon's anguish, and my reading of the environmental assessment, taught me much about flora and fauna in the range.

In this case there was little I could do to help, but other learning was extremely effective. When I visited Tokanui Hospital for the first time as the local MP, Superintendent Henry Bennett gave me a full tour and briefing before I joined him and his wife at their home for lunch. I have never forgotten one hospital room in which an intubated young adult was lying still on the bed. He had hydrocephalus. He had not had any visitors for over a decade. He was turned every few hours to stop bedsores. Henry told me he didn't think the patient had any quality of life. 'I wanted you to see him,' he said to me gently, 'because one day you may have to make a decision on laws in such cases.'

There was extensive and ongoing work in Huntly with the power project: noise, dust, roads, housing, and information. There was a long state-house waiting list. With the increasing population, public servants like police and transport workers were being relocated without homes to go to, and so were forced to leave spouses and children elsewhere. The Housing Corporation had approval for 10 new homes for state rentals but had not begun any of them. I learned, however, that the departments of Mines, Electricity, and Works and Development provided housing for their workers, that some of these completions were well ahead of schedule and the homes were unoccupied. George Gair was Minister of Housing, and I asked him on 21 April if he could take over 10 completed homes from Works and Development, and give that department the Housing Corporation homes when they were completed later in the year. He organised this within a month. That would not have happened with any other colleague.

It wasn't long before I found I was very uncomfortable and conflicted over choices I needed to make. In early 1976 I received a letter from the Presbytery of the Waikato, a group representing all congregations of the Presbyterian Church in the district, about their opposition to sporting contacts with South Africa and to the visits of nuclear ships, their support for nuclear weapons-free zones, and their wish to see the New Zealand development assistance programme increased. I agreed with everything they said, but what should I do? I couldn't write and tell them so. It would be immediately publicised, and it would not be strategically helpful for the long game. Most people didn't understand that just voicing opposition to an issue or promising to cross the floor was an exercise in self-flagellation. But I disliked getting the letters that said 'you' support apartheid sport, or 'your' party or 'your' government is responsible for this. I wanted to say, I don't agree, and I am not the party or the government and I have no influence on them at all, but this would be viewed unsympathetically by my correspondents. I was embedded in a relationship of power and patriarchy with rules and expectations. There was a real tension between Party policy and my personal beliefs. I didn't like this feeling, so I determined I would stay busy and try to focus on the electorate, where I could get a few small things done.

In the daily grind of discovering just how much discrimination against women there was to unpack, I was approached by constituents Linda and Alan Jones. They trained racehorses, and Linda was an accomplished rider. She had applied for an apprentice jockey licence from the New Zealand Racing Conference and had been turned down in 1974 because she was married, too old (she was 24), not strong enough, and there were no separate changing and bathroom facilities in the jockeys' rooms at racing clubs. Licensing women as jockeys would have to wait until the introduction of the Human Rights Commission legislation, which I felt would address such arrant nonsense.

Sometimes there was an achievement towards social justice that I didn't know was coming. During the election campaign, I had been lobbied extensively by Pākehā living in Raglan who were opposed to the claims of the local Māori, Te Roopu Matakite o te Tainui Awhiro, for the return of their lands at Te Kōpua. Many Māori families had been on this land for centuries. It was the papakāinga of the Tainui Awhiro sub-tribe. During the Second World War, 88 acres (35 hectares) was taken for an aerodrome under the Emergency War Regulations on the promise the land would be returned after the war. There were also promises of compensation for the bulldozing of the marae, dining hall, kitchen and whare that were never fulfilled. Many houses were not compensated because they were considered sub-standard (they had swept-earth floors). The tribe was moved off the area with no provision of alternative housing. In March 1949 the equivalent of a paltry $660 for the marae was awarded to the Waikato Maniapoto District Māori Land Board by the Māori Land Court. The court had also awarded $3,790 compensation for a new meeting house and construction of an access road, but it was never paid.

In 1970, without consultation with the Tainui Awhiro owners, the government vested the official title for the land in Raglan Council. The council allowed it to be turned into a golf course and a motor camp, while an airstrip remained, and signed a lease with the Raglan Golf Club. Urupā were covered by the tenth tee and putting greens. I attended one of the council meetings where the matter was on the agenda; councillors just stuck to the line that they couldn't break the 50-year lease. Raglan residents were claiming that to do so would be expensive and that, as ratepayers, they would have to pay for this. There was a lot of ignorance about Māori land claims, and a good dollop of racism in the mix. Speculation and misinformation were not helping the mess.

Numerous attempts had been made to regain the land through official avenues, including working with MPs Koro Wetere and Matiu Rata in the

Labour government between 1972 and 1975. On 25 April 1976, Māori led a peaceful protest on the land and staked off some of it. They said the protest was a plea for a diplomatic settlement of the problem. Tainui kuia Eva Rickard asked to see me to give me information that would balance the lobbying from others.

The decision to return the land was made by Minister of Lands Venn Young and announced by Minister of Māori Affairs Duncan MacIntyre on 21 May 1976. The Minister of Lands would make an application to the Māori Land Court for a revesting order. The principle was that any land forcibly acquired by the Crown should be offered back to the owners if or whenever the use or purpose for which it was acquired ceased to apply. Māori would be asked to provide compensation for the return of the land. Eva Rickard argued that return should be unconditional and of substance, not just a return of title. It would be 1987 before this final outcome was achieved, just one battle of many in a sustained effort by Māori for compensation in respect of stolen land.

The activities of an aeroplane manufacturing business in a small corner of the electorate were to have global implications in May. The New Zealand government received information that CT4 aircraft trainers were being made for the Rhodesian government by Aerospace Industries in Rukuhia. New Zealand was party to UN sanction arrangements which prohibited such trade with Rhodesia's white minority regime. The aircraft were destined to pass through the UK on delivery, and the whole question had surfaced in the UK media. The New Zealand government would withhold permission for the export of the trainers, as all intelligence showed they were destined for Rhodesia.

Every week there were ministerials – that is, letters to government ministers – to write. For me these were the last resort after I had tried all other options, or I used them to highlight a case that needed a law or policy change. Subjects included the price of milk in Raglan; the definition of a 'channel' in the Fisheries Act (a constituent had nets confiscated); hydatids dog-dosing subsidies; requests for relief of import duty on a sports cup for presentation at the local high school and for a licence to import woven woollen fabric for the Te Awamutu and District Highland

Pipe Band; an approach from the Rotary Club about whether the Royal New Zealand Air Force could fly donated pigs to Samoa; nominations for JPs; invitations for the Queen to visit on her Royal tour; more examples from women about discrimination in employment, including not being able to work in a quarry; a deluge of letters from kindergarten trainees on the relief teachers scheme; the need for stop-banking for Huntly College to avoid annual flooding of its grounds; benefits; housing; maintenance payments; compensation for land purchases under the Public Works Act and for access and compensation for the Kapuni gas pipeline; intervention with Railways for the short delivery of flour to a baker in Ngāruawāhia; subsidies for school swimming pools; complaints about the 40 per cent sales tax imposed on phonographic records; closure of the Pukemiro Post Office (30 aged people would now have to travel by bus to Huntly to cash their pension cheques); courthouse closures; the time taken to provide telephone services ... Within just a few months, I was getting a picture of incredible inefficiencies. Tariff structures were a nightmare, and were still in hangover mode from the Second World War. Licensing was a mess: those who had import and transport licences ran small fiefdoms. Transportation regulations intended to protect the railways restricted truck movements without a special licence, adding significant costs. Vast amounts of primary production were subsidised. Far too much discretionary power rested in the hands of ministers. Certainly, that meant I might lobby for gains for my constituents, but the process needed a wholesale clean-out.

Meanwhile, in Wellington, I was learning very quickly how deceitful and nefarious some of my colleagues could be. In 1974 New Zealand's first abortion clinic had opened in Epsom, Auckland. In 1974–75 there had been major parliamentary battles on abortion, and the Labour Party had ensured no remit supporting a liberalisation of existing abortion law would be supported by the Party conference. Of 87 MPs, 21 Labour and 11 National MPs were members of the Society for the Protection of the Unborn Child (SPUC). On 30 August 1974 Dr Gerard Wall (Labour) introduced the Hospitals Amendment Bill to restrict abortions to public hospitals.

The Hospitals Amendment Bill dragged into the 1975 parliamentary year, attempting to restrict abortions to public hospitals. It passed, but with an amendment by the National MP for Remuera, Allan Highet, to extend operations to licensed hospitals. In September 1975 the High Court ruled the law was invalid because it amended the wrong section of the Crimes Act. In the middle of all this, in June 1975, Labour Prime Minister Bill Rowling made the conventional parliamentary move for an explosive issue in an election year. He set up a six-member Royal Commission of Inquiry on Contraception, Sterilisation and Abortion.

Debate around abortion was going on when I went to work in Parliament in 1974, and one of the first conversations George Gair had with me was about a visit he and Allan Highet had made to the Epsom clinic. He said that the most outrageous claims had been made in Parliament about the murder of babies, and he and Allan had gone to find out for themselves what went on there. He described the staff he spoke with as 'some of the most compassionate people [he had] ever met'. He listened to women waiting for terminations. He described what he'd learned that day and the stand he took on the issue in future as one born of compassion and humanity. Even under extraordinary political duress, he never wavered.

This was the background for the agenda item in the caucus of 25 February from Minister of Health Frank Gill, a Catholic and ardent anti-abortionist, and the continuation of the male parliamentary assault on women's reproductive freedom. Gill claimed that because the Health Act did not define clinics, no controls on their proliferation were possible before the royal commission reported. He had evidence from an Auckland obstetrician and gynaecologist, Herb Green, whom he claimed as an independent witness.[6] As this debate began, I could feel George very agitated beside me. He and Allan Highet started to interrupt – they both knew Green was a SPUC supporter – but Muldoon told them to wait.

Gill reported that Green claimed there were shortcomings in equipment, techniques and doctors at the Epsom clinic. He and Muldoon were totally in the hands of SPUC. (The Catholic magazine *The Tablet* had endorsed Muldoon for the 1975 election.) Muldoon claimed Gill had inherited deficient legislation and had to act, as there was a 'strong demand' for amending legislation. 'The abortion issue doesn't win or lose elections,' he said, 'but it is an issue in which anti-abortionists changed their vote.' The government had to move, he insisted, or there would be another half-baked Private Member's Bill such as Wall's.

Gair and Highet were then given a turn to speak. Highet had been in touch with most of the gynaecologists in his wealthy Remuera electorate in Auckland: they said Green was very biased and did not speak for them. All favoured the clinic. Gair had made contact with every GP on Auckland's North Shore, which also included Gill's electorate. Not one of them wanted the clinic closed.

Mike Minogue was up next. He was very disturbed by Gill's proposal. He wanted to know why we couldn't wait for the royal commission report. Muldoon and Gill stayed with their line: the courts had said the Act was deficient, so the Minister of Health had to go back to Parliament. The proposed Bill would be sent to the Caucus Health Committee before introduction, and would not be referred, as was the usual process, to a select committee. It would be a conscience vote.[7] All caucus discussions on abortion were leaked to media within 24 hours.

By 16 June Gill was back again. He had figures showing terminations in the last nine months: 2,362 were performed in Epsom, 10 in private hospitals and 375 in public hospitals. He now claimed he was concerned at a lack of independent counselling for women seeking abortions. Muldoon instructed caucus: 'We have to put a Bill into the House that stands up as workable – then it is over to you. The Minister of Health can't let an inoperative Act sit there.' While caucus agreed the Bill could go to the House, there was plenty of resistance to passing anything until the royal commission reported.

Mike Minogue had questioned Gill's claims about complication rates, so I quickly sent him a memo:

> Twenty-six women were admitted to National Women's Hospital with complications following a therapeutic abortion at Epsom, during its first year of operation. This represents 1.4 percent of the total number

> of cases at the Centre that year. The principal early complications were pelvic sepsis, suspected uterine perforation, and incomplete abortion. The complication rate appears to be low and compares favourably with reports from other centres. During the same period, 17 women (8.4 percent) whose pregnancies were terminated at National Women's Hospital had significant complications.

The issue was up again when a draft Bill was presented to caucus on 15 July 1976. Aussie Malcolm advised that within 24 hours of the June caucus he had received letters from trustees of the Epsom clinic who made it clear they knew what was happening in caucus. My colleagues were angry and didn't like being bulldozed, and they weren't buying the Muldoon/Gill trumped-up approach. Shearer, Walls, John Elliot and Highet all advised against it. Now Muldoon was pushing another line: 'My aim is to protect marginal electorates. I don't want you to antagonise electors. I have had some success in tactics.'

When the subject was discussed at the very first caucus of the year, Gill had asked for questions relating to the Bill to be sent to him, rather than being asked in the House. I had already tried this. I subsequently approached him to ask where my answers were, and was told: 'I am not prepared to put my department to work for you to conduct a campaign of your own.' Okay then, I would do it myself.

On 16 July I wrote to 87 hospitals. I advised that the government had announced an intention to introduce an amendment to the Hospitals Amendment Act. To facilitate an understanding of the present position, could they please assist in a survey? Were abortions performed in the hospital? How many persons were involved in the decision? What methods were used? What was the complication rate? Was there provision for counselling before and afterwards? What post-operative contraceptive advice was given? More than 50 hospitals replied. Pahīatua Hospital advised that they did not operate but referred 'cases to the Medical Aid Centre in Auckland, who in [their] opinion are providing an excellent service'. Winston McKean, superintendent at Gisborne Hospital, wrote to say 'how pleasing it is that the opinion of those who work in the hospital field was being sought. Such communication and consultation were notably absent when the previous amendment was promoted by Parliament.' Many respondents said to wait for the royal commission. A number said it depended on the point of view of the gynaecologist. Rotorua's superintendent, W.J. Watt, wrote: 'Only one gynaecologist will perform these operations here, and because of this we are of the opinion that abortions should continue to be permissible in special centres. Otherwise, the pressure could create an intolerable situation for us.' Most replies were handwritten.

On the same day I sent a survey to doctors in my constituency. It was identical to that sent by Ian Shearer to his. Have you referred or would you refer patients to the Aotea Clinic? Has any patient you referred not had an abortion as a result of counselling at that clinic? Do you support the existence of a private charitable trust to provide termination of pregnancy? Twenty-nine of the 34 doctors replied, 82 per cent of whom said they had referred or would refer patients to the Epsom clinic. Thirty-seven per cent of these had referred patients who, after counselling at the clinic, had not proceeded with a termination, illustrating that abortion on demand was not occurring there. I sent this information to Muldoon.

On 1 August, Whetu Tirikatene-Sullivan and I spoke on the second day of the National Abortion Conference at Auckland University. One of those attending was a National Party supporter named Sue Wood. I did not know her, but she wrote to Muldoon that evening and sent me a copy of her letter. She wanted him to know she was 'so impressed with the manner, presentation, and quality' of my address, 'and with the tremendous reception' to it. 'I have often felt the need for a woman National MP who is well informed and sympathetic to the issues of concern to women. We, as a Party, gained a lot of ground today.'

Reproductive freedom was not the only campaign against women at the time. The Domestic Purposes Benefit (DPB) was a recommendation of the 1972 Royal Commission on Social Security, which had been set up by, and reported to, the previous National government. The legislation was introduced by the Labour government in the Social Security Amendment Act 1973. The DPB was paid from May 1974 to enable solo parents to care for children without needing to find paid employment. It was also paid to unmarried mothers and their children, women living alone with no other income, and those caring full time for incapacitated relatives. It could be paid to an unsupported separated or divorced woman or man, and the Department of Social Welfare was supposed to recover the costs from the other partner where maintenance orders were not being paid. The rate for a Domestic Purposes beneficiary with one child was $57.36, increasing by $3 for the second child and $1.25 per week for each additional child. There was an allowable income of $21 per week, and a rent supplement, but every case was considered 'on its merits'.

By the caucus of 16 June, DPB costs were $75 million per annum and coming under scrutiny. There were calls for spot checks on beneficiaries, some of whose neighbours had started reporting women whom they thought were in permanent relationships. Some of my colleagues were full of the empty uninformed clichés: 'It's mainly unmarried mothers'; 'Young women are intentionally getting pregnant to get the benefit'; 'Some of them are so promiscuous they can't name the father because they don't know who it is.' There had been 32 prosecutions for false declarations, and this apparently stigmatised all those in receipt of the benefit. Colleagues claimed knowledge of many who were defrauding the department. The Minister had ideas about granting an amnesty for those who would be honest about this.

It was obvious most of this was hot air and gossip, but it was hard to know where to start to stop it. At the next Social Welfare Caucus Committee meeting, I asked the department to run a quick pilot to see if fathers were named in the beneficiaries' files. A fortnight's survey of files in Porirua and Lower Hutt offices found that fathers were indeed named but the men didn't respond to inquiries. They couldn't be found. They had scarpered to Australia. Phew. One nightmare down.

I could see that remits attacking DPBs were on the floor for the Party conference, so the next strategy would have to be through questions in the House. On 11 August I asked the Minister of Social Welfare how many people were on the DPB because they were not receiving the maintenance due to them. Twenty-two thousand! What was the total number of those on the DPB? As of March 1976, 22,600 women and

472 men. Then I started to target the numbers of men defaulting on maintenance payments, the insufficient staff in the department to commence proceedings against defaulters, and the estimated three-year lag in issuing proceedings in a context where more than 50 per cent of maintenance orders in force were in arrears. The attack on DPB recipients was galling, but I was managing to take a lot of the energy out of the government's position by demonstrating the cost problem was men, and maintenance recovery was where government had to make savings.

At this 16 June caucus, I had a small victory. My nomination of a Hamilton lawyer, Silvia Cartwright, to the Commission for the Future was approved. There was also a commitment to a Commission on the Courts. Muldoon was worried that this would result in a massive demand for more judges, courts, buildings and staff. The lawyers in the caucus – Derek Quigley, Jim McLay, Dale Jones – spoke in favour of the commission, and others reflected community concern at delays in getting court fixture dates. Muldoon resisted: 'If we had an election today a good number would lose their seats. I feel it would be different in 1978. But that will depend on what we do [and] I don't believe anything in the Courts will help that election.' He was very concerned about recommendations that would require new expenditure. Caucus determined the commission would go ahead with a report by December 1977, and action would be confined to legislative changes in 1978.

Minister of Māori Affairs Duncan MacIntyre had the next agenda item, a need for legislation to follow up on the Treaty of Waitangi Act of 1975. The Act required a tribunal, and National's election policy had been to examine laws to ensure they embodied the spirit of the Treaty of Waitangi. MacIntyre had not, however, moved on the tribunal. Treasury proposed a deferral and using the Human Rights Commission instead. I could see this would lead to well-founded accusations of racism. Muldoon responded that in Opposition the caucus had damned the tribunal with faint praise: 'We had thought it was window dressing but decided not to oppose it because we would harm our Maori candidates. We thought this would go into the Human Rights Commission in 1977.'

He turned to Ben Couch, one of two Māori MPs in the caucus. Ben said it wasn't window dressing for Māori. MacIntyre explained that the Māori Council wanted to see claims enabled back to 1904, tribunal recommendations to be binding on the Crown, and the right to nominate members of the tribunal. Mike Minogue surprised me. He saw grave dangers in a tribunal, saying there was potential for two sets of law, one for Māori and one for Pākehā. He was not happy with giving legal foundation to the Treaty of Waitangi. He was reflecting the views of many Pākehā. Caucus agreed to hold off on any action.

Finally, there was a loyalty lecture. Some MPs (not me) had approached the Prime Minister on voting. He advised that the only commitment was to vote with the government on a vote of confidence – that is, votes on the Budget and on issues to do with national security. 'But I assure you that if we fail to vote as a team, we will split the caucus and the Government. If a backbencher is critical, the Minister has to drop him or her for the team.' Sir Keith chimed in: 'The most essential thing is teamwork. We had [some members] difficult to control, but it was essential not to show divisions. I led my Governments, but I didn't always agree on all things done by my Government.'

Other key issues had gathered momentum. From April 1976 I had been writing to those who opposed nuclear ship visits: 'The government will make arrangements for standards to be met by any ship, nuclear powered or carrying nuclear weapons before it may enter New Zealand waters. These arrangements will have the highest possible regard for the safety of New Zealanders and the impact on the environment surrounding our coast.' A New Zealand Code for Nuclear Powered Shipping was released on 28 June 1976. At the Auckland Harbour Board meeting on 20 July, the general manager advised he would have the code studied in depth and compare its recommendations with those the board had secured and which were in operation elsewhere in the world. From an initial study there appeared to be some matters that would concern the board. There were certainly matters which concerned me, and my confidence about safety standards evaporated.

The Ministry of Foreign Affairs had advised against a farewell to the

All Blacks team to tour South Africa and to play apartheid sport. The Rugby Union had indicated they would not be upset if a farewell reception was not given. Walls, McLay, Ed Latter and I are all recorded as supporting no farewell. We were drowned out by the rugby *über alles* camp. Muldoon had said in a campaign speech on 13 November 1975 in New Plymouth that the team would be farewelled, and we were stuck with that.

Six months into 1976 my novelty value meant lots of media attention and requests. In the *Sunday Times* in January I was already claiming that I had 'learned to be more patient with differing personalities, with getting things done [and] with myself'.[8] Journalists had begun to create this woman called Marilyn Waring. She 'does her homework well, and thinks long and hard before speaking. Research is of paramount importance.' I advised I didn't want to be put in a box labelled 'Women's Issues – Apply Within' but to 'encourage the pressure groups to apply their pressure elsewhere as well. I don't want it to fall to me all the time to bring up in caucus how decisions will affect women.' The story advised that 'her feelings about the events of the past few months and how they affect who she is haven't been completely sorted out yet. She just grins and says, "I'll see how it goes and take it from there. It's the only way to look at it."'

By March, after hanging out with me for one day, the *New Zealand Woman's Weekly* headlined 'The Real Marilyn behind the MP for Raglan'.[9] It described an 'uninhibited, musical, sports-minded girl, brown-eyed, honey-blonde, Marilyn Waring, 23, with a mischievous giggle. Her concentration focuses intently on the speaker. Even when we are talking earnestly on a subject close to her heart, Marilyn's voice is scarcely raised. She is a lot gentler, prettier than newspaper articles and photographs have indicated.'

Director George Andrews from TV was in touch. He wanted to make a television documentary following me through the electorate, the Opening of Parliament and my maiden speech. I told the interviewer many had said that 'at my age, I haven't had enough experience to cope with the great variety of things brought to an MP by constituents. But by the time people come to you – whatever their problem is – they've got very little regard for the fact they are talking to a 23-year-old woman. It's the problem that's the concern of the moment, not any prejudice they might have, or even about which particular party you belong to.'[10]

The Party and the electorate enjoyed the publicity, but I found it quite strange, a sort of theatre of the absurd. I was on a steep learning curve about a range of issues and how people were affected by them. It was then my job to act responsibly with what I'd learned. But 'the real Marilyn' was in a process of 'becoming', and I didn't feel comfortable with all this attention.

In preparation for my maiden speech on 2 July, I read those of the 13 women who had preceded me into Parliament and of the men who had held seats that encompassed the Raglan boundaries. In 1976 mine was a 'safe' constituency representative speech. I did advise that there would be occasions 'where further representation should be given to the youth and women of this country ... and that when I felt a pressing need to do so, I would advance the interests of these two groups'. I focused on the poverty of evidence for policymaking and the dearth of 'statistical material on what many consider the most urgent of social concerns'. I also spoke about 'polluted oceans and rivers, smoky air, scarred landscapes, concrete jungles and sterile and mechanically monotonous jobs'. I warned that:

> We see only what we are looking for. Observation is unconsciously selective, guided by the observer's perspective and point of view. It is of fundamental importance that the right questions are asked, and this will not be the case if a restrictive life view prevails in any directives for research. A trend is no less real just because you do not like its direction.
>
> As representatives, the constituents who approach us are invariably those whose circumstances were forgotten, unforeseen or unpredicted when the legislation was passed. Often that individual constituent is then caught in an anomalous situation. How often is this the result of a lack of foresight or a dearth of information, because we did not see or did not want to see that ten years hence such a situation would arise?[11]

On 2 July I also asked my first question in the House – on the Huntly bypass. On 7 July I made my first boo-boo. I was asked to speak in the free-for-all Supplementary Order Paper afternoon debate, five minutes per speaker until 5.30 p.m.[12] I made all the points I wished to inside my time and sat down. The Opposition immediately called for a Division – the formal title for a vote. Oh dear. In general, unless speaking on a conscience vote, you filled all the time allocated for speaking, whatever the quality of what you had to say.

I was enjoying the Parliamentary Expenditure Committee. The PEC was unusual in that the Minister of Finance was not a member and didn't attend, and media were excluded. We would be examining the Annual Reports and Accounts, and the Estimates of Expenditure, for every government ministry, department and agency. I learned how to ask questions in this committee by watching experienced Opposition members Jonathan Hunt, who asked plenty with great precision, and Mick Connelly, who asked more but not as well or with such strategic purpose. We could submit written questions, and I used the opportunity to get a great deal more information about Huntly than we were being given at the Power Planning Forum.

I was told that the information supplied to the PEC during the hearings on the Estimates could be used only in the parliamentary debate on the Appropriations Bill.[13] These were five-minute speeches and were not recorded in full in the parliamentary debate record. If you couldn't get all you wanted into the public domain in those five minutes, what was the situation in other speeches I might make, inside or outside the House? All other submissions and reports to other select committees were available in our library after matters before them had been reported in the House.

I wrote to the Clerk of the House for advice, and received this reply:

> Official papers prepared at the request of the Committee have always been regarded as confidential, and the assurance of confidentiality has been fundamental to the willingness of departments to supply frank and detailed information. Publication of all such evidence as a matter of rule could seriously prejudice the Committee's effectiveness. The confidential treatment of evidence as such is reinforced by the practice of my office not forwarding to the General Assembly Library copies of papers considered.

I was making early use of Questions in the House. George had asked the most questions in both 1974 and 1975, so I had been a keen observer of his use of this procedure. My backbench colleagues Jim McLay and Barry Brill were the Caucus Questions Committee, and their attitude was that having government members ask the tough questions about some of the contentious issues, with a supplementary to follow, was a good way to diffuse attack from the Labour Opposition. They would also ask ministers' offices if there were questions that needed asking, and allocate those around MPs who weren't submitting their own. We were supposed to get a minister's approval to lodge a question. If I thought they wouldn't approve, I would wait for the minister to be absent and get the acting minister's signature instead. For most written questions and all questions on conscience issues, I just followed what the rules of procedure said. You were to lodge a question with the Clerk's office by a particular hour of the day, and I bypassed the caucus process.

When Parliament was sitting, backbenchers flew to Wellington on a Tuesday morning for select committee or caucus committee meetings, also held on Wednesday morning. From Tuesday until Thursday the House sat 2.30 p.m. to 5.30 p.m., then from 7.30 p.m. to 10.30 p.m. On Fridays, we sat 9 a.m. to 1 p.m. Caucus was held on Thursdays from 10 a.m. to 1 p.m. When the government wished, they could 'take urgency', and we would carry on sitting after 10.30 p.m. from Tuesday to Thursday, or 1 p.m. on Fridays. Muldoon often took urgency on a Friday morning, believing the Opposition would shut the debate down more quickly so they could catch their flights home for the weekend. National Radio's broadcast was limited to Parliament's regular sitting hours, so after 10.30 p.m. the government would stop putting up speakers and the Opposition had to keep the debate going. However, as government backbenchers, it was our job to maintain the quorum of 20 required in the House at all times. Because of this practice, we regularly referred to ourselves as cannon fodder. All other time in Wellington, from 8 a.m. each day, including lunch and tea breaks and adjournments, was filled with meetings.

The lunacy of the rules was well illustrated during the debate on the

Superannuation Schemes Act 1976, repealing Labour's scheme. We began an afternoon sitting at the usual time. The Bill would be taken through the Second Reading and committee stages under urgency. We went all night, and all day, and all night and all day, until we reached midnight on Saturday. The House calendar still read Thursday, because the House hadn't risen. So at midnight on Saturday there was a debate about whether it was still Thursday or Sunday. The House couldn't sit on a Sunday.

I voted against the lowering of the drinking age to 18. Sir Keith had asked for my advice and was surprised at my position. In my view, New Zealand did not have a mature appreciation of the cost of alcohol damage. The liquor legislation, a conscience issue, taught me a lot about lobbying and organised vested interests, with the independent winemakers, wine resellers, chartered clubs, licensing trusts (like Huntly's), the Hotel Association, Wholesale Wine and Spirit Merchants, churches and students all active. Somehow we had to get women organised like this in campaigning, but without the financial resources.

An inundation of letters came from women teachers. The Department of Education had issued a directive that teachers 'in the service' were to be preferentially appointed to vacancies. At the time, there were 67 different employing authorities, and when you resigned from one to shift to another, you were immediately 'out of the service'. Any woman who resigned to have a child or to fulfil other family responsibilities was also on that list.

I began a correspondence and argument with the Ministers of Social Welfare and Education on the policies on childcare centres and pre-school alternatives such as kindergartens and play centres. The government's position was summed up in a letter to me on 17 June 1976: 'Our basic policy on the care of pre-school children is that the family is and should remain the paramount unit of child care in our society.'

At the Cabinet meeting on 5 July, each minister was asked by the Justice Minister to 'instruct his Departments to expeditiously examine their legislation and administrative practices with the aim of isolating those provisions and practices that discriminate against women by reason of sex or marriage or treat women in a paternalistic manner' and to report back by 20 August. Acts and regulations had to be examined to advise where the elimination of discrimination would cause problems, with an indication of the nature of the problems.

As promised in the 1975 election manifesto, the first New Zealand human rights legislation would make discrimination of a person on the grounds of sex, marital status, religious or ethical belief, colour, race, ethnic or national origins unlawful. Unlawful discrimination covered employment, partnerships, industrial unions, professional and trade associations and so on, and access to places, vehicles, facilities, land, and housing and other accommodation. It also covered educational establishments, the provision of goods and services, and discrimination in advertisements. The Bill exempted religious and social organisations not operated for profit, and in a tug of the forelock to the rural backbone of support for the Party, domestics employed in private residences (for example, rural housekeepers) would not be covered.

Amendments to be made to the Domicile Act would abolish a wife's dependent domicile on her husband.[14] The situation had been that when a woman married, she could not treat the country she thought of as her permanent home as her domicile when she married a man with a different domicile. The government also introduced an amendment to the Juries Act to provide for equal responsibility for men and women for jury service. These changes had been promised in the Party's 1975 manifesto.

Superannuation regimes had been a feature of the 1975 election campaign. The Labour government had introduced a compulsory superannuation scheme in 1975 under which employees and employers each contributed at least 4 per cent of gross earnings. The scheme left out all those who weren't in the paid workforce. These women (mostly), and those with disabilities especially, were immediately disadvantaged. They could join the scheme 'voluntarily', but quite where they were supposed to find the cash to join was a mystery. The change would cast most of them as 'dependants' on a pension, with all the stigma attached. National Party policy was to abolish this and replace it in 1977 with a universal (not means-tested) scheme called National Superannuation.

These were substantial, important legal changes, but they would not be enough to satisfy or placate me.

By 29 July, New Zealand was under more pressure in respect of sporting contacts with teams from South Africa. Foreign Affairs Minister Brian Talboys advised that even the Australians might vote against New Zealand if there were motions against us in the UN. The Canadians were very touchy, with the Commonwealth Games due in Edmonton in 1978 and a boycott from African states looking likely if New Zealand athletes attended. Inside caucus, Warren Cooper called for a summit of sports bodies. Jim McLay said no political interference meant we must not express support for any team wanting to play a South African team. Talboys and Holyoake were obviously in a different space from Muldoon, who was not at this caucus. Because Labour had stopped a South African visit, the National government was seen as reversing the policy to allow contact. Former prime minister and now Minister of State Keith Holyoake advised: 'The Organization of African Union feel pretty emotional. They won't let it rest. If there is a Commonwealth Conference that passes a motion that to play in South Africa is to be refused admission to the next Commonwealth Games, or if the UN passes a resolution against us, we are out on a limb. This is now a very real probability. We do want to see multi-racial teams. We should underline this.'[15]

Doug Carter was now New Zealand's High Commissioner in London. He'd been approached by the British Minister for Sport to call a meeting of Commonwealth ministers of sport in light of the threat posed by New Zealand to the Edmonton Commonwealth Games. Doug had told a journalist about this proposal, adding that the South African government used the All Blacks tours to support apartheid and its policies. These were Carter's personal views, fumed Muldoon, but they were useful for me to quote in the Raglan rural heartland.

Women's issues were to the fore again when, on 18 August, Jim McLay introduced his Private Member's Bill to amend the Evidence Act to regulate the admission of certain evidence in proceedings relating to sexual offences and the mode of taking evidence in such proceedings. It applied in particular to rape cases, so that the complainant could not be cross-examined as to her sexual activities with any person other than the defendant. I was very proud of Jim and was amazed that any new young male MP with political ambitions would choose this as his first stand. I was in his speaking team for the introductory debate:

> When a person is robbed, the robber is put on trial; when a person is murdered, the murderer is put on trial but when a woman is raped it is the woman who is put on trial, and if it can be shown that she has a sexual history then her credibility is doubted. By a female definition of rape, I mean that if a woman chooses not to have intercourse with a specific man and that man chooses to proceed against her will that is an act of rape. Large numbers of wives are raped by their husbands each night. The fact that the accused and the victim might have been lovers in the past does not obviate the possibility of rape taking place. This proposed amendment will end the victim's feeling of being on trial in the courtroom.[16]

The following day Gill introduced his Hospitals Amendment Bill. It was a convention that even on a conscience matter Parliament voted for introduction, and that morning the National caucus had been heavied into falling into line on this matter. Sixty MPs supported it, and 16, including National's John Lithgow, Minogue, Shearer, Quigley, Walls and me, voted against it.

Later that day, I was working in my office when a journalist knocked on the door, came in and closed it behind him. Geoff Minchin was the reporter for the *Sunday News* and was not someone whom I knew very well. He said: 'I need to tell you something, and I don't want you to say a word or react in any way. I've just seen the dirtiest newspaper story I have ever seen. It makes me ashamed to be a journalist. It is to be published in the *Truth* newspaper next Tuesday. It's about your relationship. You need to get a lawyer as soon as possible' – and he left and closed the door behind him.

I felt as if all the breath left my body. I couldn't be paralysed, though; I had to move immediately. But who could I trust? I called Jim McLay's office to learn that he was in Auckland, and began to make arrangements to see him as soon as possible. Shortly after this, Keith Davies, a television journalist, knocked on my door. He worked for a current affairs programme that went to air on Sunday evenings. He kept it quick and was not solicitous of comments. Having established that I already knew what was coming, he offered 'as much time as you might like to have on Sunday evening to comment before *Truth* is published'. He left.

I flew to Auckland and drove to Birkenhead to find Jim. I was late getting there, and he was still waiting on a cold, windswept corner. He listened and then swung into action. I believe he alerted the Prime Minister, as well as lawyers Julian Watts and Richard Heron in Wellington. I flew back to Wellington and spent several hours with the lawyers on Friday. They then worked most of that and the next day on an injunction to stop publication of the story and its allegations.[17] They interrupted Judge David Beattie on the Saturday evening, and he signed the injunction.[18]

On Monday morning, the case was before the court and, as I understand it, several pages and particular parts of the story were expunged by court order. On that Monday in Cabinet, a note came in for the Prime Minister. Muldoon asked all staff to leave the room and then advised Cabinet what had happened. The memo was as follows:

> Prime Minister:
> Marilyn Waring
> Mr. Leay has rung to say that the injunction on the *Truth* story has been overturned. *Truth* will run the story front page tomorrow 'Marilyn Waring is a Lesbian.'
>
> Mr. Chapman and Mr. Leay asked me to inform you of this so you could, if necessary, discuss it in your Cabinet and inform your colleagues.
>
> Mr. Chapman is concerned that Marilyn should be briefed so that her initial reaction follows along a sensible political response with the interests of the Party in mind.
>
> At the same time, he is concerned about the longer term consequences in relation to the marginal Waikato seats.
>
> Mr. Chapman has briefed all the Divisional Chairmen, in particular, Murray Reeves in the Waikato, so that nothing should be said that is detrimental at the time when local people are likely to be badly shocked.
>
> Mr. Leay wondered whether we should consider getting Marilyn off on the Caucus tour to the Pacific Islands or whether we would expect her to tough it out.

Muldoon went around the table to each minister individually, asking for a promise of support, and a commitment that they would keep their National Party members and officeholders quiet. George Gair told me all agreed except Frank Gill.[19] Extraordinary activity then went on from National Party headquarters, and all divisional chairmen were given their instructions to shut down the electorates.

On Tuesday morning, the day of publication, I went to the office very early so I couldn't be accosted as I arrived. It was a relief to be back inside the machine, where I knew what would happen from moment to moment. The machine had enabled the survival of the alcoholic, the wretchedly depressed and the hopelessly incompetent. It would offer some protection. Already on my desk was a handwritten note from Labour frontbencher Martin Finlay: '*Illegitimi non carborundum* – and don't sue.[20] Let me know if I can help.' My office neighbour and colleague Ed Latter, who was an officer in the Territorials, was already on duty, and had taken charge of the corridor and anyone entering or leaving. Olga arrived early. She hugged me and said, 'I don't know why it's of any interest to people. My family has been in the National Orchestra and the ballet, and I know lots of wonderful gay people.'

At some stage that morning, the PM asked to see me. He said, 'I understand much of what *Truth* has said is accurate?'

'Yes, Prime Minister.'

'I hope you are not thinking of suing?'

'No,' I said.

'Then the way to do this is not to say anything at all to anyone, do you understand? You don't say anything, I don't say anything, the Party doesn't say anything – and there's no story if we don't talk. In the end, it will just go away. As for your future, that will be between you and your electorate.' Muldoon refused to say anything about the story to any journalists. My electorate chairman Peter Hamilton arrived, told me I had his total support, kept me company and visited Muldoon.

I had a question in the House that day, and I was relieved that I was going to be able to carry on as usual. When I entered the House, the press gallery was full. I expect they were all waiting for me to ask for leave to make a personal statement. Waiting at my seat was Leader of the Opposition Bill Rowling. 'I just wanted you to know that we had nothing to do with this,' he said, 'and no one in the Labour Party will be making any comments about it at all.' I sat with Merv Wellington in the House and could see my question on the Order Paper. House procedures meant that I would get the first supplementary question as well. I asked Merv to ask the Minister to please write out a simple supplementary for me. I was in no state to do that. It was probably the only 'patsy' supplementary I ever asked.

I slept in my office a lot that afternoon and evening. I woke once to see Minister David Thomson working quietly at the door; Mike Minogue was another quiet minder. Then the flowers, telegrams, mail and messages began to arrive. They expressed anger, shame, indignation, love and support. They cut through all politics, ideologies and dogma, from men and women, old and young, straight and gay. How dare they? people asked. And to pick on the youngest female in Parliament.

What do I remember of myself for those days? My body was in motion, but my mind was in an unrelenting, uncontrolled panic. I loved New Zealand, would I have to leave? Where would I go? What would I do? I knew of no elected representatives who had survived being 'outed'. I conjured with strategies of getting engaged to a host of gay or straight male friends. I was powerless in respect of any legal action. I was highly cognisant of the stigma that attached to gay and lesbian people in society, but I could go back to university or music – they didn't mind 'us'. I ranged wildly between overdrive and catatonia; paralysis then fight. This attack cut and wounded me to my core. This was not about what I did but who I was, a lesbian and a feminist. I took Valium and made arrangements not to stay at my Wellington home in case of a media ambush.

In respect to this last possibility, I could not have imagined the reality. Except for the *Waikato Times*, no other media wanted to touch it. Some used the 'she may sue' excuse. Some journalists were gay themselves and had no spirit to follow up. Some had become friends. Most were in Geoff Minchin's camp. David Lenihan at Radio 1ZB was 'appalled at the *Truth* article'; TV journalist Gordon Dryden's telegram and press gallery member Bruce Kohn's note were two of many asking 'If there is anything I can do?' Bruce found the reporting 'mightily offensive'. Kathy Findlay from the *Listener* was 'ashamed to be a journalist this week' and expressed 'solidarity'. I remember hearing a Radio New Zealand journalist come to the end of the corridor and ask for me. 'Marilyn's not saying anything,' she was told. 'Oh thank goodness,' she said. 'You'll appreciate I had to ask.'

The *Waikato Times* did its best to get some response, with its headline 'Waring Story Rouses Anger'.[21] The Waikato National Party divisional secretary, Trevor Barber, told the paper the story was 'typical of the type of sensationalism used to sell weekly newspapers. Irrespective of their occupation, everyone has the right to privacy.' Fifteen MPs were approached for comment in Wellington. Not one was prepared to make a statement. Off the record, conversations indicated a general feeling of shock, outrage and hostility against *Truth* for running this story.[22]

Martin Gummer, chair of Auckland's Young Nationals, wrote that I had their support: 'You have been an excellent MP, with intelligent views and the courage to express them forthrightly.' Sally Mills in the Eden electorate wanted me to know I was in the thoughts of many 'friends and supporters unknown to you'. Hamilton Young Nationals assured me 'of our complete confidence'. One letter stood out. It was from Jack O'Halloran. He lived in Te Kūiti, in Jim Bolger's King Country electorate. He had been the National Party's Waikato divisional chairman and a voting member of the Raglan pre-selection committee. He then chaired the selection meeting in Ngāruawāhia. I had never considered that I might have had his backing. 'I was angered and concerned by this unprovoked attack,' he wrote. 'I am confident your electorate will be solidly behind you. There would be many people in the community who would be vulnerable to this type of media abuse. I sincerely hope you will not let this interfere with your career.'

Bill Andersen and Ken Douglas, of the Northern and Wellington Drivers Unions, respectively, wrote letters expressing 'personal support', and 'regret and anger' at the 'despicable attack'. Frank Thorn wrote as the general secretary of the 'most female organization in this country, the Clothing Workers Federation, deploring the attack made on your personal life'.

Party members in Raglan telegrammed their full and unconditional support, and their love, and advised me to keep my head high. A week later my electorate Executive Committee gathered for its long-scheduled half-yearly meeting. We had over 30 members of that group, and about a third of those present were women. I made my routine MP's report, then made a statement about the *Truth* story. Peter Hamilton also made a statement about the 'intrusions into the private life of our MP by incorrect and unsubstantiated rumours'. There was a very subtle Muldoon presence there. He had sent Peter Akland, a member of his media staff, to do nothing else but sit in the back of the meeting, and Peter Hamilton introduced and acknowledged him. Don Macky was first on his feet. He was furious. He reported how much respect I had gained for my hard work, and how much support his Pāterangi branch members and the Macky family had for me. It wasn't long before the resolution was tabled: 'That this meeting places on record its total opposition to defamatory conjecture on the private life of any public figure, and reaffirms the Raglan electorate's total support and confidence in Marilyn Waring as our MP.' It was adopted unanimously.

Back in Wellington Olga was managing the continuing deluge of mail. Letters came from organisations now: the New Zealand University Students' Association (NZUSA), the Women's National Abortion Action Campaign (WONAAC), the National Organisation for Women (NOW), the Workers Educational Association (WEA) and the Gay Liberation Front. Olga said that at a recent Christian Science meeting she'd attended, as well as around Parliament, people had asked her quietly, 'Well, is she?' Olga would reply, 'I don't know. I haven't slept with her.'

Meanwhile, the Hamilton branch of the Labour Party Young Socialists had a statement for the *Waikato Times* condemning the *Truth* story as 'despicable'.[23] 'It was a completely unwarranted intrusion into Miss Waring's private life.' The branch was also suspicious of the complete lack of public response from the National Party. Many people wondered if the Party had instigated the story. The *Sunday Times* ran more comment a week later: 'Straight talking Huntly farmer and Raglan National Party Chairman Peter Hamilton is still fuming over the personal attack leveled at the rural electorate's MP Miss Marilyn Waring. "She was very distressed. But she is a very mature person for her age, and it hasn't affected her performance at all. She was speaking in the House in question time the same day the allegations were made, and she hasn't canceled any of her engagements."'[24]

From all corners, people were trying to help. My former Victoria University teachers were publicly backing me. Professor John Roberts, Dr Rod Alley and Dr Stephen Levine wrote: 'During the years she has spent with us Marilyn Waring was at all times a highly competent thoroughly professional person of integrity. Hours of study, academic supervision, and personal sacrifice represent a substantial accumulation of knowledge and expertise about public and political issues in New Zealand. This must on no account be somehow sacrificed for the sake of the commercial advantage of a weekly newspaper.'

Truth continued to get traction on the story for six weeks, driven by the vast and highly negative mail they received.

This entire event had lasting effects on me. Now, whatever happened, I had nothing else to hide. In politics, this is a particular freedom. At the same time, I built walls so big, so high, so deep to protect myself. I locked myself away. Part of me was broken. The supportive letters coming in poulticed the poison. But something reckless was also unleashed in me, and I would use that energy for the issues ahead.

It began immediately, as we moved to the second reading of Gill's Bill to restrict access to abortion on 1 September. After discussing the resolution of the National Party conference to wait for the royal commission, I moved to consideration of what royal commissions are for. They could be a device to attract public comment, opinion and professional advice on a particular subject; a very neat political sidestep in a sensitive area; or an earnest attempt to allow a team of experts to suggest solutions to serious policy problems. I told the House:

> We have recently been advised that there is no possibility of an amendment to section 183 of the Crimes Act, which defines the crime

> of abortion, until this Royal Commission has reported. We have been told that any suggestion of an amendment to Section 42 of the Police Offences Amendment Act on the supply of and advice on contraception to those under 16 years must wait until the Royal Commission reports. We have been told in the House by the Minister of Health that any implementation of the National Party's election policy on the supply of contraceptives free on prescription must wait until the Royal Commission reports. The question then is, why there is an exception.
>
> So the questions we must all ask ourselves are these: Is it good legislation? Will it work? Is it inspired by sensible and reasonable ideas? What circumstances will it produce? Are the requirements of the Act reasonable? And will the Act be effective?
>
> There seems to be a lack of appreciation as to the practical results of channeling all terminations of pregnancies to public hospitals for approval, which in itself seems to be a contradiction of the National Party's general philosophy. In fact, on the introduction of the Bill, the Minister of Health said that the intention was to move abortions into the public sector. One of the medical superintendents who replied to my survey wrote: 'Most public hospitals have termination committees reflecting a variety of opinions and they often include one or more gynaecologists, some of whom have very conservative views on the subject. If two opposing views are rigidly held by the committee members, then very few terminations are likely to be authorized. Department of Health figures show great variability between hospitals.' Indeed, the returns to my questionnaire [to hospitals] show that, and show that one public hospital in a very small centre runs just 20 terminations behind the National Women's Hospital.[25]

The public galleries were full. When I finished, there were cheers and applause, and I felt it was for much more than my contribution to the debate. The Speaker was moved to comment: 'I have no objection to appreciation of the speech of any member being expressed elsewhere by our welcome visitors, but I believe all right-thinking members of the House object to participation in the activities of this Chamber by our guests. They are permitted to come and listen but not to participate.'

At the end of the second reading debate, on an amendment proposed by George Gair, the Bill was deferred, awaiting the royal commission report.

I received another flood of supportive letters and telegrams from the country and my electorate. Church members furious at being told what to think and do enclosed the handouts with which they had been 'hectored'. Many health professionals across a broad spectrum of expertise, including from Family Planning, and women's organisations such as Business and Professional Women were among them. This time, though, I opened letters from those who wanted to express their 'disgust and abhorrence'. I was told about 'the bitter and fanatical look on your face and in your character' (anonymous); another 'noticed the similarities between you and Adolf' (Michael Diamond, Dannevirke); my stance was 'revolting, sickening, the greatest contribution you could make would be to retire into complete obscurity' (S. Hughes, Brooklyn). Lots of people wrote that they were praying for me, so maybe they would be a karmic counterweight to the more bilious correspondents.

Silvia Cartwright had accepted the position on the Commission for the Future.[26] She wrote and asked me what I thought were the key issues for planning and study for the next 25 years. I used the opportunity to speak to the Taumarunui Women's Club 25th Jubilee dinner on 25 September to give her a response:

> We have some perception of the future. We must protect our best environmental features both from natural climatic changes and from industry. We must protect our historical heritage, small as it is. We must look at our whole internal transport system. How many container ports do we need? How many international airports do we need? Is too much of our decision making based on a blind parochialism with little or no respect for the national interest? In Foreign Affairs I think we must look to the Pacific because our relationships with our neighbours in the Pacific will become the crux of our foreign policy.
>
> Although there seems to be general agreement that we live in a period of rapid change, there is a severe lag in grasping the implications of this information. But how often are we aware of the things we literally cannot see? How many are brave enough to perceive the critical areas for planning and study as being those that are essentially attitudinal, essentially social, and essentially educative and essentially progressive?
>
> In trade, diversity of product and market is of the essence. I don't

> think we have urban structure plans or planning for land use. Housing and water are special resources for which some long-term utilisation planning is required. Reform of Parliament and reform of the House of Representatives, reform of policy-making procedures and reform of decision-making must be a critical area of change for the future of New Zealand.
>
> Perhaps I came into politics at a wrong age. Perhaps I still misunderstand the political system, but I cannot but feel more and more cynically resigned to hopelessness, which sees necessary social decisions deferred, that sees bigoted and anachronistic laws upheld, and that sees difficult decisions postponed for another day.

It was the last paragraph that caught the media's attention. Most papers ran it on its own, and got themselves in a tizzy hypothesising that I intended not to run again. I denied this, but I began to think about what things I could do if I was in Parliament only for these three years. Electoral boundary changes were due in 1977. I might not have an electorate. I could be challenged and not get the nomination. I might not be able to keep going in an environment where my principles were constantly compromised.

October was a busy time in Raglan. A mining company, AHI Minerals, had made an application for a prospecting licence in six areas, including the Pirongia State Forest Park and the Maungatautari Scenic Reserve. Legislation at the time gave a guaranteed right to mine if the prospecting licence showed economic assets. The decision was in the hands of the Secretary of Mines. Federated Farmers, local government, environmental organisations: everyone I met was opposed to granting this. It was all hands to the pump in a coordinated effort. We made submissions and stopped the issuing of the licence.

The weekend of 23–24 October saw an appalling abuse of police powers. In 1974, the Labour government had instigated dawn raids on homes where they believed Pacific peoples who were visa overstayers were resident.[27] The Minister of Police had apparently directed the Commissioner of Police to set up special squads to search for overstayers. Now the police were once again conducting random checks. No one in Cabinet knew. Many of us found random checks completely unacceptable, whether or not people were overstayers. Even some people born in New Zealand were arrested. There was a major backlash. McLay, Brill, Shearer and others had been contacted by Party officials who were not prepared to ask for donations and membership renewals because of these police actions. A young Auckland lawyer named David Lange asked what sort of a country this was where people could be held for two days without being charged, and where their only remedy was a Supreme Court writ.

Simon Upton was now chairing the Party branch in Ngāruawāhia. He wrote about the possibility of a Christmas barbecue there, and added: 'Just a final word about overstayers. I suppose you've had so much abuse and mail about it you must be really fed up, but I thought I'd just mention that I was appalled by the handling of it all and know a number of long committed supporters who have been really upset. None of us feel very keen about door knocking in the immediate future. Tact, calm and rationality ... and I'm hoping for a Cabinet reshuffle.'

It was about to get worse. In November 1976, in Parliament, an inebriated Muldoon accused Colin Moyle, a Labour frontbencher, of being picked up by the police for homosexual activity. Police had told Muldoon about this when he was leader of the Opposition. Many of us were disgusted. At caucus Jim McLay was the first brave voice: 'Your conduct in the House was unacceptable. You finished up in Bernard Levin's column in *The Times* of London.' Simon Upton wrote to me again: 'The Party is really taking an unnecessary battering, and it is really affecting long-time supporters. After the Moyle allegations, they really can't be bothered speaking well of the government and are becoming increasingly cynical. This has had a demoralizing effect on party officials and workers. I have taken to saying that [Muldoon's] statements on the Moyle issue are completely indefensible regardless of their veracity, and in the worst taste.' My *Truth* experience taught me a lot about support: I wrote to the Moyle family.

On 21 November Brian Talboys had returned from his trip to African capitals to explain the government's policy on sporting contacts with South Africa. Muldoon introduced the discussion by saying: 'We can give advice [to sporting bodies], but we fall short of saying "don't go or don't come."' Talboys advised he couldn't see how anything New Zealand now did would avert a boycott of the Commonwealth Games or pressure on New Zealand at the upcoming Commonwealth Heads of Government Meeting. He took the position that we should 'try to dissuade' sporting contacts with South Africa.

Many in caucus opposed this stance of active dissuasion as putting unacceptable pressure on sporting bodies. Talboys responded that if you say you abhor apartheid, you have to show it. Muldoon's announcement at the post-caucus press conference was that sports bodies had a 'right to decide', linked to a 'duty to consider the wider effects'.

But Holyoake would not settle for this. On the morning of 16 December, he addressed the National Press Club in Wellington, pressing for the government to 'actively discourage' contacts. If sports organisations were considering contacts with South Africa, he said, they should seek the government's views, and the government would reply that these contacts affected our national interests and put our reputation in jeopardy.

When he entered the caucus room that afternoon, Muldoon rounded on him. 'What was in your address? Was it drafted by the Ministry of Foreign Affairs? It goes further than the policy of this caucus.' He read aloud pieces of the speech. Sir Keith responded: 'There might be one passage that went a little further.' Muldoon was furious. Holyoake, as a widely respected former prime minister, was the one caucus member he couldn't bully. Muldoon then claimed that African leaders did not take the sports boycott seriously. They joked about it. Talboys rebutted him immediately: 'That is not correct. They were quite emphatic about this.'

I had had enough of these games. I had already begun responding to letters and questions saying that I opposed sporting contacts with South Africa. I couldn't change anything, but it cleared my conscience. I tried to focus on where I might be useful.

Once Parliament was sitting, I had begun to mail out Bills, parliamentary questions and answers, and some key speeches or press statements to women's organisations. I began with the organisations listed at the back of the 1975 *Herstory Diary*, and augmented this with liberal groups from the affiliated organisations of the National Council of Women (NCW), and others as they came to my notice. I sought to expand the numbers exponentially for up-to-date lobbying and advocacy, to tackle the presumption that NCW spoke for all women, and to get more women lobbying their MPs. When something was urgent, I telegrammed them all. Nothing like this had happened before. I kept this up for nine years, and at some stage the list of organisations was over 200. It would take me a lot of the night to do all the photocopying and envelope-stuffing and to procure enough copies of Bills to send.

In 1976 the issues were as varied as they were urgent.

Women needed an extension of benefits to cover prosthetic aids following breast cancer surgery.

The Superannuation Act 1956 was compulsory for all employees on the permanent staff in the public service aged between 17 and 24, with the sole exception of married women. The Combined State Services Organisation (CSSO) had proposed changing this in 1974, but the Labour government did not proceed with it. National would proceed only if it were raised again by the CSSO.

Women couldn't be appointed as meat inspection staff (all public servants) in freezing works because there was no provision of lavatories or cloakroom facilities in the vicinity of the work area.

Immigration applications for permanent entry from married women to take up full-time employment in approved occupations needed to show that arrangements had been made for the care of small children during working hours.

There was no discrimination between male and female beneficiaries with respect to blind persons. However, thanks to the income test, blind women lost their benefit when marrying a sighted man, but a man would not lose the benefit in the reverse situation.

The matrimonial property regime in 1975 was breathtakingly outrageous. Even judges of the Court of Appeal and the Privy Council had said it was manifestly unfair and unjust, but the law gave them no room for judicial discretion to award property equally because its focus was on monetary contribution.[28] There were some appalling outcomes for women, especially in cases involving farms. National Party policy now recognised that both partners made equal contributions to their relationship, and provided for a just division of property when the relationship ended. All forms of contribution to the 'marriage partnership' were to be treated as equal, and there was no presumption that monetary contributions were of greater value than non-monetary ones. A 50/50 division of property would hold unless it was 'repugnant to justice'. These were significant and internationally leading legislative changes for those who owned property.

While some colleagues wanted the inclusion of de facto couples and the extension of the division to the death of a spouse, others were totally opposed to these proposals. There was considerable resistance to the 50/50 division in the National caucus to the very end. They weren't alone. A lawyer named Ruth Richardson had made the two most significant and well-argued submissions to the Statutes Revision Select Committee: one for WEL, and the other as legal advisor to Federated Farmers. One night in late November 1976, when Ruth was absent, Federated Farmers leaders John Kneebone, Alan Wright and Rob McLuskie trawled the corridor, attempting to step back from their organisation's submission.

For National supporters, a lot of issues in the mainstream were bleak. Budgetary conditions were very tight, and Muldoon had to put more money than he wanted into the Supplementary Estimates.[29] The National Party had gone to the election in 1975 with a promise to legislate to make union membership voluntary. In 1976 there had been strikes by drivers, shearers, freezing-company employees, and pulp-and-paper mill and waterfront workers. While these encouraged and reinforced Party supporters to push for the change, it was perfectly obvious to me that a voluntary membership regime would make little difference to these unions. The whole approach obscured the fact that at some of these sites there was lousy governance and management that was not subject to close examination.

In addition, laws, regulations, and government ownership and practices were costing the country dearly. The entire agriculture industry was riddled with subsidies. Interventions were rife. Government set wheat prices, regulated the capacity of freezing companies to pass on killing charges, approved prices for metric weights of bread, tried to regulate the size of potatoes for sale, paid guaranteed supplements to farmers to carry calves, sold licences for imports, and ran many services with extraordinary inefficiency.

In November New Zealand's monthly feminist magazine, *Broadsheet*, interviewed me, asking questions that were becoming commonplace. What was I doing in the National Party? I wanted much better opportunities for equality in education and employment, I said. It's through education and employment that people can begin to escape oppression. I thought that social progress demanded a larger government revenue to pay for it. That revenue was better collected from a private enterprise system than from the subsidised and inefficient state system we had.

I observed that a lot of right-wing bigotry only ever sees a welfare system as being exploitative. The same people may rort the system within their own business, getting around taxation provisions, but they wouldn't recognise it as such. They would think that was clever.

'Should feminists even be in Parliament?' *Broadsheet* asked. I replied:

> I have very little patience with feminists whose whole line is I oughtn't to be in the system because it is a male system. The short-term decisions that are being made in Parliament affect every feminist. It's a very frustrating place to be because you feel you are bashing your head against a brick wall the whole time. I still think it is really necessary for a lot more feminists to be there. I think feminism is broader than party politics. It's more encompassing. It defies any sort of separation into party philosophical blocks because its goals are of a longer term and of greater consideration than immediate and often smaller differences of policy approach. For me the electorate is paramount. There's a real excitement about that immediate form of representation where you're in close contact with the people you are representing. Trying to represent any sort of feminist consciousness is much more difficult because you never satisfy anyone.

'Do you find it disheartening or do you expect it?' *Broadsheet* asked.

'You learn to expect it,' I said.

Then: would I say, just from the amount of work I had, that there would be sufficient justification for having an office or something concerned with women within the parliamentary process?

'The only apprehension I feel about that is you then channel the awareness just to one place. I think it's better at the moment to keep it in an open forum. Otherwise, it tends to be a dustbin way of getting rid of these problems.'

Muldoon was driving me nuts with his nonsense regarding women. I addressed this in a speech on 10 November. At the recent NOW annual conference, the Prime Minister had spoken of the 'vast range of opportunity for women in every walk of life to fulfil themselves as wives and mothers, or in the careers of their choice'. I responded: 'Men do like to speak of women "fulfilling" themselves. The term is not used of men, and used of women is, I think, rather denigrating. As for career opportunities, could I point the Prime Minister in the direction of an advertisement which appeared in Auckland recently for "Accountant 25–35 male, or really excellent female considered."'

I was winding up the first year. Doug Carter's advice about all the invitations that flooded in was very good: 'Go to any that interest you in the first year and work out if you ever want to go again.' I had been to viticultural and other field-days, April Anzac Day ceremonies, Agricultural, Pastoral and Horticultural shows, Waitangi Day commemorations, 'Top Town' games, ram fairs, cattle sales, polo, the Te Rapa and Te Awamutu Racing Club meetings, the Huntly Fire Station opening, a vintage car show, the New Zealand age-group swimming champs, school centennials, weddings, and the conferences of Pasifika women and the Māori Women's Welfare League. I had spoken at National Party fundraisers in Nelson, Whanganui, New Plymouth and Tauranga. Only one function ever cancelled me after the *Truth* story. Allan Highet was mortified it was a Party function in his electorate of Remuera.

I had attended receptions and dinners where my presence was expected – at Government House in Auckland and Wellington, the

Party's September dinner for the visiting UK Opposition leader Margaret Thatcher, and the prime minister's dinner for caucus members. I attended the jubilee service of the Waikato Diocese of the Anglican Church, and the unveiling of the memorial plaque to the miners of Huntly. Ngāruawāhia High School and St Mary's Diocesan School asked me to speak at their prize-giving ceremonies. I advised students that all of us will change our jobs and be retrained in our lifetime, so you do not have to be wedded to choices you make as a school leaver.

I had spoken in the Estimates debates on mines, electricity, works, housing, education and transport. I had asked 100 questions in the House, more than any other MP. I would wait to see what the Electoral Boundaries Commission would deliver in 1977.[30]

1977

In December 1976 I wrote a proposal for a PhD thesis and went as far as writing to potential supervisors for comments. It was a letter written in haste, and not especially coherent. It focused on the myths of a consultative democratic caucus. I was thinking that I couldn't go on and wouldn't last another term, and needed something concrete to show for my parliamentary experience. There was also the issue of whether there would even be a seat for me at the next election. Population growth meant the Electoral Boundaries Commission would need to consider creating new parliamentary seats in South Auckland. This would put pressure on boundaries in the Waikato. I felt certain I would be challenged for the nomination, even if Raglan remained unchanged.

I was serious in my thesis intent. In January 1977, I sent a memo to all ministers' private secretaries asking for copies of all speeches and press statements for the rest of the year. I assiduously took notes and kept papers that had been circulated internally on issues before caucus. I kept newspaper clippings of every post-caucus press conference with the Prime Minister. I would analyse the differences between what was said and agreed in caucus, and what Muldoon told the media and the public.

At the same time as I was planning and collecting this data, I was working hard in the constituency. I was very torn. I felt that if I failed to secure a nomination again, or retired, it would be a burden for other young women who wanted to stand. For years they would wear my failure as an excuse to overlook them.

Muldoon had revalued the New Zealand dollar by two per cent on 29 December 1976. Building permits were rising again, and the total surveyed workforce was up, mostly because of an increase in female employment. Petrol prices were forecast to rise after most of the

Organization of the Petroleum Exporting Countries (OPEC) group agreed to a 10 per cent increase in the price of oil. This would be an inflationary pressure. Unemployment figures were expected to show a small decline, especially while there was a net migration loss of over 6,000 people a month.

In February 1977 the price of milk increased one cent to nine cents a bottle, and still had a government subsidy of $35 million a year. New Zealand had a poor balance of payments deficit of $1,017 million. There had been a rise in the value of exports over the previous year to $2,038 million, while imports were at $2,579 million. The country had to reduce consumption, but its economy was so small that even the purchase of a new airliner by Air New Zealand could have a marked effect on these figures.

The initial rates for National Superannuation payments were announced. Married couples would receive 70 per cent of the average wage (net $67.62, paid into separate accounts), and single superannuitants would receive 60 per cent of the married rate (a net $39.81). I celebrated that this was the first independent regular payment of their own that many women had ever received.

South African sporting contacts were back on the agenda at the first National Party caucus meeting of the year on 27 January. Minister for Foreign Affairs Brian Talboys was away overseas. I was always anxious when this item was discussed in his absence. He tried to mediate a better path than the nightmare proposals of the pro-sporting-contact right wingers.

Muldoon advised that following the meeting of the Supreme Council of Sport in Africa in December, a letter had been received from its secretary general, Jean-Claude Ganga. Muldoon described Ganga as 'a fierce character and a hardliner'. Ganga's letter questioned whether there had been any changes in New Zealand's policy of discouraging tours or refusing visas. He advised of discussions on the possibility of a boycott by African teams of the Commonwealth Games in Edmonton in 1978. The Ministry of Foreign Affairs had drafted a reply for the Prime Minister's Department. Muldoon told caucus the letter was ambiguous. It had said that New Zealand is a multi-racial country founded on respect, tolerance and cooperation. New Zealand law explicitly forbids racial discrimination. It had asked why we were the focus of international attention. New Zealand, the letter continued, supported the international campaign aimed at eliminating apartheid of which the international sporting boycott was a part. New Zealand deplored racial selection of sporting teams, and we did not welcome or encourage teams selected on racial grounds.

The way Muldoon presented the issue – that we were going too far, and it was time Foreign Affairs got the message – was set to stir a response from the backbench. When Minister of Internal Affairs Allan Highet suggested that it was a good statement of our position, he was booed. The key point was that New Zealand sports bodies were autonomous and totally free from government control. Talboys had told these organisations that they had obligations to consider the wider implications of contact but there would never be a suggestion that the government had requested them not to participate.

When I joined the caucus, new MPs were not given a briefing as to how it worked. We learned by osmosis or, in my case, I learned from George Gair's quiet commentary on who the PM was picking to speak and why. The agenda followed set topics, though the person in the chair determined their order: apologies, policy matters, Parliament, legislation, matters arising in caucus committees, select committees. Muldoon often opened with a travel report if he had been abroad: in these, he was always the hero. Appointments to various government boards invariably took time. Sometimes there were nominations for overseas delegations. The international and regional meetings of the Inter-Parliamentary Union (IPU) and the Commonwealth Parliamentary Association (CPA) were annual events, as was the Speaker's Tour.[1]

The February caucus had a typical agenda. Who would get the trip to the CPA conference in London; who would play golf in the annual match against secretaries, drivers and the press gallery; who would go on the caucus tour of the marginal Palmerston North seat? Queen Elizabeth would be at the February Opening of Parliament and would open the new Executive Wing building, referred to as the 'Beehive' because of its design. The Queen would not inspect the Guard of Honour; MPs could not stand on the steps and watch the arrival; and no children would be permitted into the Executive Council Chamber to meet the Queen. The Queen's Jubilee Medals would be added to the New Zealand Honours List announced in June, and MPs should make nominations for these.

General director of the National Party Barrie Leay briefed caucus on where the Boundaries Commission had got to in their work. In 1976–77 both major parties had advisers sitting with the commission. Leay was extraordinarily well prepared. He could tell you which polling stations had voted which way in every marginal seat. It was obvious he played a significant role in where the lines were drawn. He also declared that the Labour adviser had not done sufficient homework, and he was confident that new boundaries would serve the National Party well. I didn't get any indication of what was happening to Raglan.

The line-up of appointments to be approved indicated the range of opportunities to reward some of the Party faithful and lots of others who were 'damned good blokes'. We'd approve names for boards of savings banks, registration, national parks and trust boards; research, advisory and industry councils; advisory committees, tribunals, commissions and more. Sometimes the legislation which governed these bodies called for nominations from the national representative bodies, but if Muldoon did not like these names he sent them back and asked for others. There was no point in protesting. If you didn't give him another name, he left the slot vacant.

As chair of the Cabinet Committee on Public Expenditure, George advised that ministers were under severe constraints in new spending. They must cut into current schemes if we were to bring in new policy. Public service staffing numbers were frozen, with a sinking-lid policy in place. Departments had to argue every new addition. Interest rates were spiralling. Bridging finance rates had reached 18–26 per cent.[2]

The Whips' office had received an invitation for a representative to attend a Convention for Peace Action. Muldoon claimed it was a communist front organisation in league with a KGB man.[3] I was starting to see an interesting pattern here. No MP signed the Official Secrets Act; we just swore or affirmed an allegiance to the Queen. But, when it suited, Muldoon seemed to have no qualms about spilling news, which can only have come from New Zealand's Security Intelligence Service (SIS), about which unions (he claimed) were financed through the Soviet Embassy, or which New Zealanders had been to 'train' in Libya or Cuba. There was a section of that caucus who would oooh and aaah at such claims, while describing some of these people as Stalinist and some as Trots and some as Marxists, and whether they were Beijing or Moscow aligned.

I sought sanity in the constituency. Whatever I could do or attend there made me happier. In January 1977 I wrote to all chairmen and secretaries of the Raglan National Party branches and Women's Section branches.

— Do you plan to have any National Party social activity this year?
— Is there an important occasion in your district this year, e.g. a school centennial?
— What regular meeting-place events, e.g. stock sales, occur in your area?
— What sporting clubs function in your area?
— What service clubs or voluntary agencies do you have in your district? When, how often and where do they meet? Are there supporters happy to escort me to open meetings?

I could learn a lot wandering and chatting at these events.

I sought another form of sanity with women: in their service organisations and their communities, and with academics and activists. In early February I attended the Women and Health Conference sponsored by the Ministry of Health. The distance between MPs' understanding of women's health issues and the knowledge of those giving evidence-based papers at the conference was galactic. There was no way to describe one of these worlds inside the other. Every day I swung between them. I cannot even say I bridged them – the distance was too large.

My diary for the year filled up quickly. International Women's Day (8 March) and New Zealand Suffrage Day (19 September) were booked early. Part of me had expected invitations to various events to dry up following the *Truth* story, so I accepted a wide range. There were annual general meetings at which I was the speaker and 'we wanted to attract a good crowd', and others I attended because I wanted to listen. I tried to avoid any schedule that had me speak and then leave. I thought such behaviour was rude and didn't give me an opportunity to learn anything. Olga thought some of my acceptances were odd. 'Are you sure you want to go to the Deer Stalkers Association?' she queried. 'Absolutely,' I explained. There were members of this organisation in the electorate. Deer stalkers were on most forest park advisory committees, forestry development working councils, noxious animals advisory committees and the Mountain Safety Council, and had plenty to say about national parks. Other acceptances ranged from the Māori Women's Welfare League, the Prisoners' Aid and Rehabilitation Society, the Diabetic Association and the Neurological Foundation, to Save the Children Fund, Disabled Citizens Society and Friends of the Earth. I was a moving sponge for information and opinions. If I could not attend, I asked for copies of any remits or resolutions which might be agreed. Olga would type, 'I would be grateful if you could convey my apologies to all present' – a courtesy, of course, but I was always aware of the constant pressure for publicity and name recognition. I presented ribbons and cups, medals and certificates. I went to events at diplomatic missions and producer boards in Wellington, and hosted busloads of schoolchildren from the electorate in Parliament Buildings.

Then, by March, we were into the by-election in Māngere in South Auckland, caused by the retirement of Colin Moyle after Muldoon's attack on him in the House. This was a solid Labour seat. The Labour Party had chosen lawyer David Lange as their candidate. He was elected with an overwhelming majority.

I had some satisfaction when the government established the Royal Commission on Nuclear Power and it began its work. The terms of reference were: 'To inquire into and report to Government upon the likely consequence of a nuclear power programme ... considering such matters as siting, licensing, inspection, environmental effects, safety factors, transport of fuel and waste, disposal of waste and any other matters which the Commission decides should be brought to the attention of Government.' The personnel appointed were likely to gather good information and were unlikely to recommend a move in the direction of nuclear power, but I would pay attention to who made submissions and what they said.

On 7 March, at the end of her tour of New Zealand, the Queen announced that Sir Keith Holyoake would be New Zealand's next Governor-General. I thought back to that caucus in December when Muldoon had turned on Holyoake in a fury at his speech on sporting contacts. It was that moment he decided he had to get rid of him, I reckoned. Years earlier, Holyoake had embraced the 'No Maoris, No Tour' movement that asserted South Africa would not determine the membership of New Zealand sporting teams. He had been the first New Zealand prime minister to protest against French nuclear tests in the Pacific, and in 1963 had announced the ban on the storage or testing of nuclear weapons within New Zealand's territory. He had no problem supporting a South Pacific Nuclear Free Zone. So long as he remained in caucus, he was going to chip away at Muldoon on all these issues. He would not have wanted a diplomatic post; Governor-General was the only position with sufficient mana and dignity to persuade him to move aside. Holyoake resigned from Parliament immediately.

Holyoake was the oldest appointee to the position, and the only former prime minister to take up the role. Rumour was that the Queen was displeased at the appointment and the precedent, and that 'the Palace' made it clear it was never to happen again. The Governor-General should be non-partisan. The tradition of informing the leader of the Opposition of the nominee was not followed either. I liked Sir Keith, but I disliked this appointment.

Polls reflected significant anger. The National Party's Pāterangi branch passed a remit at its annual meeting that 'this Branch views with grave concern the appointment of a serving member of Parliament as a Governor-General'. On 11 March I addressed Wellington Polytechnic students about my 'unease and disquiet about the parliamentary system' and reflected on comments made throughout the electorate on Holyoake's appointment. I was down to be reprimanded at the next caucus, but when the agenda item arrived Ed Latter advised he had had a 'lot of flak about the issue before Marilyn's statement'. By then five of my branches had passed resolutions or remits. Two MPs with neighbouring constituencies to Raglan – Jim Bolger in the King Country and Lance Adams-Schneider in the Waikato – responded that there had been 'nothing at [their] Branch meetings. It is strange there are such differing reactions.' Good grief, I thought. Get a grip. Look at you two, and who comes to your meetings, and look at me. Totally different cohorts of people, and especially women, support me. I don't need to foment anything. My people are on to this all on their own. So you can stop your snide little campaign. But I just sat there quietly.

At the caucus meeting on 17 March we were read a National Party women's seminar resolution: members should bring any concerns into caucus and not air them outside. I didn't feel targeted. Shearer and Minogue aired their concerns, as did the right-wingers and tour supporters. Muldoon was aware that if he shut down one side, it would shut down the others. He advised there would be no stifling of backbench opinions, and in this he was quite consistent during his leadership.

Holyoake's resignation had given Muldoon the opportunity to make some minor changes in Cabinet. One of these was to appoint George Gair as Minister of Energy Resources, Electricity, and Mines. It was a gift for Huntly, and me, and George would change the way these government agencies operated in the town.

Construction on the Huntly power site had begun in October 1973. I continued attending the regular meetings of the Power Project Forum along with Huntly's mayor and town manager, representatives from Waahi pā, Federated Farmers and the Raglan County Council. I learned a lot about the behaviour of the government agencies represented at these forum meetings.

The power station site was on the banks of the Waikato River, less than 500 metres from the residents of the Waahi Marae, the principal marae of Ngāti Mahuta and the home of the Māori Queen, Dame Te Atairangikaahu.[4] The Māori communities of Te Kauri and Rākaumanga lived on the dusty gravel-covered Te Ohaaki Road used for all major site supplies, including more than 2,000 concrete piles. These were so long they could not be carried across any existing bridge on the Waikato River, so a special bridge was built north of Huntly from Rangiriri to join Te Ohaaki Road. It would carry only the project's pile transport, and it would be demolished when these loads had finished. I lived on the other side of the river in Huntly, but the town rocked all day six days a week to the sound of piles being driven. It took more than two years to drive those piles.

In 1973, before construction began, Ngāti Mahuta and the Environmental Defence Society had both appealed the grant of water rights for the project to the New Zealand Electricity Department (NZED). The Appeal Board dismissed Robert Mahuta's evidence on Māori as custodians of the Waikato River as irrelevant.[5] The board did, however, make NZED carry out a full biological survey of the river and formulate a plan to measure changes in biodata affected by the discharge of cooling water. Robert Mahuta had petitioned the Labour government for direct input into the project planning, including the impacts on the Waikato River, emissions from the station, construction noise, noise from the operating station, and privacy and safety. Tainui offered advice on how to consult with Māori. The request was ignored.

Within days of George's appointment, he approached me in the House with a copy of the Electricity Act 1968, which governed the building of power stations. Section 11(2) allowed for an amount of up to one per cent of the capital cost of the project to be made available to the community affected. In the past, all hydro stations built under the legislation were in isolated places where a village for the workforce was established by NZED, which also contributed a boat ramp (for hydro lakes) and an information centre from this discretionary spend. That was what was proposed for Huntly, and this was in George's briefing papers as incoming Minister. He wanted me to make sure the community was on to this. He asked for a coordinated process, involving consultation with Waahi Marae, the Huntly Borough Council and the Raglan County Council, to bring him a proposal to access these one per cent funds.

In September 1977 George confirmed that the government would compensate Ngāti Mahuta for the impact of the project on their traditional way of life with a major upgrade of the marae, along with new housing, and community and recreational facilities. Waahi land between the power station and the marae would be landscaped to make a buffer zone between the two. He recognised the Waahi community's relationship with their ancestral lands and water.

The Huntly Borough Council and the Raglan County Council also received their funds in line with the one per cent grant. The Huntly Power Project was one of the biggest single construction jobs ever undertaken in New Zealand. It employed 2,000 people at its peak. The main building would rise to 20 storeys and cover an area of nearly three hectares. What a difference it made when the minister in charge was a 'people person'. This was an exceptionally good and unforeseen outcome of the Holyoake appointment, for Huntly and me.

The good moments were welcome. I was suppressing a lot to survive. Public life and expectations were highly masculine. I was in a very particular and proximate relationship with power and its abuse. I was identified with my position as a Member of Parliament, where there were few if any role models, and others were quick to judge. The language the media used to describe me was changing. The *Christchurch Star* wrote that I was 'variously written off as a feminist, backbench maverick or trendy academic, [but had] seldom been out of the limelight. There was speculation that her political career will end prematurely.'[6] Well, it might, but there was plenty to do in the meanwhile.

A woman teacher wrote from Pukemiro School. She had been denied marriage-allowance removal expenses. These expenses had been available in the past, when her husband was teaching and she was a full-time parent. Now she was teaching and her husband was the full-time parent, and she was denied the allowance in precisely the same circumstances. 'For the wife to be eligible the husband must be completely incapacitated and receiving no remuneration whatsoever,' the Education Board advised. Education Minister Les Gandar wrote to me that 'this involves a personal decision as to their domestic arrangements. The teaching service is only one sphere of state employment. Any decision made in respect of teachers would have far-reaching consequences in the other state services. There were ongoing negotiations to eliminate discrimination in the public service, and this was but one of many items being discussed.'

These negotiations had been due to start in September 1975 in the term of the Labour government, but the state unions had waited six months to make their first response to the proposals. This was typical. Unions did not want to be told they had to accommodate issues of importance to women. Many were misogynist, white and male. Neither they nor the government partner was in a hurry to look after women workers. I asked for a complete breakdown of the conditions under which a male could receive the benefit compared with a female. I asked how much longer women had to wait. I knew that four boards concerned with employment conditions in the state services had no women members. I asked how many women were engaged in the negotiating teams of the state services and the unions. Oh dear. The Minister was so offended that I might think the gender of those engaged in these discussions had anything to do with a failure to move on these issues. But an exception was made. The removal-expenses allowance was paid.

On the PEC, I was agitating for our meetings to be open to the media, or for papers presented to us to be publicly available once the Estimates debate was under way in the House. In late March, a three-member sub-committee of chairman Bill Birch, Opposition deputy leader Bob Tizard and I was established to investigate and to report back to the full committee before the House sat again in May. Leader of the Opposition Bill Rowling said the Labour Party would welcome moves to open up the hearings. The president of the Newspaper Publishers Association, J.A. Burnet, wrote that 'the proposal to lift secrecy surrounding surveillance of departmental spending was a splendid example to other Western democracies of a direction for Government to move in'.[7]

The Clerk's office, however, did not like this idea, and repeated their position outlined to me in 1976. The Audit Office reported to us that:

> When Audit officers appear before the Committee for examination on the reports, their verbal comments in amplification of their content could be to some degree inhibited if they were to be reported. Even though they are confined strictly to the facts, as they are known, for obvious reasons, they have not been cleared by the departments and may be arguable if a wrong emphasis is given to them. So long as the comments are offered 'in committee' there is no damage to the auditor-client relationship, but the publication of them before a right of reply has been exercised would be unfair and possibly harmful.

In caucus, only Mike Minogue supported the idea. Oh well, I tried.

New Zealanders were always active in the use of petitions to Parliament. Once tabled, they were sent to the Petitions Select Committee, which heard submissions on the issue. The committee could then recommend to the House that the petition be given a 'most favourable' recommendation, 'no recommendation', or a 'for consideration' report. Those reported as 'for consideration' could not be debated. Many petitioners would be excited by this response, not aware that 'for consideration' was a device to avoid a further debate on the issue in the House. Nuclear issues were the subject of three petitions reported in April: 11,800 signatories opposed nuclear-armed and nuclear-powered ship visits to New Zealand; 20,370 signatories asked to reverse the decision to permit nuclear-powered ships into New Zealand ports; and a massive 333,000 supported a petition against allowing nuclear power reactors either on land or on ships in New Zealand waters. All received 'for consideration' recommendations so that they couldn't be debated.

On 14 April Brian Talboys advised caucus that Palmerston North Boys' High School was contemplating a possible tour of South Africa by its First XV rugby team. They had sought his advice. The reply was that the government abhorred 'the policy and practices of apartheid in all its manifestations, including the selection of sports teams. We draw your attention to the will of the international community as expressed in the Resolutions of the General Assembly of the United Nations. We ask you to take into account the interest of other sporting bodies who might be affected by any decision you might take. We ask you to take into account the interpretation that will be placed on your decision and the effect of this upon the national interest of your country.' The team did not go.

But the New Zealand government was being ostracised. At the IPU meeting in Canberra, Australia, host Prime Minister Malcolm Fraser had broken away from his text to attack those who continued sporting contacts with South Africa. Fraser and Muldoon enjoyed a mutual loathing, and neither of them hid it. Fraser was far more in touch with international realities and could wear the mantle of 'statesman' – not a description one could ever apply to Muldoon.

My cathartic response to despair about these issues was to write speeches to give outside the House, to think aloud with people who wanted to think, and to look for opportunities to do research on key issues of concern. On nuclear power, I said: 'I believe at the moment if we are strong in our endeavours to educate and inform the public as to the alternatives, to seek their assistance in conservatory measures, that we will be able to enjoy a non-nuclear future.' I bemoaned the use of gas to generate electricity in large thermal power stations. I described coal reserves in the Waikato of 450 million tons, 100 tons of which were defined as recoverable, but noted that this did not take account of environmental considerations. I asked about the development of sun, wind, tide and organic-matter generation, and about using waste heat produced in so many business operations. We were 'discovering in Huntly, major mining and energy operations have large social and economic costs'.

The draft re-drawn electoral boundaries were available at last. Raglan was chopped in three, and was one of the few electorates that completely disappeared in name. The top section including Huntly would go north. Ngāruawāhia and Raglan and some of the rural areas there would go east into the Waikato electorate. A new seat (with an old electorate name), Waipā, was the one I was expected to contest. Waipā was a 'blue ribbon' seat, and would be one of the safest in the country: its new boundaries retained Te Awamutu and now included Cambridge, a wealthy rural town with a population of about 8,000.

I had attended branch meetings of the old Raglan National Party branches, but the 1977 AGM would be based on the provisional new boundaries. There wasn't anything very different about the remits. These covered housing, roading, government spending, taxation, the Farm Savings Scheme and the Livestock Incentive Scheme. Social welfare remits asked for state-run crèches for solo parents on a daily basis, and for economic relief for the parents of disabled children who were caring for or educating them at their own cost.

I had noted as each meeting was held in the old Raglan branches that most of the delegates who were appointed for any candidate election were Waring supporters. But when it came to the election of officers for the Executive of the new Waipā electorate, I could feel organised resistance. Neither the Party chairman nor the chair of the Women's Section were among my supporters.

The secretary of the Raglan electorate, Lex Riddell, was asked to continue in the position for Waipā. He agreed, but because he lived outside the Waipā boundaries he had to be co-opted to the Executive. I remembered something Valerie Forbes had said after contesting selection with Mike Minogue in Hamilton West. There were opportunities to nominate up to six co-opted members of the Executive, all of whom would be granted automatic voting rights in any selection. Valerie had told me Mike had these co-options all sewn up. At the last moment, I caught her eye, raised my hand and asked if it would be useful in the transition to Waipā for all the officers from the old Raglan Executive – Peter Hamilton as chair, Simon Upton as treasurer, John Aubrey as publicity officer – to be co-opted, along with Katherine O'Regan as my constituency assistant, and even my father. Valerie moved this amendment immediately, and the motion quickly passed.

Waipā was going to be niggly until they had a candidate. George Chapman had made one of his rare caucus visits on 23 June, and described the Party's prospects for 1978. There would, he said, be a 'real struggle following the boundary changes. On paper, we have a majority of 26, but more than 13 seats are marginal.' Party membership was in decline. 'We could drop to 100,000 – half of the 1975 tally. We must take steps to reverse the trend.'

Chapman had referred to some of us as 'caretaker' members until confirmation, but I was receiving different treatment in Waipā. I wrote to him:

> While I am invited as a delegate to Waipa Electorate Executive meetings along with my colleagues, Adams-Schneider, and Bolger (who don't attend), I am not invited to address these. I am not invited to, notified of date/time/place or discussion topics of the Waipa Electorate Sub-Executive. I have not been contacted once since his election by the Electorate Chairman, Mr. Val Collinson. I do not know to whom he refers inquiries which Electorate Chairmen inevitably receive from constituents. An electorate newsletter has commenced production unbeknown to me. I was not sent a copy, invited to contribute, or specifically acknowledged in that letter. Care was taken to point out that Waipa was without a member and quips such as 'A Politician is a man amongst men. Otherwise, he is a follower of women,' were dotted throughout.

Materials I had always received in Raglan I now had to ask for: dates of the electorate and Executive meetings; membership numbers and projections; copies of minutes of all meetings held. I had to argue about payment for wreaths I'd laid on behalf of the government and people of the constituency at three Anzac services in the old Raglan.[8] I was told in writing by the electorate secretary that I had a generous electorate allowance to cover these, as well as the costs of monthly constituency surgery-session advertisements. I asked the chair of the Members Services Committee, Lance Adams-Schneider, to put in writing for me what the electoral allowance was to cover. It was vehicle-running, secretarial services in the electorate, hospitality, clothing, domestic help and donations. My constituency allowance was insufficient to cover these, let alone the additional costs I had brought to the Executive's attention. Lance also advised that members should advertise their availability to all constituents, and that this cost was not covered by the electorate allowance.

Meanwhile, an urgent remit had been sent from Women's Sections of the Party in the Waikato asking for the weedicide 245T, which was manufactured in New Zealand and widely used on farms, to be withdrawn immediately because of its effect on pregnant women.[9] Women were noticing a relationship between birth defects and use of the chemical, and early research was confirming links between them. National Party women in the Waikato wanted a ban and an investigation. Hugh Templeton had raised the possibility of an inquiry into 245T at the 28 April caucus. Ed Latter was very opposed. He had many orchardists in his electorate and swore they needed to use it. I advised of the concern in the Waikato. Les Gandar was the Minister of Science. He said there would be an advantage in an inquiry because it would show the claims were ludicrous. He said that 'his' scientists had advised him that 'a rat would need to drink 150 gallons of 245T to be affected, so a human must be safe'. So that was that. The discussion lapsed, and we moved on.

In June the Prime Minister had been at the Commonwealth Heads of Government Meeting (CHOGM) in London, where sporting contact with South Africa was a key agenda item. Leading up to this meeting, Muldoon's story as told to caucus was that Commonwealth Secretary-General Shridath Ramphal had set up a meeting with Prime Ministers Pierre Trudeau from Canada and Michael Manley from Jamaica, Tanzanian Vice-President Aboud Jumbe, Nigerian representative Brigadier Shehu Yar'adua, and Muldoon, who had refused to have Australia's Malcolm Fraser in the group. At a pre-CHOGM retreat at the Gleneagles golf course in Scotland, these six leaders drafted a text for an Agreement. It read:

> Governments unanimously accepted that it was the urgent duty of their governments to combat vigorously the evil of apartheid by withholding support for and by discouraging contact or competition with sporting organisations, teams or sportsmen from South Africa or from any other country where sports are organised on the basis of race, colour or ethnic origin ... Each government should determine how it might best carry out these commitments. Fulfilling their commitments was essential to the harmonious development of Commonwealth Sport in the future. Heads of Government welcomed the belief, unanimously expressed at their meeting, that there were unlikely to be future sporting contacts of any significance between Commonwealth countries or their nationals and South Africa while that country pursued apartheid policies.

Muldoon released the text to the New Zealand media before it was presented to, and agreed by, all members of CHOGM and became part of the communiqué released at the end of the meeting. He wanted to ensure local media understood his interpretation of the document before anyone else could say what the agreement meant. The New Zealand Press Association reported that Muldoon had said the government would not be sending the communiqué to sports bodies.[10] Nothing in the pact, he said, 'is inconsistent with our policy, which was the freedom of sports bodies to make their own decisions'. African representatives at CHOGM noted publicly that the British and Canadian governments actively discouraged sporting contacts with South Africa and expressed their repugnance for them.

On his return to New Zealand, the Prime Minister was not quite so cavalier. Brian Talboys had sent the Gleneagles Agreement to sporting bodies. Muldoon said it would be up to the 'good sense' of those bodies to make their own decisions in light of the Gleneagles Agreement.[11] Asked whether the government would issue visas to a South African national rugby team, Muldoon replied: 'This won't happen, and we all know that. You keep on putting hypothetical questions to me, and I will not answer them. The Rugby Union is not going to invite a Springbok team here, and I have said many times that the next team that comes will come when South African rugby is totally integrated at all levels.'[12]

On 1 June I gave my Address in Reply speech.[13] I was still on about data and lack of evidenced policy: 'It means that uninformed, unresearched prejudices often form the basis of debate in this Chamber and elsewhere. It means, for example, that a totally specious, unproven hypothesis can regrettably become the principle behind something such as the DPB Review Committee Report.'

I had not withdrawn from the front line on this issue. I kept using questions in the House:

— What was the ratio of departmental officers to the 36,309 maintenance orders administered by the Department of Social Welfare on 31 March 1977? Answer: one officer to 518 orders.

— What is the length of time between audits of maintenance at offices of the Department of Social Welfare? In Hamilton, the audit is three months and undertaken manually. Arrears of maintenance can reach incredible sums.
— Does the government intend to alter the manual system of audit? The Minister is at present working on proposals to introduce a new system.

By the time the DPB Review Committee reported, most of the focus was on unpaid maintenance. The government had to set up a system of maintenance accounting. Additional Social Welfare staff (188) would be appointed, with authority for even more if necessary. First-time degree courses in social work would be offered at Auckland, Massey, Victoria and Canterbury universities, and also at polytechnics. Women in receipt of the DPB had been stigmatised, but my work with women lobbyists had stopped the vacuous claims of National MPs and made some major changes which impacted on men.

New Waring support initiatives began happening in Waipā. On 3 July a new Women's Section of the National Party was established in Ōtorohanga, in Jim Bolger's old King Country. There hadn't been sufficient interest before. Pam Disher and Frances Rawlings asked two great supporters of mine, Maureen Fraser and Cecile Braun in the Te Awamutu branch, to help set it up. Jim McLay was the guest speaker. He, George Gair and Allan Highet had made it clear they weren't staying away from Waipā, and would help in any way they could. In spite of the behaviour of the Waipā Party Executive, I was being invited to many activities in the Waipā branches that were new to me.

In July Jim McLay's Evidence Amendment Bill was reported back to the House after select committee hearings. In my address, I was over-optimistic 'that rape victims would report the crimes perpetrated against them, and will feel more justly and more humanely treated by the Courts. The legislation meant that no evidence could be given, and no questions should be put to witnesses relating to the sexual experience of the complainant with any person other than the accused, or the reputation of the complainant in sexual matters, except by leave of the judge.' Parliament had made some progress, but there was a long way to go. I continued: 'Women do not find an accusation of rape easy to make. Those who do report their rape find it is a hard accusation to prove. One safeguard embodied in the law for the protection of defendants is the chastity standard appended to the statutory rape provisions governing assault against females below the age of consent. Resistance is immaterial in the case of a child below a certain age since the law resists for her. The law does not resist for a wife in respect of rape by her husband.'[14]

In the wake of another dreadful rape event, I asked caucus for support to establish a special Select Committee on Violence. The terms of reference for the 1975 Select Committee on Women's Rights had omitted any reference to violence against women. I could also see the 'lock them up for longer' National Party supporters getting vociferous, so they would probably see such a committee as to their advantage.The Prime Minister was opposed: 'Where will it end up? The Opposition will have a field day.' But caucus supported me, and Minister of Justice David Thomson would return to caucus in December with the terms of reference.

At the 15 August caucus, the New Zealand Security Intelligence Service (SIS) Bill was on the agenda. The SIS had been responsible for the information which had led to the unsuccessful prosecution of a former civil servant for spying. An inquiry by the Ombudsman had followed. All the proposals in the Bill were based on recommendations in the Ombudsman's report, but one significant recommendation was not included. The report had proposed a change of emphasis in the work of the SIS from its 'present concentration on protest'. Ombudsman Guy Powles recommended: 'That the Act be amended by inserting a proviso that intelligence shall not be obtained regarding any person or body which is not actually engaged in espionage, sabotage or subversion unless the advice of the Intelligence Council has been obtained' and that 'until the Act is so amended the Service curtail the counter-surveillance on activities in accordance with the spirit of the proposed amendment'.

Muldoon and the right wing were opposed to this recommendation.

They really were adrift from the 'mainstream' they thought they represented. From Wharepapa South, 21 National Party supporters who would be in the new Waipā electorate wrote: 'We feel most strongly that the New Zealand Security Intelligence Amendment Bill denies the freedom of speech, the right to personal privacy, the right to question the activities of those in authority, and most importantly our democratic right to public scrutiny and access to the appellate jurisdiction of the Courts.' I wondered if they had bothered to write to their current electorate MP, Jim Bolger. Mike Minogue put up a significant fight for all the Powles amendments. He was unsuccessful, and was harangued in and out of the House for not crossing the floor on this issue. But I watched his strategy, and his ability to play a long game, as he won the trade-off of a commitment to the introduction of freedom-of-information legislation.

The other major change in the legislation was the introduction of an interception warrant, which had to be applied for every year, in writing, to the Director of the SIS. Muldoon tried to have this application made to the Minister (himself), but the caucus pushed back and ensured it was the courts which would determine the issue.[15] An interception warrant could be issued if the court was satisfied by evidence on oath that the warrant was necessary for security or intelligence, that the value of the information justified interception, and the information was unlikely to be obtained by any other means. One warrant would have a 90-day limit. I hoped the involvement of the courts might also give effect to the Powles recommendation focusing on espionage and not on legitimate, democratic activism.

In 1977 the credit-rating agency Moody's gave New Zealand an AAA rating. I doubt it was warranted. But it was time for my annual Budget speech.

> May I say to all in the House: you are representatives of the present and the future, not the past. What I say tonight is as a representative of more than half of the New Zealand population aged under 35. There is a vital need to study the economic and social implications of an aging population. Projected forward 20 or 30 years, I and my generation will not be able to afford the cost of the care and income maintenance of

> all those over 60. Assisted by improvements in medical science, the numbers of those over 60 will keep growing.[16]

In an early reference, I was looking at the contribution of the unpaid work of women: 'We must come to grips with discrimination on the grounds of race and sex. Alvin Hansen remarked that if a careful calculation of [all outputs] were made over the last 10,000 years, in most places and times, it would probably be found that women produced more than half of the real gross national product.'[17]

I also reflected on what was happening to the farming districts on the west coast in both Raglan and Waipā. 'While we heartily invest money in agricultural production for the rurally isolated, we slowly deprive them of their social needs. We close their small schools and their rural post offices, and consequently, the store and garage go too. The access roads deteriorate.'

It didn't bother me to be critical of aspects of the Budget: 'The underdeveloped state of social research and social statistics in New Zealand is deplorable. In the same budget in which $3,055 million, or nearly half the total amount, is expended on three votes – Social Welfare, Education, and Health – the vote for Department of Statistics and research in this area has been reduced. For too long this department has had insufficient services and insufficient attention. The poor state of social research is one of the key impediments to the development of coherent social policies in New Zealand.'

At the August National Party conference, Sue Wood had been elected Women's Vice President. She asked to meet the eight women dominion councillors, Colleen Dewes and me. We discussed the vexed question of the membership of the Party's Policy Committee but thought the prospect of change was bleak. There was a significant – and widening – gendered gap in National's policy focus. That said, the Citizens and Aliens Act gave New Zealand women the right to pass their citizenship on to their children on the same terms as men. In the past citizenship could be conveyed by descent in the female line to a child born overseas, but only if the mother was unmarried.

The Human Rights Commission Bill finally emerged from caucus for introduction to Parliament. It contained prohibitions against discrimination on the grounds of race, sex, marital status and religious or ethical beliefs. Both Duncan MacIntyre and Jim McLay argued for the inclusion of sexual orientation, but it was a tough enough job in caucus to get the other grounds included and to get the Bill out the door as promised in the 1975 Election Manifesto. Most MPs received scores of template letters pushed by various churches opposing the legislation. I could see the legislation might solve the issue for Linda Jones, the wonderful jockey in my constituency, but I didn't see why we should wait for the legislative process. I wrote a letter to the New Zealand Racing Conference, enclosing a copy of the Bill, drawing attention to the discrimination in employment provisions, and advising that given their policy they might want to make a submission. Linda told me that when the meeting got to that item on the agenda, the chairman effectively said, 'We won't have any choice about women jockeys, so we may as well move to change the rules now.' And they did.[18]

The Territorial Sea, Contiguous Zone, and Exclusive Economic Zone Act 1977 was passed. This extended New Zealand's fishing zone to 200 miles (320 kilometres), making the economic zone fifteen times the size of the country's land area, and the fourth-largest in the world. Special provision was made for the establishment of an Exclusive Economic Zone beyond the outer limit of the territorial sea of the Ross Dependency in the Antarctic. This was a unilateral declaration. The Law of the Sea Convention had not been finally agreed.

The Town and Country Planning Bill was introduced in August. It too was something to be proud of, with its focus on:

- the protection and enhancement of the physical and social environment
- the preservation of the natural character of the coastal environment and the margins of lakes and rivers and the protection of them from unnecessary subdivision and development

- the conservation of productive land and the prevention of unnecessary encroachment of urban development on such land
- the prevention of sporadic urban subdivision and development in rural areas
- the maintenance of the special relationship between Māori culture and institutions and their ancestral land; and
- the prevention of the cities expanding beyond the optimum geographical area.

This was a partner with the Reserves Bill, focused on preservation and protection of threatened areas of natural, archaeological or historical value. It also established the Queen Elizabeth II National Trust to protect such features on private land.

It was comforting to have some moments of pride. There were plenty that resulted in the exact opposite.

In the Prime Minister's constituency of Tāmaki there was a sensationally beautiful piece of land known as Takaparawhā or Bastion Point. It overlooked the Waitematā Harbour, and contained a memorial to Michael Joseph Savage, New Zealand's first Labour Prime Minister. It was the last reserve area on the Auckland waterfront. Ngāti Whātua, the local iwi, were the original settlers and owners.

As at Raglan, Bastion Point had been requisitioned by the military in 1941, but at the end of the war the government, instead of returning the land to the iwi, gave it to the Auckland Council as a reserve. In 1952, again just like at Raglan, the council destroyed the marae, and all the homes and people were evicted. Compensation was offered, but many Ngāti Whātua never uplifted this. Why would they? It was their land! Ownership continued to be disputed, and this led to an occupation by members of the iwi and their supporters, beginning on 5 January 1977.

The Minister of Lands, Venn Young, brought the matter to caucus, but it was obvious Muldoon was directing the responses. In June, Young described a small hard core of protesters as occupiers, who he said were determined eventually to be carried off. Hyperbole abounded. McIntyre claimed: 'They are looking for a Sharpeville.'[19] Talboys alleged the protesters were trained in Beijing or Moscow. There were some level heads: 'Why do we want to put houses there? Māori people will say we ripped them off.' But Muldoon directed that the Auckland Council would file an injunction asking the protesters to leave. It would take some time for this to work its way to court. I felt anxious and depressed by these exchanges, especially when MacIntyre and Talboys were part of the madness.

I was often tied up in constituency work by the nonsense of sales tax and exemptions. For example, an agricultural contractor might import a large excavator. The 10 per cent sales tax on machinery would not apply in the case of machinery used in dairying, agriculture, farming, forestry and fisheries. So my contractor would have to prove, and sign a declaration to the effect, that a particular machine would be used solely for agricultural purposes – no roadworks, river clearance, or housing development with that excavator. There was an exemption from sales tax on outboard motors for fishing vessels, and tax refunds might be granted on outboard motors purchased by commercial fishermen for use on vehicles engaged exclusively in commercial fishing operations. An applicant had to provide his local collector of customs with a current certificate of registry for his boat, a boat fishing permit, and evidence in the form of financial statements or certificate from an accountant or solicitor establishing that at least 80 per cent of his earned income was from commercial fishing operations. Approvals under this exemption were limited to two outboard motors per year per vessel. The applicant was also required to sign a deed of covenant that the motor would not be disposed of or used otherwise than for commercial fishing purposes for not less than two years. But the fisherman dies, and the family need to sell the motors for income. Now I need a death certificate, but we have to wait for the coroner. The time it took to make these cases, and to wait for a determination, was way out of line. It created inefficiencies and increased the pressure inside the National Party to introduce a universal indirect tax regime.

By September 1977 the DPB review had become maintenance law

reform. It was clear that the legal process was the major problem in recovering maintenance. The person receiving the benefit (usually the wife/mother) had to bring an action to the courts. This process could involve several months of negotiations between solicitors before the issue of court proceedings, then several more months waiting for a court fixture. Eight thousand benefits were being paid where no maintenance order had been sought. The courts could handle approximately 3,000 defended cases per year. The caucus had no choice but to agree that:

- court proceedings for maintenance should be issued immediately an application for a benefit is made
- the action should be brought by the Social Welfare Department, not the woman herself
- the procedure should encourage husbands or fathers to allow claims to go undefended
- the amount claimed should be set out in the application – it would be $55 weekly
- the husband or father would have 14 days to decide whether to defend the action
- this would be an alternative procedure; it would not stand in the way of spouses who wanted to claim more than the benefit doing this.

Meantime, the abortion issue was back on the agenda. The Contraception, Sterilisation, and Abortion (CS&A) Commission had reported in March 1977. Once its report was published, I advised in correspondence that: 'My personal stance on the abortion issues is that, where it can be shown that there are sound medical, psychological or socio-economic reasons why the pregnancy should not proceed, then it is a decision for the woman concerned, and the facilities for such a termination should be provided at reasonable cost and be available in sufficient number for this.'

In April, Des Dalgety, Muldoon's lawyer and Society for the Protection of the Unborn Child (SPUC) president, hosted a dinner at his home for Muldoon, Frank Gill and the Roman Catholic Cardinal Delargey. It was here that they worked out the strategy for dealing with the royal commission report.

Gill, they decided, would introduce the Bill based on the report. Dalgety and SPUC would get busy drafting their amendments and lobbying MPs so that they would have one of their anti-abortion supporters move all these amendments – something Minister Gill couldn't do. Gill would introduce the Bill in October, which would give SPUC plenty of time to get organised and lobby. Muldoon, who had made himself Leader of the House, and so controlled the daily parliamentary Order Paper, would take urgency and run the debates all night to get through them as fast as possible. There would be no reference to a select committee.

SPUC, Dalgety and Muldoon had settled on Chief Government Whip Bill Birch to be their man. In November 1977 Birch sent a letter to all medical practitioners with a copy of his proposed amendments, which set up an Abortion Supervisory Committee (ASC) and panels of certifying consultants, and left out the general practitioner (GP). By then, 1,300 of an estimated 1,500 GPs had referred patients to the Epsom clinic. The proposed panel system had operated, for example, at Wellington and Hutt hospitals, which processed, on average, 26 women per year from 1971 to 1975, while 312 women were referred to the Aotea Clinic from the Wellington–Hutt region in 1974. Polls consistently showed over 65 per cent of New Zealanders favoured the woman alone, or the woman and her doctor, making this decision.

On the first reading of the Bill, Mike Minogue made his feelings about Muldoon's tactics plain: 'I certainly resent the fact that I am saying this at twenty-five to two in the morning when I can hardly think what I am saying. I suggest that this is no time for decision-making.'

I spoke after Mike:

> The New Zealand Association of Scientists in August 1977 stated that unsupported statements, imprecise definitions and uncritical evaluation of contradictory research findings are to be found in this report.
>
> The proper formulation of the issue involved in the abortion question is not whether or to what extent abortion should be permitted, but

> whether or to what extent the freedom of decision that modern medicine makes possible should be abridged.
>
> If in the final analysis there is one principle that is to be acknowledged to be the standard by which the political arrangements as a whole are judged, and by which the fitness of proposed laws are measured, it is the principle of liberty paraphrased in the 1975 National Party manifesto as freedoms.
>
> When, from a consideration of personal freedom, there is doubt about the specific content of legislation – and there is in this case – or substantial disagreement about the broader premise on which the legislation must be justified – and there is in this case – the presumptions of liberty must prevail. The acid test in the last analysis is whether the House is prepared to pass legislation that flaunts this principle as it affects women and as it affects the legal and medical professions. Justice is considerably slower than procreation. A woman pregnant against her will cannot wait for a court to make up its mind; she goes out and finds an illegal abortionist because it is faster and cheaper.[20]

I then sought leave of the House to table six affidavits I had referred to in my address which demonstrated the royal commission's proposals wouldn't work. Just one MP's objection can stop this. Muldoon objected.

As the Bill and debate moved to the committee stages, anti-abortion MPs moved quickly to make the legislation even worse. Dalgety succeeded in getting his draft of the long title of the CS&A Bill accepted, including the phrase 'having full regard to the rights of the unborn child'.

A crucial clause proposed by Gerard Wall 'that all possible means of resolving the risk to a woman's health must be exhausted before an abortion could be approved' was passed at 5.58 a.m. by 34 votes to 26. This amendment prohibited abortion when the serious danger to the mental or physical health of the woman could be averted by any other means. Its practical effect was to outlaw abortion totally.

At 6.05 a.m. a clause moved by Labour MP Sir Basil Arthur removed foetal abnormality as grounds for termination. We lost again 34–26.

The inclusion of rape as an automatic ground for abortion was voted on at 7 a.m. We lost 37–22.

Whetu Tirikatene-Sullivan's proposal putting the abortion decision in the hands of a woman and a doctor of her choosing lost 45 votes to 15.

George Gair was trying to find some middle ground. He moved amendments all night to:

- replace the proposed system of panels, and to substitute this with two doctors agreeing that the abortion was justified
- remove the proposed supervisory committee, and to transfer its licensing function to the Director General of Health
- add social workers to the list of persons authorised to supply contraceptives to children under 16 years of age, to direct or persuade such children to use contraceptives and to advise such children on contraceptive matters
- require the Director-General of Health to grant a renewal of a clinic licence unless he considered there were grounds for not doing so
- remove criminal liability from a female who attempted to procure her own miscarriage.

They were all lost.

In addition to those 13 MPs who were ill or overseas, 14 male MPs who were present in the House at the beginning of the debate were no longer recording votes and had apparently 'gone home'. Among these was the Prime Minister, whose last recorded vote on a division was shortly before 2 a.m. His first recorded vote later on Wednesday morning was at 10.31 a.m. I alerted the media, who asked him what he had voted for and when. He couldn't remember.

The third reading passed on 15 December 1977 and became law on 1 April 1978, although the all-important abortion-related amendments to the Crimes Act (which contained grounds under which abortions can be granted), and in particular the Wall amendment, took immediate effect. This meant that as soon as it was passed, the Contraception, Sterilisation, and Abortion Act of 1977 proved both unclear and unworkable. No one would or could operate legally.

At the caucus meeting on 20 October, Bill Birch reported from the

Party's Dominion Executive that they felt 'we have lost a lot of ground as a Party. Conflicts within the Party on the SIS and Abortion Bills have been damaging events. We have lost momentum', and there were difficulties in the renewal of memberships.

Muldoon delivered a major economic package in October 1977, an attempted reflationary budget even while the Consumer Price Index (CPI) was at 14.4 per cent. Unemployment was at a post-1945 record and expected to grow. Muldoon always resisted policies that might have halted the negative trends in the economy if they would add more to the jobless queues. Key features of the October announcement were:

— a one-off supplementary family benefit of $25 per child paid to mothers
— a five per cent tax cut
— adjustment of the reserve asset ratio at the Reserve Bank to allow for an additional $25 million, to be available for mortgage and farm lending
— reduction of the government security ratio on life-insurance offices by one per cent, with the offices requested to invest the $24 million released in industrial projects with an export orientation
— reduction of security ratios for trustee and private savings banks, releasing about $64 million for mortgage lending
— abolition of the restriction on trading-bank investments in local authority bonds
— expansion of the Māori training scheme, as well as carpentry and joinery courses
— accelerated maintenance in public-sector buildings, using private-sector contractors
— a farm-employment wage-subsidy scheme
— an increase in the Export Suspensory Loans scheme.

Some policies George and I had worked on in Opposition were in the package. The Housing Corporation would make loans to single people. Finance would be available for those in tied accommodation to purchase their own home, and this would be open to people who were at least 45 years old and within 10 years of retirement. The purchase of a first home or section for the construction of a first home would be exempt from stamp duty. The package introduced a vendor mortgage scheme to encourage older persons to vacate family homes and leave an investment in the property as a mortgage, and shift to smaller accommodation. But mortgage interest rates were high, and economic and financial forecasts for the next year were not good.

I was still collecting all my proposed thesis material, but what else might I do if I had just one more year in Parliament? There had been a Cabinet memo about the Implementation of Recommendations of the Select Committee on Discrimination against Women, 1974, but more than just the government needed to respond. I knew that Canada had followed up its Commission on the Status of Women some years later with an audit called *What's Been Done?* Access to parliamentary questions and some progress on legislation suggested by the select committee would make it possible for me to do something similar, so I began to act on this.

The select committee had received 128 submissions and made 53 recommendations. I dissected each of the recommendations, asking each the same question: on whom was it incumbent to act? I used this list and wrote to these entities, inquiring precisely what they had done. I also wrote to each of the bodies which had made submissions to the original select committee to seek their opinion of progress or otherwise. Where departments were slow to answer, I lodged questions in the House. Where other bodies were slow, I sent a follow-up letter. Where companies were concerned, I selected 30 of the largest from the Companies Register, equally divided between the North and South Islands. Nineteen replied. A selection of replies included: 'Until women have further advanced their status in New Zealand business life, our shareholders are unlikely to appoint a woman to our board despite the fact that more than 45 percent of our 25,400 shareholders are women' (Watties). Another read: 'Dear Miss Waring, In reply to your letter of 27 January, we have done exactly nothing, Yours, etc., Sir James Doig' (UEB Industries). Where clubs, organisations and associations were concerned, I chose 17 at random, and 12 replied. Where voluntary organisations were concerned, I chose at random 36 that received government assistance. Nineteen replied.

Action was not explicit in the recommendations of the select committee. For example, of 14 recommendations on women in employment, only three had substance. But I was gathering more information. For example, only about 14 per cent of industrial awards (out of 100) contained provisions for maternity leave. No one had any idea at all how many children under five had mothers in paid work. No financial allowance could be made available for mothers of primary school children on full-time correspondence-school courses. The Department of Labour posters advertising the final step for equal pay had managed a distasteful 'put sex in the pay packet' slogan.

The Ministry of Foreign Affairs was hanging on in opposition to renouncing ILO Convention 89: 'There is no way of escaping our commitment to it. New Zealand will remain legally bound by the provisions of the Convention until 1981, and any action which would place New Zealand in breach of its obligations under the Convention would be an extremely serious step which would run directly counter to our traditional position as an upholder of the rule of law.' What a load of twaddle. Other Western advanced economies had renounced this.

Women were paying for the budgetary subsidies offered to those earning income. The family-benefit payment of $3 per child had not shifted since 1972. In 1977 it would need to be increased by another $2.25 per week to keep up with the subsequent increases in the CPI. This would cost about $120.7 million a year. So women were the losers in the redistribution of government resources. Mothers could wait.

I thought it would be a good idea if the women MPs, Whetu Tirikatene-Sullivan, Mary Batchelor, Colleen Dewe and I, could meet with the Committee on Women, and I initiated this in November.

I maintained a regular correspondence with the small local newspapers in Raglan and Waipā. I sent them all my interventions in the House – especially questions – if they were relevant to their circulation. In 1977 I had spoken in the Estimates debates for Mines, Social Welfare, NZED, Education, Housing and the Arts. I also spoke on the Health

Amendment, Ministry of Energy, Electoral Amendment, Evidence Amendment, New Zealand Planning, and CS&A Bills. With respect to Waipā, I was trying to be a dedicated, reliable, hard-working local MP. I was now certain there would be a contested selection early in 1978.

Meantime, there was a local celebration in order. Katherine O'Regan had contested her riding for the local government elections for the Waipā County Council, and became the first woman member of that body. We were delighted. I also wrote letters of congratulation to each of the successful local-body candidates within my constituency. Many local government representatives were closer to the people than I could be. I valued their feedback.

As the year drew to a close, Sir Roy Jack, Speaker of the House, died on 24 December 1977. We would have a by-election early in 1978.[21] It would be an interesting test of the government's popularity going into the election year.

1978

On 23 December 1977, Muldoon had announced a nuclear-powered submarine, the USS *Pintado,* would visit Auckland on 16 January 1978. The visits to Wellington of two US nuclear-powered cruisers, *Truxtun* and *Long Beach* in 1976, had been met by public protests, and union stoppages had meant the host port was idle while the ships were present. Despite the USA's 'never confirm or deny' policy on whether vessels carried nuclear arms, it was well known that not all cruisers carried nuclear weapons. But nuclear weapons were invariably carried on submarines, and there would be weapons on board the *Pintado.*

The Auckland Harbour Board was advised that the berth approved for the *Pintado* by the New Zealand Atomic Energy Agency (NZAEA) was at Jellicoe Wharf. The board countered that, for safety reasons, the Wynyard berth should be evaluated. The government's reply was that Jellicoe Wharf 'conforms to the safety considerations set out for all nuclear-powered ships in the NZAEA 500 Code'. But the code said such vessels must not berth or anchor within a 600-metre radius of a high-density or residential area. The Jellicoe Wharf berth meant downtown Auckland became a high-risk area, even within the parameters of the ridiculous safety assessments.

In early January, the president of the Auckland Trades Council, Bill Andersen, advised that members were worried about their personal security, as well as the security of their families. 'No one seems to be asking why the sub has been sent here.'[1] Watersiders voted overwhelmingly to not work Jellicoe Wharf and to declare it off limits during the six days of the submarine's visit.

We were supposed to be reassured by the planning. On 12 January, Northern Regional Commissioner of Civil Defence Commander J.L.

Quinn advised: 'The area around the submarine would be monitored constantly during the visit, and if a nuclear accident should occur, people within a 600 metre radius would be asked to walk immediately to the Parnell Rose Gardens and the Shortland Street or the Britomart Place car parks. A shuttle bus service would then take them to decontamination centres – either in the periodic detention centre in Parnell or the Auckland City Council depot in Cook Street – where, if contaminated they would have a shower and receive two potassium iodate tablets and a change of clothing.'[2] Pills would be distributed to various authorities in preparation for the submarine's visit.

Auckland Harbour Board, which had received complaints from major shipping companies, sought compensation from the government for the loss of income from mercantile shipping during such visits. The managing director of Star Shipping, for example, hoped that the board would sustain 'the usual efficient commercial port operations during the future visits by naval vessels'. But Muldoon had a different agenda and wasn't bothered by economic losses if he could play his political games.

The Rangitīkei by-election was to be held on 18 February 1978. Sir Roy Jack had won the seat by 1,756 votes in 1975. Bruce Beetham, the leader of the Social Credit Party, had been the runner-up and was standing again. His party had taken over seven per cent of the national vote in the 1975 general election but won no seats. Muldoon was confident Rangitīkei was a traditional National seat and there would be no problem retaining it. He was wrong. Bruce Beetham won the by-election with a majority of 1,335, taking 48 per cent of the vote to National's 38 per cent, with Labour at 11 per cent. It was a rude surprise for the Prime Minister.

Rural New Zealand was not happy. In late 1977 seasonal industries, particularly in provincial areas, were badly disrupted by weather. Fifty per cent of the registered unemployed were labourers, factory workers or freezing-industry employees affected by the late resumption of seasonal work. The 1977 Budget, at $382 million, was a very rapid reduction from the $1,001 million spend National had inherited in the 1975–76 fiscal year. Muldoon had then spent a further $506 million in the October 1977 'mini-budget'. A very low Gross Domestic Product (GDP) meant a reduced tax take from companies and workers. Also, with rapid inflation, there was a fiscal drag, which kept moving people to higher tax brackets when they received increases in income. Thousands of people were leaving New Zealand, and there was increased expenditure on unemployment. The new superannuation scheme had kicked in as the largest single item in the Budget, leaving no room for manoeuvre with other expenditure.

In early January I was invited to a meeting at Labour frontbencher Martyn Finlay's beach house at Piha, along with his Labour colleague Warren Freer, Jim McLay, George Gair, Sue Wood, Bob Harvey (a Labour Party supporter and advertising guru), and ALRANZ secretary Anna Watson from the Epsom clinic. The agenda was New Zealand's impending abortion nightmare, and what might be done to organise and mobilise the anger about that. By the time we left that evening, we had a plan, a name – REPEAL – and the simple goal of a nationwide petition with the single aim of repealing all the CS&A and Crimes Act changes made in December 1977. We drafted the petition 'prayer'.[3] We had no budget, but put together a list of people each of us would approach as possible patrons of REPEAL. My job was to return to Wellington in January and build the electorate organisers for the petition; I also had to find people prepared to have their name in public. I knew some possibilities. My colleagues gave me many more. I searched my mail for others. Most of these approaches were 'cold calls', made in the middle of the school holidays. I found this hard, but it had to be done.

Everyone returned the calls; one person used a radio-telephone from Milford Sound. If a GP I contacted couldn't take the risk of becoming a patron, they would suggest the name of someone who would. I had to have a full list so that everyone would come (at their own cost) to Wellington for media training, to meet each other and to ensure we were all singing the same tune before the launch in February. People were so outraged, an extraordinary list of high-profile people signed on as patrons: Federation of Labour president Tom Skinner; Challenge Corporation chairman Ron Trotter; Auckland and Christchurch mayoresses Barbara Goodman and Judith Hay; the last four retired women MPs from Labour and National; the former Dean of St Paul's in London, Martin Sullivan; more industry, union and farming leaders; professors of law and medicine; Māori including Henry Bennett, Ranginui Walker and Māori Women's Welfare League president Mira Szászy, until there were 50 in all. I also invited the Rev. John Murray from St Andrew's Presbyterian Church and lawyer Brenda Cutress to front the movement, and found an office we could have in Wellington for no cost, to be staffed by volunteers. I took the petition to a day at the Thames Summer Races, expecting to be sent scurrying for interrupting a social and leisure event. But it was the exact opposite. People signed up and wanted empty forms to take away.

In the three months from the first week of February until mid-May, REPEAL collected 318,820 signatures. Petition forms were handed over to Parliament's four women MPs who presented them on the same day.

The CS&A Act had been passed early on 15 December 1977 and was to become law on 1 April 1978, but the Crimes Act changes, which specified the grounds for abortions, took immediate effect. By January 1978 consultants at National Women's Hospital in Auckland were refusing to carry out abortions for fear of breaking the law. With the new Wall amendment – 'and the danger cannot be averted by any other means' – doctors said it was too dangerous legally for them to risk operating. Under the Act, a woman needed the signatures of her GP and two certifying consultants before finding an operating surgeon. By the time the legislation came into effect in April, the Abortion Supervisory Committee (ASC) had failed to appoint certifying consultants in Taranaki, Nelson, Marlborough and Timaru, and North Otago and Whanganui had only one each. The ASC, in response to public clamour, recommended changes to the Crimes Act, with foetal abnormality to be included as a ground for termination, and deletion of the Wall clause. We would be back to abortion in the House again in 1978 with legislative amendments. Meantime, the Sisters Overseas Service (SOS) was set up to raise money and to offer advice to assist women to fly to Australia for an abortion.

For months I had expected to be challenged for the National Party's nomination for the candidate for Waipā – the new electorate that incorporated 44 per cent of the votes cast in 1975 in Raglan. In January

I was writing to well-wishers, 'If I win I win, and if I don't, then there is plenty more left in life for me to do.' I was upset to lose the opportunity to represent Huntly and Ngāruawāhia where, despite their various challenges, I felt far more at home, even if I would never win the booths in those towns. Waipā was very different. Yes, there were pockets of poverty, but this covered an area with much higher living standards.

There had been an upsurge in the membership of Waipā National Party branches to qualify more voting delegates. My challengers were three worthy, middle-aged Pākehā men: a transport operator from Te Awamutu, a garage proprietor from Cambridge and a surveyor from Ōtorohanga. The hidden message was obvious: they sold themselves as 'good family men'. I did not wholeheartedly embrace working for this nomination, but I had been encouraged and heartened by a delegation led by the mayor of Te Awamutu, Ned Freeman, who was not a Party member. One morning when I was conducting my constituency meetings in the council rooms, he had assembled a very significant group of local government and business leaders, farmers and Party stalwarts, Māori leaders, feminists and teachers – constituents whom he knew I had helped – to advise they wanted me to stand for Waipā. Ned had also asked the local media along. I was genuinely surprised by some of the people who joined that group. I often underestimated the number of people who supported me quietly.

For this contest I didn't visit any voting delegates I thought would not support me. Women were organising. I remember a meeting at Margaret Whitfield's home in Wharepūhunga. On a slope in the garden, the men were seated on chairs in front of me, with the women standing behind, arms folded, containing them there. There was a gender division, with women supporting me even in the branches new to me, but men still held the largest number of delegate votes at the selection meeting on 6 March.

Muldoon told my caucus colleagues to stay away from this selection. It was between me and the electorate. Tony Friedlander, however, came to talk to me. Until 1970, his father had been the Party's Waikato divisional secretary, and their name was well known in National circles. Tony asked if there was any branch where I was having problems with support. I told him I didn't feel there was much at Te Kawa Crossroads. He called the chairman of that branch and invited himself to the annual meeting, and advised me he was going to tell them that he needed me back in Parliament. Senior MPs warned him not to go. He recalled: 'Someone obviously phoned my father before the meeting and he drove down from Hamilton to meet me beside the road before I reached the venue, to advise me to keep my nose out of another electorate's business. His advice was that my intervention would be resented [in Waipā] and could count against you and probably harm my own career prospects. Interestingly enough, rather than change my mind, his advice helped me to improve what I intended to say. Following the meeting, which he attended as a guest, he commended me for the way I had handled the meeting but expressed concern that I probably hadn't endeared myself to some in the Party and caucus. I never did ask who had contacted him.'[4]

I was working in my office in Parliament on 3 March when Michelle Boag, who worked in the National Party headquarters in Wellington and was prominent in the Young Nationals, knocked on my door. She didn't say much, wished me the best for Monday evening, handed me an envelope and left. Inside were the two questions that would be handed to candidates at the selection meeting, one from the Party president and one from the prime minister. Neither was difficult or challenging, but it was useful to gather a few more briefing papers to swot for the answers.

At Tūrangawaewae Marae on Saturday, the Māori Queen, her eyes twinkling, gave me a pink corsage 'to wear on Monday night' at the Te Awamutu College assembly hall. It would be perfect with the very expensive deep-blue dress I had bought from a fashion store, Memsahib, in Wellington. Late Monday afternoon a TV crew arrived at my home. Reporter Bill Ralston had set it up. He said he was confident I would win the nomination, but there wouldn't be time to drive the film from Te Awamutu to Auckland for the 10 p.m. news bulletin. So he interviewed me as the victor and got his film on the road, hoping he would be able to make a phone call to confirm I had won before the late news broadcast.

I did not find it easy to write this selection speech, and I thought it was staid and boring. I compared the Waipā selection with that of Raglan.

'The position is only altered by time and by the responsibility I now find in carrying on my shoulders, not only my performance as the representative for Raglan, but also the record of the National Government's two and a half years in office.' I reminded people of the change in the demographic data. 'Compared with Raglan, Waipa is predominately urban, and the combined population of its three major centres is 18,000. It is wealthy, and second on the list of per capita expenditure for New Zealand towns.' I advised, 'There is no future for Waipa or New Zealand in speaking of going back to anything.' I supported the key principles of the National Party as 'elusive objects in practice' and as 'ideals we chase in daily administration. But in politics, one learns very quickly to look at what people do, not what they say. We believe in private enterprise, but we temper the purity of that philosophy in New Zealand with a wide range of taxpayer-subsidised concessions and incentives.' I surmised that in politics it is frequently the office, not the individual, that accomplishes change, but the office must be deserved by the person applying for it.

My conclusion stated the obvious:

> The significance of the vote this evening goes far beyond who becomes the National Candidate for Waipa. The New Zealand public will weigh first who Waipa accepts and second who Waipa rejects. The polls show that three-quarters of a million New Zealand voters are presently uncommitted. Waipa matters in terms of our Party's credibility in its boast of having the broadest base of political support. National's image is on trial. Tonight you must be confident of the reasons for your choice. You must be proud enough of those reasons to justify them, under intense scrutiny, to the Waipa electors, to the National Party, to the Prime Minister and Government Caucus and Parliament for years to come.

The evening was not prolonged. I won the nomination on the first ballot. Later in the evening, scrutineer and supporter George Mandeno said to me, 'You cut that fine. You made it by one.' Thank goodness for those co-options at the first Waipā AGM. I knew I had five of the six, and they had got me home.

The next morning the *New Zealand Herald* reported on the selection held in front of 700 National Party delegates and members. I liked the bit where it said: 'The weight of her support staggered leading party officials who, only three hours earlier, had suggested that three ballots, the maximum when four nominations are considered, could be necessary.'[5] The mail and telegrams that greeted my nomination were amazing – from foreign missions, judges' chambers and the parliamentary press gallery – as well as from National colleagues and from Labour MPs. The Waipā office holders who had organised the AGM resigned. I was grateful and relieved. Now I could get on with my work. I didn't like a lot of it, but I would be the person who would decide when and how I would leave Parliament.

Caucus also had work for me to do. I would be one of the election-year speakers at universities. Ministers were not to go. For the first time, too, I put my hand up for the ballot for one of the overseas trips, and I was selected to join the parliamentary delegation to Europe later in March to lobby on an anticipated sheep-meat regulation by the European Economic Community (EEC) which might affect New Zealand.

The five-MP delegation would visit the capitals of the smaller EEC countries: Ireland, the Netherlands, Belgium, Luxembourg and Denmark. It was my first experience of this kind, and I liked it. I had no difficulties reading and remembering briefs. I did other research myself, in addition to what was supplied by the Ministry of Foreign Affairs and our diplomatic posts. I learned a lot of unexpected things. A parliament (as in the Netherlands) did not have to sit adversarially, for example. People in Europe truly did remember the sacrifices made by my grandfather's generation. He survived at Gallipoli and in France in the First World War, but other relatives had drowned in Belgian mud. At Ypres, I was affected with great sadness by the stories of the battles, and vowed I would never be part of any decision to send young men and women to war. I learned a lot about trade, tariffs, protectionism, customs duties and the nature of these negotiations. International Politics had been one of my majors at university, and now I was in the midst of some real stuff, however minor it might be.

The sheep-meat delegation MPs were not present at the 29–30 March caucus. There Muldoon advised that Parliament would meet on 10 May – timing that was related to his decision on an early-June Budget. He told caucus that while all indications suggested an upturn, unemployment would still be high. Many sectors of the economy were in poor shape, he reported, but overall economic management looked good. Muldoon consistently overestimated his capability in this sphere.

Much of this caucus was spent reviewing the Rangitīkei by-election and what to do about Social Credit leader and new MP Bruce Beetham. The Opposition would be expected to find him a position on a parliamentary select committee. Muldoon advised caucus: 'Keep things lively, but intelligent. The press will be on his side. Treat him as a backbencher. Don't listen with rapt attention. He'll find it a little difficult and lonely. Don't make it easier.'

Beetham would share his seat in the House with the sitting MP from Pakuranga who had been defeated when challenged for the National Party nomination as a candidate for the 1978 election. He had formally resigned from caucus and the Party, but would speak by arrangement with the government Whips as an Independent National. Muldoon called this 'quite a tragedy', especially given what he called his 'willingness to stop opposition to sitting members'. It's as well I wasn't there to hear this: I would have choked in the front row.

All members of caucus were asked to submit ideas for policy for the election in November. In early 1978 I offered the following for Education: 'The most important function of education is to develop the desire and capacity to learn. Formal education should be preparation for self-education through life focused on versatility, adaptability and how to learn. For my generation and those in school, the whole nature of work by which we earn a living will be altered. We must be educating for the world the young will know, not that of the past.' I prepared a paper on bicultural and multicultural education for the caucus committee, but it was not adopted. I and other women in the National Party were pushing very hard on early childhood services for both care and education, but this was a mess. There was no overall coordination of either. Minister of Social Welfare Bert Walker said that the provision of childcare centres would weaken the 'families in our community, the very structure we should be seeking to strengthen'.

Sexism and paternalistic attitudes permeated government policy. A letter to the editor of the *Press* in Christchurch explained that:

> Currently New Zealand is desperately short of therapeutic radiographers. Late in 1977, a British radiographer was accepted for a post in the Christchurch Radiotherapy Department. However, the lengthy immigration processes were terminated since this woman's husband could find no employment here, rendering them undesirable immigrants. The Department of Immigration's attitude is blatantly sexist. Why should already overloaded staff be forced to continue working under pressure because the patriarchal Government refuses to admit that a woman's place in society is where she chooses, not where men choose to put her?[6]

There was sexism in the defence forces. I had significant reservations about women serving, but could not allow this to influence my response to requests to work on equality for women who wanted careers in the army, navy or air force. There was a blanket prohibition on women in combat zones, so in both the navy and the air force this operated as total exclusion. In May Ian Shearer forwarded to me a reply he had received from the Minister of Defence, on behalf of a constituent, 'whose daughter Jacqueline wishes to take university studies under naval sponsorship ... The Navy provides university courses only for male entrants. This University Training Scheme is designed specifically to produce professionally qualified, career, combat officers, and is therefore restricted to males.'

A 16-year-old in Te Awamutu and another young woman from Wellington were in touch in July. They wanted to join the Royal New Zealand Air Force (RNZAF). Why didn't the RNZAF accept training applications from women as pilots or air crew, and why couldn't they apply for the University Training Scheme? The RNZAF was the route used by young men to become pilots for commercial airlines, after serving the basic required years. It was an easy way to accumulate the flying hours needed to be accepted, and to get paid en route. As a result, retention of pilots and navigators in the RNZAF was very poor. Any woman who wanted to fly for Air New Zealand had to pay thousands of dollars to instructors and to aero clubs to accumulate the required miles. Ian stayed on the case with letters and questions in the House, to no avail.

Unemployment figures were growing, but it was difficult to discover what impact this was having on women. A lead story in April in the *New Zealand Listener* commented: 'Increasingly families surviving on a single income are becoming the new poor of middle-class New Zealand and, in a country of rising unemployment, the most likely employee to get the push is the married woman. The only thing that can be said for sure about New Zealand's unemployment problem is that no one knows how big it is. The Labour Department doesn't know. [The 1976 Census recorded] 14,560 men and 12,650 women (2180 of whom were married) as unemployed. The numbers registered with the Labour Department at the end of August 1976 as unemployed were 3709 men and 2130 women.'

But the census figures probably underestimated the problem when it came to married women, as many who wanted paid employment would enter their occupation as 'housewife', reflecting an unhealthy community stigma around being 'unemployed'. The Working Women's Council in Wellington were organising on the issue, urging unemployed women to register. The unemployment benefit was not a handout but an entitlement. 'All women, particularly married women, should register, as in some cases, even married women are entitled to the unemployment benefit. There is nothing to be ashamed of in accepting your legal entitlements.'

There were two key points at issue here. One was to ascertain what was happening for women – were they losing their jobs at a faster rate and, if so, in which sectors? We couldn't gauge this at all. The other was that there was a discriminatory outcome between men and women claiming the unemployment benefit. When a married man lost his job, he was paid out at the married rate for himself and his spouse. When a married woman lost her job, and her husband was the 'housekeeper', she was not eligible for the married benefit. This anomaly between men and women was the same for sickness and invalids' benefits, including eligibility for a housekeeper allowance. The 1975 policy had committed us to change this: it would arise again later in the year.

MPs were often asked to be available for interviews with postgraduate research students. I received one such request in April from Helen Clark, now a lecturer in Political Studies at the University of Auckland. Helen's PhD thesis was on the political role of farmers in three western societies, New Zealand, Great Britain and Sweden. She had been in those last two countries on a scholarship, conducting interviews with MPs 'who were farmers and/or who represented electorates in which substantial numbers of farmers resided'. This interview was the first time we met.

The next caucus was on 13 April. Muldoon reported that the National Party's Dominion Council was 'in a flap' after the Rangitīkei by-election loss. Party president George Chapman wanted to come to caucus. Muldoon opposed this. He hated having the president or general director present. He always chose two of his strong supporters as caucus representatives to the Council, and they rarely reported criticism of the prime minister accurately. However, Valerie Forbes was now on Council and made very balanced reports to our Electorate Executive: these were often at odds with what we were told in caucus. Muldoon's position was that the Party was best to concentrate on the organisation.

At this caucus meeting Ian Shearer was on the case about banning advertisements for cigarettes. He was indefatigable on this issue. There was also a Health Advisory Committee on Smoking and a resident of Hamilton who kept up a tremendous lobbying and petitioning campaign. Ian wanted to ban smoking on public transport and in hospitals, and was supported by a number in caucus. But cigarette sponsorship drove many high-profile New Zealand sporting events, and Muldoon didn't want the backlash. His advice was to say it was 'under consideration, like [the registration of] chiropractors'. Such tactics were used whenever there was a lot of public pressure to act, particularly in an election year.

On 11 May the Party's Dominion Executive met. The Prime Minister generally attended for a short time, talked at them, and then left. This time he did report back that there was some pessimism and worry about Social Credit. He had also advised the president that he was not to allow leadership to be up for discussion in Party executive meetings. That was a matter for the parliamentary caucus.

A significant amount of the caucus meeting on 18 May 1978 was spent on the continuing occupation of the Ōrākei Marae on Bastion Point.[7] We were advised by Minister of Lands Venn Young that tribal leaders had attempted to get the elders and protesters together, and that the elders had refused protest leader Joe Hawke's case. Muldoon told us that the 'people left were communists and anarchists. The government would now move the protesters out forcibly with Police but would have to use the Army to move caravans, a bus, and other materials. Lands officers would inventory possessions and demolish buildings. This was a historic landmark and the time was up. It would all happen in one day. The Police Commissioner was confident it could all be done in accordance with the law.'

The day chosen was the next caucus, Thursday 25 May, the 506th day of the protest. The reason, we were told, was that the government had been awaiting a reduction in the number of protesters. I suspect it was because Muldoon could be shielded from the media for the first hours of the eviction because he'd be attending caucus. Ian Shearer was up: 'There are children on the point,' he said, 'and there is an area that is tapu, where there is a memorial to a young girl who lost her life there. That must be left.' There was a knock at the door. The Whips handed Muldoon the first of the pieces of paper that would arrive that day. 'So far 30 have been arrested,' we were told.

We moved on to other agenda items. Typically these included industrial disputes or negotiations; this month the focus was on workers in the meat-processing industry and those belonging to the Port Employees Union. In the National caucus, it was always the fault of the unions.

Another knock at the door: 'There have been 83 arrests. Demolition of the outer building is completed. There are 200 more inside the building.'

Minister of Māori Affairs Duncan MacIntyre had Mount Egmont on the agenda.[8] Changing the name of this iconic peak to Mount Taranaki had been an issue since a petition in 1975. Compensation to Taranaki iwi with respect to the mountain under the Treaty of Waitangi had been increased 50 per cent. MacIntyre was proposing that the government (symbolically) returned Mt Egmont to Taranaki Māori, who would then give it back as a gift to the nation as a national park, with its original Māori name. Senior local electorate MPs in the region didn't want this to happen in an election year, but Tony Friedlander supported it.

The Prime Minister wanted caucus to consider two matters of importance. The first was that the land in question did not stop at the foothills of the mountain but included a lot of land surrounding it. The second was that the area proposed for a national park had potential for energy exploration, and there might be a problem around the ownership of mineral rights should any attempt be made to access such resources. Norman Jones could be relied on to represent the right wing. He wasn't supportive of MacIntyre's proposal, he said, and 'the majority of New Zealanders are not very interested in the Maori wars'.

Ben Couch was one of only two Māori in the caucus. He quietly rebuffed Jones. There were many significant grievances, he said, and they had to be fronted. He supported the Minister. MacIntyre responded that the petition of the 1974 hīkoi, led by National Party supporter Dame Whina Cooper, included many land grievances and we could not ignore them. 'If we are going to do it, now is the time.' Muldoon sent the issue back to Cabinet to bring again to caucus.

There was a quiet undercurrent in the room. Ōrākei Marae was in Muldoon's constituency, and you would have had your head taken off if you tried to argue with him on this. But the sense of discomfort at what was happening at Bastion Point on this Thursday was obvious. It felt as if the Taranaki issue could assuage some of the guilt. It would assist those who wanted progress on Treaty issues, and those who were environmental activists and had no issues with locking up national parks free from energy exploitation. It would not be the first time Māori had made an extraordinary gift of land to the nation for a national park.[9] When the matter came back to caucus on 22 June, the support for MacIntyre was overwhelming.

Another message showed more arrests at Ōrākei, and expressed confidence that the whole process would be completed in a day. By the end of the day, 222 people had been charged with illegal trespass.[10] It was a shameful day for New Zealanders and for the government I was part of.

Parliament had opened on 10 May, and 18 May was set down for speeches from the party leaders. As I came into the House that day, I recognised a group of women from WONAAC waddling into the gallery as if they were in the final stages of pregnancy. Hmmm – what this was all about? I didn't have to wait long. They lifted their shirts as one, and purple balloons emblazoned with 'Abortion a Woman's Right' rose to the high vaulted ceiling. I was delighted. (Others were horrified.) The balloons floated around there for weeks because, short of trying to fire at them with a missile, nobody could get them down until they ran out of air. I didn't get much to smile about in my work, but the sight of them kept me going every time I entered the House.

We were back in another abortion debate. The legislation had proved inoperable. Muldoon didn't think the changes – in particular, the excising of Wall's 'by any other means' clause and the inclusion of foetal abnormality grounds – were necessary, but said he would vote for them 'if they will persuade more of the medical profession to do what they should have done as doctors'.

Whetu Tirikatene-Sullivan introduced four amendments, which would have made rape, extremes of age, contraceptive failure, and social or economic circumstances all grounds for abortion. All four amendments were lost. The clause on rape was defeated by two votes. I had decided to vote for all Whetu's amendments but not to speak. I was almost catatonic with anger on this by now. But a decision by the Abortion Supervisory Committee provoked me so much I roared into the mess in the House again:

> Dr. Peter Wilcox applied in good faith to become a certifying consultant. He took the House at its word. The law was liberal, reasonable and workable. He responded to the pleas of the Supervisory Committee and the Auckland Hospital Board, knowing that right now in Auckland there is no operating doctor, and at least 12 women that I know of in the area, who have a certificate issued by two certifying consultants are

> awaiting an operating doctor.[11] They are entitled to a legal abortion, and there is no one to operate. Knowing that, Dr. Wilcox applied five weeks ago to become a certifying consultant. He is highly qualified and a highly respected medical practitioner. He has been the superintendent in charge of the maternity hospital for 11 years, and he has done over 2000 maternity deliveries. He is experienced in the early termination of pregnancy. The Auckland Hospital Board thought highly enough of him to approach and appoint him to the position, but he has been turned down by the Supervisory Committee.

With my voice cracking, I concluded:

> Women in New Zealand have had abortions since the first settlers arrived. They have continued having them regardless of what has happened in the House in 1974, 1976 and 1977 and they will continue to have them regardless of what happens this time, whether it is in Aro Street, in Ponsonby, in a rural cottage with a friendly GP, or in a hospital, until those of us with cash can no longer fuel them to Australia. They will have them because they need them and they want them. The women of New Zealand will not in any way subject themselves to a law in which they have no voice and for which they have no respect.[12]

I thought I had properly blown it then, but my backbench colleague Derek Quigley came up to me and said, 'I was just sitting it out, but when I heard you I realised I had to get back into the fray as well.' We battled as best we could, with all four women MPs again in the same lobby on every vote.

Of course, I received loads of the organised rote-written anti-abortion letters. Many of them were poisonous. I threw them away, except for the only three I received from my constituents. I took care with those to respond.

I was able to draw on my EEC delegation work when I made my Address in Reply speech on 30 May.[13] I was already playing to the new Waipā electorate, where many people were engaged in and dependent on agriculture. With Huntly gone from my orbit, Mines, Energy, Electricity, Works and Development were no longer a focus, and I had a sense that it was on rural matters that I would meet the most resistance from electors – and where Social Credit would be popular.

I complimented our diplomats, of whose work I was genuinely proud. I advised the House: 'I am concerned that we all understand. Europe is saying it does not owe us a living, that we can no longer go on producing increased volumes for European markets and expect top prices. We are diversifying. We are expanding markets in Asia and the Middle East, and our diplomatic posts are exploring all avenues for further market opportunities.' I quoted Jim Gemmell, president of the New Zealand Manufacturers Federation. 'It is no use blaming the EEC for our misfortunes or complaining about practices that make it more difficult to sell on world markets. We must face the fact that the cause is our inability to increase productivity and expand our overseas markets ... We will not achieve our objectives by an increased Government role in the economy.' If I was going to be critical of the meddling and interventionist policies of Finance Minister Muldoon, then it was good to have someone of repute doing it for me. It was my job to assist farmers to access the multitude of subsidies and incentive schemes available, but I would also comment quietly in safe company that I wasn't comfortable supporting social-welfare programmes for sheep. Many farmers in my electorate thought the subsidies were too many, too scattered and too high.

Whenever I had an opportunity to speak in the Estimates debate, I took them. The Estimates were effectively the House sitting in the committee stages of the annual Appropriations Bill (the Budget). There were a certain number of sitting days set aside for these, and the Opposition drove the agenda, based on the issues they wished to use to embarrass ministers. I could also press ministers on elements of policy that had not been enacted, speak of major issues of importance to women, or prime the constituency parish pump. I was happy to do any of this.

On Justice Estimates I argued that there should be a retirement age for Justices of the Peace, and that more Māori and women should be appointed. I congratulated the Marriage Guidance Council, the Prisoners' Aid and Rehabilitation Society, and the Neighbourhood Law Offices, who received some funding from this Vote, on their work. I understood these references helped to secure ongoing funding. On

Education, I hammered away on the whole pre-school area again. In my contribution on Health, I noted that from 1 August 1978 contraceptives provided on medical grounds on a doctor's prescription would be eligible for the pharmaceutical benefit. Likewise, pregnancy tests would qualify for a health benefit.

In 1978 I was a member of the Statutes Revision Select Committee. There were very diverse Bills to attend to. The Marine Mammals Protection Act 1978 allowed for the establishment of sanctuaries; prohibited the hunting of marine mammals; and legislated for management plans and strategies for the protection, conservation and management of marine mammals in New Zealand waters. That felt good.

I spoke on the Social Security Amendment Bill in July. Ian Shearer had introduced a Private Member's Bill that would allow payments be made to all those caring for children and adults with mental disabilities who required 24/7 care. The government adopted part of the Bill but excluded adults requiring care, as recommended by the Royal Commission into Hospital and Related Services in March 1973. Parents in my constituency had told me about the high costs of caring for intellectually disabled children: of going to Hamilton, where services are available; of a large car for a child who cannot sit; of fees for doctors and specialists; and the costs of continuous replacement of household crockery and furniture because of breakages by strong and excited youngsters. Higher insurance premiums have to be met, and special equipment, footwear and clothes, and special diets are often necessary. Frequently sections have to be fenced and gates padlocked.

> In addition to all that there are problems of short stay placement costs, and relief for the family to enable it to go into town or to attend family gatherings. Those problems are immeasurable in terms of financial assistance. Problems are caused perhaps by resentment by other children in the family, and the fact that these are overcompensated or undercompensated for. Economic restraints are imposed on a one-income family, and there is often the problem of finding a baby-sitter for the psychopaedic child. There is no doubt that the family faces a

> changed lifestyle that revolves around that child and this cannot be calculated in terms of dollars.[14]

Opposition MPs, such as Russell Marshall, referred 'to their disappointment that, in taking over the Private Members Bill the Government has decided to confine it to children. Members on this side of the House have mentioned that a great many people have to care for not only disabled children but also for disabled adults.' Yes, that invisible unpaid work again.

The horror and idiocy of the CS&A legislation and its outcomes continued. On 28 July the Department of Education sent a letter to all schools: 'Under Section 3 of the Contraception, Sterilisation and Abortion Act 1977, it is illegal for any person, including any teacher, to supply instruction in the use of contraceptives to any pupil under the age of 16 in any school, unless that person does so with the prior approval of the principal or head teacher of that school given after agreement with the School Committee or Board of Governors.'

Te Awamutu College sent me a copy of their reply:

> We can probably accept, with some reluctance, the requirement that teachers be 'cleared to teach'. This is not as easy as it sounds. The School Certificate Geography syllabus demands reference to 'population distribution and growth' and food problems. Any average to bright 4th and 5th former is likely to raise population control by contraception.[15] We are asked to censor what goes on library shelves. We cannot in all seriousness accept that the Encyclopaedia Britannica should not be placed in the library for the free use of all pupils. Would a teacher, or librarian commit an offence if, in answer to a pupil request, he or she placed this material in the hands of any pupil? Is any teacher at risk using this material in a classroom for normal teaching purposes (e.g., Science or Social Studies)? Is the school at risk by having such materials on library shelves?

I lodged a written question to the Minister of Education about Britannica and the other titles: *Man and Society*; *Population, Resources, Environment*; *Man, Medicine, and Morality*; and *Biology and the Social Crises*. Minister Les Gandar replied: 'I am advised that all but two of the titles listed in the question would seem to constitute materials for "instruction in the use of contraceptives."'

In caucus on Thursday 20 July 1978 the Prime Minister was in the chair. We had some pieces of legislation to deal with, and first up were amendments to the Accident Compensation Commission (ACC). We were expanding the geographical coverage to include the Exclusive Economic (fishing) Zone (EEZ). Antarctica was excluded, but oil rigs would be covered.

The next item was the Misuse of Drugs (Listening Devices) Bill. This was to allow police to enter premises to install listening devices. They would need to obtain a warrant from a Supreme Court judge for assistance in detecting the importation and distribution of Class A and B drugs. Colleagues Gandar and McLay spoke in opposition. These powers were not available for mass murder, they said. There was an additional issue, in that the Post Office Act inhibited mail interception. The caucus recommended Customs could open suspicious mail and then repost it. The police also argued for the introduction of a new clause to protect undercover officers who 'had to be able to smoke cannabis to continue to have the trust of criminals'. The select committee had seen a very fine line between allowing this to happen and police officers having the opportunity to incite, counsel or procure an offence by, for example, asking someone for drugs. There were also some major issues about breaches of privacy and listening devices. The Caucus Committee on the Misuse of Drugs was concerned that all policy was police driven. No attention was being paid to treatment and rehabilitation. Methadone maintenance could not be administered anywhere other than a medical facility. There was certainly no treatment available in prisons.

When the Misuse of Drugs Amendment Bill reported back to caucus on 21 September, it contained provisions that any police officer 'in the performance of his duty' had a defence to a charge brought against him under the Misuse of Drugs Act. No undercover policeman could be prosecuted under the Act except with the leave of the Attorney General.[16]

We had another round of industrial disputes, this time in the meat industry. Government ran interference with unions and employers in meetings with Minister of Labour Peter Gordon, Agriculture Minister Duncan MacIntyre and the Prime Minister. Wage-increase demands were at 12 per cent. Many of these meetings were conducted with large amounts of whisky consumed.

Party president George Chapman and director Barrie Leay were welcomed to the next caucus, on 27 July, to discuss the Party conference and preparation for the election, which would be held on the final Saturday in November. The Prime Minister advised all MPs to 'stay away from abortion'. Later that day he called me up to his office and told me he didn't want abortion to be an election issue. I was incredulous. 'It is one,' I replied, 'and there isn't anything I can do about that. I didn't create this mess.'

The next caucus item concerned some of the West Taupō forests that were in my new Waipā electorate. Minister of Forests Venn Young argued that loggers needed a 'sustained yield' for specialist timbers. He claimed that failure to do so would necessitate imports. Ian Shearer queried the effect on the endangered kōkako and drew attention to an oversupply of native rimu on the local market.[17] Why was further exploitation needed? Young then acknowledged the surplus of native timber and reiterated the major issue was a sustained yield.

Environmentalist Stephen King was already camped high in a magnificent rimu in the threatened Pureora Forest, gaining a lot of national attention. The last National government had suffered a huge loss of support as a result of the 'Save Manapōuri' campaign, and there was little appetite now for a re-ignition of cross-spectrum political activism.[18] Many New Zealanders would mobilise on environmental issues. Caucus was divided, and the issue was sent back to the Caucus Forestry Committee with an instruction for 'non-committed personnel to be present'.

The result came quickly with a new Central North Island Forest Policy. A state forest park including Pureora, Tīhoi, Wharepūhunga (in Waipā) and Hurakia, Taringamutu and Waituhi state forests was established immediately. The amount of native timber cut from native state forests would be reduced as rapidly as practicable. Logging would be withheld from sensitive wildlife habitats, at least until the likely effects had been studied and for not less than three years. Reserves would be set aside for scientific, wildlife, educational and recreational purposes. The area would include large areas of virgin lowland forests throughout the central North Island. All forms of government price control on native timbers would be removed to allow prices to rise as the timber production fell.

I was very grateful I wouldn't begin representing Waipā with yet another fight on my hands in the furthest southern reaches of the constituency. I hated getting up every morning in Wellington to the prospect of a workplace of constant battle. It was taking its toll. It was about this time that Mike Minogue described our job as 'turning 360 degrees 24/7 to stop even worse things from happening'. It was a good description of the daily dynamic of what he and I tried to do.

The final issue for this caucus was the Orakei Block (Vesting and Use) Bill, the follow-up to the removal of protesters from Ngāti Whātua land at Bastion Point. The Bill was necessary to avoid the Town and Country Planning Act, which would have required hearings and a right to appeal. Auckland City Council favoured this route, but Muldoon wanted to close it all down. The land would be run as a public reserve by the city council in perpetuity. Hearings would be in Wellington only, and would not be open to the press, to avoid demonstrations and protests.

On 9 August the *New Zealand Herald* ran a story in which a senior Cabinet minister described me as the 'most valuable piece of political property going. Political insiders believed she could be among first of the "1975 intake" MPs to be promoted in a National Government.' There were plenty of critics, of course. This was noted.

> Yet they ignore her growing influence in caucus, her ability to sway party colleagues with logical and well-researched arguments. This year she was particularly critical of the remits chosen by party headquarters for debate by delegates where government had already announced policy, meaning delegates were being asked to 'rubber stamp' government decisions. 'That takes the initiative away from the conference. It becomes the conference of endorsement,' she said. Apart from abortion and solo mothers, all her public skirmishes with cabinet ministers have been on electorate matters.

I had no ambitions at all for promotion. There was a practice that once given a Cabinet portfolio, you would always accept and defend 'Cabinet collective responsibility' for any decision made. If you could not accept this, you would leave. I thought my behaviour made it especially obvious I would never put myself in a 'collective responsibility' trap; I could never serve this prime minister in any portfolio, or subject myself to any more stress than I already had as a member of this caucus. But the expectations were always of what men had done for decades. The usual thinking went (and I heard this often): 'Well, yes, I'd have to compromise, but look at the opportunities I might have to advance [name the issues] important to me.' It was expected that everyone there was ambitious for power, and colleagues simply did not believe me when I said I did not share this.

In early August we were advised that the Social Security Amendment Bill would include provision for married female breadwinners to receive payment at the married-couple rate for sickness and invalids' benefits, with payment for a non-qualified husband. A provision would be made for women on a sickness benefit to be paid a housekeeper's allowance on the same basis as men. But Cabinet decided not to allow married women to receive the married-couple rate of unemployment benefit, with payment for a non-qualified husband. Apparently, this would entice a married man to become voluntarily unemployed in the knowledge that his wife's chances of obtaining suitable employment were less than his own.

Aussie Malcolm fought back: 'Since we have not extended this provision to the unemployment benefit, we have not completely implemented the policy undertaking to remove sex discrimination. The Social Welfare Caucus Committee would like to discuss this matter further.' Barry Brill held the very marginal seat of Kāpiti, where his Labour opponent, Margaret Shields, had a lifelong commitment to advocacy for women. He could see the electoral impact of this exclusion. He was lobbying too. He wrote to the Minister:

> It is certain that the exclusion from the Social Security Amendment Bill will be heavily criticised. To enable me to defend the Government's decision, I should be grateful if you could let me have a further

> elaboration of the view that provision for married women 'could lead to abuse of the benefit.' In particular, is it likely that a married man would become 'voluntarily unemployed' merely to increase his wife's unemployment benefit to the married rate? If this is so, is it not even more likely that married women are doing the same thing at present?[19]

Whatever these colleagues' motives, I was relieved when it wasn't just me all the time on the front line.

I had listed the Select Committee on Violent Offending as a caucus agenda item for 22 August. The committee had been told to produce a preliminary report before the election, and I was very worried about the direction this might go. I advised caucus that:

> All submissions (except one) received and heard by the Committee have been from those employed in enforcement. We haven't heard from offenders or those engaged in rehabilitation. We haven't heard from Maori and Pacific communities, and we can't expect them to come to Parliament Buildings to have that conversation. There's a real risk of serving up old ideas for new problems. We are exposing a range of issues not heard by Parliament previously. We should not damage the impact of the final report.

Committee chair Ben Couch and another member, John Elliot, agreed with me. The Prime Minister responded that the committee 'wasn't there for social work. The public has no sympathy for violence. There is a middle way. Denis O'Reilly may help here. We need an interim report.'

Denis O'Reilly, a Pākehā, was a patched member of the Black Power gang. He had become a detached youth worker, focused on providing meaningful employment for the gang members. In 1978 he had set up the Te Kaha Trust work cooperative, and the select committee had visited its site in Wellington. Denis and other gang leaders had also shared whisky with Muldoon on the ninth floor of the Beehive, discussing the issues of alienated and dispossessed young Māori in the cities.

The committee had also visited the Epuni Boys Home and the Kohitere Boys Training Centre, both residential centres for young offenders. There were over 20 residential institutions nationwide, most of them for males. I was also independently visiting the Miramar and

Weymouth Girls' Homes, and the Arohata Women's Prison, where I knew the woman who managed the pre-release unit. From this, I was introduced to the Aroha Trust, women who were also getting contracts for work. I knew Helene Wong, the only woman in the PM's Advisory Group, and one evening we went to a Trust dinner that included a meeting they called for with Black Power members. 'No more rapes, no more beatings-up' was their message.

At the girls' homes I was told that it was common for girls to run away as their release date was approaching. I had been able to meet with some of them on my own, without staff. They told me that it was frightening to think of going home: it wasn't safe for them, and they would be 'thrashed or raped'. I told this story quietly at caucus. A colleague said, 'Normal women don't think like that.' No one said a word.[20]

We moved to the next agenda item, which was the recommendation for the select committee hearing the REPEAL petition. Tony Friedlander asked if it was a conscience vote, and was told it was not. Muldoon asked what instruction caucus wanted to give the committee: should it be 'for consideration' or 'no recommendation'? George Gair pointed out that the SPUC petition in 1976 had gained a 'most favourable consideration'. He asked why the REPEAL petition could not be referred to Parliament rather than to the government for a decision, since it was Parliament's legislation. The caucus decided on a 'for consideration' recommendation, which meant there could be no debate. The *New Zealand Herald* reported that 'the huge Repeal petition was quietly shuffled into a legislative backwater yesterday afternoon'.[21]

The draft Women's Policy was up for discussion. Oh dear. We couldn't commit to revocation of ILO Convention 89 because the International Labour Organisation was a tripartite body and governments could not commit the other two parties, the Federation of Labour (FOL) and the Employers' Federation. Muldoon and Holyoake's replacement, farmer John Falloon, did not like the proposed changes in death duties in line with the new matrimonial property provisions. Muldoon wanted to know why we needed to extend non-molestation orders. The Minister for Social Welfare, Bert Walker, argued: 'Any move to have married women receive unemployment benefits on the same grounds as men looked like an open invitation to abuse, increasing the numbers of unemployed.' Les Gandar objected to the whole Education packet. 'Do we need a women's policy?' asked the Prime Minister. 'Yes? Send the whole policy back to the Minister of Justice.'

Eventually Justice issues dominated. There would be legislation for no-fault divorce, the right of either spouse to receive maintenance based on need, and the removal of discrimination in custody hearings. As the Royal Commission on the Courts had recommended, we would establish a Family Court system with specialist judges and jurisdiction over cases involving separation, divorce, maintenance, paternity, custody, access and adoption. The grounds for non-molestation orders within households would be extended. National 'recognised' that law-enforcement procedures 'deter complaints relating to rape and domestic violence'. More women police officers would be recruited. Voluntary Rape Crisis and Women's Refuge centres would be assisted. The police would be required to record all domestic violence reports, whether or not they resulted in a prosecution or conviction. The increases in women appointed to boards, commissions and tribunals would continue.

The final policy document was very watered down. My only consolation was that Labour's was no better.

The Social Security Amendment Bill was back from the select committee and before the House. I was still battling the absence of married women from their right to an unemployment benefit. I advised that if the Opposition moved an amendment for inclusion, I would support this, or perhaps move my own amendment. The PM advised caucus that 'Amendments will be unacceptable.' I went ahead and prepared and submitted my amendments. To my horror, the PM waited until I had leave from the House, changed the parliamentary Order Paper for that day, and moved the legislation through the committee stages in my absence. The government would always have defeated my move, but it shut me out of the debate and offered the Labour Opposition some days to pillory me about 'disappearing' for the vote.

After my selection as the candidate, Waipā gained 116 new Party members and had just two resignations. In August, going into the election campaign, Waipā had 2,063 Party members. Any more than 2,000 was considered extremely healthy. I was very lucky with the team who supported me. I had a wonderful new Party secretary in Jim White. Four women and seven men were on my sub-executive, and nine of these were staunch Waring supporters. Chairman Arnold Myers said he was never bored. Wherever he went – to his Power Board meetings, his bowling tournaments, or just walking down the streets of Cambridge – people would approach him to talk politics. We began to prepare for the campaign.

We gathered the lists of all clubs and societies from the Public Relations offices in Cambridge and Te Awamutu, but knew these did not cover the full expanse of the electorate. In July, all branch officials received a letter asking them for a list of the following: What do you have, where is it and who should be contacted for visits to schools, kindergartens, playcentres, hotels, Returned Services clubs, cosmopolitan or social clubs, firms, factories and other businesses employing more than twelve, sale yards and weekly sale days, old folks' homes or rest homes, hospitals, government departments, government farm blocks, hydro stations, forest nurseries, and so on. Officials were then asked to indicate if I had already visited those places in 1978, or would have been there in the days allocated for electioneering in their branch area. Katherine O'Regan joined the campaign committee and pulled all this together and made the lists. In my first campaign, for Raglan, many cynics had remarked that the only time they saw a politician was during the campaign. I resolved this would never happen with me. Constituents would have plenty of gripes about my representation, but this would not be one of them.

Our campaign for 1978 was a major logistics exercise. Daily spreadsheets showed the date, driver, the campaign hall, meetings and visits; where and with whom I would have breakfast, lunch and dinner. What I didn't eat (offal, cheese, cream, corn, brassica vegetables) and an allergy to cats were detailed. Columns showed where I would sleep, and who was in charge of the banner.

Above: Talking to workers while on the campaign trail in 1975 – this photo was run with the caption 'enough tea to float a ship'.
New Zealand Herald, APN-1000334

Below: The front cover of my election pamphlet for Raglan in 1975.
Marilyn Waring collection

Above: National Party leader Robert Muldoon's typical campaign appearance involved a collection of giant charts that were changed as he spoke, acting as a kind of early manual PowerPoint.
Stuff Ltd/Alexander Turnbull Library, EP/1975/1599/6a

Below: Still somewhat dazed by being elected to Parliament – at the National Party headquarters in Hamilton on election night 1975.
New Zealand Herald/Alexander Turnbull Library, PAColl-6340-02

Celebrating my win on election night 1975, with campaign committee secretary Katherine O'Regan (left) and chair Peter Hamilton (front). Katherine's then-husband Neil O'Regan is at the rear. *New Zealand Herald*/Alexander Turnbull Library, PAColl-6340-01

Above: Competing for selection as the National Party candidate for Waipā in 1978: three Pākehā 'family men' and me. From left to right: Keith Magee, Jan Wild, Marilyn Waring and Morris McFall. My corsage was a gift from the Māori Queen. Marilyn Waring collection

Below: Speaking at a community meeting at Mangakino, with (from left to right) Western Māori candidate Timi Te Heuheu, chair Fin Phillips, and MP Rex Austin, who was only the second Māori to have won a general electorate. Attending meetings in this isolated and struggling community was important to me, despite the challenging 80 kilometre drive home. Marilyn Waring collection

Declaration of Allegiance

I, Marilyn Joy Waring, do truly affirm and declare that I will be faithful and bear true allegiance to Her Majesty Queen Elizabeth the Second.

Marilyn J Waring ♀

Declared before me, Charles Philip Littlejohn

this 16th day of May 1979

C Littlejohn

Above: When being 'sworn in' as a parliamentarian for my second term in 1979, I made an affirmation rather than swearing on the Bible – and was only the second MP to have done so. Stuff Ltd

Below: My declaration of allegiance on being 'sworn in' in 1979. I made a point of adding the Venus symbol (♀) after my signature. Courtesy of the New Zealand Parliamentary Library

MARILYN

will represent

YOU

WARING FOR

WAIPA

My campaign pamphlet for Waipā in 1979 opened out to a poster, featuring about 150 men, women and children who had volunteered to come to the Te Awamutu Racecourse one Sunday morning to be photographed. Marilyn Waring collection

We planned an all-in-one pamphlet that would open out to an A3 poster. To get the photo for this people were asked to come to the Te Awamutu Racecourse at 10 one Sunday morning for a fun photo shoot. About 150 men, women and children fanned out on a raised mound behind me. The photographer stood me on a chair in front of them to gain the desired effect. The poster announced 'Marilyn will represent YOU!' We copied different news stories and surrounded those with photographs taken at work in the constituency. On 15 August I'd had a day with Rex Austin and Timi Te Heuheu in Waipā.[22] Timi was the son of Sir Hepi Te Heuheu, the paramount chief of Ngāti Tūwharetoa, and was the Party candidate for the Western Māori electorate. National candidates in Māori seats rarely had a budget, so I ensured we got a photo of the three of us to go in my publicity pamphlet. We also reproduced commentary from newspapers: 'The most improved National MP in Parliament is also the youngest. Miss Waring has a quick brain, works hard and has improved her debating techniques greatly since she entered Parliament. If she stays in politics, she will be one of the dominant members in the next century,' the *New Zealand Herald*'s Judy Addinell had written.[23] Ian Templeton had written: 'Miss Waring [is] said by some Ministerial colleagues to be one of the best political brains in Parliament.'[24] I had a couple of gallery journalists in my loop, but Ian and Judy were never close to me, so I was surprised to read such comments. We printed 10,000 pamphlets, which were manually distributed into letterboxes by volunteers.

After I had made campaign visits, the branches supplied me with the names and addresses of hosts or guides, all of whom received a letter thanking them for their help and hospitality: 'I enjoyed the time spent with you and the conversations, and appreciated the opportunity you gave me to meet yourself and others.' Olga took care of these. She told me Sir Keith had adopted this practice. I still asked Olga what he had done, and learned well from this.

As we came into September, my weekly programme was sent to officials. It recorded the seven days of activities by a.m. or p.m., including all committee meetings. In general, leave priorities were given to MPs in marginal seats, and to ministers, but Party headquarters had advised I was to be used in other constituencies. I was seen as a money spinner and a speaker who would attract hundreds of women to a meeting. National could collect funds when I came to town. From August to November 1978, I spent days in 17 other electorates.

In Waipā, I was trying something different at public meetings. On one occasion I asked Minister of Local Government Allan Highet to speak, and invited all the local-government elected members and their staff to come along. I asked Jim McLay to come and speak on the new matrimonial property law, and invited all the lawyers from Hamilton and in the electorate. These meetings were great for learning about the issues in much more depth. The participants, who were well informed, asked questions I hadn't even thought of, and they in turn appreciated that these weren't 'National Party' meetings.

I had a terrific campaign committee, which included some from the old Raglan team. Again we made and erected all our billboards and disobeyed the guidance on avoiding panel meetings with other candidates. Cecile Braun had noticed that the Prime Minister, who grew lilies, had given some of his seed to Thailand. She wrote to ask him for seeds for Waipā; a local nursery propagated them; and these were sold for a tidy sum. The team also saw how weary I was getting with all the meetings outside of Waipā, and built in afternoon resting times, or fun days such as November's World Rowing Championships in Cambridge. Katherine made that phone call again, requiring a public announcement for me to get a message, so that everyone knew I was there. I had helped lobby Allan Highet to secure the finance needed for the venue, and I loved most sport, so I was very happy to sit there 'at work' in the sun. It didn't happen often.

By the time Parliament rose for the election, I had spoken to service clubs for men and women across the country. I was booked to address three school prize-giving ceremonies. I had unveiled the plaque for the Pirongia State Forest Park, now protected from mining licences. I'd attended the compellingly testing Skellerup Young Farmer of the Year final, meetings of the Waikato Valley Authority concerned with the management of the Waikato River, and watched a newly installed rotary milking shed near Te Awamutu milk a thousand cows in two hours. Being an MP continued to be a privileged learning experience, and this, and the people of my electorate, helped me endure the days in Wellington.

The prospects for any new National women MPs at the elections were looking bleak. Colleen Dewe's seat in Lyttelton required less than a one per cent swing to Labour for their candidate, Ann Hercus, to win. Leslie Miller, whom I had met through WEL Tokoroa, was an outstanding candidate for Taupō, but a less than two per cent swing would return the seat to the former Labour MP. It wasn't any consolation that, apart from in Lyttelton, I couldn't see Labour having any new women in Parliament either.

My Labour opponent in 1978 was Dr Anthony Rogers, a Hamilton physician and the father of an old school friend.[25] The Social Credit candidate was John Kilbride, a dairy farmer who would rake in the anti-abortion, anti-feminist and pro-rugby votes, and would be aided by the swing away from National in rural areas, largely based on dislike for Muldoon.

New Zealand's apartheid sporting links continued. Trevor Richards, from Halt All Racist Tours (HART), had written to caucus in May, drawing attention to New Zealand sporting contacts with South Africa in golf, gliding and women's softball. He had also made representations at the United Nations Anti-Apartheid Committee. There were requests from caucus to see if he could be arrested for treason! In July, Nigeria had withdrawn from the 1978 Commonwealth Games in Edmonton, but there was no mass walkout of other countries opposed to New Zealand's policy of non-interference with sporting bodies. I was grateful for Foreign Affairs Minister Brian Talboys' press statement on 11 October 1978 as we approached the election. It marked a Day of Solidarity with South African political prisoners. Talboys spoke of the 'bankruptcy and inhumanity of these policies. The plight of political prisoners in South Africa is one aspect of its abhorrent apartheid system.' He condemned this and other practices of the South African government.

On 11 October the new Canadian high commissioner to New Zealand had an appointment to meet the Prime Minister for the first time. Irene Johnson had an MA in Economics from the London School of Economics and been a public service commissioner in Canada. The Prime Minister's private secretary opened the door and announced her arrival. Muldoon continued with his work. Then he put his head up, looked at Irene, and growled, 'I hope you're not one of those feminists, are you?'

What's Been Done? was finally collated and analysed. I had presented the results of my work to the inaugural conference of the Women's Studies Association in Hamilton in August. It was then edited and published by the Committee on Women in October. On the last day of Parliament in 1978, I sent a carnation buttonhole to all retiring MPs on both sides of the House, and most wore them.

In 1978 the electoral rolls were breathtakingly inaccurate. Several hundred thousand more names appeared than there were eligible voters. The discrepancies had occurred as a result of constructing the rolls according to the new seats and boundaries. In the 87-seat 1975 election, National had won with a majority of 23. In 1978, in a 92-seat Parliament, the majority would be 10. National won 51 seats, Labour 40, and Social Credit retained Rangitīkei while taking 16 per cent of the overall vote. Labour took more votes than National, but under the FPP voting system it was electorate wins that counted. There was a 7.8 per cent swing against the government and an 8.7 per cent swing to Social Credit. National had five ministers and two backbenchers retire. Three of these were in marginal seats that were subsequently lost. We lost five sitting MPs, including Colleen Dewe. I held Waipā with a majority of 4,906 – comfortably more than half of all votes cast. The Waipā Labour vote collapsed as women moved to support me, and Social Credit came second. I was now the only woman in the Party in government.

National had 10 new male MPs. They were still a generation older than I was, but they didn't represent the 1930s Depression and Second World War generation, and had joined the National Party because of their economic ideologies. The opening item for the caucus agenda on Thursday 30 November 1978 was in my name – 'Election Result'. George Gair and I again chose to sit in front of Muldoon in the front row. But first Muldoon had his say. He welcomed the new MPs. 'The things that happen here are absolutely secret. Most of the press are not supporters of the National Party. We will be Government with a smaller majority with an entirely new situation in the House.' He described the 'pairs' system, operated by the Whips of each party, who reached an agreement on how many members from each side could have leave at any one time. 'Don't make appointments which clash with business in Wellington unless it is vital. In caucus, you are entitled to say what you want to, but if you miss a decision you can't come back later and say you didn't agree.' He went on: 'We try to get a consensus. We try to avoid votes if we can. Voting against your colleagues in the House is a serious matter and should not be taken lightly. Politics is a team game all the way. You're either in the team or not.' He advised new MPs to take things quietly in their electorates, and warned against making close friends on the other side of the House.

Then we got to my item. What I didn't know was that there had been a heated debate, led by Dorothy McNab and Valerie Forbes, at the National Party Executive meeting following the election. They did not want Muldoon holding all three offices of Prime Minister, Minister of Finance and Leader of the House. They were highly critical of his squandering the huge 1975 majority because of what they saw as his arrogance and insensitivity.

I spoke of the problems experienced by all candidates in trying to defend the character of the Prime Minister, and that this had been consistent in all the electorates I had visited. I said it had got in the way of discussion of policy issues. Every candidate I had supported in those electorates, as well as Party supporters, had complained of this. I asked for a change in the PM's behaviour.

Ian Shearer followed, saying there had been criticism in his electorate that he was obliged to record. Minister and Waikato MP Lance Adams-Schneider responded that criticism of leadership had always been a feature of politics. Aussie Malcolm had a bob both ways: he 'disagreed with Marilyn. But we must acknowledge the sense of anxiety, which she expressed.' Muldoon used his bully-boy tone in response. Caucus should learn that the Party would have to accept him as he is. He was not proposing to change.

Colleagues obviously talked to media afterwards. Ian Templeton reported:

> At the first post-election caucus of the parliamentary members of the National Party, Muldoon ruthlessly chopped off a debate on his leadership style in the election campaign. Marilyn Waring, the 26-year-old member for the true-blue farming constituency, probably blew her chances of promotion in a Muldoon administration. But at least she can face her constituents and say that she had a go while other backbenchers, many of whom had expressed privately much the same sentiments as she offered, remained silent until they joined in the 'hear, hears' when the Prime Minister launched his rejoinder. Some of them, of course, are hoping for preferment.
>
> Marilyn Waring has time on her side and is probably sensible to distance herself from a leadership style, which could grow steadily more unpopular. Some political observers believe she has the kind of talent, which could if she wants to put it to use, make her the first woman to lead the National Party, and eventually take her to the top seat in Cabinet. It is their reluctance to recognise that Waring can communicate with large segments of the population, with whom they are far out of touch, which could contribute to the National Party losing its tenuous grip on the treasury benches at the next election.
>
> Marilyn Waring would probably resist being used by the party to recapture the women's vote. But she could communicate more easily with other groups, that National is in danger of losing, the young people, the single parents, the minority groups who feel at risk when Muldoon starts counterpunching.[26]

After this caucus, I walked to Courtenay Place and bought myself a new Takamine acoustic guitar. I could see it was going to be a rough three years.

Cabinet had been announced in December. When George Gair was appointed as Minister of both Social Welfare and Health, he asked Muldoon if I could be appointed his under-secretary. I told him I loved his faith and loyalty towards me but I was very pleased I wasn't forced to refuse the role.

Muldoon wasn't finished. On 19 December he announced nuclear-powered submarine USS *Haddo* would visit Auckland in January 1979. The Auckland Harbour Board had been working all year to get the New Zealand Atomic Energy Agency to visit and discuss 'the future policy on the allocation of commercial berths in Auckland for nuclear-powered warships and the regard that will be given to the commercial demands on the port without the associated disruption of commercial shipping and operations'. This time five container vessels and five bulk ships would be affected. The board wanted indemnity reimbursements of costs and loss of trade and income as a result of such visits. They would be ignored.

1979

In early January the Auckland Harbour Board and waterfront unions were unanimous in their opposition to berthing the nuclear submarine USS *Haddo* at Jellicoe Wharf for its five-day visit.[1] It was unsafe. Board general manager Bob Lorimer advised that the NZAEA regulations precluded any work within a certain proximity to the nuclear vessel. Raglan Harbour representative Angus MacDonald told me the board members were not prepared to be used by Muldoon. They knew submarines were nuclear-weapon carriers, and the board wanted compensation for loss of trade and money during the period. The majority of the board were National supporters, but they were opposed to nuclear-armed and nuclear-propelled vessels in their harbours. In public, however, they continued their argument based on indemnity and economic losses.[2]

The government passed special regulations extending the Auckland Harbour Board geographical limits before the submarine's arrival. The harbourmaster's jurisdiction over craft approaching Rangitoto Channel increased, expanding the area in which he could prosecute those on protest vessels. When waterfront unions denied all services or assistance to the *Haddo*, the board formally requested the Royal New Zealand Navy to supply and arrange surface escorts and tugs. It was the job of the police to deal with protesters.

On 19 January New Zealanders took to the water in yachts, launches, motorboats, kayaks and surfboards in a Peace Flotilla to confront the *Haddo*. Police helicopters buzzed the yachts, trying to disturb the wind in their sails and turn them over. Police Zodiacs scooted around in an effort to push craft out of the way. Protesters, not devoid of a sense of humour, threw yellow paint bombs which landed on the submarine.[3] Eventually, protester Stephen Sherie managed to climb aboard the vessel's hull. There would not be another submarine visit, and no other US ships would come for 20 months. Neither the Carter administration in the USA nor the Australian government could see any strategic use for further visits, although Muldoon never gave up pestering for them. Increasing numbers of New Zealanders did not want nuclear weapons or nuclear-powered ships near the country.

My plane was fogbound for the first hours of the caucus on 1 February. The new Whips, Tony Friedlander and Dale Jones, were selected. But some of the comments about Muldoon's behaviour during the campaign had had some effect. He blamed the media for the way he was portrayed. He announced he would have fewer press conferences. He spent a lot of time outlining the dire predictions for the economy, with a rapid deterioration in the balance of payments forecast.

Since the 1975 election National's policy had been to abolish compulsory membership of trade unions. The idea was that this would disempower the unions, and make it easier to control the freezing, waterfront, construction and engineering unions in particular. I thought those lobbying for the change were in cloud cuckoo land, because it would only affect the unions whose workers were isolated from each other and easily intimidated or exploited, such as those in clerical and cleaning jobs – mostly held by women. By early 1979, the country had a regime where unions could not enter into award negotiations until they had held a ballot on voluntary unionism. Muldoon had selected what he thought were 'easy wins', but he was receiving some rude shocks. Eighty per cent of members of the Bank Officers Union had voted in their ballot, with a clear majority (57 per cent) voting for compulsory union membership. Even National supporters were voting for compulsory membership. Their basic interest was the maintenance of the union, and the Party's assessment on this was way out.

Muldoon had met with the Federation of Labour (FOL) and claimed it was a major achievement to get agreement to conduct ballots across the board. I wasn't surprised. The FOL knew what worker sentiment was, both with Muldoon as PM and with rampant inflation. Workers did not want to be vulnerable to having to negotiate on their own. Ballots would be a nuisance for the FOL but would only strengthen their hand. Muldoon decided the Clerical Workers would be next to ballot – he thought he might get a victory there – followed by the Storemen and Packers, and the Drivers unions. Labour issues suited the bully in Muldoon. 'We lost votes at election time from some who thought we weren't tough enough on industrial matters,' he claimed.

New appointments were a feature of any caucus meeting, and there was an interesting moment when we were told that a former National MP was to join the board of the Waikato Trustee Savings Bank. The regional banks were a favourite for these sinecures. When Mike Minogue challenged why we couldn't appoint the best person for the job, he received a loyalty lecture. 'We have a tradition of loyalty in this caucus. The loyalty that holds after retirement. It lets people down lightly. I am very pleased we have this tradition, and it has served us well. Unless we have loyalty, we are finished as a party and a caucus.' Mike was never bothered by the bully. He replied, 'I'll ignore the implications: do we appoint Party people or assess other considerations?'

At the next caucus meeting, Muldoon announced who would chair the parliamentary select committees. I was utterly astounded to hear that I would chair the Public Expenditure Committee. Apparently at his first meeting with his new Whips, the PM had asked Tony Friedlander who he thought would suit the role. Tony suggested me and Muldoon just nodded and wrote it down. This meant I would also chair the Caucus Economic Committee (CEC). George Gair had indicated I should chair the Health and Welfare Committee as well, and I agreed to this.

Media were also surprised at the appointment. The Christchurch *Press* headline read: 'Waring has a Mind of Her Own and Intends to Keep It That Way'. The story claimed:

> The announcement last month that [Marilyn Waring] would chair the powerful Public Expenditure Committee came as a surprise to her. 'I scarcely expected promotion,' she says. Had the proposed appointment made her less cynical about the workings of Parliament? 'I've got a reputation for asking a lot of questions. I don't know whether that's what

> he wants, but that's probably what he will get.' ... She is not interested in any possible political reasons behind the appointment. 'The fact is that it's there now and I'm going to do my best at it.'

The interview changed focus:

> 'One of the difficulties of increasing women's representation in Parliament is that women can feel extremely disdainful of much of what they see of the system,' she says. 'It is extraordinarily compromising to put yourself in the situation to try to change and yet be part of something you can't admire. But the advantages for everybody in incorporating the other half of the population into the decision-making process cannot be overstated. At present, the system tends to appoint only those women it knows will preserve the system,' she says. 'It is terrified of many other talented women who could disrupt the status quo.'[4]

The *New Zealand Herald* reported:

> Unlike some of the other Select Committee chairmen chosen last week at the Government Caucus, the youngest MP did not lobby for the job. She ruefully questions the use of the word 'powerful' and wonders if the adjective can be used accurately to describe any Select Committee.

However, the reporter contended, the committee does have power:

> Its objective is to ensure that money appropriated by Parliament is spent as Parliament intended, with due exercise of economy and without waste or administrative extravagance. It can question permanent heads of departments without the shelter of the Cabinet Minister, and it can take both a retrospective look (through its examination of the audited Public Accounts) and a prospective look (through its perusal of the Estimates). For a backbencher, the committee and its various subcommittees offer access to a goldmine of information. But she questions the use of gaining information vital to the public interest if it cannot be aired effectively.[5]

I could see all this could mean I would be buried under work. I heard that Elizabeth Sewell, an active feminist with extensive networks, was moving to Wellington and looking for employment. We met, and I asked her to think about whether she would be available to work with me, especially on the key issues always to the fore for women. I advised her she would never be asked to do any National Party work. I couldn't see how I could stay afloat as the only woman in the government caucus, keep up in the electorate and the House, chair PEC and caucus committees, do research, and advance feminist issues without help. I could rely on Research Unit staff as secretariat and to work on briefs for caucus committees, but that left a huge load. We had to make some progress on funding women's refuges and rape crisis centres, and collect data to support this. The State Services Commission Working Group on Early Childhood Care and Education was finally meeting, and we needed them to recommend a diverse and flexible range of early childhood services. There would be a raft of changes to family law opposed by the organised right wing. I never knew where the next crisis would occur. Elizabeth knew she would learn a lot on the inside. I asked her to take a couple of weeks to think about it.

I was getting more familiar with the Waipā electorate as I travelled its length and breadth. In rural areas people were diversifying, planting raspberries and blueberries, growing leucadendrons and carnations, and raising deer alongside the traditional dairy, sheep and beef farms, the thoroughbred racing studs and the maize fields. To the west was Kāwhia, known as the resting place of the *Tainui* waka, a small settlement with a high number of speakers of te reo Māori. Kāwhia's Maketū Marae was an important meeting place for annual poukai (visits by the Māori King or Queen to Kīngitanga marae). The road to Kāwhia wound through Oparau with its many conservation blocks of native forest. Visiting friends at Aotea Harbour, I could sit and hear just water lapping and birdsong in an environment of exquisite colour. I found this restorative and healing.

The community of Mangakino was another focus. I would drive there from Kihikihi through a landscape pocked with plugs left after intense volcanic activity millions of years ago. Paddocks with weathered standing limestone outcrops carried sheep and some beef. Mangakino had been built as a hydro-power station village for workers building a series of dams on the Waikato River from the 1940s to the 1960s. Many of the few hundred people who lived here now were beneficiaries and superannuitants. It was very difficult to get a permanent doctor or fill the staff vacancies at the local high school. There were no offices of government services in the town, and the bus to Tokoroa ran only twice a week. There was a residential care facility for men with disabilities, but other than basic services there was no chance of employment in the town. I met constituents in the private bar of Mangakino's only hotel. In winter the 80-kilometre drive home, winding through pine forests in thick fog with nothing but the central white line to guide me, could take a very long time.

National Party supporters in Waipā, and especially the Women's Sections, maintained a serious calendar of activities with coffee mornings, luncheons and fundraising dinners. They were open to inviting academics, appointees to government bodies or other opinion leaders who might provoke them. They didn't want an exclusive menu of National MPs. When I spoke at or attended such meetings, I felt nurtured and relaxed, and grateful for the brief respite from Wellington.

I had a busy February. I attended the annual Viticultural Field-day in Auckland, addressed the Kellogg Farm Leadership course at Lincoln University, and met in Wellington with Auditor-General Fred Shailes and his deputy Jeff Chapman about changes we could make to PEC processes and outcomes. I met with the Waikato Manufacturers Executive, the board of the Auckland Farmers Freezing Company, and representatives of the construction industry in the Waikato, and began the round of annual branch meetings in the constituency.

Elizabeth agreed to come on board, and in late February I became the first backbencher to employ their own full-time research officer.[6] I had only my parliamentary income ($18,365), and I split it three ways between Katherine, Elizabeth and myself. These payments were not tax deductible.

There were some items in caucus that could waste hours, and the issue of shop trading hours was one of these. The majority of New Zealanders wanted building supplies and general hardware, as well as gardening supplies, to be available outside a Monday-to-Friday 40-hour week, but everyone in caucus had an opinion, example or story to highlight their case. An ongoing issue was the range of products now available at petrol stations (for example, magazines and periodicals), in competition with retailers who could not stay open after hours. It was a favourite Muldoon trick to put up a subject that would attract many speakers, delay other issues and be inconclusive, so that was how we started caucus on 1 March.

New MP Geoff Thompson had the next item and wanted clarification on the role of caucus in policymaking. He asked about restructuring the economy and said he would like a steer on what the government's intentions were on this. The PM answered that caucus sets the policy for the election. The last three years had been a tidying-up exercise. The big issues would come to caucus, but the degree to which this could be done would depend in part on how much he could trust caucus not to break a confidence. Ian McLean, also a new MP and, threateningly to Muldoon, an economist, commented that 'the election manifesto didn't tie our hands too tightly. We're now moving into a new phase. What is done in the Budget in 1979 would establish the policy settings, not just for a year, but for several years. We would have support for quite significant moves in freeing up the private sector.' Muldoon responded that he was broadly correct. But we had a basic dilemma. The OECD and the Planning Council would recommend what Ian suggested, but we would have 'all of the pain by next election and few of the benefits. We would inevitably undermine sound businesses. I am keen to restructure, but on an approach that avoids damage.'[7] This was a very clear explanation of Muldoon's resistance to change, and of his priorities as long as he was Minister of Finance.

There was more to come on this theme from the new MPs when we discussed the proposed Post Office courier service. Don McKinnon called it an intrusion into private enterprise. Derek Quigley said it was out of line with our philosophy and he was surprised the proposal hadn't been withdrawn immediately. Mike Minogue said it was time to limit, not expand, state agencies, and we should be in orderly retreat. Doug Kidd agreed and said he'd be happy to defend a government decision to cancel the proposal, especially when private enterprise was capable of handling the service. Muldoon growled: 'We do many socialist things in this caucus. It's a practical problem. We could sell Air New Zealand and Telecom, but we don't ... This issue will be in front of us in a number of areas. There is an element of cross-subsidization in many things government does. This applies to postal services and telephone rates. The larger electorates are being subsidized in these services by the bigger cities.' But he asked Ben Couch to look at it again, and the backbenchers asked me to put it on the agenda of the CEC.

There were two items in the name of the new Minister of Justice, Jim McLay. A large number of submissions in the Family Proceedings Bill from the Exclusive Brethren religion (whose members never voted) wanted adultery retained as a reason for divorce. A further key issue was that while rape was covered in the Crimes Act, women wanted clarification in the Bill that rape be extended to the period of separation before divorce.

The second item concerned a brilliant report on the Adoption Act 1955 by Patricia Webb.[8] She advised that adoptees should have access to adoption records. There were very strong feelings from a group of men in caucus. Interesting it was. I always wondered about the lives and stories that lay behind such positions. Aussie Malcolm argued that it was essential to maintain the security of the mother from children who might go looking for her. The government should confirm that the advice came only in a report and that didn't mean we were obliged to take action. Ian McLean, on the other hand, fully supported access. I knew women who forever hunted streets and crowds with their eyes, looking for the child they had given up for adoption. Genetic health inheritance warranted access too, I thought. I also had women friends who never wanted to be found by their birth child, and I knew I would disappoint them with how I would vote if I had the opportunity. But for now, the issue would be cast aside.

Elizabeth was moving on the rape crisis and refuge issues by 9 March. She wrote to all the organisations she knew of, asking for their aims, work and structure, costs and how they were financed, by whom and how often services were used, and any special services offered. She made it clear all replies would be treated as confidential, and information would be aggregated to a national picture. This would be more information than was held in any government agency. We had spoken with Allan Highet and asked if the Lotteries discretionary fund could resource a national meeting of these organisations so they could decide what issues they needed to raise with central and local governments. The information we were gathering would support the application. Elizabeth organised the meeting in Porirua within a few weeks of Highet's approval, and the National Collective of Refuges was formed.

On 28 March there was a meltdown in a nuclear reactor at the Three Mile Island Nuclear Power Plant in Harrisburg, Pennsylvania, USA. The event was mentioned briefly in caucus. Human error, as well as malfunctioning gauges and valves, had led to the release of radioactive gases into the atmosphere. Pregnant women were evacuated. Few people believed assurances that the radioactivity was not a health threat. Massive demonstrations followed. I noticed that an Australian paediatrician named Helen Caldicott, who worked at Harvard, addressed 200,000 people at the largest rally, in New York's Central Park.

In late March the National Housing Commission announced work would begin on research into the specialised housing needs of particular groups, including single parents, students, those with disabilities, ethnic minorities and people requiring emergency shelter. 'Emergency shelter' also included housing for some women's refuges. There had been ongoing development of different and more appropriate architectural designs for these groups, but that was always as far as it seemed to get.

Chairing the Caucus Economic Committee was difficult. First, there was the expectation from the new MPs – from a different generation, with tertiary qualifications, and hard workers – that evidence and the Party might well convince Muldoon to change course. They were energetic in these endeavours. I also felt that a more qualified chair would have been Ian McLean. Ian came with 'evidence'. He was an agricultural economist with an extensive farming background. He had worked in the Ministry of Agriculture and led a Food and Agriculture Organization (FAO)/ United Nations Development Programme (UNDP) project in Tanzania. I was impressed with his analysis and proposals, but they were not in a direction Muldoon was heading.

Chairing both the PEC and CEC meant a change in the focus of questions from the media. During a National Radio interview on 30 March I suggested there should be limits to the areas where government is permitted to compete with the existing and legitimate business activities conducted by private enterprise. In early April I chaired the CEC on the issue of the Post Office courier service. There was a large attendance, and the opposition was overwhelming. On 19 April the issue was back in caucus. Postmaster-General Ben Couch argued there was a place for both services. The Prime Minister intervened: 'We should have stopped this argument at the last caucus. But this is far too serious. This is a normal extension of Post Office activity. There are implications for the profitability of the mail service. We are trying to keep up to date and modern. Why stop now? I sense that is the view of caucus. Don't get caught up in a wave of emotion. A government in this country cannot govern solely in the interests of private enterprise.' He then asked for a show of hands on the issue. A large majority of caucus voted against the service. The PM nodded. 'I shall announce this at the National Conference.'

The Committee on Women (COW) was represented by the Minister of National Development, Bill Birch. He wrote asking if, on his behalf, I would organise a meeting for caucus members to hear from COW on their work. A whole ministerial office and staff, and he couldn't do that. It was obvious Birch could not be the 'Spokesman on Women'. The PM advised he had decided the role should go to Minister of Justice Jim McLay: a large amount of legislation 'in this area', Muldoon said, made him the obvious choice. There was no Ministry for Women, and no staff provided with the 'spokesman' title. Given the choices available, I was very happy to have Jim in the role.

At the end of April, the CS&A Act came into force. I wondered if there was some way in which I could test some of its provisions, and made a statement advocating that women might investigate menstrual extraction techniques to be used in the first one to four weeks after a missed period. Minister of Police Frank Gill advised a senior Wellington police sergeant on Saturday of Marilyn Waring's 'exhortation to women to learn how to perform abortions on themselves ... I told him I had complaints by people who had believed the law had been broken.' Asked to specify which complaints he had received, Gill amended his reply to say he had received inquiries from the media asking what he intended doing about my comments. Aahh: he had taken the bait.

The *New Zealand Herald* editorial called my action 'extreme, unbalanced, and too radical'.[9] Letters to the editor flooded in. Many writers were 'shocked', 'appalled', 'ashamed' and 'disgusted'. But a Mt Roskill woman wrote, 'I am sorry the National Party has not 20 more Marilyn Warings in its ranks', and a woman in Whitianga was 'horrified that men say their piece on this absolutely female problem. Ms. Waring is courageous. She knows what desperation means to women who are experiencing an unwanted pregnancy.' Menstrual extraction upset some officials in the Waipā electorate. At the next full meeting, Ian Forbes, a Te Awamutu GP (and Valerie Forbes' husband), came along. When the issue was raised, he asked for permission to speak and calmed everyone down.

At the same time, Sisters Overseas Service was at a crisis point. Volunteers answering the telephones each day could not cope with the number of women asking for advice on how to seek an abortion. SOS Wellington reported to the ASC that between April 1978 and March 1979, 110 cases of those in contact had been directed to local GPs, and 351 in the same period had been helped by SOS to have abortions abroad.[10] Of these, 266 women came from outside Wellington.

The 1979 oil-price panic following the Iranian Revolution in January was biting deeply and quickly. Petrol stations were closed during weekends. This was a major issue for rural transport operators in my electorate, but there was lower consumption nationally. The May caucus set out some further options. The Prime Minister was not interested in rationing, so 'carless days' were being mooted.[11] Our best advice was that the problem would continue, and possibly worsen as disruptions to supply spread to other supplying nations.

By 3 May caucus MPs had finished their annual round of branch meetings. We could tell from the conversations and remits that while recognising the issues of the oil shock, people wanted significant changes in policy direction. Ian McLean raised the issue of local Party unrest in respect of economic policy. What are we to do, he asked, when matters of significance are not discussed here in caucus? Muldoon responded with a trust and loyalty commentary.

The media often attempted to provoke me to comment on issues I had no argument with. One of these concerned Jim McLay 'jumping on a jet on Monday night and heading for distant Sri Lanka for a Commonwealth Youth Conference. Aged 34, he just scraped under the barrier.' The *Sunday News* reported that Marilyn Waring has been the principal choice several years in a row to head the New Zealand delegation to the function. Nominations are made by Foreign Affairs, Internal Affairs, and the National Youth Council. But each year her nomination has been blocked by the Prime Minister. I was surprised to learn I had been nominated, and heartened that such people had confidence in me, but I was not bothered by the outcome.

I had too much else to do. In the Family Proceedings Bill before the Statutes Revision Committee, there was no provision for a de facto spouse to apply for a non-molestation order. I was told in caucus that these women were 'protected' by the laws of trespass and assault. Some strange moral code meant my male colleagues shaded this standpoint by arguing 'the difficulty of determining what qualified as a de facto relationship'. I submitted written questions to every minister whose agencies administered policies that took account of de facto relationships, from superannuitants, tertiary students, to housing loan and tenancy applications, and more. I asked how they determined what a de facto relationship was. In all cases the couples were treated as married, with one exception: under section 5 of the Evidence Act 1908, a spouse could not give evidence for the prosecution in a charge against his/her partner, and this applied only to 'spouses of a marriage solemnised in accordance with the law'. So it was an issue of right-wing morality. Caucus were satisfied to see women who wouldn't get married have less protection than those who did.

Parliament opened on 16 May 1979 – our last formal sitting day had been 14 December 1978. In 1975 I had not known there was an alternative to swearing on a Bible when being 'sworn in' as a parliamentarian. In 1979 I learned that I could make an affirmation, and I did this. I signed the parliamentary register of the 'affirming', and noticed that only one name, John A. Lee, appeared above mine, twice.[12]

The select committee 'to consider the incidence and causes of violent offending' made its final report to Parliament on Friday 18 May 1979. Whetu Tirikatene-Sullivan and I had been the women members of the committee. We had heard 155 submissions; held eight meetings away from Parliament Buildings (this was unusual), including with gang members and work trusts at the Tapu Te Ranga Marae, Island Bay; and made visits to Auckland Prison and Waikeria Borstal. The committee's terms of reference specifically asked for submissions on domestic violence. The committee recommended refuges for the victims, and that the government assist with their funding. Many refuge-centre submissions had emphasised the problems experienced with non-molestation orders, and claimed that these were too hard and took too long to obtain to be an effective protection. There was support to extend orders to de facto partners, and for women to be able to access these 24/7. The relationships Denis O'Reilly and other detached youth workers and gang leaders had developed with Muldoon evolved to active participation by Black Power, the Aroha Trust and others, in submissions to and visits for the select committee. We then reported that it had been demonstrated to us that: 'The gang organisation can provide a constructive and productive means of drawing together people, mostly young, who [have had] loss of identity through migration to urban areas, absence of family or tribal influence, [whose] socioeconomic disadvantage, unemployment or resort to alcohol or drugs, cause them to fail to fit into accepted social environments.' We wrote about the 'wholly desirable results of the work co-operative' where young people benefited from the sense of purpose, stability and guidance offered.

These were issues and ideas that many in the National Party were probably not expecting to be a priority focus. There were placatory remarks in the report: 'It is without question that much gang behaviour has aroused anxiety and apprehension in the public mind.' But in response to calls for more police powers, 'the committee was advised by the police and accepts that their existing powers were sufficient to deal with gang violence'. I thought this committee was a good use of the parliamentary process, and some of this report would be immediately useful in lobbying for resources and better legal and agency responses in critical areas.

At the caucus on 17 May Ian McLean again raised concerns about taking flak in National Party branches. He said there needed to be attempts to avoid a growing rift in the Party. These feelings ran much deeper than needing clear moves towards private enterprise. There had to be change. Colleagues representing Whāngārei and Levin and I spoke of the impact of the 40 per cent sales tax on caravans and boats. The Munro's caravan plant in Ōtorohanga had given notice to 60 employees. Muldoon's resistance to a tax overhaul and move to a Goods and Services Tax meant he was casting about for anything that might remotely be called a 'luxury', and taxing it, in a context where unemployment resulted.

On 23 May there was a debate to criticise the delay in calling Parliament together. There had been a gap of seven-and-a-half months since Parliament rose in October 1978 and Labour MP Richard Prebble moved a motion condemning the decline in the economic situation. As chair of the PEC, I was now expected to participate in such debates after several ministers had spoken. I was fairly matter of fact. Food prices were up. Our annual bill for oil had moved in six years from just over $90 million in 1973 to more than $700 million; inflation was 'down to' 10.4 per cent; prices had increased 22 per cent and wages 29 per cent. Increases in the costs of power were necessary to restore financial stability in electricity. There had been some user-pay changes in transport taxes; the sales tax on commercial vehicles had come down. More effective competition was proposed between road haulage and the railways. Beef prices were up; there was higher dairy production. Mary Batchelor was the next Labour speaker. She congratulated me on my 'efforts to make excuses for the government, a very good try on her part, considering that she had an impossible task'.[13]

There was never any pattern to the issues brought to my attention, or certainty about what I could do with that information. I couldn't 'solve' much myself. In May I had a letter from a lawyer outlining the consequences of an amendment to the law on succession to Māori lands introduced in 1967. He wrote that my constituent's mother, the owner of valuable undivided interests in Māori freehold land, was widowed in 1950. In her old age, she married a widowed relative. When her second husband died, his will left all this property to his own children. She subsequently died intestate. Under Māori practice, the land which would have passed to my constituent and her siblings passed to complete strangers. I took the matter up in letters to the Ministers of Justice, Lands, and Māori Affairs, and to Māori colleagues in the House.

Another constituent had been turned down for a farming loan by the Māori Land Board because she was a woman. I drew the attention of the board and the Minister to the Human Rights Act 1977. The Māori Land Board finally agreed that it was no longer acceptable (or lawful) to decline an application on the basis of the sex of the applicant. The loan was approved.

During the weekend I would receive telephone calls from Māori constituents whose relative had died in Waikato Hospital, where there needed to be an autopsy. The family would be waiting throughout the weekend to receive the body to take it home to the marae, but all the pathologists would be off duty and not back until Monday morning. Women who had just given birth would come to the office to tell me that the same hospital did not respect their wish to protect their whenua (afterbirth) by taking it home to bury – a special cultural practice. It was often just sluiced away. I would discuss these events with the senior staff at Waikato Hospital, the Minister of Health, with Whetu Tirikatene-Sullivan and Koro Wetere, and, probably most effectively, with Māori Queen Te Ata at her home at Waahi Pā.

I continued to use questions to highlight issues which needed change and for which MPs were directly responsible: for example, the nomination of Justices of the Peace. In 1977, 92 per cent of JPs were male, and 8 per cent were female. Ninety-four per cent were Pākehā, three per cent were Māori, and those remaining were of other ethnic groups.

My Address in Reply speech in late May focused on 1979 being the United Nations International Year of the Child (IYC). This had not been mentioned in the Speech from the Throne, nor by any of the speakers before me in the debate.[14]

Visiting schools in my electorate was one of the most enjoyable parts of my job. I also spent a lot of time listening to parents, especially mothers, who were battling for their children to have equal access to services and assistance. Katherine O'Regan, whose son Andrew had dyslexia, chaired the Waikato branch and was on the National Executive of the Specific Learning Difficulties (SPELD) organisation. She introduced me to its work with children and adults who had a problem with basic psychological learning that was manifest in difficulties of speaking or writing. Speech therapists employed by education boards did not assist with SPELD students, and many schools refused to allow children out during school hours to see one of the few trained SPELD teachers. (They allowed music students out for lessons.) Katherine used to tell me when I went off to visit Waikeria Borstal that probably 10 per cent of the inmates were in the SPELD spectrum.[15]

I had heard many stories of parents from all socio-economic groups working voluntarily to 'make up' the space for the additional and different needs their children might have, and that were not catered for in the mainstream. The voluntary work involved was significant and entirely invisible to policymakers. My speech, I hoped, was also a way to acknowledge them.

I praised the adaptability of children, and our need to nurture diversity and initiative in the education system. I spoke of the needs of the system to respond to those who were not mainstream. I asked the government to ratify ILO Convention 103 and in particular Article 5 – any person nursing their children could interrupt their work for this purpose at prescribed times, and these interruptions would count as working hours.

I spoke of violence against children.

> Although the flogging and whipping of adults were abolished in 1941, the use of corporal punishment on children shows little signs of diminishing. Before an outside agency is entitled to take notice of a child's desperation, the child has to be delinquent, or have a broken limb. Persistent cruelty, even of the most pernicious kind does not entitle a child to any kind of protection or redress, provided the cruelty stops short of unreasonable physical violence. How children ever manage to acquire and maintain a sense of justice and social responsibility in the teeth of such a regime is beyond my comprehension.

At-risk children were a concern too – those in domestic-abuse situations, the young boys in refuge centres who had never known a non-violent male in their lives, and children exposed to pornographic influences in the media and the advertising sector. I recorded the disturbing figures of youth unemployment, and gave the latest figures for under-20 males and females in the Waikato. I asked the government to give urgent consideration to expanding its additional job programme to the retail, wholesale and financial sectors, because in my electorate employment opportunities for young people were found mainly in the servicing industries. I recognised the efforts of tens of thousands of parents, professionals and voluntary workers who gave children the very best they could.[16]

On 31 May 1979 the new MP Winston Peters was welcomed to caucus. Brian Talboys was in the chair and wished him a 'long, healthy and rewarding stay'. Winston had been placed second in the election for the seat of Hūnua, and had won it in a magisterial recount.[17] I had first met him at a candidates' conference in 1975 when he stood for the Northern Māori seat. In that campaign, I thought he had the most compelling political message in any election advertisement I had seen. It occupied a full page in the *New Zealand Herald* and ran just once. It had a photograph of blankets, muskets, tobacco and feathers – with which colonists paid Māori for thousands of hectares of land. It resonated with the spirit of the October 1975 hīkoi protesting the alienation of Māori land. I'd had no other contact with Winston, but he was now the third Māori in National's caucus.

The national economy was deteriorating quickly. Since the Iranian Revolution, 5.7 million barrels of oil per day had been withdrawn from world supplies. From January to July oil prices had more than doubled. There was a weekly caucus update on the energy situation: an aviation-gas tanker was on its way; stocks of diesel were deteriorating; the distribution of stickers to introduce carless days was happening. New Zealand's terms of trade and balance of payments were heading into precarious territory.

Yet at caucus on 7 June the Prime Minister claimed that the National Party's Dominion Executive was in 'good heart'. I suspect this was a reflection of the fact he had been out of the country, he hadn't been holding press conferences, and the Hūnua electoral petition had been successful. Muldoon had been visiting the USA and had raised agriculture protectionism issues. He had not been successful in his campaign to have even more nuclear ship visits.[18] This despite his work on the outgoing US ambassador to New Zealand, Armistead Selden, a Nixon appointee, former US Navy man and avowed anti-communist. Muldoon convinced him to write a very strong letter to US Secretary of State Richard Holbrooke, claiming that 'access by the US Navy to partner ports was vital to ANZUS'. Holbrooke, a Carter appointee, replied that in light of the Three Mile Island incident this was not an appropriate time to raise the issue. This response was leaked, probably by the Americans. Muldoon was also busy countering the fact that nuclear ships were banned in New York City. Safety and meltdowns were not the reason, he explained; rather, it was the possibility of sabotage. Did he think that wasn't a possibility in New Zealand?

On 15 June I led the debate reporting back from the PEC on financial management and control in administrative government departments. The 1978 Report of the Controller and Auditor-General had raised significant issues. We found that financial management in administrative departments was mediocre and lacked positive leadership. Estimating procedures were too rigid and complex, and accountability to Parliament was inadequate. We recommended that when a policy proposal had been approved in principle by Cabinet, all resource-use implications should be submitted as a single package, rather than piecemeal. We wanted changes in the presentation of departmental reports to Parliament so they were structured in terms of departmental programmes and activities.

The committee decided that in our future work we should look at the list of programmes in each department to find out when and for how long they had been authorised to operate. What were the original objectives? Some had been running for years without this kind of examination. We also wanted to identify programmes that had similar or conflicting objectives within the whole sphere of financial management – for example, the control of fresh water where the Ministry of Works and Development, river catchment authorities, the Department of Internal Affairs, the Ministries of Agriculture and Fisheries, Health and Environment, and local authorities were all involved.

We were critical of the State Services Commission, which was reluctant to accept that special attention was needed to recruit and retain highly skilled accountants in government departments. Figures showed that the turnover of accountants was high and that many departments had acting accountants without professional qualifications. Many were part-time employees.

In 1979 we also made a start recording the Estimates hearings on tape. A typed transcript was subsequently given to each member within a few days of a particular meeting. This was a very constructive innovation that eliminated any argument about 'what the committee was told', while still leaving interpretation open. The Clerk's office met the costs.

I also sought time with each minister to put the following question: 'If you were a member of the Public Expenditure Committee, what questions would you put to your own departmental officers during the Estimates hearings?' Three-quarters of the ministers saw me; one didn't want to see me unless his senior departmental officials were there. Some were clever enough to give me questions that would lead to demands for more resources from the Opposition during debates in the House, potentially strengthening their agency bids the next time around. Some had no idea what they would ask.

Another change I wanted to explore was whether we could have other select committees engaged with us on the Public Expenditure examination of the Estimates. This would not only do justice to the 45 different agencies that would appear before us, but also allow the specialist select committees – for example, Transport, or Health and Education – to use their more in-depth knowledge of some programmes by conducting those hearings. I met with each of the committee chairs, and all agreed they could take this on. We would do it as a pilot, and if it worked well we could do this each year, rotating the agencies back through the PEC after two years, to ensure different eyes examined the evidence. I brought the proposal to caucus on 21 June. The only resistance came from former PEC chair Bill Birch.

On 21 June, Len Bayliss, chief economist at the Bank of New Zealand, gave an address to the Federated Farmers conference in Wellington. George Gair and I had met with Len several times when we were working on housing policy in 1975, and he had subsequently taken one of the positions in the Prime Minister's 'Think Tank' from 1976 to 1978. I liked Len and his straightforward approach, regardless of his audience. He told the farmers an 'inadequate rate of farm profitability primarily reflected on a substantially overvalued exchange rate'. This rate was set by Muldoon.

Farm subsidies led to increasingly serious distortions in farm investment and production, and this had become a major budgetary problem. Estimates varied as to the total cost of various farm subsidies, but they were thought to be around $400 million annually. There were about 83 different farm subsidies and incentive schemes in place, in addition to the large interest-rate subsidies from the Rural Bank. They tended to be allocated on an ad hoc basis, in part reflecting the political clout of each component group of farmers. Products with below-average or low profits tended to receive more subsidies than products earning above-average or high profits – a situation Ian McLean had called an admirable social-welfare distribution policy.

Len advised that a major reason for the rise in farm costs by $450 million annually was because farmers had to purchase protected domestically produced goods, rather than imports competing at a lower price. He quoted Ian's analysis which showed an emphasis on increasing stock numbers, rather than on increased production per stock unit. The subsidy regime encouraged spending instead of economising, and this led to a wasteful use of fertiliser. Interest-rate subsidies played a significant role in accelerating the rise in rural land prices. In my electorate, we had people engaged in 'capital gains' as opposed to 'production' farming.

It wasn't just the urban electorates of the Party looking for fewer subsidies and regulation. A lot of farmers in Waipā shared these sentiments and were looking for change.

Back in the electorate, I was feeling more comfortable. I had some wonderful supporters, and I felt very lucky to work with, learn from and spend time with them. Waipā electorate secretary Jim White had started a newsletter, and I always enjoyed seeing what he had chosen to put in it. In June 1979 he selected items from the Speech from the Throne:

— The government will be giving particular attention to strengthening trade relations with countries in North Asian, Middle East and Eastern European regions.
— Government had to reassess and re-arrange its capital works programme to ensure that only essential needs are met. Priority has been given to those programmes, which have an export potential, the capacity to help reduce the level of unemployment and reduce the demand for imports.

Jim advised Party members that at the Waikato Divisional Conference spontaneous applause greeted a comment by the president that many Party members were saying to him that we should tackle the economic issues, get the job done and not worry about the consequences, echoing Ian McLean's comments in caucus.

The next major function would be in Te Awamutu, where I asked the branch to host Jonathan Elworthy MP, the chairman of the Select Committee on Ancillary Licensing. With Katherine's help in assembling the list, I would write to all sporting bodies, clubs, wine and spirit merchants, restaurateurs and hoteliers with details of the committee's terms of reference. All parliamentary votes on alcohol licensing were conscience votes, and I wanted to assess electorate feeling on this issue first hand, as well as have my electorate people heard by the chair of the committee.

A lot of deep thought and discussion went on in my electorate about how politics and representative democracy could be improved. This encouraged me to speak about alternatives, despite the inevitable criticisms. I believed that the seasonal farming needs that saw Parliament run from June to November were gone, and I was not impressed with arguments that the timing of the Budget debate should be a reason for inflexibility. I favoured a parliamentary year divided into 10 one-monthly cycles, with a week in the electorates and three weeks in Wellington, and allowances made to be in recess during some school holidays. The Wellington period could be used for sittings of the House or select-committee work – whichever happened to be the most pressing. Two planned sessions, one mainly legislative and the other budgetary, were an alternative approach. I advocated for computerised voting to save MPs hours wasted voting in the lobbies: 'It is inexcusable that the House spent nearly 32 hours in primary school type queues in 1974, more than the equivalent of a whole week of parliamentary business.' I was also critical of the composition of Cabinets – both the lack of people to select from, and the lack of expertise among them. I thought we could consider appointing half a dozen ministers from outside Parliament. They would be entitled to attend Parliament and address it during debates.

Out-of-nowhere decisions needing a great deal of energy for response were regular. The Secretary of Defence, on Defence Council orders, had announced a new policy to discharge from the armed forces any person who was homosexual or suspected of being homosexual, and whose behaviour was deemed detrimental to discipline. John Elliot and Ian Shearer were asking questions in the House about this. They were told that homosexual behaviour was prejudicial to service discipline and could not be tolerated: it would lead to an inevitable collapse of respect. There had been an inconsistency in the treatment of males and females and this had to be remedied. They wanted men and women to be subject to the same discharge rules.

On 27 June I wrote to Ria McBride at the Human Rights Commission:

> My first question concerns the rights of Armed Forces to approach you, Government Departments, members of Parliament or any other similar authority other than through their Commanding Officer. This lack of opportunity for direct representation is an unjustified breach of human rights and one to which I would wish you to direct some inquiry.
>
> The second matter concerns the Defence Council Order itself. I believe that it is the first time in the Western World that there has been a back-door attempt to effectively legislate against homosexual activity between women so that it penalises them in the employment of their choice. I hope the Commission will find it possible to give this matter an early investigation.

Within a few days, another issue exploded. In early July in Rotorua a Supreme Court judge refused name suppression of a 19-year-old physically disabled young woman in a rape trial involving nine motorcycle gang members. The complainant was profoundly deaf and suffering from an allied speech defect, and had a congenital heart condition. Her father, full of anguish, rang me and wrote to me. The officer in charge of the investigation was stunned at the decision on suppression and took leave from the police force. I followed up with a question to the Minister of Justice, asking if he was prepared to bring in amending legislation to stop anything like this happening again. On 10 August, lawyer and MP for Rotorua Paul East introduced a Private Member's Bill to stop the publication of the complainant's name in sexual offence cases.

Speaking in support of Paul's Bill, I recalled a meeting I had attended earlier in the year in Auckland.[19] It was a seminar for judges, magistrates and police, with a focus on sexual assault. There were just a handful of women in the room. A police doctor who examined rape complainants spoke cynically and callously about victims he had examined – including one 'where the vaginal wall was so loose the speculum fell out'. He made it clear he didn't believe sex workers could be raped. He was a shocking advertisement for why women would not report. Some of the women at the meeting threatened to leave. I intervened and asked for this offensive presentation to stop, and I asked for an apology. Afterwards, Elizabeth and I began a focused effort on having women GPs available for the police medical examination in cases of sexual assault.

Elizabeth had finished the survey of seven major refuges, and simply having data was making a difference. The Welfare Services Distribution Committee was formulating a policy for grants from lottery profits under a prescribed formula. The Mental Health Foundation gave $2,500 to each refuge. We laughed that Elizabeth was also being asked to research material for Jim McLay's speeches as our 'spokesman'.

I made my Budget speech on 18 July. I claimed that 'the Budget was largely anticipated as a restructuring Budget – it is a far too cautious a document to justify the restructuring description'. Movement was too moderate. Our key economic data made grim reading, and the oil crisis continued. This would always be a tough Budget to write. I supported the gradual, positive move to reduce levels of protection across industry sectors.[20] I also supported the 'crawling peg' exchange-rate system and a more flexible system for importing raw materials, components, plant and equipment. It would still leave some industries with protection of about 300 per cent.

I spoke of the need to consider indirect taxation, a 'value-added tax', a 'retail tax' or an expenditure tax. I was not happy with government expenditure as a percentage of GDP and with further expansion of government activity. I deeply understood Muldoon's reluctance to make any decisions that would trigger further unemployment. But inefficiencies, especially caused by regulatory and protective instruments, and the costs of these at every level, were cumulative, and each failure to act meant it all just got worse, with the constant impact at the community level. I referred to examples from constituents: from the production of pottery, lampshades and carving; restrictions on garden centres, rugby clubs, motor lodges and export sawmillers. In Waipā, these issues were brought to my attention far more than they had been in Raglan.

Finally, I reflected on the government's pursuit of DPB recipients who were in 'permanent relationships', whatever that was supposed to mean. 'One is all right as long as one had Tom last night, Dick tonight, and Harry tomorrow, just as long as one does not have Tom or Dick or Harry all week; but it is all right if one has Allison – as long as she is not a member of the armed forces.' This passed by most MPs in the House, but parliamentary staff listening to the radio transmission hooted with laughter.

In an issue of *The Republican*, editor Bruce Jesson had suggested I was a feminist.[21] In the 28 July edition, there were two letters to the editor of note. Sandra Coney wrote:

> Radical feminism argues for a profound restructuring of society. Thus radical feminists are not, as Jesson claims 'Only concerned with the question of male domination.' Which is precisely the position, which enables a clear stand to be taken on a woman like Marilyn Waring who is involved in a right-wing capitalist party. The National Party philosophy on women is that a woman's place is in the home. Any woman that supports such a Government is working against the class interests of women and thus does not warrant support from the Women's Movement.
>
> The reason Bruce Jesson has heard little criticism of Marilyn Waring's position is not because radical feminists lack a coherent position on such women but has more to do with the fact she is a woman and is vulnerable to attack for many other reasons. This causes a certain paralysis with regard to openly expressing that position.[22]

Christine Dann wrote:

> Although Marilyn Waring receives extensive media coverage, she is certainly not regarded as a leader by radical feminists, lesbian feminists, socialist feminists or even a majority of feminists pure and simple since she does not accurately or adequately represent their views.
>
> Waring is thus not a leader in any real sense. She sometimes expresses views which any feminist and most women would endorse – on abortion for example – but in other areas (her passive support for the SIS Bill for example) she has been severely criticised by feminists, who feel no loyalty towards her as [they] would towards a leader who genuinely represented all their interests.[23]

The experience of chairing the PEC gave me more, and different, subject matter for speeches. Because the public was excluded from our meetings, there was limited understanding of what we did, and at a public lecture at Waikato University in August I made it clear that we took our jobs very seriously. I was well aware there was a great deal of concern about the government's accountability to the public.

I sometimes wondered if the absence of the media at meetings meant there was little posturing. There were no passengers on the committee; everyone paid attention and participated. I had especially admired the way Jim McLay had chaired the Statutes Revision Committee when I attended, and I tried to be communicative, open, patient, thorough and consistent in my chairing work. For the first time, two women were now permanent members of PEC. Ann Hercus was smart, attentive and experienced after her work on the Price Tribunal and the Commerce Commission. She had been a member of the Society for Research on Women and helped in organising the United Women's Convention in Christchurch in 1975. She and I would work together to ensure a thorough series of questions on women in the agency under scrutiny and on the impact of the agency's policies on women. We didn't have to set this up. It happened spontaneously. It was such a relief not to be the only one having to raise these issues over and over again.

On 28 August the Estimates for the Justice Department were debated in the House. I moved a reduction in the Vote of $218,328, the amount required to service the Abortion Supervisory Committee.[24] Normally moving a motion against the government in such circumstances would be heretical: the Estimates debates are part of 'supply' for the government and as such a matter of confidence. But this was a conscience issue.

I did tell Justice Minister Jim McLay that I would be doing this, but I didn't discuss the matter with anyone. Nor did I expect support or a seconder. It was another opportunity to focus on the ASC, this time on duplication of services in public expenditure. In moving the amendment, I advised I did not wish to trifle with the committee of the House, or to abuse the Estimates examination procedure. I did not wish to place the Minister in an invidious position.

There was, I said, no need for a magistrate to preside over the ASC. The committee was charged with reviewing the abortion law, but this was the job of Parliament. Applications for licences were the job of the Department of Health, as was establishing standards for facilities. The ASC had not ensured adequate counselling facilities. I said I could not let such an abuse of public funds go unchallenged.

Three following speakers referred to my amendment: Warren Freer supported it; Mike Minogue said the matter had already occupied much time in the House and the proper course was to amend the legislation. Jim McLay replied that he had to maintain the Vote for his department, even though he voted against the abortion legislation in 1977, 'and would do so again'.

At the caucus meeting on 30 August, we were advised that there was to be another round of the Standing Orders Select Committee. Standing orders were the rules and procedures for running Parliament. There were new issues with the ministers finally moving to the new Executive Wing, the 'Beehive' building. Division bells had long rung for five minutes as an indication a vote was to be taken; now Cabinet members had to walk further to reach the Debating Chamber. A scientific experiment was conducted. The oldest of the messengers in the parliamentary staff were taken to the ninth floor of the Beehive. Using the stairs, they were timed on how long it took them to reach the Chamber. It was thus determined that the bells would ring for seven minutes.

Another innovation was that voting in the parliamentary lobbies would now start when the bells began. In the past, we had stood in queues until the bell stopped, and could start voting after only the doors were (literally) locked. We were asked if there were other issues important to the caucus.

One colleague asked if there would be any consideration of participation in and time limits for Address in Reply and Budget debates. We were all expected to participate, and the speaking time for each was 30 minutes. Twenty minutes was plenty.

Aussie Malcolm led the charge on the issue of the parliamentary quorum. There always had to be 20 MPs in the Debating Chamber; the

Speaker would adjourn the House otherwise. This meant it was the government's job to maintain the quorum, as the Opposition could go down to one speaker and one Whip. Aussie wanted the quorum down to 10. Tony Friedlander, Jim McLay and I agreed. Government backbenchers were released in relays to go to the dining room for a meal during urgency when the House sat past 10.30 p.m. and sometimes into the next day. We asked for a meal break for urgency. There was a vigorous discussion on why the parliamentary year could not be more aligned with school terms so that MPs could spend time with their families. It was all a waste of breath.

I did a lot of reading while sitting in the House, able to tune in and out of the debates according to the subject and my interest. In the afternoon and early evening it would be briefing papers and correspondence; in the evening some new feminist reading; and, as it got later, I would switch to my pile of local newspapers and the myriad trade journals and magazines we all received. I completed a great deal of knitting sitting there, multitasking my way through the long hours.

I spoke in the Estimates debate on Health on 11 September, focused on fluoridation, which I said had 'done much to eliminate dental decay in young people'.[25] This arose from a briefing in the Health Caucus Committee and was a particular concern for George Gair as minister. I asked what difficulties he was having in persuading local bodies such as Rotorua and Christchurch to fluoridate the municipal water supply. I also spoke of growing gynaecological waiting lists, and asked if the rural practice subsidy could be available in Mangakino so that they might have a doctor. I noted with thanks departmental funding for Plunket, for departmental studies of child abuse, and for the Family Planning Association.[26]

Later in September, after a visit to speak in Christchurch, a journalist at the *Press* asked if she could have an extended interview.[27] We covered a lot of topics. I criticised the failure to devalue the floating exchange rate. I was pleased with progress on Closer Economic Relations (CER) which would lead to free trade with Australia. I spoke of chairing the PEC as being extremely complex and invigorating. I told her, 'I don't believe in

State capitalism – in excessive amounts of enterprise capital in the hands of the Government. We are also over regulated and over controlled.'

On abortion, I said, 'I just know if women want terminations they are going to get them legally or illegally, and since that is the fact, I would like them to have them in the safest, healthiest and most supportive environment.' Referring to the racket that greeted my statement advocating menstrual extraction, I replied, 'Of course there are dangers. I outlined them at the time. I would advocate the technique in the appropriate environment with the appropriate supports.'

I described my work as having 'good days and bad days, like anything you do'. How can you be so sure you represent women? the interviewer asked. 'I can only reflect my experience as a woman and the experience of women who let me know what their experience is.'

I explained that I thought of my term in Parliament as one day at a time. 'There may well come an issue in Parliament on any given day, a point of principle on which I find it impossible any longer to be a representative in New Zealand, an issue which I'd have to ask some very serious questions about.' Would I name one such issue? 'Arming the police.'

When asked, 'Does Mr Muldoon frighten you?' I replied, 'No. I don't really know the man. I only see him about three hours per week.'

Back in the House, I continued to ask more questions than anyone: on the number of secondary school crèches (there were 18), police recruitment training on domestic violence, microprocessors, industry development reports, road user charges, music teachers, and medical tests for drivers over 70. Questions in the House were the fastest and easiest way to get a reply to all kinds of esoteric issues people raised with me. It was also the end of a process of trying to work through the system until there was no other strategic route left.

For example, in Ōhaupō, the primary school was on top of a rise set above the peat swamps of the area. In winter there were frequent thick fogs, laced with the smell of burning peat. The school was outside the restricted speed limit for the settlement, on the opposite side of the only footpath and on the main highway. I had stood with the children and staff on the road, trying to get everyone across safely. I watched as they collected data on traffic movements in the mornings. I had signed and presented petitions. I had lobbied the National Roads Board. Then the inevitable happened, and a child was killed. When would we get a tunnel under the road, I asked the Minister. Will it need another fatality?

Sometimes I was so shocked by an answer given in the House I was unable to recover for a supplementary question. On 30 October I asked George Gair as Minister of Social Welfare: 'Under what circumstances are venereal disease [VD] tests performed on children admitted to children's homes, and do the females have the right to refuse such tests?' George replied: 'A routine medical examination is part of the admission procedure. When the age of the child and circumstances suggest it is prudent to check for VD, a medical practitioner does this. The total number of children tested in any one year is about 1200, of which one in six is found to have VD. There is a right to refuse the test.'[28]

I was featured in an interview in the *New Zealand Woman's Weekly* in October.[29] The journalist said it was plain that the pressures of being a vocal and determined public figure were exhausting. She described my 'disconcerting frankness' in speaking about this. 'It's burning me out because I don't know if I'm doing any good,' I said. 'Sometimes I'll be driving along a country road, and I think "One day I'm going to wake up and realise this is all an exhausting dream." In as much as I know what is going on, I tell people. I'm honest; I'm impatient with political game playing.'

The *Australian Women's Weekly* also published a story in October describing me as 'an outspoken feminist activist with a healthy sense of the ridiculous, [who] is thought by many to be the woman who could one day be prime minister of her country. Today she is the best known and probably the most influential woman in New Zealand.'[30] They obviously hadn't read the letters to *The Republican*.

I attended a select committee hearing on the Police Amendment Bill and the Crimes Amendment (No. 2) Bill, both of which covered searches of women held by the police. I was anxious that the gender of those conducting searches be written into the legislation. There was already such a section in the Customs Department legislation. Police attending the committee advised they didn't need this to be written in, because policemen left the room. This was garbage. I knew from some of the women at the rape conference in Auckland, from a range of women I had spoken with during my research for the Select Committee on Violence, from the women from the Aroha Trust, and from women I had met inside Arohata Prison that not only did policemen remain in the room but there were also instances of sexual assault. So I said I didn't believe them, and that it happened often.

So began an attempt to belittle and heavy me by the cops. A good feminist friend inside Police HQ advised there were meetings on 'how to get Waring'. I was asked to provide evidence, and the Police Association secretary said he didn't believe the accusations.[31] 'The practice is outlawed – absolutely taboo.'[32]

I wrote to the Minister of Police:

> I have expressed some grave concern over apparent breaches of police instructions during searches of female offenders. My understanding of police instructions is as follows; that on the occasion of any search or strip search of any women the search is to be performed by a policewoman or another woman of good repute, and any policemen are to retire from the room to the watch-house.
>
> During the last two years, in particular, I have had reported to me by young females numerous breaches of the above. These reports can be divided into two main categories: searches after arrests for drug offences to search for more narcotics, and searches after violence offences to search for weapons. I have also had numerous reports of a third nature in any area where police instructions are unclear. This concerns those cases where search warrants are executed on a house and women are disturbed in bed naked and are hindered in a variety of ways from clothing themselves for considerable periods of time.
>
> In my reported comments, I spoke of the indignity of complaint and victimisation. I have heard the Commissioner's denial that officers are ever in breach of police instructions regarding search. I accept that he made that assessment to the best of his knowledge and belief.

I wasn't the only voice. Parents of young women who believed the stories of their daughters' treatment in custody wrote to me. A friend, Jo Symmans, worked in the pre-release home at Arohata. On 2 November she asked the 36 women in her unit if they had been searched in the presence of male police officers. One was searched by two males only; three were watched by male officers in the room while they were strip-searched; one was watched by male officers in the room while she was strip-searched and internally examined.

The police and the Minister wanted names, dates and particulars. I wrote that they were not mine to give. 'They were given to me in trust because I need to know that such events occur,' I said, and 'I don't believe all policemen are angels.'

My letter concluded: 'I value my credibility on an issue of women's rights far too greatly to sensationalise an issue where I believe that breaches of these rights are occurring in too great a number. I hope that this week's publicity has resulted in a heightened awareness on the part of female offenders of their rights, and of policemen and their duties.'

This publicity was the last straw for the Ōtorohanga branch committee of the National Party in the Waipā electorate. Six members resigned because 'We cannot control Miss Waring.'[33] I was relieved they had gone, and the chairman, Arnold Myers, was blunt. Charges that democracy had not been practised in Waipā were, he said, 'a bloody lot of rot. The 14 other branches are happy, and that's a fair indication.' The Ōtorohanga branch chairman 'had no previous experience in politics and kept coming to the electorate with botched up ideas'. The committee members had done the right thing in resigning. 'They have been opposed to Ms. Waring right from the start, and it has been difficult for us to work with them for some time.'[34]

The Ōtorohanga branch Women's Section president Pam Disher told the press that I had the solid support of 70 members. 'From experience and working with Marilyn, they [the section] find her easily accessible, attentive and sympathetic to the needs and feelings of the constituents.'

The *Waikato Times* took up the matter in its editorial: 'The final judges are the fickle faceless – the voters. And they have a liking for an MP who is different from the grey mainstream.'[35] By 20 November, a new committee was elected, and they were a terrific group of people.

It was good to have a committee whose members I respected, and it was my constituents who really made my life bearable. *Broadsheet* had reported in 1976 that I had said my priority was my constituency so my support of some issues would be compromised. My caucus thought the issues I supported would be frowned on by my Party supporters. But I was able just to be myself in Raglan, and then in Waipā. I remember deputy chairman Colin Murray saying at an Executive meeting that he didn't spend years battling overseas to come back to trammel an MP's right to free speech. He mightn't agree with what I said, but he had fought to protect my right to say it. I was also helped by the fact that Ian Shearer and Mike Minogue were in neighbouring electorates in the Waikato Division. When 'my' (yes, I spoke of them possessively) people went to a Party division meeting in Hamilton, they couldn't be picked out or picked on.

The caucus of 15 November had several foreign-policy issues on the agenda. Unless it was about ANZUS, CER, apartheid rugby or trade, this was unusual. We learned that an explosion that was compatible only with a nuclear weapons test had been detected, and it was thought to be the work of the Israelis and South Africans. We needed election monitors for the first elections in the new Zimbabwe. In Iran, as the revolution gained momentum, New Zealand would be 'correct' in maintaining a relationship and not much more. There had been no requests from the Americans for involvement, and while we would try to be helpful, we had to look after our oil supplies. Lamb exports to Iran were being paid for on US letters of credit. We were worried about the safety of our diplomats.[36]

I had been invited by my former political science teachers to contribute chapters to books they were editing on the state services and democracy.[37] This gave me another avenue to explore PEC issues and the processes of allocating resources across the state sector.[38] On the PEC, I followed up on information Jim McLay had given me. He had noticed in his briefing papers on becoming Minister of Justice that a Management Audit Report had been conducted. When he asked for it, there had been enormous resistance to giving this to him. Jim suspected that some of his ministerial colleagues didn't know about these audits in their agencies. As I looked into this for the PEC, it appeared even the Controller and Auditor-General's office didn't have them. On a 'trial basis' we were sent just the recommendations from four departments. In 1980 we would ask for the whole document from all of them.

In other PEC work, we were monitoring the introduction of pilot projects with new expenditure-control techniques. A bulk financial allocation was introduced in the Customs Department, and revolving funds to 19 farm development schemes in the Department of Māori Affairs.[39]

We also wanted changes in the form and content of the Public Accounts to include some very basic items, such as a statement of source and application of funds. We wanted to review rushed expenditure towards the end of the financial year to ensure the budget allocations were used up. What pressures caused this? We had found leases of office premises by government departments unoccupied for long periods. Some of our discoveries were breathtaking. I knew the Ministry of Works and Development (MWD) Architectural Division did design work for other agencies. It had never occurred to me that only trading departments were charged for some architectural services. If the client was a non-trading department, these costs were not allocated or specified for the job and were met by MWD.

Sometimes on PEC I just enjoyed getting answers to questions I'd had for some years. What justified the existence of the Te Rapa air-force stores base? There was no commercial airstrip within 20 minutes of it, and no air-force airstrip for 90 minutes. Why was there an air-force store in the most commercial/industrial area of Hamilton? What justified the retention by 19 departments of their own construction or maintenance forces? What liaison existed between the departments of Health, Education, Social Welfare, Police, Māori Affairs, and Sport and Recreation, hospital boards and local authorities in their community work programmes?

I had found being the only woman in caucus gruelling, and both George Chapman and Barrie Leay wanted more National women in

Parliament. I suggested that we hold a weekend training school for women who might be interested in standing for selection. They agreed to fund this, and Michelle Boag would organise it from the Party headquarters. I made a list of women I thought would be good. I did not know, and they were not asked, if they supported the Party. In late November they were invited to a women-only event for potential women candidates in early February 1980. This meeting would have valuable long-term consequences. Everyone in the group was in some way active in women's non-government organisations, and it was a serious two days of frank discussion, including on media and publicity, running for selection, information and where to find it, and how to handle offers of help. Ruth Richardson and Katherine O'Regan would become MPs; others ran for Parliament, or in Sue Wood's case, also became Party president. There were women who would be future mayors and commissioners, who would lead their professional bodies, and whom caucus would approve as appointments.

Towards the end of the year New Zealand celebrated a few 'firsts'. Sonja Davies was the first woman elected to the Federation of Labour. Jean Herbison was appointed first woman chancellor of the University of Canterbury. Joan Anderson became the first woman elected as moderator of the Presbyterian Church. Jan Everard and Sue Freeman became the first women accepted for pilot training with Air New Zealand. A Maternity Leave and Employment Protection Bill was introduced into Parliament, providing for a minimum of 26 weeks' unpaid maternity leave with job protection during that leave.

But the reasons given by the Railways for not employing women were prehistoric. They advised me that they did not wish to employ females on manual jobs because women undertaking heavy tasks could cause embarrassment to customers when handling luggage. Women couldn't work on night train services because of the risk of family strife caused by men and women employees working in close association in conditions conducive to misconduct. The ability of women staff to cope as bartenders or bar managers on trains was open to question. There were no women in locomotive crews – locomotives had to wait for long periods, and rostering a woman at night with men would jeopardise the reputation of staff.

The oil price rise had created a number of crises in the economy. At one stage the country had been down to 35 days of fuel remaining. Our dependence on others had led to a range of projects that the government now planned to introduce: this became known as the Think Big programme. It meant that the PM wanted to speed up planning processes and get rid of regulatory obstacles and Acts that meant delays in moving on the projects. Caucus battled and won amendments to many clauses in the National Development Bill. But the Bill proposed that if an Order in Council was made, and it differed from the recommendation of the Planning Tribunal, the minister was not accountable to Parliament. Mike Minogue, Ian Shearer, myself (and the Law Society, Federated Farmers, the National Council of Women, tens of thousands of New Zealanders) saw Opposition MP Geoffrey Palmer's amendment as a solution. It proposed that the Order in Council should be of no effect unless, and until, affirmed by a resolution in Parliament: this would ensure accountability to Parliament. We voted in favour of the amendment. It lost 46 to 41. I did not receive any criticism or sanction from the Party at parliamentary level, or at electorate level where most Party members were keenly aware of the potential for Muldoon to abuse power. They were very supportive of caveats on his reach.

In December I received an invitation to join Barrie Leay and a guest for lunch at Plimmer House restaurant in Wellington. This was not somewhere I could afford; it sounded like a special occasion. The other diner turned out to be the first secretary of the British High Commission. He wanted to formally invite me to make a visit to the UK and to Brussels early in 1980 as an official guest of the British government. I should advise my fields of interest, and they would organise and fund the programme. I was delighted. With this trip to look forward to, it was a cheerful end to the year.

1980

I would be leaving New Zealand on my study tour on 10 February. The British government had provided an around-the-world ticket, with an expectation that I should take the opportunity to visit and learn in other capitals. I wanted to attend the Commission on the Status of Women in Vienna in February, and I would work around that. The year began with putting my itinerary in place and preparing the electorate for my absence.

In my contribution to a newsletter to electorate Party members on 7 January I wrote that the cost of National Superannuation had raised government's percentage expenditure of GDP to a record 47 per cent; inflation had risen to 16 per cent; there was net emigration, and the number of unemployed had risen. The question of the leadership of the country was still dominant, and Social Credit had strengthened enormously. Our decision-makers in all spheres were from a very distinct class: 'white, male, middle aged and salaried. We needed to add much more variety, alternatives and differences to current leadership if New Zealand was to achieve only some of its vast human potential this decade.'

A special issue of the *National Business Review* had chosen 54 newsmakers of the decade, so the newsletter included Colin James's assessment that I was 'Parliament's most flair-some member, who has more courage and compassion (and some would add, incaution) than most of the rest put together'. The annual summary of MPs as wine types announced a Gold Medal for a Waring Sparkling Cuvée. It was: 'Pretty dry and has a sharp edge which adds to its popularity. Better than average fruit for this type of wine and has further development in front of it yet. Not favoured by a few traditionalists, but good value.'

I advised I would be absent until 1 May. I sent each Party official a copy of the select committee report on the liquor legislation, and invited guidance from branch members on various options raised on the 'conscience issue' votes. I met with Katherine, Olga and Elizabeth and worked out a clear spread of roles in my absence, and this too was sent to all my Party officials.

On 9 January I sent a memo to all ministers asking them to outline briefly the major pieces of legislation they would introduce in 1980. If there were any surprises, Elizabeth might start preparing for them.

The Family Proceedings, Family Courts, and Guardianship Amendment (No. 2) Bills had been introduced as a 'family law' package in late 1979. It proposed establishing Family Courts, with Family Court judges, which would have jurisdiction over separation and divorce, guardianship, custody, matrimonial property and consents to marry. There would be one ground for divorce at the end of marriage: that there was an irreconcilable breakdown and the parties had lived apart for at least two years. Pre-trial procedures would be replaced by a mediation conference before a Family Court judge. Religious and right-wing submissions opposing these and other changes were inevitable, and Elizabeth would need to monitor these.

In maintenance cases, the Social Welfare Department would be able to issue administrative notices for the attachment of wages. Interim non-molestation orders could be made without both parties being present, and interim orders could be made for the exclusive possession of the home. Children would need to have their own counsel appointed in custody and access proceedings.

I was also still dealing with Inspector Anderton and the search practices of the police. On 10 January I wrote to him again. I advised that I had had further contact with 18 women in the North and South Islands, and received varying responses. I had, I said, outlined 'the merits of a statement by affidavit, but also showed them [the women] the transcript of our discussion, where no absolute assurance as to safeguard from harassment for complaining could be given. Because this inquiry was not one conducted under provisions of the Police Act I was not going to insist on anything.' I went on:

> There are some generalisations, which may be made. Almost all complaints involved the Criminal Investigation Branch. They were not confined to any area in New Zealand. Most of the women were under 20 at the time. It has appeared to me in the course of this investigation that the object from the police point of view was to pinpoint particular officers who have been involved in breaches of instruction rather than change the rules. This is not my object at all. I did not, and cannot understand any unwillingness on the part of the Police force to have the legal safeguards as regards search similar to those provided by Customs legislation. My concern is the protection of the dignity and the rights of the women who may find themselves in such a situation.

Caucus met for a two-day caucus on Wednesday 23 January. On Thursday, I was stunned when Muldoon advised I would be replaced permanently as chair of the Public Expenditure Committee because of my UK Guest of Government research tour. Each year the UK (and the USA, and the apartheid South African, governments) invited a government and an Opposition MP on such a trip. In my four years in caucus, no one had ever lost a select committee chair as a result.

On Friday morning I wrote to the PM, saying I found this unjust and unjustifiable. My first concern was how Waipā constituents would read it. I advised that Waipā had the highest Party membership in the Waikato Division. There was no strong movement for a selection challenge, but my removal from the chair of the PEC would provide a sure catalyst for any who wanted to oppose me. The PM's decision would draw attention to my absences overseas and be seen as a demotion.

I explained that I had already considered the implications of my absence from the chair, and worked to ensure that it would be of little consequence. Sub-committee work would continue, and I would miss no more than six full committee meetings. A great deal of my programme in Britain, Athens, Brussels, Rome and Washington concentrated on learning about alternatives in expenditure control. On the eve of my departure, I said, he was choosing to strip me of the status which had made many of these engagements possible.

He replied by a handwritten note that afternoon. 'Dear Marilyn, I have your letter. Why did you not raise these points when you spoke to me? I understood you to agree to my suggestions. Please see me on my return.' I had been dumbstruck, and surrounded by colleagues when I was given the news. It had not been an appropriate moment to argue.

I was still away when Muldoon returned to New Zealand, and he took the matter to the caucus meeting on 14 March. He said he wanted to canvass opinions on the PEC chairmanship. The caucus minutes recorded two surprises among those who supported me, none among those who were opposed. Richard Harrison, the Speaker, was the first surprise.[1] I was doing a good job, and there was a need for continuity in the chair, he said. Ian McLean advised that work had continued without a stutter in my absence. The sub-committees were doing their investigative work, and I would be back for the Estimates hearings. Frank Gill and Bob Bell were up early with 'she should be replaced'. Bolger thought another member should have the kudos for the year, and Adams-Schneider suggested this should go to Dale Jones. Second surprise: Dale said no, he was happy for me to continue. George Gair suggested 'we all owe Marilyn something for our electoral support', and that it was a political minus to replace me. Minogue agreed and said I was an asset in the PEC position. Rob Talbot and Jonathan Elworthy argued I had forfeited the right to the chair; John Elliot and Tony Friedlander said I was on a legitimate tour, and the Whips had approved the leave. The PM concluded that there was 'too much politics' to have a change. I would be left in the chair.

I had left Auckland on 10 February. Apart from 24-hour stops in Bangkok and Istanbul in early 1974, I had never visited the so-called developing world. Reading or film cannot convey the full-throttle exercise of every sense, of being in an entirely different space – this was something entirely new. My first stop was Bangkok. I met staff at the Asian and Pacific Centre for Women and Development. I visited the Bhirasri Institute of Modern Art for the opening of Brian Brake's photographic exhibition of Māori carving. But the image I have retained for the rest of my life is of a scene in a Lao weaving on the apartment wall of a New Zealand diplomat. A traditional, recurring image was of fields with elephants in a line, their trunks linked with the tail of the one in front. Local people would be walking with them, holding hands, and with children. Above them were large bright stars. In this weaving, the elephants' trunks lunged skywards, their mouths trumpeting. People looked up with faces that looked like Munch's *Scream*; children clasped adults. Bombs rained down from B52 bombers.

On 13 February I was on a small plane to Kathmandu, reading briefing papers on the New Zealand government development programmes in Mount Everest (Sagarmatha) National Park, the forest nursery and the Himalayan Trust Hospital. Through the Colombo Plan, New Zealand had been assisting with milk processing in Nepal since 1958, and I was interested in what was going on at the Balaju dairy in Kathmandu: it had been the subject of some discussion in the PEC.

I'd been in touch with New Zealander John Lindeman, who was working with a Dutch friend, Cas, building the Summit Hotel in the Kupondole area of the capital, using all Nepali labour and products. In time they planned that Nepali people would own the hotel.[2] John had organised appointments with Ministers of Agriculture and Industries and Commerce, in addition to the round of meetings organised for me by the New Zealand High Commission in Delhi. He would be at the airport to take me immediately to my first meeting. I had a page of Nepali greetings: please, thank you, left, right, forest nursery, hospital, etc. I was rehearsing those. In Thailand, I had felt awkward with no Thai language apart from 'sawadee ka'.

When we landed, the airport seemed free of security. John escorted me through, and we proceeded through what seemed to me a medieval village, extraordinary to my inexperienced western senses. I was transfixed. This may explain my distraction when we arrived at the Industry Minister's office. The room reminded me of the office of my first headmaster. There were files of paper from floor to ceiling. I clasped my hands together, bowed and greeted the Minister with 'Sagarmatha' (Mount Everest). John just contained himself, and the Minister bowed back. 'Namaste,' he said.

John and Cas had been thinking about what tourism initiatives they might pilot with a view to handing these over to locals. One major issue was how to import the necessary materials. Nepal is trapped between

China and India. Roads were dangerous and often impassable. Air freight was prohibitive. But they had managed to import a river raft, and wanted to raft the Trisuli River with a view to a possible tourist venture. No one they knew had done this before, and I had never been whitewater rafting, so I was on. We would go on Saturday 16 February.

We were up early and swung along roads it was best not to think about until we reached Charaudi. The villagers had barbecues alight along the river. They were fasting, because today the tiger was eating the sun – that is, there was to be a total eclipse. I marvelled at how a nation with no mass media knew the tiger was eating the sun today and no one must watch it. It was going to take some time to pump up the raft, and I did not want to intrude, so I went for a walk around the outskirts of the village. I found a nice large log and sat down and took some photos. I was fascinated by what was happening to the light meter on my camera. A group of grandmother, mother and daughter were waving to me. I waved back. Then the grandmother and the young girl came towards me, the old woman chuckling loudly. I thought she wanted me to take her photo. I got a good shot. But she wanted to show me I was sitting on the village beehive.

The raft ride was awesome. The Nepalese with us knew the river, and before each set of serious rapids we would pull to the side while they walked ahead with John and Cas to work out how we would run the next course. Physics was never my strong suit, so I did not realise that, when we broached a waterfall, velocity meant the person at the front of the raft, holding two ropes – that was me – would shoot into space, before landing back where the rest of the raft had gone over. I had a great day.

John took me to the central market in Kathmandu, where small clay pottles of beautiful fresh yoghurt were available every day, an end-product of the New Zealand programme. Driving up a valley to the dairy, we saw the roadside end of a simple, covered, gravity-fed pipe rising up the slope from the road for several hundred metres. At different points above, farmers poured their milk down this chute. I thought simultaneously about the trust implicit in doing this, and the opportunities for a loss of product between the roadside and the plant.

I was advised that the King's brother was the key decision-maker concerning the dairy, and he wanted the plant's output to be bottled, not packaged. The second-hand equipment sent from New Zealand was insufficiently reconditioned, and the existing bottling line was being replaced under the direction of a Hamilton company. This was an early lesson in how development could work. The diplomatic line was that countries asked for assistance. But nepotism played a major role, and donors could be caught when the powerful beneficiaries changed their minds about what they would like.

Small amounts of electricity sometimes worked in Kathmandu. In the evenings we would go for a walk around the city, often relying on candles in the courtyards of houses to light our way. It felt very safe with John and Cas. One evening I stood outside a courtyard, watching an extended family and maybe neighbours. One played a madal (small drum), several played bamboo flutes; one bowed a sarangi (stringed instrument), another played rang jhyamta (small cymbals). Children danced. It was a long story. At the beginning everyone knew all the words, but as it progressed only the older women knew them, and they would bring everyone back to a chorus. I had played in a medieval music consort with Steve Rosenberg, Graeme Stentiford, Robert Oliver and others at Cambridge Music School in 1975. This art form was urban culture in Kathmandu in 1980.

But it was not a romantic environment. There was little or no sanitation, and no sewerage schemes. Malaria was prevalent. The infant mortality rate was high. Roads were built with shovels, not even wheelbarrows. Everything was carried on the back. Men operated treadle sewing machines or old Imperial typewriters in small booths.

I left Nepal for Athens on 18 February. I had been travelling for 10 days, and already I had been taught anew in myriad ways that would influence how I thought about and interpreted my political views and activities in the future. Greece would offer yet more insights. Inflation there was running at 19 per cent. Overseas investments were falling, and oil prices had risen dramatically. Sixty per cent of tax was collected indirectly. Parliament was debating family law, the dowry, divorce, domicile, abortion, and custody and maintenance. All the banks were on strike, and the lawyers marched on Parliament.

I had sought the assistance of our diplomatic posts in making appointments, with priorities on public expenditure, technology change and employment policies, and the women's movement. The presence of a half-competent MP could also offer our diplomats an opportunity to get in doors to lobby again on issues important for New Zealand. Greece was to enter the European Economic Community in 1981. Our ambassador explained that we were in delicate stages of negotiations on the price and volume of the next season's lamb export. So off we went to the Ministry of Foreign Affairs for discussions with Minister Georgios Rallis and his officials. I had appointments with the Greek equivalent of our Planning Council, and with my Greek parliamentary counterpart on the introduction of zero-based budgeting into their parliamentary budget cycle. One evening I would be addressing the Multi-National Women's Liberation Group.

Our Embassy had arranged a special luncheon for me with Lady Amelia Fleming, widow of Sir Alexander Fleming. She had sheltered New Zealand soldiers when working with the Greek Resistance during the war, had been imprisoned by the Greek military junta in 1967, and on release in 1971 was stripped of her citizenship and exiled. Amelia had been elected as a Socialist MP in 1977, and was very active in Amnesty International (AI) and on human rights issues.[3] While I had supported AI for some years, Amelia was the first prisoner of conscience I had ever met, and our time together made me even more resolute in my support of the organisation. I felt very privileged to listen to her stories and to have time with her at her home.

My meeting the following day was with Opposition MP Virginia Tsouderos, a feminist and former journalist. She closed the door to staff and my Embassy companion. She didn't waste any time. 'How do you manage with all those men?' she said. 'Alone and so young? They cannot be as bad as the ones here maybe?' This was a blinding, transformative flash of realisation for me. I had never discussed it, but I had always thought *I* was the problem, that other women wouldn't have the same experience as me as a parliamentarian if they complied with all the stereotypes of what a woman was supposed to be. I was deeply grateful for this insight.

From Athens, I flew to Vienna. I had asked for accreditation to the New Zealand delegation to the Commission on the Status of Women. Colleen Dewe was the New Zealand delegate, and Helen Fawthorpe came from our New York UN office to assist. Helen and I had been at university together. I arrived in Vienna to be told that Colleen had been hit by a tram and was hospitalised with a broken leg. Helen sent a request to Wellington for me to replace Colleen. It came through at the final moment. Jim McLay told me he had to walk over broken glass to get it approved.

This was my first experience of the extraordinary assembly of a United Nations commission meeting. Although many there would have been used to the rhetoric this was my first exposure to the points of view expressed in, for example, some of the debates about Zionism. It became clear that what I had learned in putting together *What's Been Done?* was more up to date than our briefing papers, and so I just wrote interventions from my knowledge. Helen told me it was most uncommon for copies of New Zealand's speeches to be requested by Lesotho, Greece, Malaysia, the World Council of Churches, Colombia, the Netherlands, Britain and the USA. I finally met Australian feminist Elizabeth Reid, who was a senior UN official for the commission and would be principal officer for the UN Half Decade Conference on Women to follow mid-year in Copenhagen.

What was surprising was that the local newspapers at home ran material from my speeches. The *Te Awamutu Courier* reported the first intervention:

> The proposed programme and strategies confirm the status of male-dominated decision-making frameworks rather than attempting to break down the system. Too much in the proposals is dependent on women being given something rather than taking or making it for themselves. Too many proposals would benefit only those in the middle and upper social strata who have access to the decision-making process.

> The myriad of voluntary organisations in New Zealand as in other countries is proof of the need women have to join together in pursuit of objectives they have defined, but which are not being met by other systems' structures.[4]

The *Waikato Times* ran excerpts from the second:

> The Board of the Broadcasting Corporation of New Zealand is male and appointed by a male Government Cabinet. The owners and directors of private radio stations are men. The Boards of the major publishing companies of daily newspapers are male. The editors of the thirty-six major metropolitan daily newspapers are male. The major executive positions in both BCNZ television channels and Radio New Zealand are all held by men with one exception: the head of programming for Radio New Zealand is a woman.
>
> Media can clearly be seen to work as a conservative force for upholding stereotyped images of women and men in New Zealand Society.
>
> Positive signs of change were the emergence of feminist bookshops, women publishers and printers, 'learning webs' established by women as disseminators of information, regular newsletters published by women's organisations, and 'women in the media' groups formed by women journalists.[5]

The expected resistance to my appointment to the delegation came from the Society for Promotion of Community Standards. Patricia Bartlett wrote that a more emotionally mature woman with wide experience and involvement with different women's organisations, especially those involving family life, should have been appointed.[6]

From Vienna, I travelled to Rome for meetings with parliamentarians, ministers and officials, and with representatives of the Union of Italian Women. On 14 March I arrived in London, where a solid programme to meet my requests had been organised. There would be meetings at the Department of Health and Social Security, the Home Office, and with the secretary-general of the Commonwealth Parliamentary Association and the director of Amnesty International.

I began in Manchester because the Equal Opportunities Commission was there. But the highlights of Manchester were an evening at the

Royal Exchange Theatre for the world premiere season of *The Dresser* starring Tom Courtenay, and the opportunity to meet Professor Enid Mumford at the University of Manchester. Enid was the first woman to be a full professor in a UK Business School. I knew of Enid's work when she famously conducted action research for nine months with coal miners working underground. Now she was researching the effects of computing systems and IT on work design.

I travelled to Brussels for meetings at the European Economic Commission to discuss agricultural questions, EEC relations with New Zealand, equal employment opportunities for women, and consumer policy. I was fascinated with the idea that the EEC might be able to lift the legislative standards member states had for women's rights, and for the human rights of the citizens of the EEC.

Back in London I had the obligatory day at the Houses of Parliament: a tour of both the House of Commons (lucky MPs, no daft quorum) and the House of Lords; lunch (not as good as Bellamy's) with MPs; and a meeting with the Clerk's Office and members of the Public Accounts Committee.

The event that would have a major effect on me was attending the Commonwealth Society conference 'Alternative to Chaos', based on the Brandt Report, *North–South, A Programme For Survival*.[7] The keynote speaker was former UK PM Edward Heath, who had been a member of the commission. I received a copy of the publication. I noted that it contained a page about the special concerns of women, and realised that Elizabeth Reid, who had been the first appointment to a women's rights post at the Commonwealth Secretariat, probably had to bang heads for weeks to achieve even that.

My handwritten notes outlined the conference focus. The three most pressing issues were: 1) the food required to meet the vast increases in populations expected in the South; 2) the raw materials required to satisfy the industries of the North and the development of the South; and 3) the problems of energy. The North–South dialogue had increased in intensity because of high inflation, high interest rates, unemployment, no growth and an oil price rise. Oil had become the one product that people who had it didn't want to produce. Kuwait had cut production by

25 per cent. Saudi Arabia was cutting back after the Iranian revolution. Iran was down to a third of its previous production. The South wanted commodity agreements on about 18 products which were mostly from the primary sector, and impossible to stockpile. (Hmm – like New Zealand.) As an alternative, the South would like to see processing and marketing concentrated in their areas. I was reading and hearing far more points of view on international politics than ever before, but the absence of women was an ever-present feature.

The last days in the UK were spent visiting the Arts Council; the National Council of Women and the Abortion Law Reform Association; the Chiswick Refuge Centre; Cookham Woods and East Sutton, a women's prison and borstal, respectively; and the day dependence clinic at University College Hospital.

From London, I flew to New York, where Helen Fawthorpe had prepared a wonderful programme for me. I attended the preparatory conference for the UN Half Decade Conference on Women meeting. I had lunch with Carol Bellamy, the first woman to be elected (in 1978) as president of the New York City Council.[8] I attended an editorial board meeting of *Ms.* magazine. At a luncheon hosted by Ronnie Eldridge, then director of community and government affairs for the New York Port Authority, I met some remarkable women working in such 'untraditional' jobs as chief air traffic controller at Kennedy International Airport. This group were in roles New Zealand women still only dreamed of.

A Kiwi connection meant I was invited to give a lecture to postgraduate students and fellows at the Woodrow Wilson School of Public and International Affairs at Princeton University. Then Elizabeth Reid had made an appointment for me to visit the Institute of Politics (IOP) at the Kennedy School of Government at Harvard, where I spent the day meeting director Jonathan Moore, and talking with students, staff and fellows. Elizabeth had been a fellow at the IOP and had asked Jonathan to consider me for such an invitation. I remember sitting there thinking what a relief it would be to have that opportunity, but a young feminist backbencher from Aotearoa would not meet the threshold for such an invitation. Previous fellows included Shirley Williams and Lee Kuan Yew.[9]

From New York I travelled to Washington for a frantic round of meetings: the Congresswomen's Caucus; the Senate Appropriations Committee, with Patricia Derian, who had a history of civil rights and human rights activism, and was now assistant secretary for human rights and humanitarian affairs in the Department of State. I addressed a meeting of the American Newspaper Women's Club. I met with staff of the White House Office of Management and Budget, the directors of the Congressional Budget Office and the Senate Budget Committee, as well as the director of policy in the General Accounting Office. I called on elected representatives serving on Budget committees. I was a sponge and soaked up everything on offer. I was always happy in a learning environment, and I would have plenty of material for the inevitable speeches once I got home.

Within days, I was telling travel stories in Waipā, and at branch meetings and fundraisers in Puahue, Kihikihi, Ōtorohanga, Pāterangi and Wharepūhunga. I had faxed to Wellington more than a dozen handwritten newsletters about where I was, whom I was meeting and what I was thinking, and Olga had typed these and sent them on. They had been read and passed around. Katherine had acted as a messenger for constituents who needed help, and Elizabeth had handled inquiries in Wellington.

Elizabeth updated me on key issues. Since the Gleneagles Agreement, two rugby personnel and one jockey had been to South Africa. The Ministry of Foreign Affairs had written to these men prior to their departure, outlining New Zealand's obligations under the agreement. On 9 April Brian Talboys advised the NZRFU that he was 'deeply concerned that a South African tour is even one of the options which will be considered'. They had to take full account of New Zealand's responsibilities under the Gleneagles Agreement. 'Sporting contact with the South African Rugby team gives the appearance – however much this is unwarranted – of condoning the apartheid policies of the South African Government.' But the Rugby Union was paying no attention.

The Human Rights Commission had been hopeless on the question of the Defence Council orders banning homosexual men and women from the services. In February they had replied that they were satisfied that the discharge documents would give little chance of a future employer being aware of allegations of homosexuality against the man or woman concerned. We gave up on them.

Those attending the graduation ceremony at Waikato Technical Institute on 8 May 1980 got to hear some of what I'd learned and seen on my overseas trip:

> I have learned that at least three competing systems of dairy herd management in the United Kingdom and about 20 in the United States control machine milking of cows by computers which record the yield, compare it with the cow's previous output, make allowances for lactation cycles, and feed her with the appropriate ration of feed automatically. I had seen portable translators capable of displaying instant equivalents of words in any five languages.
>
> Drivers of cars could press labelled buttons to find out how much petrol they were using, their average speed and how many miles they could travel before needing to refill. The microprocessor was reckoned to be able to spawn 2000 new products each year.
>
> This technology also raises major political questions as to who will be in control of the information and data in New Zealand, where the entire broadcasting system and telephone system are controlled by the state. Privacy will be one of the gruelling legislative problems to be grappled with as this technology encroaches more and more on our lives.

My travelling observations and conversations saw some change in the focus of my questions in the House. What were the language training policies for New Zealand diplomats posted overseas? Answer: training was available in 25 languages, including two-year international courses in Mandarin, Arabic and Japanese. What were the government's intentions on opening a diplomatic post in Southern Africa? It was a desirable goal, but current severe restrictions on government expenditure meant we were unable to do this at the moment. What were the latest estimates of the numbers of Afghanistan refugees crossing the border to Pakistan following the Soviet invasion? This question was provoked by the Afghani refugees I had seen in Kathmandu. The numbers given were 736,707 to 57 refugee camps in Pakistan.

On 31 May I was to deliver the keynote address at the Young Nationals Conference in Picton. Wellington Airport was closed. I always had a full speech text prepared, and faxed through a number of pages from an office in the airport terminal so that someone else could read it. On this occasion I asked:

> What do you share with those who are currently making decisions about your lives? You will always represent a different age. You move from a different life experience in a different environment and probably at a different pace. Who will talk for you and where are they?
>
> Will some people insist that we are all one people when it is blatantly obvious that we are two quite distinct cultures? Take a look at the planet's issues of Iran, Afghani refugees, famine, destruction of ecological systems, trade restrictions, military conflicts, hundreds of millions of people pre-occupied with survival and elementary needs living in permanent insecurity. Robert McNamara, the President of the World Bank, had described millions of the world's poor as having a condition of life below any rational definition of human decency. Your future is intimately involved with so much in the international sphere that may seem remote to you.

I was increasingly seeing the results of having leaders two generations older than me planning for yesterday. The briefings I'd had in my travels just confirmed this. Simon Upton was in Picton and wrote thanking me for my 'clear-headedness and perspicacity. Please keep saying those things.'

I took up this theme again in my Address in Reply speech:

> The boundaries between external and domestic considerations are becoming increasingly blurred. Trade and politics, in international relations, are inextricably mixed. Economic power, control of markets, access to markets, have become the very substance of international politics ... The contraction of important and traditional markets and the lack of optimism for our terms of trade, make our trading position precarious. Earning a living in a world in which politics and economics now go hand in hand is a very complex business for a nation of only three million people. In Antarctica, we have an important presence to be maintained that gives us a very large sea zone control, and we have

> key relationships with small island nations of the Pacific region. We accept per head of population a large number of refugees. Japan and Indonesia now take as large a proportion of our exports as Western Europe. The People's Republic of China is our second largest market after Japan. The Prime Minister recently chaired a meeting on the status of the Palestinian Liberation Organisation. Fifty-nine countries have diplomatic accreditation to New Zealand. We have 47 posts abroad staffed with personnel from the Ministries of Foreign Affairs, Defence, Customs, Agriculture and Fisheries, Treasury, Labour, Scientific and Industrial Research, as well as the Tourist and Publicity Department and the Department of Trade and Industry.[10]

Nothing had changed in the National government caucus, however. On 12 June we were considering the Maternity Leave and Employment Protection Bill. Aussie Malcolm drew attention to the 1975 manifesto commitment to provide pregnant women with job security plus 26 weeks' maternity leave. After hearing all the submissions, the select committee wanted to make some changes in the Bill. The first of these was to introduce paternity leave, initially with ten days' unpaid leave at the birth of the child, with one month's notice to be given. Derek Quigley opposed this as a cost to the employer. Bruce Townsend pointed out that the provision would apply to only two per cent of the workforce, and the majority of submissions had been in favour of it. But paternity leave was voted out on caucus voices. Pressure to reduce the 26 weeks of maternity leave also continued. For a woman to access maternity leave, the Bill required 24 months in employment.

Shop trading hours were back in caucus on 19 June. Minister of Labour Jim Bolger was in charge of this issue. He said there was a public mood for liberalisation and he would like it extended to Saturday for trading on any basis between 7 a.m. and 9 p.m. The Prime Minister was always a liberal on this: 'We know dairies flout the law and will continue to do so. Church groups know this and ignore it. It's an interesting theological approach, to use a bus to go to church and buy a can of beans on the way home to save cooking. I want Sunday included too.'

Paul East, representing the tourist city of Rotorua, wanted local authorities to decide according to their different circumstances. George Gair just said free up the regulations and leave it for the individual retailer to decide. I was in this camp. Winston Peters argued that there was a danger of getting too far in front of the public, and he opposed our stand. In the end, opening up Saturday trading was agreed unanimously. Muldoon advised caucus it was not good to leave the law as it was on Sundays 'when we know there is illegal trading. We have got to reform properly and legalise what we want.' We would return to the issue later.

In caucus there were still issues where the Victorians could have a win. One was in the attempt to get rid of enticement – an ancient property law about a man owning his wife – as a grounds for divorce. There was only one case of its use in the country's history. Paul East called it medieval. Other colleagues objected to any law that made marriage breakdown easier, or advised that 90 per cent of people believed they did have 'property' in their marriage partner and would want to hold on to this right. In a show of hands, enticement was retained – for now.

The same group got another chance on 10 July. The opportunity to extend the Family Proceedings Bill to ensure the availability of non-molestation orders to de facto relationships was recommended to caucus. The Prime Minister set the stage. He advised there was 'some merit on practical grounds for the protection of women in de facto relationships. Can we say that de facto is to be denied what a married person can obtain by way of protection? On balance yes we should cover de factos, but should it be in this Bill?' Jim McLay responded that all women should be covered in the same legislation. But no: always they were there. 'These are people who are wanting the protection of the State without complying with marriage laws. We should not wrap up in marriage laws the acceptance of de facto relationships.' The majority of caucus voted for a separate Bill.

I had been so energised by the new ideas I had encountered on my trip, but within days I was already flattened by having to work with these men. I had been trying to suggest some creative ways of accruing more revenue for the government. I wrote to the Minister of Transport asking if he would consider making personalised registration plates available on request at a special charge. I had seen these on my travels. He replied that he knew they were in other countries, that substantial fees were charged for them and that they were something of a money-spinner. 'New Zealand, however, does not have a large enough motoring population to carry a profitable system of this kind. The Motor Vehicle Register in Palmerston North was not computerised, and the question of personalised plates cuts across the basic policy of maintaining a permanent plate system.'

The end of June was time to submit my tax return. It shows that in 1979–80 my total gross earnings were $21,405.24, my personal tax was $7,205.54, and my compulsory superannuation deductions were $2,354.56. I also received a non-taxable electorate allowance of about $570 a month, and a sessional allowance for nights spent in Wellington while on parliamentary duties. Payments made to Katherine O'Regan and Elizabeth Sewell to assist me in my work were not deemed deductible expenses.

The media were on their rounds, and this time the *Otago Daily Times* caught me just before I left for UN women's conferences in Oslo and Copenhagen in early July:

> Walking into Parliament Buildings is like taking a step back in time on to some exclusive 1930s passenger ship. It's as if Marilyn Waring has set up a 1970 student's flat on board. Her room is tall, thin and lined with pictures. A large portrait of Marilyn Monroe hangs over her desk. Picture postcards of famous women are stuck up in rows. Emmeline Pankhurst, Virginia Woolf, George Eliot, Jane Austen, Bronte Sisters and more. There's a Robin White print of a mother and child and two photos of Wellington. She looks exhausted. A senior Cabinet Minister once described her as the most valuable piece of political property going. 'They think I'm extremely valuable at election time. They'd probably prefer I was buried somewhere in between times.'
>
> 'I don't feel intimidated by pomposity.' Waring says: 'I'd had work experience here. If I'd walked straight in off the street, it would have been different. There are intimidating aspects, which have nothing to do with the building or people – like being continually broadcast. In New Zealand, I'll always have to live with what I've said in this house. In 30 or 40 years' time, I don't want to look back and find I was making an

idiot of myself. You must be your sternest critic. You're the only person who truly knows your motives. The only one you must be immediately answerable to at the end of the day. I like to be able to sleep easily at nights.' Her schedule is packed tighter than a dagwood sandwich. How does she cope with exhaustion? 'I don't. I get sick. If there are eight flu bugs going around I get them all.'

I ask if she has personal ambition. She says 'No' quickly, then hesitates. 'I would like in my lifetime to learn to create something real, to make something that's there when you've finished.' New Zealand's first woman Prime Minister? 'I can't imagine ever moving from the back bench. I don't aspire to become Prime Minister. I don't want it.'

I ask what she regards as her greatest achievement. 'I don't think you can claim anything as your achievement. It's the office which wins battles, not Marilyn Waring. I fail daily to convince this Parliament that their attitude to women denies them and the country a multitude of options for policy, for the budget, involvement, ideas – everything that women can contribute. We are all the poorer for that.'

How could total equality ever come about? 'If I knew the answer I'd be rich and famous. Marilyn French said she'd like to feminise the world. In claiming equality, we are not asking to be like men. We would like our values to be treated as equal. It won't happen in my lifetime. Women enlarge options because they think differently and see different things. It doesn't just go for women either. We are blind to our own indigenous culture. We deny youth too. We say they lack experience, but I say the point of view is valid regardless of experience.'[11]

Women activists had mounted quite a writing campaign to have me included in the New Zealand delegation to the UN Half Decade Conference for Women in Copenhagen. Colleen Dewe would be the delegation leader, joined by others from the Māori Women's Welfare League, the National Council of Women, Women's Electoral Lobby and Committee on Women. It wouldn't have bothered Muldoon to leave his only woman MP out of the group. I had also been invited to represent Oceania at a United Nations Institute for Training and Research (UNITAR) meeting on 'Creative Women in Changing Societies' in Oslo just before the conference. Elizabeth Reid had suggested me as a last-minute replacement for Germaine Greer, who was unable to attend.

I boarded the flight from Copenhagen early. My jaw steadily dropped open as I recognised the faces of writers Nawal El Saadawi, Ama Ata Aidoo, Robin Morgan, Ann Oakley and Phyllis Chesler from their book-jacket photos, and the former prime minister of Portugal, Maria de Lourdes Pintasilgo, from international magazines – and realised they had to be going to the same meeting. Once there I met and listened to women with years more experience of walking the hard yards for women's rights; of being exiled, imprisoned, reviled; of understanding the days spent refusing to be seduced by relentless male power. There was wisdom here, with Maria de Lourdes speaking of the creativity in encounter, the courage to be vulnerable and transparent to retain a high degree of emotional health. Nawal acknowledged that even when we have external support, we are still fighting as individuals on our own strength. We worked together for four days, and I heard stories that would give me strength in the years ahead. I understood how incredibly lonely I was, and that I would go back to that, beyond this momentary and unexpected oasis. I would be the only one of the group in Oslo who would be in a country delegation for the conference. Many of the others would attend and speak at the parallel NGO Forum.

In Copenhagen, I was briefed by Elizabeth Reid, principal officer for the conference; her colleague Marcella Martinez; and by Sue Kedgley and Jan Beagle, two New Zealanders working in the UN Secretariat for the meeting. I knew our delegation would be split up among committees working simultaneously. It is almost a contradiction in terms to ask of a UN conference, 'Where will all the action be?', but I was advised to attend the First Committee, which would be drafting the Preamble. Colleen took me aside quietly. 'This is your scene,' she said. 'I have been told to keep you on a tight rein. You pull, and I'll just give you more rope. You do whatever needs to be done here.' So I set out to see what that could entail.

I read all the documents. The Preamble contained all the paragraphs which foreshadowed any UN conference on anything: North–South issues, apartheid, recognition of Palestine, fundamental human rights and abuses. If there were to be votes and divisions in the final session, they were likely to be on these Preamble paragraphs. Much of the language had been set in stone for years, but I figured there would be a way in if I looked at it very carefully.

I found it. I sat up most of the night writing the intervention. I took the words of the North–South economic debate of exploitation and oppression, and made the parallel, using the same words, of the treatment of women by men. I cleared it with Colleen, and with Helen Fawthorpe, now sitting with me in the First Committee. The text had to be approved. It was telexed to Wellington, where another good feminist sitting on the UN desk advised that 'it hadn't been possible to get the Minister's views', and we should go ahead. On 25 July the following amendment was submitted by New Zealand:

> Add the following text to paragraph 11:
>
> It can be said that existing theories of labour and capital do not adequately trace the linkages between women's work as reproducers and producers and production systems in world economies; similarly, the dominant histories of exploitation do not adequately trace the subjection, exploitation, oppression, and domination of women by men. Women are not simply discriminated against by the productive systems but subject to the discrimination that arises by virtue of being the reproductive force.

Then, sitting with Helen, I delivered our intervention. It was an amazing feeling to be able to speak feminism in New Zealand's name:

> Imbalances in global economic power between developed and developing countries have their origins in inequalities in operational control over means of production: imbalances in global power structures between men and women have their origins in inequalities in control over the means of production and reproduction. We must address the imbalances based on the discriminatory perspectives of sexism.
>
> Economic organisation by itself is not responsible for women's subordinate position in development, but it interacts with a supportive ideology of sexual bias to create an adverse environment.
>
> To discuss the impact of strategies of development on the status of women in society means confronting the totality of women's exploitation within the context of the world system of how we relate to each other in every sphere.

We can draw on our own examples. The rural woman in New Zealand has a contribution that is unrecognised, invisible, unquantified and unpaid. She is often unremunerated family labour. The input and support of her contribution are to that food production that is vital to New Zealand's economic survival; she is a central figure, a pivot, but is in no sense recognised as an 'equal' partner in that production. Tariff barriers and protectionism policies in agriculture imposed by the North further threaten the living standards of these New Zealand women.

I want to address myself to the minds and hearts of people who are delegates here. I want to speak of being doubly oppressed: of being oppressed because one is poor, and a woman: of being oppressed because one is black, and a woman; of being oppressed without a home, without one's land; and oppressed as a woman.

We must address the problem that every woman everywhere must confront; the problem of woman as both mother and worker, reproducer and producer. While the economic organisation of a society may change, for every woman this system of control does not change.

Without our confronting these issues, development will continue without benefitting the majority of the people, the women of the world.

Women's exclusive association with the domestic or reproductive sector is at the crux of women's subordination and its perpetuation.

Men don't die in childbirth. Maternal mortality is the leading cause of the low-life expectancy among women in developing countries, just as anaemia and malnutrition are the causes of their chronic fatigue.

Women continue to satisfy the basic human need to reproduce human society and continue to see reproduction unpaid, undervalued and unacknowledged.

Given the framework of the United Nations institution, universities, multilateral agencies, multi-national corporations and our Governments, it is still men who will decide the targets for women; it is still men who will decide what our role will be – who will decide what benefits will accrue to women as beneficiaries of development. In all this talk of equality, we are still to be patronised.

It is not good enough for progressive groups to ignore women's particular needs and subordination by saying that the 'general' struggle for change will take care of women's oppression.

In moving our amendment, we call for the elimination of all exploitive dependent relationships, including that between men and women.

I had no idea how this would be received. There was a standing ovation. This was all very unusual in the UN. I was told to look up to see the women in the translation booths on their feet, clapping. I had ensured they all had a copy of the text beforehand. The first call was given to the delegate from Lesotho. 'I don't like getting sentimental about amendments,' she said, 'but this is a beautiful one. Wearing my women's coat and not my diplomatic coat, and remembering the women of my village,' Mrs Morrison Tobe told the committee, 'I must support it.' Ghana, Malaysia, Papua New Guinea and most European nations gave unqualified support. Brazil didn't like the 'reproductive force' bit. The USSR said some words couldn't be expressed well in Russian: the Russian translators gave me the response. India said it was 'too exclusive' – that is, it dealt only with women. But there was a swell of support from Caribbean countries and from the women-led African delegations. Helen's colleague in the UK New York mission said Britain didn't like it but wouldn't oppose it. As the days wore on and we battled our position, this fellow finally said to Helen, 'I'm going to have to ask my government to complain to yours about what she is doing.' Helen laughed. 'She is the government,' she replied.

Writing in the *Observer*, Janet Watts described the scene: 'The conference plenary sessions in which the country's delegate had 15 minutes to speak were certainly a farrago of political tub-thumping, tedium, grandiloquence, and lies. There were a lot of games being played, and a lot of those games had been designed by the boys. The intelligence of many of the women delegates was impressive, but they were being forced to spend it on manipulating a machine. Geopolitical demagoguery hamstrung proceedings with procedural ploys.' My speech galvanised the meeting, she said, and 'suddenly out of the woodwork there were the men. Male diplomats in their best pinstriped plumage sat at the tables representing their countries.'[12]

Georgia Dullea from the *New York Times* came to meet us. 'As a member of the key committee working on the conceptual preamble to the World Plan of Action, Ms. Waring has succeeded in sending to the plenary sessions an amendment that addresses the subject of sexism while avoiding what she calls that "unmentionable word." "Its chances are good," a United Nations source said. "That means we may get a little feminist stuff in the plan. Waring came in with something creative."'

Dullea continued:

> For two weeks now, delegates from the developing countries have been maintaining that the roots of women's oppression spring not from the men in their countries but from the so-called 'isms' – colonialism, neo-colonialism, and imperialism. Waring has borrowed the rhetoric of the third world and shaped it in a feminist perspective. The New Zealand amendment refers to 'the subjugation, oppression, and domination of women by men.' The New Zealand Member of Parliament sees nothing especially creative about the amendment. 'Somebody had to say it,' she remarked with a shrug. 'Frankly, when we proposed it, we didn't know if we had any support or not.' The reaction surprised her. 'The delegate from Ghana told me: "it is the universal experience of women."'

But as Watts noted, it was all just part of the game. In the other committees, members of the New Zealand delegation were adding the words 'sexist' and 'sexism' to obvious paragraphs. In the late hours of the night a male triumvirate of senior delegates from India, the Soviet Union and the Holy See were objecting to the New Zealand amendment – all that was left to settle other than apartheid and Zionism. A senior woman diplomat from Mexico was in the chair. When the Vatican delegate argued that reproduction was not work, she explained: 'Not work, but it is hard labour.' So it stayed. 'Said' became 'argued', 'existing theories of labour and capital' became 'predominant theories'. I had even taken some writings by Marx which came in handy with the delegate from the Soviet Union, who was very surprised when I hauled the book from my briefcase during negotiations. I have no idea why I thought these might be useful when I packed in Wellington – just instinct. His gall was heroic, as a footnote was inserted into the document to record that there was no wife-beating in the Soviet Union!

But our amendments would not make any difference to women's status anywhere. One day they might be useful for activists coming afterwards. I knew how important words on the page could be in advancing our rights: a story here, a precedent there, a subtle change in language somewhere else. The New Zealand amendment made it through to the final document. In the end, New Zealand was advised by Wellington that we had to abstain on the Programme of Action because of the wording on 'Zionism'. I left Copenhagen feeling tired and drained, but much of that may have been the anticipation of having to be back in Parliament, with no more breaks on the horizon.

Soon after my return, I made my annual Budget contribution.[13] I was much more focused on international debates than on defending the government's record. I included some of my observations from the Copenhagen conference, and asked: 'How can we overcome inefficiency at all in our national Budget statement while we deny ourselves the intelligence, the experience, the sensitivity and the vision of half our members in decision making, in negotiation, in planning, and practical action?'

In early August the NZRFU announced they would invite a South African apartheid rugby team to visit New Zealand. I issued another press statement saying I was totally opposed to this. Brian Talboys was doing his best. Jim White had selected one of Talboys' statements for the Waipā newsletter in early September:

> Apartheid is a system that dictates that, if your parents are black, then, before you are born, the shape of your future is determined – not because of any weakness or strength that the child will have when it reaches maturity, not because of the limitations of his intelligence or unrivalled intellectual capacity, not because of the richness or the poverty of his all-round ability, but simply because his mother and father have black skins. Those stark facts have sunk deep into the consciousness of the people of Africa. It is a system they hate. They hate it in all its manifestations ... It is a thoroughly humiliating experience for a human being to be treated as a second rate citizen in the land of his birth. He is determined to fight against that system to change it. To New Zealanders I say: I am absolutely sure that you would fight against it if you were involved, and I am equally sure you would not have a high opinion of people who were prepared to tolerate those conditions.

The Public Expenditure sub-committees had been busy in my absence, and their reports were presented on 20 August. On financial management in the Forest Service, findings showed commercial operations and the accounting systems in use were generally unsatisfactory.[14] The committee had been unable to appraise the return on total funds employed, and management's ability to ascertain true costs was seriously affected. The key recommendation was that an independent financial structure be implemented. The majority of the committee (the government members) recommended that the government consider the establishment of a limited liability structure company for the Commercial Division and exotic production forests. We were using the few tools available to try to push for much-needed reforms resisted by Muldoon.

The second report was about financial management and reporting in education, and schools in particular. The Audit Office report of March 1978 had advised Parliament these were matters of 'extreme concern'. We all knew teachers handled funds for schools – bus trips, sports trips and museum entry: a whole range of cash funds were collected. The committee sought widespread advice, and found that many of those handling funds in the education system were not properly trained, and guidance and control from the Department of Education had not been as effective as it could have been.[15]

In August we were into the Estimates debates, and as PEC chair I was liaising with ministers on the key questions asked by the Opposition during hearings, suggesting a speaking team to the Whips, and keeping myself busy and interested. In the debate on the Railways Vote, I queried the estimate of $37 million for what was called the 'social services subsidy'.[16] Treasury had commented that effectively a great deal of Railways business wasn't subject to competition because of social service requirements – the government's decision that Railways would continue to operate unprofitable lines as part of the public transport system.

On Trade and Industry, I asked about the rumour that ministers had been asked to examine committees under their control.[17] Were they efficient? Did they still have a job to do? Was the original programme outdated? Were consumer interests 'sufficiently represented'?

It was a good moment to see the Audit Office, the PEC and departments making efforts to break out of the old moulds. In the case of the Customs Department, I reported that:

> The PEC had approved the block allocation pilot scheme. Operational managers had been brought to Wellington and trained in financial management, and were responsible for the control of their own expenditure. Placing of the control of most expenditure items under the block allocation scheme had given operational managers the flexibility to spread their funds in the way that best suited their ports of entry. They could make decisions on their own budgets and their performance, and would not be prescribed by an itemised budget.
>
> The scheme had freed the department from bulk purchasing from Government stores. That meant it could shop around. Typewriters had been purchased from local stores at much better prices than from the Government Stores Board. Cars that would otherwise have been laid up in Post Office garages for repairs had been fixed in one or two days in local garages, without the need for rental cars. The PEC had been told that when a departmental vehicle had been damaged when officers had been travelling to carry out planned surveillance of an overseas vessel at another location, the Public Service Garage had quoted about $380 for the repairs that would have taken about three weeks. A private firm had quoted $150, and the repairs had taken two days.[18]

My questions in the House continued. I learned that of the 285 apprentices taken on yearly in Railways, only four young women were working: two in signwriting, one fitter, and one fitter and turner. There were three applications for the 1981 intake. Parents and spouses could not be coerced into signing firearms permit applications, but this didn't cover de facto partners. Had the Minister of Internal Affairs seen the advertisement in the *Herald* on 1 September for advisory officers in the area of employment assistance to small cooperatives, which concluded with the words 'assistance may be given to a married man to move his household'? It was, I was told, a departmental error; an old and incorrect form of wording had been used. The position would be re-advertised using the word 'person'.[19] There was more. Were affirmative steps taken to ensure young women were recruited for apprenticeships in energy development? Could the Minister confirm that the interviews conducted by Department of Labour officials, and employer and union representatives, who were all males, had seen no women accepted, despite some applying?

I had another small nomenclature dispute. In 1979 I had managed to have the front page of the Public Expenditure Report describe me as 'chairwoman'. The draft reports I had for 1980 described me as chairman. I argued. The Speaker advised me no precedent had been established, and that there was 'no warrant in terms of the Standing Orders for describing you in any other manner than as Chairman of the Public Expenditure Committee'.

Throughout August the National Party was involved in another by-election, set for 6 September. Muldoon, against the wishes of Foreign Minister Talboys, had appointed Frank Gill, the member for East Coast Bays, as ambassador to Washington. I was delighted to be rid of him from caucus, whatever the means, and Muldoon assumed that East Coast Bays was a safe National seat. Muldoon had announced an increase in the tolls on the Auckland Harbour Bridge, which would have a major impact on these voters, and had been involved in public battles with journalists just before the by-election began. He opened the campaign to a half-filled hall, then left for seven weeks overseas.

At the caucus meeting on 4 September, Norman Jones reported back from the Dominion Council meeting. He had bad news, he said. Party organisation and membership were in a bad way, and this had been brewing for some time. Electorates had Party membership targets to be achieved before they could go to selection advertisements for the 1981 election. Fifteen were ready, but we were two months behind schedule. George Chapman and Barrie Leay wanted to speak to caucus. Dominion councillors felt that parliamentarians were not listening, and expected the caucus to get their message. Cabinet ministers were not communicating; and there was a lack of communication between the Prime Minister and the Party president, with blame on both sides.

With Muldoon overseas, Talboys had attended the meeting as acting leader. He said he agreed with most of what Norman had reported. 'Feelings in the electorate had changed in the last months, and the Party is going through a rough patch. We need our organisation. A Building Fund request was also getting at Dominion Councillors.' Talboys advised that there was more concern expressed than for some time. 'They feel we've lost direction as to policy and they are concerned about bad press on the media battles, and the bridge toll rises.'

On 6 September, National lost the East Coast Bays by-election to Social Credit's Garry Knapp. When contacted for comment, Muldoon blamed the Party organisation and the National Party candidate. Party officials were enraged, and responded in the media.

Talboys was still in the chair for caucus on 11 September; the Party's president and general director were present at the start, and had been told they were very welcome. Chapman said this had been one of the worst weeks he had known as president. He intended to speak frankly. The mood of the Dominion Council was very pessimistic, as it had been in 1971, and this was devastating for the organisation, for membership and money. Morale had been seriously set back; now we had a serious setback in East Coast Bays. Why had the public mood shifted against us when Labour was in disarray and when Social Credit's policies were not understood?

Against high inflation and high unemployment, he said, our policies were seen as incoherent. Many actions of the government had penalised our supporters over the past 18 months. The public view was we were looking after big business. We were burying our case in trivia. The East Coast Bays result was our third warning. The first was Rangitīkei; the second the General Election. These were the implications. In the short term we could have, at best, a narrow win in 1981. What did we have to do for 1981? We needed clear enunciation of our policy nationally. We had to sell the Party. He concluded: My access to caucus is not of concern to me, but I was hurt when three invitations were withdrawn in 1979. It is unfortunate this is now an issue. We must fix it – the Party expects to see it fixed.

Mike Minogue responded. We had these political irritants like Muldoon's personal attacks on people. We had legislative irritants such as shop trading hours and education changes. There were tax irritants acting as disincentives, especially for the small man. Quigley said our activities flew in the face of National Party policy. McLay argued that we must avoid trivia. We must present real challenges. Over the past three months he had experienced something close to rebellion among his Executive and branch members. They were younger, free-enterprise-orientated Party members, much like the cohort in East Coast Bays. People were rebelling against the way we had been governing, he said. Barrie Leay described the electorate and Party as 'sour', as they had been in the 1972 election. I had experienced much of this feedback in Waipā. Remembering the dreadful cringe I generally felt at Party conferences, I thought the Party had to bear some responsibility too. So I advised I expected it to sharpen up. 'Our remits are not socially alert. They alienate people,' I said.

That afternoon my focus on the Ministry of Foreign Affairs Estimates was on China.[20] New Zealand Ministers of Foreign Affairs and Agriculture had visited. Muldoon had been one of the first world leaders to meet the new Chinese leader, Premier Zhao Ziyang. There would be a visit from Vice-Premier Li to New Zealand. Trade was increasing, cultural exchanges were encouraged, and there looked to be opportunities in China for New Zealand agriculture and forestry technology. I also promoted the request made to government to remove tariff barriers and protection on 18 products from developing nations.

An hour later, in the Housing Estimates, I criticised the disjunction between government policies on housing finance and architectural design, and actual housing needs.[21] There was a multitude of types of family formation, and more flexibility was needed. In the Health Estimates, I spoke of my concern that there were young men in Waikeria Borstal who were not in the right place. 'Disturbed people should not be incarcerated' there, I said. With the help of government grants, courts 'should be able to place people in supportive institutions'. Alternatives to imprisonment were a critical need.[22]

Muldoon was still overseas for the caucus of 18 September, so Brian Talboys was again in the chair. He chose to begin with the 1981 Springbok tour. He said there had been a shift in public opinion against it. One caucus member claimed New Zealand was being used as whipping boy. True, we are a whipping boy, Talboys responded, but we are a very small country and are vulnerable in the rugby arena. And we could be seriously criticised in this area.

There was serious fallout from National Party officials and supporters, especially in the Auckland Division, after the East Coast Bays by-election defeat. I learned about it mostly from Valerie Forbes and my chairman Arnold Myers. There were lots of phone calls, and around me in the caucus there was a movement to unseat Muldoon. I knew nothing about that, but my colleagues would have known where my sympathies lay. I was approached and asked to write the following letter to one of them, Eric Holland, MP for Fendalton:

> I wish to advise you that I should like you to know that I am among our colleagues who would seek to have the matter of the leadership of the National Party raised at a Government Caucus meeting. I should like to authorise you to hand this letter to the Chief Government Whip at such a time when you receive 25 such requests.

Eric received 28 letters, a clear majority. But Muldoon was advised of the situation, had his own supporters round up the waverers, and by the time we got to the first caucus after his return he had 33 votes.

By 16 October, Muldoon had cemented his numbers for this first caucus meeting after his return. Brian Talboys was now in Europe. The first item on the agenda was the result in East Coast Bays; it was in the name of Don McKinnon, who had the neighbouring electorate. He advised of knowing there was a shift in support away from National in East Coast Bays. Frank Gill's appointment as ambassador saw further erosion, and Gill had never been a popular MP. In the campaign, the issues were lost. Media relations were poor; the Harbour Bridge tolls announcement soured support; and at the campaign opening meeting in East Coast Bays Muldoon gave the wrong speech. Contritely Muldoon murmured, 'I thought I had lost them.'

McKinnon continued: 'It was the wrong speech, and the message spread. The story was far more on you than issues. If that is the environment next year, we won't win East Coast Bays, and we will lose Albany. All the factors of the upset are blamed on you. We received only two subscriptions for 40 house visits at the weekend.'

The Prime Minister responded: 'Everything went wrong. I didn't know Social Credit figures.[23] I felt we had enough up our sleeve. I should have known the Social Credit vote. I was concerned at the turnout for the meeting, but it was a good evening. I wanted to raise the issues of the SIS and the USS *Truxtun*, and there is no joy on the economy.[24] We were all wise after the event.'

Dale Jones was next. People want to talk about taxes and unemployment, and staff shortages at National Women's Hospital, he said. Paul East suggested that the major lesson from East Coast Bays was that the tide was slipping away. We had to pull up our socks – 'you too' to the chair. 'We need forward-looking policies and to avoid personalities. I am very nervous. We have no support canvassing. People are fed up. They want a strong united National team.'

The Prime Minister nodded: 'Basically I agree with you.' Norman Jones was direct: 'You'll just have to pull your head in.' Winston Peters reported a 'bad reading from canvassing. Ten people last Saturday got only six members. With this swing, a lot of hard work is wasted.' Jim McLay said it was very similar in Birkenhead. Membership was stuck on 1,350. He agreed with Don McKinnon's assessment of the campaign opening: 'They didn't like the style of speech. In fact, people walked out. People voted against your style.'

Muldoon was playing the compliant, conciliatory game, but now he saw a diversion, and an opportunity to be the tough leader to break through a stalemate with the Party. He straightened: 'You are all saying you won't get to membership numbers [set at 2,000 for seats held] to go to selection for 1981. Let's see – [show of hands] – more than 50 per cent are not in selection. The Party will have to drop this requirement. We have to get this done.'

Derek Quigley doubted he could hold Rangiora with a 1,160 majority. It was a question of leadership. He had a letter from key branch chairmen, 'some who had been with the Party for 35 years, expressing very strong opposition to you [Muldoon]. We can't win with you. They are criticising me for supporting you.' The Prime Minister replied: simplistic statements do a lot of damage. This kind of letter does that. Politics in government is not simplistic. Ben Couch took the floor. 'We are here as a team. We should put our country ahead of personal interests.' Hugh Templeton chuckled at my quiet 'That would be a nice change.' Michael Cox had a majority of 1,300 and had only 1,250 Party members: 'I am down the chute. People are unhappy about the direction of policy, and we lack unity.'

Aussie Malcolm tried to point out the debate was now on two issues: leadership and the future. But Muldoon had a diversion, and there was a great deal of self-interest in the room. 'Let's get a message to the Party,' he said, 'that it is the view of caucus to get selections under way without reaching the membership numbers. Who supports this? About 10 to 12 against. The majority want it done by Christmas.'

But George Gair brought us back to leadership. He had to communicate the Dominion Executive resolution to 'request the National Party Caucus, as a matter of urgency to review the style of government, its policies, and the communication of policy to the electorate, to ensure that the National Party avoids what will otherwise be certain defeat in 1981'. George faithfully reported the challenge to caucus, the depth of feeling, the lack of money and members. 'It's bad out there.' Poor George. Even though Muldoon had to sit through a critical session with the Party Executive after his return, it never helped to have to be the messenger in these cases.

This, however, was the trigger for the next, well-orchestrated act. David Thomson was invited to advise caucus of a telephone call he had made to Brian Talboys in Germany. He had asked him, 'Please tell me where you stand on the leadership of the Party?' He reported Brian as saying, 'I think we are better to stick where we are. I am concerned that if we make a change, we will do ourselves more harm than good. If caucus is determined to make a change, I will not refuse. My advice to caucus is that we should continue with what we have. It's basically about style and attitude. Let Rob find out for himself. If he's prepared to adjust let's stick with him.'

I had nothing to add. I had just received a letter from the IOP at the Kennedy School of Government, at Harvard University, offering me a fellowship in their spring semester (February–May) 1981. The prospect of being offered a place was so remote I had not even engaged in wistful thinking about it. Apparently, the coverage from the Copenhagen conference had been noticed. But I would need to do this very carefully. It was asking a lot of Waipā to let me go, though many had said they thought it was important when I had educative international opportunities. I suspect some thought it would help to keep me as their MP for longer. I called my former university teachers in political science and asked if they would mind writing an endorsement of this opportunity, the first for a New Zealander, and about the reputation of the IOP and Kennedy School and its staff, and about my suitability for the role. I asked if I could first share this with my electorate Executive to get their feedback and, if I was supported, eventually release it in a press statement. They did this quickly and generously.

I was up in the general debate on 22 October:

> There has been an increase of 4.5 percent of women in the full-time paid work force, and 5.6 percent in the part-time paid work force. Those results were against all the odds. They are gains without the provision of child care, with International Labour Organisation prohibitions on night work, lack of support systems, no maternity leave, and a whole range of jobs that women are not allowed to work in. In 1971 women did not appear at all in the census figures as flying instructors, television and film directors, urban and rural valuers and planners, or in the timber industry, as rabbit and opossum hunters, netmakers, glaziers – but they are in the last Census.[25]

In November *New Zealand Engineering* ran most of an address I had given at their conference, focused on changes we had made in the PEC. I would relinquish the chair from January 1981.

> Now we have a much more detailed series of questions on financial management and accounting practice in the public service as part of the examination of departmental estimates, because methods of controlling public expenditure are inadequate. The main objectives of the system in place, devised in the late 1960s, are in ensuring legality. The system lacks current year budget information for cross comparison purposes, recording of commitments entered into, comparisons of the previous year to date and monthly figures, cash flow budgeting figures, timeliness in reporting.
>
> Governments and policy-makers seem to accept control as a responsibility after an incurred cost – such as a prison or hospital – but there is not the same acceptance of prevention as a social responsibility before the cost occurs.[26]

On 4 November, I spoke on the Shop Trading Hours Bill. I enjoyed telling the House about an incident in Te Awamutu when a businessman who was selling lemons and oranges on a Saturday morning, and giving away clocks and watches with them, was prosecuted for illegal trading. It illustrated the stupidity of the law, he said. And I agreed with him. He was the chairman of a local branch of the Labour Party.[27]

I was doing my job, but I was not happy. I wrote to some friends: 'How do I cope with the contradictions implicit in a feminist belonging to a political party? How do I explain that the policies of leadership, concepts of power, what is said in the programmes, what is done, how things are done are all offensive to me? How much am I part of the problem?'

At caucus on 6 November, a key item was the Maternity Leave and Employment Protection Bill, which had now been reported back from the select committee. Jim Bolger advised I would be bringing in amendments at the committee stages, and one of these involved the concept of parental leave. Employers argued that provisions to keep a position open during maternity leave were too arduous. The National Party Conference was opposed.

The Prime Minister felt we should pass the Bill as reported back. John Elliot, Derek Quigley and Bill Birch said the Bill should be dropped completely. They were joined by Winston Peters, who added,

'This doesn't win the women's vote.' 'Who would support Waring's amendments?' asked the PM. 'Sue Wood supports them,' I replied, and then I outlined them. I would replace the word 'maternity' in the title of the Bill with 'parental'. Any male employee who was the father would be eligible for 14 days' leave without pay. This must be signed by the mother.

The PM intervened: caucus had discussed and rejected paternity leave. Mike Minogue said he wouldn't have trouble supporting such leave. Another of my amendments would bring the length of time in work before entitlement down from 18 months to 12 months. This had been supported in submissions by the Committee on Women, the National Council of Women and National Advisory Council on the Employment of Women, all of which supported the change in the name of the Bill and this small measure of parental leave. Muldoon said we would proceed with the Bill as reported back.

In the constituency we were getting close to the 2,000 members we needed to go to selection. There didn't seem to be any likelihood of a challenge this time around. I had also sounded out my electorate officials on the Harvard offer, and they were unanimous in their support. They saw the invitation as quite an honour. We were also organising a four-day visit to the electorate by Canadian High Commissioner Irene Johnson. We would take in the Otway Stud, farm stays, some beautiful natural scenic stops, the Ōtorohanga Kiwi Recovery Project, and dinners and other events with a wide range of people. Meanwhile, I spent time with the 27 staff of the laundry at Tokanui Hospital. They were all to lose their jobs when the work was taken to the central hospital in Hamilton.

On 14 November, Jim McLay circulated new amendments for the Family Proceedings Bill (No. 2) on domestic violence. There had been sustained lobbying from refuges and women's advocates. The memo advised: 'There is a need for her [the woman] to get back into the home without delay. We propose an exclusive occupation order. If the Court is satisfied that the respondent has used violence against or caused bodily harm to the applicant or child of the marriage, the order can be made. There would also be a new Non Violence Order to deter harassment and threats, or those breaking exclusive occupation orders. Police could arrest a person suspected of a breach, and they could be detained in police custody for a period not exceeding 24 hours.'

At the caucus on 20 November, we were told it would be politically impossible not to join the Labour Party in a conscience vote in Parliament on the issue of enticement that we had discussed back in June. Thank goodness: then sanity would prevail. It was shameful this was a conscience vote, but enticement would be thrown out by the majority of MPs. I also obtained caucus support to undertake the teaching fellowship at Harvard. I released this news and the statement from my former teachers. There was some criticism from Social Credit in the electorate, and some questions about double dipping. Fellows were paid a stipend, which would be easily consumed in rent, food and public transport. I would still be paying Katherine and Elizabeth. The hubbub subsided.

On 2 December we began the second reading of the maternity leave legislation. I reminded the House that in the Select Committee on Women's Rights in 1975, the then (National) members for Stratford, Fendalton and Miramar had supported the position that 'paternity leave should be regarded as a corollary [to the provision] for women of paid maternity leave. The 1975 National Party manifesto promised to provide unpaid paternity leave at a time of confinement.' I admitted: 'My own inclinations are to go further than my Supplementary Order Paper proposes, but it is a hard lesson, learnt fairly early in this institution, that there is a vast difference between what should be, and what might be, accomplished.'

I then outlined my proposals, and concluded: 'The emphasis on the female parent to the exclusion of the male parent is not only contrary to the principle expressed in the Guardianship Amendment Bill (No.2) but to the principles enshrined in the Human Rights Commission legislation. We are keeping the factors that inhibit a movement towards equal opportunity in permanent imbalance.'

But I would not get the chance to move my amendments. I fell foul of that old trick again. The government changed the Order Paper when I was on leave, and moved the Bill through the committee stages. The

Opposition's taunts of 'Turned up, after the committee stages' meant I responded with:

> I want to place on record that, because of an undertaking on 19 September, for which I was given leave, I was in my electorate and unable to move a Supplementary Order Paper in my name. In addition, earlier in the week I was led to believe by the Government Whips that the Bill would not be dealt with while I was absent from the House. I very much regret that I was not here to move my changes. The absurdity of having a spokesman on women was demonstrated in the debate last night, when my colleague could not find it possible to move my Supplementary Order Paper, or to vote in line with every submission from every woman's organisation in New Zealand.

It was a tired and demoralised caucus which met in December. Muldoon advised the estimated costs for policing the Springbok rugby tour had come in at between $1.5 and $2.75 million. He said he had given these figures to the Rugby Union.

There would be a Cabinet reshuffle. We couldn't move until Brian Talboys' decision to retire was public, the PM said, and we had three other ministers retiring. We needed a new deputy leader for next year. McKinnon advised, 'We are tired – we should wait.' Norman Jones noted Muldoon had already anointed Duncan MacIntyre.

I wouldn't be present at caucus in February 1981. I asked for, and had approved, proxy votes for those who wouldn't be there.

Meantime, Mike Minogue's long game on official information made progress. *Towards Open Government*, the report from the Committee on Official Information considering 'the extent to which official information can be made readily available to the public', and in particular to 'examine the purpose and application of the Official Secrets Act 1951', had reported. It urged the government to make official information available unless there was a good reason to withhold it. Legislation would also be required to repeal the Official Secrets Act.

On 23 December, Jim White, National's electorate secretary in Waipā, advised there had been just one nomination for selection – Marilyn Waring. This felt like an important moment. I had told myself that part of leaving on my own terms would mean winning an uncontested nomination. That was done.

I dreaded the Springbok tour and the General Election, but I would have the first four months to build up for whatever the rest of 1981 would hold.

1981

In early January I had meetings with Katherine and Elizabeth on what to monitor and respond to while I was away: watching briefs were important as we headed towards a November election. I wanted a close eye kept on Waipā through the local newspapers, and Katherine's presence on the Waipā County Council certainly helped monitor issues and changes. She would also respond to and forward constituents' queries. The legislation before select committees, and for possible introduction in 1981, was on Elizabeth's list. She would deal with feminist networks and gendered discriminatory practices as well. Olga had moved to California to be with her family, so Jane Wilson had joined my parliamentary office. Transcribing and distributing newsletters through the electorate, liaising with Katherine and Elizabeth, and dealing with invitations, lobbying and other communications, were her responsibilities. I could never have contemplated accepting the Harvard invitation if I hadn't had a lot of confidence in the skills of these three women.

It was a busy time. I had a briefing lunch with US Ambassador to New Zealand Anne Martindell who, with Canadian High Commissioner Irene Johnson, shared the experience of being banned from the Wellington Club. The Club had always offered membership to those heading diplomatic posts in Wellington, but these diplomats had always been men. The club was 'private', so the Human Rights legislation didn't apply. I don't think Anne and Irene cared at all, but I saw it as a national embarrassment. Ronald Reagan was about to be sworn in as US President, and I asked the Ministry of Foreign Affairs for a briefing on their expectations for New Zealand–US relations under his administration. I was also working with Jim White on a *Where Waipa is Going* publication; mapping the course I would teach at the

IOP; organising accommodation in Cambridge, Massachusetts; and conducting a round of surgery sessions in Waipā. I left New Zealand on 21 January.

Elizabeth called within days to say there had been a Human Rights Commission (HRC) decision and a victory for Anne Barry. Firefighters' union officials vied with railway workers for Neanderthal of the Year. P.A. Stanley, a Canterbury Fire Brigades Union official, had explained his opposition to the employment of women as operational firefighters. Male firefighters would have to 'carry' women at crucial times. Training instructors might be inclined to give women an armchair ride. A certain amount of sexual activity would take place (leading to unrest among the wives, and undoubtedly the odd divorce) as a fireman might be pleasuring his female counterpart. Who would clean the women's sleeping accommodation? Women were likely to burst into tears, and would be unpredictable and depressed during menstruation and menopause.

Anne Barry had been a volunteer firefighter, and in August 1979 she had applied to join the operational firefighting section of the Auckland Brigade. She couldn't take the pre-entry test as she was one inch (2.5 cm) below the minimum height. In September 1979 she applied to join the North Shore Brigade, which did not have a minimum height requirement. In October 1979 she was rejected because her vision was below standard. The Fire Service Commission argued there was an all-male tradition in the service, with strongly held attitudes, and sleeping and bathroom facilities that did not provide for women. Reports to the HRC showed that Anne Barry's eyesight did reach the standard required by the Fire Service. Discrimination by reason of sex was unlawful, and the HRC found that Anne should be accepted for training as an operational firefighter.

I arrived in the Harvard's IOP at the Kennedy School of Government on 22 January. I signed my name in the visitors' book with some embarrassment, behind international names I recognised such as George McGovern, Carter assistant Midge Costanza, Shirley Williams, John Lindsay, Helen Suzman, Carol Bellamy and Dan Rather.[1] The other

Fellows would not gather for another week; I went to New York to visit New Zealanders at our UN Mission and others working for the UN, including Jan Beagle and Helen Fawthorpe. I also wanted to catch up with Marcella Martinez to ask her to come to the Kennedy School as a presenter in my course. Before the Copenhagen conference secretariat appointment, Marcella had been Jamaican deputy ambassador to the UN; she was now heading the office of the Jamaican Tourist Bureau in New York. I also enjoyed two unforgettable experiences: with Helen, I went to hear blues singer Alberta Hunter at The Cookery, and I went to the Brooklyn Museum and was deeply affected as I viewed, read and engaged with Judy Chicago's feminist installation *The Dinner Party*.

Back in Cambridge, I met the other six 'Spring Fellows'. John Culver had been a member of Congress for Iowa for 10 years and the Senate for six; he had also been a member of the National Democratic Advisory Council, and was a member of the Advisory Committee to the IOP. Eugene Eidenberg was a former secretary to the Cabinet in the Carter administration, responsible for coordinating the implementation of domestic policies, especially between agencies. Robert (Bob) Manning had been editor of the *Atlantic Monthly* for 16 years. He had been the United Press correspondent for the State Department, the White House and the UN, and had been a writer and senior editor for *Time* magazine. Bob was working on a huge military history of the Vietnam War. The other former journalist of the group was George Weeks, a diplomatic correspondent specialising in African affairs, but most recently chief of staff to the governor of Michigan. I was relieved not to be the only woman. Susan B. King had been very active in campaigns to reform the financing of US elections, and was a recent chair of the US Consumer Product Safety Commission. Susan was witty and wise, and I would spend more time with her in the months ahead. The other foreigner was Major General Joseph Garba, a former Foreign Minister of Nigeria, and president of the UN Security Council in 1978. He had been the leader of African moves in the UN in 1976–77 to impose sporting and cultural boycotts on South Africa, and was also one of the key figures initiating the African boycott of the Edmonton Games. I would have access to these extraordinarily experienced people for four months. Where would I start?

Within days I listened to a panel of Susan King, Gene Eidenberg and Joe Garba discuss Carter's foreign policy initiatives. I started to see what roles we were to play. The IOP Fellows were part of Harvard's outreach to the community. The courses we would teach were open for anyone to attend. They were not formal degree courses, with assignments or exams. We would have the opportunity to attend these ourselves, or indeed audit any course on the Harvard campus. My course focused on issues in international feminism – an attempt to move my class away from US myopia. My enrolment of 50 was high, and at the first meeting we enjoyed lots of laughs as men and women introduced themselves and spoke about why they had come. Two women had a Kiwi parent and missed the accent.

I taught for two hours on Monday nights, following a dynamic two-hour dinner with the other Fellows and their guests. Every Thursday we also dined with a key guest who would speak to us on current topics: energy policy, Caribbean politics, El Salvador, aid policies, union activities. This was as diverse a group of people as you could imagine. I was especially interested in the discussions on Central and South American politics, which I knew little about; the Harvard community was particularly active on matters in these regions. I had lunch every Wednesday in an undergraduate House, talking with students. Every fortnight I led a roundtable discussion at a different House on any political subject requested: comparative government, political and economic theory, public expenditure, international aid policies. I also spent time assisting women writing doctorates or dissertations on aspects of feminist theory and practice. I felt most useful introducing them to UN and international NGO documents, or recent international literature.

There were some logistics issues. I wasn't a resident or on a work visa, so I could not open a bank account. I had to take my monthly Fellow's allowance with all my identity documents to the correct bank branch, which was some ride away on public transport. They would cash my cheque, and I would keep the notes under my mattress to see me through the month. I couldn't access the libraries without a social security number, but I soon learned the librarians kept false numbers that would work in the system for people like me. There were scores of libraries at Harvard. I spent a good part of each week in some of these collecting bibliographical material I could carry on using once I got home. My studio apartment meant I walked through Harvard Square and past many bookshops every day. This was heavenly for me. I was reading Ellen Malos on *The Politics of Housework,* Janet Radcliffe Richards' *The Sceptical Feminist – a Philosophical Inquiry*, Kathleen Barry's extraordinary *Female Sexual Slavery*, and *The Best Kept Secret*, Florence Rush's book on the sexual abuse of children.[2]

Every week I had to choose from too many events. I went to panels on 'The Politics of World Hunger' and 'An Alternative Foreign Policy for the Five Major Regions'. I went to hear Jim Clad and Tim Francis speak at the Fletcher School on New Zealand foreign policy, and former Jamaican Prime Minister Michael Manley at the IOP Forum. I listened to feminist Andrea Dworkin's lecture on 'Pornography and Male Supremacy'.

In March I wrote back to the electorate that I felt privileged, lucky and much enriched. 'It is so wonderful to walk down a street unrecognised, to take the seat that faces the whole restaurant knowing you won't be interrupted. I feel at ease for a short time, and very hopeful that what I am learning, not just about politics and policy, but about myself, a little unbound, will be beneficial for all of us.'

I certainly wasn't missing anything back in Wellington. The caucus of 4 February tried again to have Muldoon grapple with key economic challenges: getting agricultural production up, stopping massive subsidies, combatting rising inflation in the costs of materials and protection of the domestic market. The PM was resistant to any measures that would increase the number of registered unemployed. I was very pleased I wasn't there for the discussion on birching.[3] Minister of Police Ben Couch had seriously floated this as an idea, explaining that he had to be seen to do something in an election year and, if not birching, then what? There had been some supportive response to the idea in polls and the media. More medieval madness. Of course, some in caucus thought this was well worth serious investigation as a punishment for some crimes. It was an election-year winner. There'd be no problem administering it – there was always someone who would do it. Mike Minogue replied that research hadn't shown that birching would reduce crime. Bashing people had a mindless appeal. Aussie Malcolm agreed that the instinct for revenge was strong but he didn't think people seriously wanted the government to consider birching. Paul East doubted the courts would impose the sentence even if it was there. Muldoon argued that support for the idea in the polls made it a difficult political issue. Fortunately, the proposal was not supported by caucus.

At this caucus Brian Talboys stepped down as Deputy Prime Minister. Lance Adams-Schneider, one of the old guard retiring in 1981, nominated another old-guard MP, Duncan MacIntyre, saying the PM would want him. Jim McLay nominated Derek Quigley, arguing this would give a leadership balance between the North and South Islands, between urban and rural representation, and between different philosophical approaches. Tony Friedlander nominated Jim Bolger, who was eliminated on the first ballot, and MacIntyre won the second round. I had left my proxy vote for Derek Quigley.

In mid-February one of the vice-presidents of Harvard called and asked for a meeting. He handed me an anonymous letter, postmarked 10 February, from Tokoroa, addressed to The President, Students Committee, Harvard University. I had received a letter from the same person. In printed capitals, it said, 'Miss M Waring MP for the Waikato [sic] electorate is a self-confessed lesbian and her electoral secretary is her girlfriend.' Mine also invited me to 'Get [expletive].' My visitor advised that Harvard had no interest in it, and if I received any form of harassment I should ask for help.

I was following US politics closely and noted President Ronald Reagan's first budget decisions, which would see an increase in unemployment. The economy still had double-digit inflation. On the afternoon of 30 March, in Washington, an assassination attempt was made on the President. He was hit by one of six bullets, and suffered a punctured lung and heavy bleeding. Three other people were hit. There was a big screen in the IOP, and students flocked there to follow television coverage. Many were in tears. I understood a lot of these were tears of grief that 'something like this' could happen in their USA.

I was quite clear that I was living in a foreign culture. Even state politicians represented hundreds of thousands of people. With few exceptions, a politician's 'awareness' factor (the percentage of constituents who know a representative's name) was no more than 10 per cent. Only 51 per cent of those eligible to vote in the 1980 November presidential elections did so. I certainly thought that the boast of constitutional principles, separating Church and State, was nonsense in practice. I felt overwhelmed watching more than 10,000 Carter political appointments leaving major decision-making positions to make room for 10,000 Reagan political appointments – not on boards and commissions and committees, but in key departmental positions.

Then there were the comparisons with private business running the telephone companies and the key transport networks; the presence of tortious liability for accidents, eliminated in 1974 in New Zealand by the Accident Compensation Scheme; the breathtaking expense of medical care; a country of voluntary unionism but the most extreme demarcation disputes; the chopping of infrastructure maintenance in every major city and state budget; and a new Secretary of State who refused to enforce desegregation of schools. Busing of students in and out of neighbourhoods to end desegregation was still a key strategy in many cities and states. I just headed for any seat on public transport, and wasn't bothered who I sat with or how far down the bus I went. But I noticed I attracted some strange looks from both white and black passengers: the 'whites at the front' practice was alive and well in Boston, Massachusetts.

There were other New Zealanders at Harvard. John Holdsworth, deputy director of the Development Finance Corporation, was participating in a four-month advanced management course at Harvard Business School. Jim Clad from the Ministry of Foreign Affairs was spending a year at the Harvard Institute for International Development.

Colin Knox was attending the two-year course at the Kennedy School, and his wife Helene Wong was with him. I had a real sense of pride watching them with their peers. John described how some of his colleagues spent more budget in an afternoon than he spent in a year. But a Kiwi's across-the-board experience, compared with specialisations, meant their contributions to debate were wise without being status quo, and their general international knowledge was very impressive. We all felt that so much of the view of the world from Harvard was in the East–West militarist-threat sphere, while our North–South trade and development approach, and future focus on the north-west Pacific, gave us a different view of the world. Don McKinnon came to spend a day with me: he had always wanted to visit Harvard. Sue Wood arrived to spend three days in Boston on her US trip hosted by the United States Information Service.

In April I went to watch the Boston marathon, hoping to see New Zealander Allison Roe. I carried my transistor shortwave radio (a constant companion – I didn't much trust US news reports) and could hear that she had broken away on what was called 'heartbreak hill', and was travelling at a sizzling pace. I must have been the only mad, screaming Kiwi at the finishing line as she broke the course record by eight minutes. I thought it would be nice for her to see another New Zealander, so I walked to the security line around the tent where the winners were to be crowned. I picked a random security guard, said I was a Kiwi and an MP, and I would like to get through to congratulate Allison. He smiled. 'Yes, Marilyn,' he said. 'I know who you are. I worked with US Operation Deepfreeze in Christchurch.' He picked up the rope and lifted it over my head. 'Go,' he said, and I found and embraced her, and watched as she was celebrated as the winner. I was so proud of her.

Another day the IOP was visited for two hours by a New Zealand Rotary group exchange team. I discussed casein with John Boddy from Inglewood; multicultural education with Evan Thomas from Spotswood; concepts of 'economic units' and 'self-sufficiency' on Indian and Māori land in respect of planning regulations with Paul Quinn from the Department of Māori Affairs, as well as the current state of the Namibia talks at the UN, and the NZRFU's continued invitation to host a racist

South African rugby team. I was also lobbied strongly by Rose Economou, an outstanding CBS journalist who was a Nieman Fellow at Harvard for the year, who had won an Emmy award for her documentary *Agent Orange: The Human Harvest*. The world's only remaining manufacturer of the ingredients of Agent Orange was Dow Chemicals, in New Plymouth, New Zealand. This company also manufactured the 245T that rural National Party women in the Waikato had wanted to be banned. I watched her documentary. I would see if I could make any more progress on this when I got home. The movie confirmed that the women in the Waikato who continued to lobby were right in their analysis of links between the chemical and birth defects.

I took the expectation to be part of the outreach of the IOP seriously. I was interviewed by *United Press International*, by the *Boston Globe* and by *Ms.* magazine. There had been a 30-minute television interview on international feminism on Channel 2, Boston, and on 8 March I spent an hour on Boston University radio for International Women's Day with Marcella Martinez. I toured City Hall and the Massachusetts Senate for discussions on expenditure control. I met with the Women's Caucus of the Massachusetts House of Representatives and Senate. I was so envious to see lots of women from each party working together. One Monday I returned for Senate roll-call to address the whole body, choosing agricultural protectionism and East–West military positioning as my subjects. I was on a panel at Princeton University in April with British MP Shirley Williams and with Elizabeth Reid, and spoke at the International College in Vermont and the Political Science Department of Wellesley College. Maria de Lourdes Pintasilgo, whom I had met in Oslo, visited. I was very hungry to hear these more experienced women speak about their lives, keeping their integrity, strategising, listening to the language they used. English was Maria de Lourdes' third language, but she often gave me lessons about my use of it. 'Use the word "pre-literate",' she suggested. 'All people would read if they had the chance.'

In early May, Victoria Irwin, a staff writer with the *Christian Science Monitor*, interviewed me.[4] I discussed women's work and its invisibility in GNP data: 'Work is measured in terms of gross national product, but women's work is not included in there. The world is dependent upon women at home and in agricultural production. But they are not considered.' Then I tackled war, and the invisibility of two major issues facing women as the victims of war. 'The first is rape by both invading and national armies. This happens in massive numbers. The second issue is refugees, who are mostly women and children.' I also warned against feminists ignoring cultural differences among women. Irwin wrote: 'Ms. Waring sees women encouraged by stories that filter through about women helping women. She lists examples of market co-operatives run by women in Africa, women fighting the effects of alcoholism in India, and a coalition to combat rape in Mexico. Everywhere you look there are stories of women working cooperatively.'

There were, I told her, major international concerns common to all people, 'the environment, the arms race and nuclear reactors. But to an extent, there is a difference even on these issues since the decision makers are male.' I also pleaded the right to change my mind on issues when I found new evidence and information: 'I have no patience with people who say that politics must be black or white.'

I needed to go to Washington to visit researchers at the World Bank and the Worldwatch Institute. I had been invited by John Kenneth Galbraith to spend half a day talking with him about GDP. But I wrote to my electorate that 'I'm homesick, not for the job, or the election, but for the green and hills, and fresh air and space.'

The *Evening Post* ran a further interview as I neared the end of my Harvard Fellowship.[5] I said I was concerned 'about the horrendous militarism of the United States and the horrifying and frightening global nuclear arms race. These issues have combined to produce the general pessimism of the women's movement in the United States.' The article continued:

> Will New Zealand see a 'new' Marilyn Waring when she returns home after what she describes as her 'phenomenal' experience? 'Yes, she will be much quieter,' she said. Has she changed politically? 'You are changing all the time politically,' she replied. She disclaimed the label of the 'world's most articulate feminist' saying 'I don't think that's true

> at all. There are women all over the world who have been working in the field for much longer than I and have a much better appreciation of the issues.'
>
> Of her future in politics, she said, 'I have promised my electorate I will stand again in November and serve another three years. I have always said I will be in politics all my life, but I may not always be in Parliament.' She firmly discounted any ambition of becoming New Zealand's first woman Prime Minister. 'I'm not that sort of person,' she said.

Back in the National Party caucus, the extent of opposition to the Springbok rugby tour was finally hitting home, along with the government's failure to adhere ethically to the words of the Gleneagles Agreement. At its meeting on 9 April, the PM advised that 'the tour will damage us from both sides'. One colleague surmised that the withdrawal of a $10,000 Sport and Recreation payment to the NZRFU had hurt. Muldoon replied that 'the reverse would have hurt us more'.

In mid-May in New York, I called to see Nigerian UN Ambassador Akporode Clark, who was chairing the Special Committee on Apartheid, and Ambassador Gbebo of Ghana. I made it clear I was against the tour, and I did not believe the government was acting in accordance with the Gleneagles Agreement. However, I pointed out that no representative of the committee had visited New Zealand since the Olympics boycott of 1976. I said that a lot of New Zealanders, who resented being picked on, did not know about the work done in other areas – the committee's work in stopping arms shipments to South Africa, its talks with Swiss bankers who could help stop deliveries to South Africa, the cultural boycott, the work on divestment. The only people committee members talked to were Cabinet ministers, diplomats and members of anti-apartheid groups. This was not a case of New Zealand and sport being picked on. But the committee had not succeeded in getting that message over to the people of New Zealand.

I also asked if they were going to review the time and venue of the Commonwealth Finance Ministers meeting, due to take place in Auckland within a week of the tour ending. If the ministers arrived, it would look as if it was business as usual and the meeting would be used by Muldoon to confirm his claim that the rugby would have no impact on New Zealand in other ways. Shifting the venue would be a personal affront, while continuing would be claimed as an endorsement that New Zealand had kept to the Gleneagles Agreement. I also thought if the meeting was held it would undermine the efforts of the anti-apartheid movement in New Zealand.

I did not tell David Barber, the NZPA reporter in Washington, about this last part of the meeting when we spoke at the end of May.[6] I summed up the ambassadors' views about the New Zealand government's attitude to the tour by saying: 'Spending several million dollars in police money for protection and security alone will be seen as a government endorsement of the tour. The government has a lot of other things it can do before it gets to visas. If services offered by state corporations were withdrawn it would stop the tour anyway.' The Public Service Association had been completely rebuffed when it asked if members could withhold services in observing the Gleneagles Agreement. The ambassadors knew that airlines, radio and television broadcasts, and other government-owned transport and hotel services had not been withdrawn either.

The *Auckland Star* ran an editorial comparing Muldoon's behaviour with mine.[7] 'Mr. Muldoon is both for and against the tour. He is thinking about nothing else except Election Day. He is devoid of principle. Waring says New Zealand faces severe political and diplomatic repercussions in the United Nations and the Commonwealth if the Springbok tour goes ahead. The spending of several million dollars on police protection and security will be seen as government endorsement of the tour, she claims. Who can deny it?' The editorial repeated my comment that the UN Anti-Apartheid Committee spoke to a select audience, and many New Zealanders truly believed they were being singled out. 'What a comment when a backbencher speaks for New Zealand and its Prime Minister takes refuge in an attitude that daily appears more supine.'

In early May I spent four days in Ottawa with Edward and Anne Latter, now leading our High Commission in Canada. I spent a day with the Canadian Commission on the Status of Women, and half a day in each of the Canadian External Affairs Department and the Canadian

Parliament. I also talked with representatives of the New Zealand Lamb Co. Ltd in Canada. Canadian producers owned fewer than half a million sheep, so New Zealand was competing with the US for a small market. The company was involved in promotional work in restaurants, hotels and universities, and with dieticians and home economists. If our lamb wasn't continually advertised, I was told, it simply wouldn't sell. But the Canadian domestic producer was looking for protection from the New Zealand exporter. I was out of all patience with the distance between the rhetoric and the performance of Western nations in their embrace of Friedmanite economics.[8] South of the border, New Zealand faced tariffs on beef, casein and lamb, but our own performance in dismantling protection was poor.

In Ottawa, I was briefed on my planned trip to Jamaica.[9] Marcella had been persistent in asking me when I would visit and I was booked to go before I returned home. In 1975 Jamaica was an important $12 million market for New Zealand. Since then trade had declined to $3.3 million in 1980, and this was mostly butter and cheese. I was updated on the current Commonwealth connection, the change of government from Michael Manley to Edward Seaga in 1980, and our aid projects. The Jamaica Dairy Project had input from Barry Marx and the team at Ōtorohanga Engineering (OTENZ), and was part of a modest aid programme on dairying in the Caribbean. OTENZ was constructing two herringbone dairy sheds as demonstration units in Jamaica, at a total cost of $200,000. I would also meet with another New Zealand company, Groomes, involved in a major World Bank afforestation project. On top of that, Marcella had linked me with key figures in the Caribbean Music Festival.

I arrived in Kingston, Jamaica, to find the whole country in mourning. Bob Marley had died. From every possible loudspeaker came 'No Woman No Cry'. I made my way to the hotel. I pulled out my briefing notes with telephone numbers to confirm meetings. No one replied anywhere.

In elevator conversation it was assumed you had arrived for Bob's funeral. 'Where you from?' they asked. 'New Zealand.' 'Huh, butter and cheese,' they laughed. 'Dat's a long way.' I tried making calls again.

I was surprised when the phone rang for me. It was Gordon Bilney, the Australian High Commissioner. 'I suppose you got the message from your High Commission in Ottawa?' he asked. No, I hadn't, but Gordon continued: 'I'll pick you up in the morning then.' Whoa, I thought, I must be going to the funeral. 'So what do you suppose it would be appropriate to wear?' I asked. 'I guess you can wear whatever you like to an Ethiopian Coptic funeral,' he replied. In the newspaper, I had seen that when Marley was ill in hospital in New York, PM Edward Seaga had visited him and offered him the Order of Merit for his contribution to Jamaican culture. 'Do it, man, do it,' Bob had replied. The funeral was for the Right Honourable Robert Nesta Marley. It was a state funeral, and as such countries would send representatives.

On 21 May Gordon collected me in a bullet-proof Mercedes to travel to the National Arena, which would seat about 6,000. Seating was clearly demarcated. In the two rows in front of me sat the Cabinet, then came the rows of foreign government and diplomatic representatives. Behind us were MPs, high-ranking government officials, cadets from the National Police College (truly), and then the white-clad members of the Rastafari Twelve Tribes of Israel. To my left family and relatives took the first rows, along with international and national musicians and music-industry representatives. The Jamaican College of Music Band, which would lead the hymns 'O God Our Help In Ages Past' and 'How Great Thou Art', was behind them. The full balconies had been opened to the public.

There were two flags, the green, gold and black of Jamaica and the red, green and gold of Ethiopia, above the two 'stages'. The lower was ready for a band – guitars and pick-up cords, speakers, microphones – and the upper level was where Bob Marley lay in a large and elaborate coffin, in front of an altar dressed for the Coptic religious ceremony. I would describe this contribution as High Church, bells and smells, for while I didn't understand the speakers, the rituals were all too familiar.

There had been applause from the balconies when Michael Manley entered the arena, and there was applause again as he was announced to read from Thessalonians. Skip Cole, clad in white, changed his assigned reading to 'deliver passages from Corinthians and Isaiah, particularly dear to Rastafarian friends'. The reading was accompanied by calls of 'Jah Rastafari' from the members of the Twelve Tribes of Israel. PM Eddie Seaga delivered a memorable eulogy which reflected his early social-science degree pedagogy, his extensive experience in the music industry in Jamaica, and his recognition that the people of Marley's Trenchtown did not support him. Musicians who had played in Marley's old band accompanied Bob's mother, Cedella Booker, singing 'Comin on Home'. The I-Threes, Bob's all-female backing group, sang 'Rastaman Chant'. Finally, the casket lid was opened as Rita Marley and her children walked up to say a final goodbye. Rita unwrapped a large white towel – I could have sworn it had an image of Superman on it – took out three large twists of ganja and laid them in with Bob. It would take many hours after this service for Bob Marley to get home to his final resting place.

I did get to visit the dairy sheds and met with the forest restoration team, and had an interesting Caribbean briefing from Gordon.

I had a lot of time to think in the months at Harvard, free from the frenzy of constant response and action when reflection takes a back seat. I had decided after the challenge in 1978 that I would stay in Parliament until I could leave on my own terms. I had been uncontested in my confirmation as the candidate for 1981. It was a safe seat. But leaving in 1984 was now an option. After nine years, no one could say I couldn't stick with it. I didn't want there to be any prejudice against young women standing for Parliament in the future because I was seen as not being able to last the distance. Meantime, I was finding being part of the Party under Muldoon extremely dark. I was so tired of all the manipulation and half-truths, and I was questioning the competence of the Party in government. It might appear different if we were, as I expected us to be, in Opposition from 1981. I'd have to assess it then. But during the attempt to change the leader in 1980, Brian Talboys had told me that whoever replaced Muldoon, and whatever the circumstances, Muldoon would set about making their life miserable.

I was dreading what lay waiting on my return: 56 days of the apartheid rugby tour of New Zealand, and an election in November. Elizabeth had been offered the chief executive position at the YWCA, and I would miss her too. In my absence, 10 women candidates had been selected to run for the National Party. Muldoon claimed five of their seats were winnable; I thought there would be just one new woman: Selwyn's candidate, Ruth Richardson. At least Simon Upton had won the nomination for the safe seat of Waikato: I would welcome his presence in the House.

There would be a lot of rugby lovers in Waipā, many of them National voters who supported the tour. My electorate chairman, Arnold Myers, had a son who had been an All Black. I cringed at the idea I would have to be on platforms around the country defending the government. I was also getting feedback that my Social Credit opponent had been making a lot of my long absences abroad for two years in a row. To keep myself safe I decided I would focus my major speeches in the Address in Reply and Budget debates on telling the story of what was happening in Waipā. For the campaign I could use parliamentary questions to get as up to date as I could on issues in the electorate. In general, I would not be available to speak at election gatherings anywhere else. That was as far as I could go with decisions for now. I had a lot to catch up on.

Parliament opened on 28 May. Early May polls showed 51 per cent opposed to the rugby tour, 32 per cent in favour and 17 per cent didn't know. Forty-seven per cent of the population thought unemployment was the nation's major problem. The rate of inflation for the year ending March 1981 was 15.2 per cent.

I had asked Katherine and my Waipā supporters to ensure we got moving very quickly in the electorate. In early June there was a campaign committee meeting, and an electorate sub-executive meeting a few days later. Decisions were made: Did we need a pamphlet for MW? Yes. Would there be cinema slides? No. Radio advertisements? No. Hoardings? Yes. How many? Where? Bumper stickers? No. There would also be a National Party pamphlet. This and other material was all to be hand-delivered, so coordination was needed. What work would be delegated to the branches? We organised a training session for volunteers later in the month.

I got my first feedback on issues from these Party meetings: Muldoon and leadership, unemployment, and my absence. Valerie Forbes was there to update us on what was being said and done in Wellington regarding the campaign. I was happy to get stuck into work in the constituency.

I visited OTENZ to report back on the dairy sheds. I attended and spoke to the Liberal Studies class for the two senior years of Te Awamutu College. I went to the Ruakura Agricultural Field-days and the Waipā races; held meetings with constituents in Ōtorohanga, Te Awamutu and Cambridge; and addressed a Women's Studies course at the University of Waikato, a public meeting in Te Awamutu and the Women's Section dinner in Te Awamutu. The people at the dinner were my supporters, and they defended and endorsed my acceptance of the Harvard Fellowship. They wanted to know where I might have progressed my thinking, and wanted me to share this with them. It was always my experience that my electorate supporters, not just National Party members, were impatient with clichés and empty political rhetoric. They wanted to think, reflect and respond, and they appreciated being respected for their intelligence and experience.

I spoke of the budgetary differences in expenditure on defence and the environment; about how different it was to see armed police and fallout shelters. I described differences in working conditions. I shared discussions I'd had with Massachusetts state legislators about the difficulties they had in the absence of a universal superannuation scheme, of needing a raft of subsidies for older people – for medical treatment, for transport, for housing, for food. Their job had been made the more difficult by a $1.8 billion cut in the food-stamp programme for the following year. I relayed US campaign stories. My colleague at the IOP, John Culver from Iowa, with 12 years in Congress and six years in the Senate, spent US$1.75 million going to his defeat. He told me of a colleague uncontested in the primaries for the Senate race who had to spend over $1 million simply on publicity. My Harvard colleagues laughed in disbelief when I advised that we had a prohibition on the expenditure of more than NZ$4,000 in the last five weeks of our campaigning. I'd watched a budget presented to the House which included a major military build-up at the same time as Vietnam veterans had their pensions cut.

I saw some important differences between the interests of New Zealand and the US under the Reagan administration, an instance being the US failing to agree to a final settlement of the outstanding issues on the Law of the Sea. As a small country, New Zealand was vitally concerned to have its claims protected by a widely ratified multilateral agreement. I believed developing countries saw the exploitation of deep seabed resources as a new departure in international economic activity.

New Zealand, I said, had a major role to play in ensuring that the nations of the South Pacific did not find themselves buffeted about by superpowers seeking military supremacy in the South Pacific. Similarly, we had to be sure that we did not involve ourselves in development that simply increased the need for imported energy to create an export product that could not cover the cost of production. We needed to ask ourselves when we were involved in agricultural development whether cooperatives were better suited in that country than land tenure.

I had learned from the Canadians that they and the Norwegians had demonstrated that the unpaid production of women accounted for something like 40 per cent of their GDP. Our existing model presumed productive output from the introduction of each additional paid worker in the workforce, and this could seriously skew per capita productivity measurements. I gave an instance of a woman who had worked for 10 years in a voluntary agency, appointed to the newly created post of administrator of that voluntary agency. She was now paid for what she had been doing for 10 years. Then she hired a paid housekeeper to do tasks she had formerly done herself. Was there any increase in production?

I reminded the audience how we all felt when a company tried to take out a prospecting licence on Mt Pirongia. The economics model couldn't capture what effect that mountain had on the weather, the production of fresh air and clean water. Where were the discussions of qualities of life instead of standards of living? How much were we running the risk of losing sight of the truly valuable because it had no capital value? I concluded that we did not need to model our future on anywhere or anyone else's theory. We had been a country of a very independent spirit and should not waver in this.

I gave my Address in Reply speech on 17 June.[10] I mentioned that delicensing in the freezing industry, opposed by both Labour and Social Credit, had produced immediate results in Cambridge. Lamb units would be increased from 100,000 to 400,000 at Aotearoa Meats.[11] An extension costing $6.5 million would result in new North American, UK, European and Middle Eastern markets. That would enable another 20 people to be taken on immediately, and all workers would be offered full employment for 12 months.

I told of a compressed natural gas (CNG) station opening in Ōtorohanga and coal exploration in the King Country; a sheep farm conversion to five dairy units; the manufacture and export of silage feed-out wagons, and pre-fabricated cowsheds and rotary milking platforms for sheep and goats. I noted horticultural expansion in kiwifruit and blueberries; and that $25 million had been spent on the Māui gas extension from Te Awamutu to Kawerau, providing employment and business for the electorate.

Then I spoke about how a government scheme, the Project Employment Programme (PEP), had benefited Waipā. Led by the engineers in the Waipā Council, eight projects with 235 jobs had been created in a short time, and more were coming. One targeted willow clearance on Pūniu River banks, funded on a 50:50 basis with the Waikato Valley Authority. This was labour intensive and had 107 people employed. In another programme, on Bulmers Island in Lake Arapuni, dead gum trees were being cleared and native trees planted by 70 workers. At Lake Koromatua 19 women were clearing blackberry and scrub to be replaced with native trees. Derelict cars left around in all corners of the Waipā County had been collected and stripped and were ready for squashing. The engineers were also training: 12 people enrolled in a first-aid course and 10 in a chainsaw course.

Shortly afterwards, Labour and National colleagues asked me into the lobby to tell them more about the scheme. I told them that buses were provided for transport, which created employment for drivers.

On every bus were at least two cooks, and lunch was prepared for the crews every day. Care had been taken to make sure there were women-only group options. My constituents told me their partners on PEP were less violent: they were fed and physically tired, and spent more time with the kids. My colleagues wanted to know who should they get hold of at the council? When could they have a copy of my speech to send to their council? Poor Waipā was inundated with visitors for two months, but they kept expanding the schemes, including running buses from Raglan and Hamilton to collect more workers. I received a handwritten note from the Governor-General, David Beattie, telling me he rarely tuned into Parliament but he happened to have the radio on for my speech. He wanted to tell me what a positive contribution it was, and how refreshing.[12]

I guess he listened to the end, as I hadn't just addressed Waipā. There were two amendments dealing with a proposed rugby tour of New Zealand which were before the House:

> I want to try to disavow some of the serious myths. The first concerns so-called merit selection and multi-sport in South Africa. While a Rugby Football Union composed of 24,000 black and coloured players does not play in the national competition for whites, there is no multi-racial sport. There is no multi-racial sport when black teams play white teams. Until integrated schools provide multi-racial teams, and until there are integrated school teams, I will not be fooled by claims that multi-racial sport exists.
>
> For those who claim that sport or New Zealand are being singled out, I invite them to do their homework on issues tackled by the United Nations Anti-Apartheid Committee. It worries about political, diplomatic and consular representation. It operates mandatory arms embargoes. It talks about nuclear relations and trade relations, especially in gold and oil, about investments, banking, airlines, shipping lines, emigration, and cultural, educational, sporting and other contacts. We are not singled out, nor is sport singled out.

I noted that it might not matter to any New Zealander (except one) that the Commonwealth Finance Ministers meeting would be moved from New Zealand, that Alison Quentin Baxter might lose her seat on the International Law Commission, that New Zealand would disqualify itself from election to the Security Council in 1983, or that our athletes' attendance at the next Commonwealth Games was jeopardised.[13] 'It matters to me, and I do not believe the price that all New Zealanders are asked to pay – that of the game of rugby – is worth it.'

At this point, Nigeria was threatening to lead a boycott of New Zealand sportspeople and to change the venue for the Commonwealth Finance Ministers meeting. At the caucus on 11 June, the PM had mentioned that the final rugby test on 12 September would be just before the Finance Ministers meeting. 'They'll come,' he said. He made a quick return visit to London to meet with Sonny Ramphal at the Commonwealth Secretariat to stop the boycott threat and his precious meeting, so the government jacked up a debate on the Gleneagles Agreement. It was a load of prevaricating nonsense. I didn't need to speak, but I advised the Whips I would not be present for the vote. I was in my room talking with Ann Hercus when the Whips arrived. MacIntyre was acting Prime Minister. This was his regime. I was marched into the lobbies. Ann told the media: 'While I was with Marilyn, it became crystal clear she was neither going to be given leave from the House, nor leave to cross the floor, nor the ability to abstain.' When asked what we were doing she said: 'It was a meeting of two people who very often feel the same way about the same issues, who both have an abhorrence of apartheid, and the occasional desire to say the parliamentary system is mad.'

Media and colleagues did get strange when Ann and I spent time or had lunch together. 'What's cooking here? Is this a feminist convention?' I enjoyed Ann's company, her intellect and discussion. We never discussed 'inside party' business. We were not gossips; we liked good books. We voted the same way on conscience issues. What was so threatening?

Muldoon was back for the caucus on 19 June. He had received a cable from Kenneth Kaunda, PM of Zambia, with an appeal to stop the tour. Kaunda would be deeply disappointed if the tour took place, and he counted on the New Zealand government's cooperation to 'discourage' it. It would have a negative effect on the Commonwealth, and this might include the Finance Ministers meeting. Muldoon summed this up as: 'His style is warm, but he says, stop it, interfere, and now involves the Finance meeting.' Muldoon added that he was complying with Gleneagles and that any action on the Finance Ministers meeting was an insult.

I had the first question. 'Will you visit the Rugby Union and ask them to stop the tour?' The PM replied: 'If I saw the Rugby Union, it could send our policy down the drain.' I stayed on my feet: 'If the tour comes, it will be a disaster. Why not tell them?'

The PM agreed: 'It will be a disaster as a tour, because of disharmony, demonstrations, and violent scuffles. Suppose they call off the tour as a result of my meeting? We would be seen to depart from our policy, to put them under pressure. I don't think the caucus wants that. Thatcher would oppose moving the Finance Ministers meeting from Auckland. I can't be sure of Fraser and his love affair with Africans.'

It had not been helpful for Muldoon in London to hear reports that an MP was being forced into the lobby on the tour vote. He made it quite clear when he returned that for backbenchers there were guarantees of flexibility, and that this sort of coercion was not to happen again.

When things were surreal, there was always the mail to ground me. The June–July stack included brucellosis and Johne's diseases in cattle, payment of reader-writers for students in examinations, the cost of cadet uniforms, Concert Programme coverage in the backblocks, and Māori-language curriculum development for secondary schools.

I lodged a series of questions in the House to the Minister of Foreign Affairs. I learned that New Zealand had condemned the Israeli bombing of the Iraqi nuclear power station under construction, and that although we adhered to the Nuclear Proliferation Treaty (NPT), we had not made any protests about potential proliferation of nuclear weapons by way of the sale of nuclear power stations. When I asked what policy stance New Zealand had on the cessation of food aid as an international strategy in support of or opposition to particular governments, I was told by the acting Minister, the PM, that the government did not provide food aid through any bilateral aid programme, and the question was not an issue that had any bearing on policy in relation to the aid programme. That was not the point, of course. Policies on sanctions, for example, or on closing borders and on the right to food were the point – issues on which every UN member needed to have a policy. I just left it.

The tour was the major agenda item for caucus on 2 July. Geoff Thompson had met with sports bodies. They wanted Brian Talboys to speak publicly to all other codes so they could set out their views in response. Other sporting codes were worried about consequences for their athletes and wanted the opportunity to get the message across to the NZRFU, with more coordination. Brian was not present but he advised he was well disposed to do this.

Muldoon replied that it was unwise for the government to ask for such pressure. It was an action contrary to our policy. 'Tell them, "You chaps get at the NZRFU, have a joint march on them," but don't use the Government. Some things are getting untidy. Mr. Fraser is now into the act. He has changed his ground: his policy doesn't preclude refusing to issue visas. We used the word "discourage" not "prohibit". That was New Zealand's position, and Australia's. If the Commonwealth Finance Ministers don't meet in Auckland, then I'll put withdrawing from Gleneagles to Caucus. Meanwhile, I asked for human rights to be on the CHOGM agenda in Australia in October. Ramphal replied that human rights were a standing agenda item. Malcolm Fraser wanted North/South as an issue as well.'

On 9 July the PM explained to caucus that he had received some letters, all couched in pleasant terms, from the Prime Ministers of Zimbabwe, Jamaica and Nigeria. He believed that the Commonwealth Finance Ministers conference would be moved from Auckland to the Bahamas. Sometimes sitting where George had put me in 1975, directly in front of the PM in the front row, I just stood up without the call and took the space. This was one of those times.

I recorded that I was opposed to the government's policy on sporting contacts, and had opposed the manifesto commitments on public platforms in both 1975 and 1978. I agreed with the Gleneagles Agreement. I read the key words: 'to work vigorously by withholding any form of support for, and by taking every practical step to discourage contact or competition by their nationals with sporting organizations, teams or sportsmen from South Africa'. I was clear: 'We have not implemented Gleneagles. Does $2.5 million for police activity discourage contact?' The PM cut in: 'It would be totally irresponsible to withhold that money.' I continued: 'National broadcasting, the national airline, the hotel corporation? I am nowhere near visas yet! That was the Party policy line in the sand – visas. We have not implemented many possibilities of Gleneagles, stopping well short regarding all the other discouragement available. The policy is we are opposed to the tour! And I sit here and have to listen to people discuss marginal seats.'

Dale Jones commented that MPs 'who say they support the tour are opposing Gleneagles and are one big embarrassment to Caucus'. Paul East followed: 'Stop flaunting support for the tour.' Tony Friedlander said simply, 'Pull your heads in.' The only agreement reached was that the tour supporters should shut up.

We would reassemble that evening for the 30-minute pre-Budget caucus. Quigley, McLean and McKinnon had been among those consistently calling for alternative economic approaches. We were given the headline items. Inflation was over 15 per cent. There was a new 40 per cent tax on computers, and 10 per cent sales tax on new plant and machinery. The Development Finance Corporation was charging 14–19 per cent on loans to importers. Because of the price of oil, the transport sector was 24 per cent of GDP. Unemployment continued to rise, and there was substantial net emigration. Budget spending on superannuation had doubled and totalled 17.3 per cent of government spending. There were now 13 industry studies on protected and inefficient industries. The PM said he was caught between the message that went 'If they are uneconomic, get out' and the unemployment that would result. Muldoon was checking off the one-liners before reading the Budget. He advised there would be a tax rebate on first mortgages. I had recently bought my first home, and suspected that for most years I'd been the only non-property-owner in Parliament. 'Oh good,' I muttered as he made that point. The PM looked up: 'I'm reasonably confident, but not certain, you'll vote National.'

I had been deeply hurt and ashamed at being forced into the

Government lobby on the Gleneagles vote on 19 June. I wouldn't take that again. It is an extraordinary reflection of the trust I had in my Waipā officials, who did disagree with me at times, that I could write the following to them on 3 July:

> I need to know as soon as possible from each of you, where you see the allegiance of a member of parliament to be – to the country, to the electorate to the government caucus, to government policy (these are often quite different) or to oneself.
>
> I have been able to give much thought to this while away, and it is important to me that I have your thoughts. I propose to spend some time in my speech in Cambridge on 11 July on this subject. It is a vexed issue, but there are breaking points. I have made some decisions as to what they are for me, and I need your honest appraisals this week.

They replied, by handwritten letter, in remarkable numbers, and I was deeply moved and grateful. People had noted that I seemed very possessive of my supporters and constituents. I called them 'my' constituents, but they were the reason I gathered enough energy to keep going.

At the Cambridge branch dinner on 11 July I was able to share replies from my officials to the letter I had written about allegiance.

- The order in which you have listed the questions is very much in line with my view: country, electorate, government caucus, and then government policy.
- The electorate – these are the people you have to represent – the people who are your people and I believe your allegiance to them is very strong. They trust you to work for them. They do not have the power to direct your work. You MUST always remain a person, not just a walking talking automaton.
- To be able to have your own considered opinion concerning these issues is terribly important and would be more important to me as an individual than some government policies or caucus feelings.
- To thine own self be true.

- — If you lose sight of your own philosophy and ideals, how can you be sincere and credible in your approach to problems?
- — Toe the party line and vote against your own beliefs and at times your own conscience. I guess that must be devastating.
- — Finally, I believe that each of us should have personal opinions on important matters and that if it is really important to us, we should be prepared to say so. You have to make the decision; we are there to back you up on that decision. This does not mean that we are necessarily in blind agreement with you.

Who were these amazing people volunteering to understand and care for me, well beyond just Party support? They gave my weeks some balance. I shared what they had written, and concluded:

> Where else am I likely to have the privileges I have: of learning more of life in five years in this job than 17 years in an education system; of sharing the diversity of life with individuals here and elsewhere; of the privilege of international conferences and delegations and education and opportunities that would never had been mine otherwise; of losing more battles on behalf of my age-group, my gender and what I perceive as my country's best interests than I care to remember, but having the chance of another three years with the guarantees of flexibility that ensure a retention of integrity to go stubbornly into the battle again.

Soon after this I was called to see the PM to be advised that his office had received details of someone who threatened to kill me. I didn't see any credibility in the story, but I was to have 24/7 attention while it was investigated. It was ridiculous. A member of the Diplomatic Protection Squad in Wellington, or a CIB detective in an unmarked car in the electorate, followed me down parliamentary corridors to the bathroom to clean my teeth, or in a car when I went for my morning run in Wellington or Cambridge. In the Waikato, they took me to meetings. The best moment came when Party supporters tried to elect a detective who had driven me to a meeting in Ōtorohanga to the committee. After 10 days I told the PM I was comfortable there was no real threat and the minders could go.

The Springboks arrived on 22 July. I was part of a government that had refused visas to four North Korean sports competitors in March 1980, and had proscribed sporting and cultural exchanges with the Soviet Union after the Soviet invasion of Afghanistan. Hypocrisy, lies and double standards were all in evidence as we engaged the nightmare.

The second match of the tour was scheduled for Hamilton on Saturday 29 July. At about midday I went to the central meeting point at Garden Place where the protesters were assembling. I knew hundreds of them – from Taupiri and Ngāruawāhia, from school and the electorate, from Waikato University and churches, from the women's and anti-nuclear movements. I wandered around talking with them, and then walked on the pavement with the media from Garden Place to Rugby Park. I was in a superb position to see the moment the march leaders swung to their left, threw grappling ropes over a section of the two-metre-high wire fence, pulled it down with ease, and began to move up a steep embankment, pushing through the crowd to invade the field. Most people I knew in the march did not know of this plan, and many made split-second decisions on how far they would go. I could see many rugby supporters now wielding anything they could to beat back the protesters, so I moved quickly to enter the grounds legitimately (I had been given a ticket) to see what I could catch on my camera. The mood of the crowd was growing hateful. There were not enough police available to arrest all the demonstrators who were now in the middle of the ground, facing out in a solid circle. When the Commissioner of Police was told a light plane flown by an anti-tour pilot was on its way to the ground, he called the game off. Most of the protesters on the field were hurt by flying missiles and fists as the police made a half-hearted effort to secure a passage for them from the grounds. I was picked up, half-strangled as an effort was made to pull my camera off me, and hurled down the embankment by a rugby supporter, his furious abuse trailing behind. Rugby supporters continued assaults on protesters up and down the streets. It took some hours for all my friends to reassemble and be accounted for safely.

On Sunday morning Arnold, my Party chairman, called. He wanted me to attend a meeting at his home in the early afternoon. When I got there, he had the all-male, rugby-loving electorate officials who had lost their Hamilton game assembled, and it was a set-up, a kangaroo court. They were going to take it all out on me. They were outrageous and way out of line – then in drove dear Jim White, my electorate secretary. Arnold had talked to him on the phone that morning when Jim was in Kerikeri, over four hours away. He could sense what was going to happen, left immediately and drove to Monavale, where he busted up the bullying inquisition immediately on arrival. Labour MP Russell Marshall called that night to see how I was. He said he felt very proud of me and very ashamed of Labour. They had all been forbidden to take part in, address, observe or actively participate in any of the demonstrations. He'd heard a report I had been hurt, and he was just checking I was okay.

There were many reports of what I didn't do – so many I felt it necessitated a personal explanation in the House at the earliest opportunity on Tuesday 28 July:

> Since Saturday's events in Hamilton I find myself accused of addressing protestors in Garden Place, leading the protest march, engaging in illegal activity, entering Rugby Park without a ticket, being seen in the centre of the field with protestors behind the communist flag, and seeking refuge in [a local] home after a very bloody assault. I categorically deny all these. While I recognize that my total opposition to this tour is well known, I wish to place on record that I kept with members of the press to watch the demonstration and policing, and stayed at grounds until the game was cancelled.

A special caucus was held at midday that day. Duncan MacIntyre was in the chair. And the question for us was: 'Do you believe the National Party conference should continue? Mr Chapman wants a view.'

MacIntyre advised that a Cabinet committee of himself, the Minister of Defence David Thomson, Ben Couch for Police and Jim McLay for Justice had received a Police Association deputation the previous day. They wanted the government to gather together the churches, the Halt All Racist Tours organisation (HART) and the police for talks, seeking postponement of the tour and just one big match. The FOL and the churches had also sent a deputation to the government on Tuesday morning, saying this was New Zealand's unhappiest experience. The government should call off the tour.

I was up first: 'Just where does this stop? We were lucky there were no deaths on Saturday. We have one man with a fractured skull, and given the mood of that Hamilton crowd, the cops are lucky they weren't beaten. Is it a death you need before you stop this craziness?' Backbencher Robin Gray spoke up: 'Otago Divisional Chair Dorothy McNab agrees with Marilyn: send them home.' Aussie Malcolm said: 'There are many good people opposed – our supporters – they are not all stirrers.' Jim Bolger claimed, 'The movement is now controlled by subversive groups.' MacIntyre agreed: 'HART has lost control. The Communist Party and the Socialist Unity Party and others are operating it now.' What a load of garbage. If they had been in Hamilton, they would have seen people with nothing to do with those parties making up their own minds, thank you. The supporters from St John's Theological College who made the centre of the field carrying their huge wooden cross took their orders from a very different authority!

On Wednesday evening, 29 July, a well-led demonstration tried to make its way up Molesworth Street outside Parliament Buildings. This time the police were out with shields, batons and helmets, and Thursday morning's newspapers led with photos of the bloodied faces of women and men who had been clubbed. MacIntyre claimed no undue force had been used on the Molesworth Street demonstrators.

At the caucus the following day, George Gair wanted to know how the government would react in the event of a serious injury or death. He thought a willingness to talk was important, and there should be a call from the government for a truncated tour. Ian McLean agreed. MacIntyre, still acting PM, advised that the police were to do a new appraisal of which rugby grounds could or could not be secured, and to speak with the Rugby Union about their responsibilities – for example, in allowing alcohol to be taken into the grounds. Alcohol bottles and cans had been the projectiles aimed at protesters on the field in Hamilton. He informed us that during the week 23 people had been arrested in

Auckland at Air New Zealand's offices, and 18 were arrested in the Rugby Union building in Wellington.

When the new assessments came in on the security of rugby venues, Muldoon had decided the army would be called in to lay barbed wire around grounds. While there were risks securing some venues, such as for the next game in Palmerston North on 1 July, the Saturday of the National Party conference, the only game to be cancelled would be in Timaru, a seat held by Labour. All games in National marginal seats would go ahead. John Falloon argued that the Party conference had to receive police protection at the expense of the game on 1 July. The Friday session of the conference was cancelled, after the Party hierarchy acted on police advice of a possible risk to the security of the conference delegates. At the Saturday match, barbed wire surrounded the ground, and lines of police were equipped with riot shields and helmets. Most New Zealanders had never before seen this form of policing exercised in the country.

This was a very crazy period. I was daily filled with such shame that New Zealand had hosted apartheid sport. I was filled with self-contempt for being part of a government that did nothing to stop it – nothing! But all the other stuff went on. I was on panels with the other Waipā candidates in Te Awamutu and Pirongia. I spoke to Rotary and Lyceum clubs, and to the Press Club luncheon in Wellington, where I repeated the comments I was making in the House in opposition to the tour.

My Budget speech in August continued the paean-to-Waipā theme. Development grants were being used to grow garlic, asparagus, cut flowers and chicory for export. I mentioned the opposite impacts as well: the closure of the Munro Caravan Factory in Ōtorohanga and a small textile factory in Mangakino. But I also hit back at the right-wingers denigrating the UN because of the work of its Anti-Apartheid Committee:

> In the *Waikato Times* of 3 August, Mrs. Wilcox, an officer for the Society for the Protection of Individual Rights, is reported as hitting out at the United Nations for being the biggest collection of hypocrites, murderers, liars, and thieves, that this country has ever had the

> misfortune to be associated with. The members of the United Nations High Commission of Refugees working in Ethiopia and Kampuchea are not hypocrites, murderers, liars or thieves. Those representatives of the World Health Organisation who have helped to eradicate major diseases throughout the world, those who attended the Geneva Conference to ensure that infant formula was not advertised in countries where there is no pure water, those representatives looking for a solution on the Law of the Sea Conference, which is of vital interest to New Zealand, are none of those things. The United Nations is our chance to put our case to the body of the world opinion. New Zealand has a right to be there.

Then I drew a contrast between the activities undertaken to outlaw apartheid and the lack of action for the women of the world:

> When will the male leaders of the world turn their attention to those millions of people who have no vote, who are invisible, not simply in their societies and their economies, but who are made invisible by their dress and excluded from the political processes in Bahrain, Kuwait, the Oman, Qatar, Saudi Arabia, Emirates, Yemen Arab Republic and those who have no voting power, women.

My Budget speech was bracketed by a Party electorate meeting, and an Executive meeting focused on the logistics of the campaign. Commentators had no doubt I would win Waipā:

> Marilyn Waring holds the Waipa seat against what might appear to be all odds. She is an outspoken occupant of the National backbench. An avowed radical feminist she has open clashes with Muldoon. Her efforts to move National policies in more liberal directions have not been conspicuously successful. She is a nationwide figure. Her style in the House is uniquely her own. Her voice is powerful, her mind is sharp, and she speaks bluntly and with great emotion in language often as critical of her own party as the opposition. She has strong local organisational support.[14]

By 13 August hundreds of Special Police had been sworn in, largely, we were told, for station-based administration jobs. I knew there was also a problem for the force in that many police had family members active in demonstrations on the streets, and they could not be in the front line anywhere. All police leave was cancelled. The costs of policing the tour had spiralled to over $7 million. All this nightmare outside, and at the caucus on 20 August colleagues wanted to know about preparations for the election campaign. Election day was 28 November.

Michael Cox asked when anything was going to happen. 'There has been no tie-up between the main party campaign and our electorates, no details of the pamphlets we have to deliver, and we are into the $4,000 expenditure-cap time frame.' The PM fudged: 'How much must we need to know? The TV commercials are very secret, and the impact will be lost if these are leaked. Labour and Social Credit are short of funds. Advertising could come down to talking heads.' Paul East asked when the candidates' conference would be held, and was told not until October. George Gair hinted that there were some policy decisions yet to be made and this made publicity planning difficult.

The Prime Minister wasn't bothered: 'We are ahead in every area in the latest McNair surveys. They are the best we've had. We do not need to fear the loss of provincial seats.'

The bishops of the Catholic and Protestant churches of New Zealand sent a delegation to the Governor-General to voice their opposition to the tour. The Governor-General sent the message on to the PM. The PM had also received a deputation from the mayors of Wellington and Auckland, who had said that they were extremely concerned about the threats to people and property on the days of the test matches in their cities.

At the 27 August caucus, Muldoon said he hadn't heard from Police Commissioner Walton recently, but the police were very confident they would manage until 12 September, the last game. Muldoon had agreed to call a meeting after the tour – a 'mini Gleneagles' – to get the cooperation of sporting bodies in a calmer atmosphere, and to ensure Labour leader Rowling didn't take the initiative. There was just no limit to the cynicism and hypocrisy of this man.

On 3 September the PM left caucus early, and we were considering nominations to the Committee on Women. After listening to the names suggested, I got up and gave a little lecture about how it didn't do us any good not to have women's movement activists and supporters on the committee. Labour did know this population, it was obvious, and it was an electoral advantage for them. I was completely unprepared for the reaction, which was that Neil Austin and Ian McLean immediately nominated me. I knew it wouldn't last, but sometimes my colleagues could surprise me. After caucus concluded, I was called up to the PM's office. I had notes on a substitute name ready before I walked in his door. He accepted my nomination for my replacement.

By the end of August I wore dark glasses on the weekly flight from Hamilton to Wellington, because I would involuntarily weep through the trip. I was running further to work each morning, hoping the endorphins would help, trying to time my arrival, shower, and then breakfast at a point where the MPs' dining room would be almost empty. Every day I would eat something, then go to the bathroom and stick my finger down my throat to vomit. I could not stand what the government was doing any more. I felt shattered. I was deeply sad and very depressed. Every close friend I had opposed the tour and was on the streets as often as possible. After the Hamilton assault, I didn't observe the confrontations at close range again. I tried to heal a little each weekend in the garden, tuned to the radio news broadcasts relaying the battles between police and demonstrators as I weeded and fed the asparagus bed.

I was ashamed and despairing to be complicit in this nightmare: the manipulation, the abuse of foreign leaders, the public release of SIS material on the background of a handful of protesters, the breathtaking lack of integrity and principle in the name of holding a few marginal rural seats. I had done everything I could think of. I wrote an affidavit for the group before the court in Wellington trying to stop the game there. I was offered five minutes on television and took it to respond point by point to Muldoon's lies. At the same time, I was so proud of the New Zealanders demonstrating in their thousands, restoring our image in the world of human rights, demonstrating moral decency in resistance, as they faced down baton-wielding police.[15]

I was still cannon fodder in the government backbench, retaining the quorum in the House. I had long prided myself on being able to knit, read and listen to the House at the same time. I now chose very complicated

Fair Isle or cable patterns that required so much concentration it was impossible to read. I sat there, counting stitches and rows and manipulating my needles.

The immediacy of work filled those awful days. The Estimates Debates were on again. I spoke on Health, noting the work of staff at the WHO in seeing through the resolution on infant formula.[16] I argued that nurses should be paid more, and that we needed to rethink care of those with disabilities. In the Estimates on Social Welfare, I was concerned that voluntary organisations receiving centralised funding would give away the power to run themselves.[17] I asked if any legal changes might follow from the recommendations of Ann Ballin's steering committee on the International Year of Disabled Persons (IYDP). Had the Cabinet Committee on Family and Social Affairs considered policies such as domestic power pricing, urban transport, and environmental audits to be included in social audits?

I had news in early September that put my despair into perspective. Nawal El Saadawi was one of six women arrested with 1,500 others in a general purge in Egypt. They were arrested under the Code of Ethics without any formal charge and accused of contributing to civil unrest. They could be held for five years, and for a year without any access to legal remedy. Even if freed, they could still be subject to legal vigilance, circumscribed in movement to a particular area, have their passports withheld, property confiscated and bank accounts closed, and have no public speaking or media contacts. In 1981, feminist activism was not considered grounds by Amnesty International to qualify as a political prisoner. Women had to use their own networks to get the message out. I wrote to the Egyptian ambassador in New Zealand and sent the details out on my New Zealand women's mailing list, now in the hundreds, with university feminists, health collectives, unions, women's centres, lawyers, teachers and journalists added. I went through the names of all those who had registered for the Copenhagen women's conference and wrote to those from the South Pacific, New Zealand and Australia, asking them to join me in protesting Nawal's arrest in the strongest possible terms, and to assist in securing her early release.

In September and October we kept moving in the electorate. I spent days in Monavale, Ōtorohanga, Kāwhia and Te Kawa Crossroads, and spoke at two Federated Farmers candidate forums. As if the tour and the election weren't enough, we also had a Royal tour in October, as the Queen was on her way to the Commonwealth Heads of Government meeting (CHOGM) in Melbourne. Parliamentarians had to have lunch with her in Wellington on 15 October, and I had to be at the Rukuhia airport in the Waipā electorate when she landed there on 19 October. I was obliged to wear a hat (a small white headscarf), and shake her gloved hand, and curtsy.

CHOGM gave no ground to Muldoon. He did not get to lambast the meeting with the screeds of human rights material he had gathered together. It looked as if he spent more time speaking to media than attending the conference, and he left early. Commonwealth leaders made it clear they were impressed by the strength of the public opposition to the Springbok tour in New Zealand, and they endorsed the Gleneagles Agreement again.

I spent much of October gathering up-to-date information on Waipā for the campaign through ministerial questions. I found out how many kilometres of Māui gas pipeline had been put in place in the Waipā electorate, and what end users had converted to gas in the Te Awamutu and Cambridge districts. I had an update on the Pukekura Forest Nursery, producing nine million tree seedlings annually, as well as natives. It could produce 24 million *Pinus radiata* seedlings a year if required; there was a permanent workforce of 11, with 50 employed at peak times. The Minister of Justice told me there was a wide range of work and training for Waikeria Prison inmates (but only tailoring, typing, cooking, laundry and market gardening were available for the women in Arohata Prison). I asked for the total numbers of men and women registered as unemployed, or on PEP work, and the total numbers of those in paid employment in Cambridge, Mangakino, Kāwhia, Ōtorohanga and Te Awamutu. I learned that only three polling booths in Waipā had disability access. What were the options for those who couldn't attend a booth on polling day?

Of course, the major message for the campaign was supposed to be the Think Big projects, but these were always going to be marginal. The need to develop and use Māui gas, and to increase storage and refining capacity at Marsden Point, were critical for the country. But more and more projects were added in a sort of grab-bag approach – and decisions seemed to be taken with backs against the wall. The government became the developer, borrowing very large amounts internationally when the country's overseas debt was already ballooning. It also made concessionary arrangements with private companies – the power price arrangements for the aluminium smelter and the expansion of the steel mill. International interest rates began to climb again. Inflation in construction and engineering with the pressure of the programmes did not help. The costs of machinery imports blew out the balance-of-payments deficit. The viability of the different projects was judged on expectations that oil prices would remain high. For Muldoon, the projects were also an attempt to tackle the continuing rise in unemployment.

On 22 October Mike Minogue and I voted against a key clause in the National Development Amendment Bill. The Bill proposed changing the subject of the Environment Commissioner's inquiries from the environmental implications of a National Development Act project to the accuracy and adequacy of an environmental impact report. The clause had the clear effect of making the powers of the commissioner uncertain. The implication was that the government did not wish the commissioner to consider any ancillary social impact or downstream resource-use environmental effects of a project, but only the effects on a specific site. Just a few hours earlier Mike and I had refused to vote on the ruling of the Privileges Committee on an anti-Springbok tour protest in the public gallery of the House. The visitors had stood and prayed silently, and had been banned from Parliament Buildings. On a more encouraging note, we had introduced the Freedom of Information legislation Mike had worked so hard for. We also had a Domestic Violence Bill and a Wild and Scenic Rivers Bill introduced, which I could talk about with some pride. The House rose for the election on 23 October.

On Saturday 31 October I had to go to a luncheon and a dinner in the electorate. I was trying to clean my house. Sometimes it is the smallest things that turf you over the edge. The vacuum cleaner broke down. I slumped down the wall. 'I don't think I can keep going,' I said to myself. 'I don't think I can move any more.' I was still immobile some minutes later when there was a knock at the front door. I crawled along and hauled myself up. I couldn't believe it. My Wellington GP stood there. I had no idea she was travelling through. Within an hour she had me admitted to a private hospital in Hamilton for a week of complete rest. Waipā had planned a quiet, efficient campaign, and we kept it simple from then on.

On election night I had a clear majority of 2,768 with over 48 per cent of the vote. Social Credit was second and Labour third. I lost four booths to Social Credit and one to Labour. It looked like anti-abortionists and rugby lovers, and National voters who didn't like Muldoon, or me, went to Social Credit, while many Labour women voted for me. But the overall New Zealand result was not at all clear as I left the courthouse electorate count to join Waipā National Party supporters at the hotel lounge in Te Awamutu. A two-party swing of less than one per cent from National to Labour was all it would take to change the government. As I was coming down the corridor, the television commentator was announcing Fran Wilde's win in Wellington Central against a National sitting member. I let out a small cheer, heard by Maureen Fraser at the door. She turned and said, 'But she's Labour.' I hugged her, and said, 'If there are not more women there I will have to leave. I can't stand this for much longer.'

The final result took some days to emerge. National took 38.8 per cent of the vote and 47 seats. It won Taupō by 14 votes. Labour took 39 per cent of the vote for 43 seats; and Social Credit, with 20.7 per cent, took only two seats – an outcome of the FPP system. There were four new women MPs: Ruth Richardson for National, and Fran Wilde, Margaret Shields and Helen Clark for Labour. Ann Hercus, Whetu Tirikatene-Sullivan and Mary Batchelor had all been returned, so we had doubled our numbers. Once the Speaker was appointed, the government had a majority of one. I had a lot of thinking to do.

I missed the first post-election caucus as I was attending a Regional Commonwealth Parliamentary Association conference in Hobart. Ruth

Richardson, one of six new MPs in caucus, wasted no time in asking to see the Treasury reports on the state of the economy. Muldoon replied they were confidential, and Hugh Templeton added that the secrecy gave Treasury the 'freedom to report'. The PM noted that the reports referred to high internal interest rates, devaluation, running down cash balances and internal liquidity under pressure. There was no cause for alarm, he said. Ruth did not give up. 'When will we be able to discuss these problems?' she asked. She was told she could put it on the caucus agenda.

The Egyptian ambassador wrote on 7 December. Nawal was released from prison. He congratulated me on holding my seat and wished me 'all the best in the service of your people'. I would need all the good wishes I could garner for the next parliamentary term.

I relied on the endorphins from my morning run to get me through the day for much of my last five years in Parliament. *New Zealand Listener*

Above: With a group of curious Nepali onlookers in February 1980 as I waited for a raft to be inflated – expatriate New Zealander John Lindeman thought rafting on the Trisuli River had potential as a tourism venture that locals could run. Marilyn Waring collection

Below: The 1981 Harvard Kennedy Institute of Politics 'Spring Fellows'. Back row, from left: Senator John C. Culver, Eugene Eidenberg, Susan B. King, Major-General Joseph Garba. Front row: Marilyn Waring, Robert J. Manning, George Weeks. Photograph by Richard M. Feldman

Above: The media were somewhat fixated on my appearance – this 1980 photo ran with the copy 'The "new look" Marilyn Waring in her office last night unpacking ready to shuffle papers again after her overseas trip.' Stuff Ltd

Below: In 1982 we persuaded the Speaker of the House Sir Richard Harrison to move a plaque commemorating the 75th anniversary of women's suffrage from a back corridor to a more prominent location. We also campaigned to get the Women's Suffrage Petition of 1893 brought up from the cellars and displayed in the main lobby to mark the 90th anniversary. The group comprises (from left): Mary Batchelor, Ann Hercus, Marilyn Waring (foreground), Ruth Richardson (obscured), Helen Clark (background) and Margaret Shields. Stuff Ltd/Alexander Turnbull Library, EP/1982/1275/23-F

Above: Protesters at the Hamilton game of the 1981 Springbok Tour pulled down a fence and scaled an embankment to invade the pitch. I entered the grounds legitimately through the gate as I had a ticket, and ran around to follow the protesters and take photographs. I am centre foreground, in the two-tone jacket.
New Zealand Herald, NZH-1000064

Below: With the match called off, the mood of the crowd turned ugly. This photograph captures the moment when I was half-strangled as a rugby supporter tried to pull my camera off me (to the right of the frame, with my arm raised), before I was sent hurtling down the bank followed by his furious abuse. More than thirty years later the supporter approached me outside a restaurant and apologised.
Photograph by Kees Sprengers

Above: Women MPs leaving the debating chamber after Doug Kidd's anti-abortion bill had been voted out by the House on 19 October 1983. From left to right: Mary Batchelor, Ruth Richardson, Fran Wilde, Marilyn Waring, Helen Clark and Ann Hercus. *New Zealand Herald*, NZH-1088007

Right: Labour MP Whetu Tirikatene-Sullivan, who was on leave during the defeat of the two abortion bills in October 1983, was another strong supporter of reproductive rights for women. Photograph by Ans Westra, Alexander Turnbull Library, AW-1770_05

Above: Prime Minister Robert Muldoon telling Party President Sue Wood that it was a mistake to put disarmament and arms control on the agenda of the 1983 National Party conference in Dunedin. *Otago Daily Times*

Below: After announcing my retirement from politics in February 1984. Photograph by Paul Estcourt, *New Zealand Herald*, NZH-1044189

I was invited to write an account of my time in Parliament for the *New Zealand Listener*, which became the cover story for the 26 May 1984 issue.

Courtesy of the *New Zealand Listener*

Leaving my office on 13 June 1984 for the debating chamber, where I would cross the floor with Mike Minogue to vote against the Government on Opposition MP Richard Prebble's Nuclear Free New Zealand Bill. The bill was defeated by one vote, but in 1987 the Labour Government would pass the New Zealand Nuclear Free Zone, Disarmament and Arms Control Act. Photograph by Paul Estcourt, *New Zealand Herald*, NZH-1101063

1982

This would be my last term. I told no one. With the government's majority of one, I wanted a watching brief over a number of issues, and asked not to chair any select committees. I got myself on to Public Expenditure and Foreign Affairs, likely to be the only committees where confidence questions of 'supply' and 'national security' might arise; Health and Welfare, which would have a lot of legislation in front of it; and the Members' Services, Library, and House select committees. I would not be taking leave to address countless organisations across the country. I wanted to stay close to Wellington and try not to miss committee hearings and caucus meetings.

In late January we held a Waipā Executive meeting and made the programme for the annual branch meetings in February–March. Party officials reported that there was not much enthusiasm for the government, so we should just keep it all low key. There would be Party events in Cambridge and Te Awamutu, a wine and cheese evening in Ōtorohanga, and an electorate barbecue. The Ōtorohanga Maternity Hospital was threatened with closure, and there were public meetings to attend. I would also sit on the King Country Regional Development Council with Labour MP Koro Wetere and check in with local government councils.

Surgery sessions began. Two constituents farming in partnership were being questioned about their 'qualifications' for a Lands and Survey ballot farm because they were dyslexic. Both husband and wife had passed the qualifications after being examined on an oral basis, but officials were discriminating. We could pass human rights legislation and spend a year trying to lift consciousness through the IYDP, but people were constantly battling to achieve equal outcomes.

The January 1982 IMF Survey of New Zealand wrote of institutional rigidities, problems with government regulations and restrictive private-sector practices. This was part of the background for the caucus meeting on 4 February, where MPs had placed tax reform on the agenda. The PM opened the discussion:

> We have undertaken to do a few specific promises in response to party and public criticism. We set up the Tax Task Force. We have to move because of the Budget time table and make decisions before the Task Force report in April. We have to tidy our thinking. We can do the arithmetic later, but we can make decisions in principle earlier.
>
> We are now adrift at the upper end of personal taxation where people are paying too much tax. We have looked after the lower end of the scale. There is plenty of criticism of our reliance on direct taxation. The deficit is very large, and it will be difficult to get it down. Revenue is up, and expenditure is down.
>
> On the issue of indirect tax, the Task Force has looked at a rate across the board. A major question is, do we have exemptions? Obviously, it is easier with a single rate. There will always be anomalies and evasion, and these are difficult to police. Should we tax services as well as food? Indirect tax would have a major impact on the CPI and then we are faced with wage compensation. We need a wage–tax trade-off. In a move to indirect tax, it is the wage earner who takes the reduction, not the farmer or professional.

George Gair emphasised the social costs when moving from direct to indirect taxation, with the 'burden on the rank and file'. He was concerned that means-tested benefits (the DPB and unemployment benefit, for example), linked to the CPI, would rise to compensate any change, but superannuation was linked to wages. Superannuation could diminish in relative terms.

Derek Quigley wanted to tax all benefits, to have sharp reductions in government expenditure, and for some state functions to be taken over by the private sector. 'We have to deal with the fundamentals,' he said. 'The economy is shot full of many iniquities, and we need to attack these. We all know these should be challenged at the same time and this would achieve a more neutral effect.' Simon Upton thought the best political benefit would come from reducing government expenditure.

Muldoon responded that the amount of the deficit was not the issue. But there was a large dispute over where the cuts should fall. Duncan MacIntyre chimed in: 'Agriculture receives $900 million in support. Should we cut there?' Muldoon continued: 'The approach here is borrowing for capital expenditure. Be careful not to oversimplify deficit situations.'

Mike Minogue appreciated the political realities outlined as a starting point. 'We are losing support in major urban centres as a party. The perception of wage and salary earners and youth is that they are caught by tax and increasingly resentful at some privileged evaders such as farmers. Reform should take account of the urban mood.'

Muldoon agreed there had been a lot of heat generated on this in the campaign. 'The problem was satisfying disgruntled urban voters without losing those they are disgruntled about. We could have a tax on fringe benefits?'

Ruth Richardson thought we should be moving to help create wealth, to reward risk-takers. She favoured a value-added indirect tax and a flat direct rate of tax. Public expenditure needed to reduce as a percentage of GDP. Information was needed for caucus and the public. She wanted the task-force papers released to caucus so that we might make a more informed contribution.

Muldoon retorted that Ruth was welcome to see the tax papers and the 17 options, but all except five were non-starters. The PM did not want to waste time with irrelevancy and didn't believe the papers would improve contributions to the debate. He advised that the difficulty of a direct flat rate of tax was achieving enough revenue and being fair to low-income earners; it was not good political thinking to make decisions on the basis of middle-class urban people: 'We don't want to lose otherwise Labour voters.' Muldoon assured caucus that taxing capital gains had been eliminated from the options.

Even without the full task-force papers, we knew of the extent of the 'fundamentals'. The proportion of income tax paid by companies had declined to 10.24 per cent of total income-tax revenue. The proportion of all revenue paid by individual taxpayers had risen to 89 per cent of the whole. Companies paid a flat rate of 45 per cent (50 per cent for non-resident companies). Individuals were subject to a highly progressive scale, with a marginal rate of 60 per cent on assessable income over $22,000. On my parliamentary salary and allowances, with no other income, this was my rate.

The Tax Task Force papers showed that the percentage of income tax paid by companies, which enjoyed accelerated depreciation write-offs and investment allowances, was directly related to the availability of tax incentives. The papers also had strong criticism of the effects of New Zealand's trade-protection shelters on the export sector. We would return to the tax conversation in future weeks, but I could already sense Muldoon's resistance to any changes.

I was choosing my acceptances of invitations carefully. In February I opened a women's art exhibition and spoke at the Craft Council of New Zealand meeting. I addressed a meeting of the International Council of Women. Parliamentary messengers told me that I usually had the third-largest volume of incoming mail, after the PM and the leader of the Opposition. Sometimes I was incredulous at the contents. Mr Yardley from Whāngārei sent a letter he had received from the Department of Social Welfare: 'I note that your wife is shortly to attain 60 years of age. She is therefore entitled to National Superannuation in her own right. Would you please have her complete and return the enclosed form to this office?' He was appalled. The department said an old template had been used by mistake.

Gwyneth Wright, a journalist with *Straight Furrow*, the weekly newspaper run by Federated Farmers, had written an extensive survey for women in agriculture. It was run in one issue. The response was overwhelming, and created a picture of scores of hours of unpaid farming work by women, in addition to their household activities. It showed that any arguments for farming inputs based on per-capita production were wildly astray. In addition to farm labour, rural women in New Zealand were engaged in a bewildering number of tasks that made the farm function but were all treated as unproductive: answering the telephone, seeing callers, keeping farm accounts, paying bills, deciding who does what each day, listening to workers' grievances, deciding all crop or stocking policy for the coming year, health-and-safety policy planning, keeping stock records, growing fruit or vegetables, preserving farm or garden produce, making bread, providing meals for workers, entertaining business visitors, keeping poultry, and undertaking a multitude of crafts for the household.

I felt as if I was getting a better understanding of the treatment of all unpaid work in the national accounts, but I mistrusted some of the conclusions I had come to, thinking, 'It couldn't be that stupid. I must be missing something.' I asked for a meeting with John Chetwin from Treasury to guide me. He quickly confirmed all my fears about the treatment of unpaid work. He agreed it was outrageous – and added quickly, 'My wife gave me *The Women's Room* by Marilyn French for Christmas. I get it.'

'So what would happen,' I asked him, 'if value for women's unpaid work was estimated in the national accounts?'

'We would probably just produce two sets of accounts,' he said, 'one with it in and one with it out, so that the world would say, "Just ignore the first one of New Zealand's. They count women."'

'Do we have a copy of the UN publications containing the rules of the United Nations System of National Accounts?' I asked.

'Well, Treasury certainly doesn't have this,' John replied, 'but I'll ask others.'

A few weeks later he came back to tell me there wasn't a copy in the country. I asked him to check with his Australian colleagues, but there was no copy of the rules in Australia either. He told me that the two editions of the accounting framework, published in 1953 and 1968, ran to several shelves of encyclopedic volumes. All of these were held in the UN Library in New York. I thought it was odd that nations ran their national accounts without a copy of the rules!

The Caucus Justice Committee had to meet in early March. The government finally had the domestic violence legislation before the select committee. The police wanted discretion as to whether they could release a person in a shorter period than 24 hours after he or she had breached a non-violence order. The committee held fast to 24 hours. Having Ruth Richardson in the room already made a difference. Although she was upset at being placed on the Statutes Revision and Official Information Select Committees, and would have preferred the PEC, she would be so sharp on legislation. I also thought her presence on the Official Information Select Committee was extremely important for the success of that legislation.

The first March caucus was again trawling for budget savings. There was a proposal to charge for prescriptions. Paul East, representing Rotorua, talked about the costs of taking children to a GP and said he expected that few prescriptions would be picked up when costs were already a pressure. Muldoon, MP for one of the wealthiest electorates in the country, responded that he had never had any such complaint. 'Well, this is just an example of the differences in the people we speak to,' I said. 'There are many examples in my electorate.' Colleagues followed: Venn Young was very concerned at chronically ill children being disadvantaged. Robin Gray from conservative Clutha had examples of GPs who were not prepared to charge. Simon Upton, representing some of the old Raglan electorate, confirmed children were not going to GPs. It was all hearsay, but it was all we had. There was no data anywhere.

Parliament opened on 6 April 1982. Could eight women MPs make any difference? Our four new colleagues came with expertise and experience. Ruth Richardson had helped set up the Women's Electoral Lobby (WEL) and been very active in the organisation's effective submissions to select committees. She had most recently worked as Federated Farmers' legal adviser, and had been on the National Advisory Council on the Employment of Women (NACEW) and the government's Committee on Women. Ruth had strong principles – about democracy, gender discrimination and the economy, for example. She did her homework and had no time for the various deceptions she would begin to see in Muldoon's behaviour. In her maiden speech, Ruth said: 'As a society, we must commit ourselves to three sorts of positive action for women – positive recruitment, positive selection, and institutional change. Failure to act in this cause is both an economic waste and a social injustice.'

Helen Clark was a political science graduate and a lecturer at the University of Auckland. She had been active in HART and had worked her way through elected positions in the Labour Party. Helen had stood in an unwinnable seat, Piako, in 1978, and in 1981 had won selection for Mt Albert, a safe urban Auckland Labour electorate.

Margaret Shields had been a member of Labour's Women's Council and a founding member of WEL and the Society for Research on Women. She had been both a convenor of the United Women's Convention in Wellington and a member of the New Zealand delegation for the United Nations Conference on Women in Mexico in 1975. Margaret happily described herself as a feminist.

Fran Wilde was another political science graduate and had worked in the Labour Party Research Unit in Parliament. She had been a founder of the Kidsarus Collective, publishing non-sexist children's literature, and of the Wellington Adoption Support Group. On the day we were sworn in as MPs, Fran would join me in making an affirmation, becoming only the third member in the New Zealand Parliament who did not swear on the Bible. In her maiden speech, Fran spoke of being 'aware of the contradictions involved in having any kind of feminist consciousness and being a member of this establishment, which is essentially a male-dominated hierarchy'.[1]

I felt less burdened knowing more women would be asking questions in the House and on select committees, speaking out on key issues of gender justice, and filling some of that space of constant vigilance.

At the 7 April caucus, I brought a recommendation from the PEC that we change the annual budget balance date from 31 March to 30 June. 'Where does this come from?' the PM barked. I advised him that the PEC had been considering this for several years, along with other financial management changes, such as the accrual accounting and block allocation pilots. Twenty-four departments supported the move. 'Overwhelmingly the answer must be no,' the PM declared. 'That would be quite impossible to work into our parliamentary year.' Other colleagues on the PEC didn't bother to argue. We always knew when it was hopeless.

We received a report on the Party's Dominion Council meeting, the first since the election. There was a major concern at the loss of urban seats, a lot of nervous twitching, and concern at a lack of action on tax reform. 'The tax issue is insoluble,' Muldoon proclaimed. 'The full report will be public Tuesday. We'll be open to reactions for a month.'

Ruth tackled the PM on raising the qualification age for superannuation. 'There are no sacred cows. It is reality now,' she said. It didn't get any traction.

Given the government's slim majority, I expected the Labour Opposition to introduce private members' bills to embarrass or goad backbench National MPs across a range of issues on which we might have taken public positions. I certainly expected some form of nuclear-free legislation, and had thought about how to deal with this. My game plan was focused on that issue so that I wouldn't be easily pushed about on others.

When Mike Moore introduced a National Development Amendment Bill to curb the power of the Executive on Think Big projects, I responded that I had given considerable thought to the implications of members crossing the floor of the House in this parliament.[2] I was aware that the Opposition saw it as a moral victory when a National member crossed the floor on legislation. I referred to Rule 242 of the Labour Party Constitution in which candidates pledged to vote with the majority of Cabinet or caucus on all occasions. At least, I said, I was in a position where crossing the floor was possible. I had certainly 'expressed reservations' on particular clauses of the National Development Bill but I 'was not prepared so early in the session to be part of a charade'. Social Credit members, I continued, were apparently free to vote from issue to issue, but it was impossible to know what they would actually do. 'It makes it impossible for those Government members with courage, to know whether, in crossing the floor of the House, they could bring about what they sought to do, because Social Credit members may not be with them in the lobby, and on no-confidence motions, they will be in the billiard room.'[3]

Some challenges seemed endless. Educating and caring for pre-school children was still a mess. A key recommendation of the State Services

Commission Working Group on Early Childhood Care and Education was that responsibility for the administration of childcare centres should be transferred from the Department of Social Welfare to the Department of Education, and that childcare should be funded in line with other early-childhood education programmes. Cabinet decided the time was not appropriate for either the transfer of responsibility or an increase in the level of funding.

The discrepancies were extreme. The on-the-job national training scheme for childcare workers received only $20,000 from the Lottery Board. In the 1981–82 financial year, the Playcentre training grant was $192,000. In 1982 there were 125 kindergarten teacher trainees; a rough estimate of the cost of their government-funded training was $900,000. Most childcare staff spent far longer with children than those at Playcentre and kindergarten. I managed to get a barely increased grant of $25,000 for the New Zealand Childcare Association to assist it in maintaining its training programme, but I could not get any minister to pay attention to the need for major change across the sector.

As if that wasn't enough, I despaired at the announcement by the Human Rights Commission on 21 April of their policy on sexual harassment:

> Standards of social behaviour cannot be expected to be only those that would be acceptable to the Victorian middle-class. But there are nevertheless standards. Behaviour of gross impropriety, of brutish crudeness, of offensive suggestiveness or blatant physical contact, is not to be condoned on a persistent basis. One must not become narrow, and there must be a reasonable acceptance of people as they are. The standards that are proper will vary according to people and place, to time and circumstances. Nor should an isolated incident or occasional event be taken out of context or given undue weight. Any complaint of sexual harassment must be looked at in terms of the degree of seriousness.
>
> For sexual harassment to amount to unlawful sex discrimination, through affecting the conditions of employment or subjecting someone to any detriment, there must be something more than occasional acts or uncouth behaviour or mere banter. There must be a threat or the

> creation of an unpleasant working atmosphere to the extent that the employee's ability to engage in their work is impaired or affected. The sexual harassment must be of a serious nature, and it will usually be persistent.

At caucus on 15 April, the PM had launched into the nuclear-free zones (NFZ) that were being declared weekly by local councils across New Zealand. 'The local body stances are nonsense because we were one of the first signatories of the NPT. New Zealand declared itself to be free of nuclear weapons, but this would not affect existing defence pacts or transit of vessels on the high seas,' he claimed. The NFZ strategy was a small gesture of New Zealanders' growing resistance to ship visits. By now more than 50 per cent of the population lived in these zones, including most of my electorate. I watched as two long-time National Party supporters, the mayors of Hamilton and Huntly, used their casting votes to take their districts nuclear-free. Australian pediatrician Helen Caldicott had spoken about nuclear weapons to overflowing halls throughout the country. Also showing nationwide was the short documentary *If You Love This Planet*, made by the National Film Board of Canada, which featured a lecture Helen had given in New York. Director Terre Nash had won the 1982 Academy Award for best documentary after the film was designated 'foreign political propaganda'.

Labour's Richard Prebble announced he would introduce a Private Member's Bill on a nuclear-free zone that would prohibit the entry of ships or aircraft carrying nuclear weapons into New Zealand. The discussion came to caucus on 29 April. Warren Cooper, now Minister of Foreign Affairs, said the US would have to disclose if there were nuclear weapons on the ships: 'We can't opt out of ANZUS in this way.' Muldoon responded: 'If the Government did not allow a ship into New Zealand, ANZUS would be in jeopardy.' He wouldn't want candidates who didn't support ANZUS at a future general election.

No problem, I thought, I won't be there. I spoke next. I would support the introduction of the Bill and referral to a select committee, because the matter needed a public airing. 'The nuclear threat is the biggest issue on the planet, so there must be a public discussion, and we need to be involved.' Paul East, Ruth Richardson and Mike Minogue agreed we must have a public forum and consider these issues. But Paul asked: 'Can we deal with it as parliamentarians? Don't let the Prebble Bill be introduced. Would Marilyn agree to support the Government and speak in the debate and say she has persuaded caucus [that] a sub-committee of the Foreign Affairs Committee be established to consider the issue and the UN report on it?'[4] Absolutely, I would. That was the next step in the plan.

I spoke on the Bill that afternoon:

> The Bill is a sincere attempt to grapple with what I believe will be the central issue of world politics for the remainder of the century. It is based on the possibility of realising a resolution by the General Assembly of the United Nations to create a nuclear weapon free zone in the South Pacific.
>
> A Government Notice of Motion is to be tabled in the House with a major background document on Disarmament. A subcommittee of the Foreign Affairs Committee, augmented with MPs from the Defence Committee, will be established, an idea proposed at the last meeting [by Helen Clark]. Briefings will take place. Submissions will be invited from informed and concerned New Zealanders. The undertaking I have been given is that there will be a chance for all the issues of the United Nations Disarmament Conference to be discussed. At the end of the debate on the introduction of this Bill, the parliamentary procedure would have seen an end to this measure, because it involves an appropriation. I believe we have found a broader base on which Parliament can share [Richard Prebble's] concern.

It was a busy day. I also made my Address in Reply speech and noted what a special occasion it was to be in the House when the number of women MPs had doubled to eight.[5] I also welcomed Ruth and Simon to the caucus. I made comments about the social expectations of volunteerism from women and Māori to keep communities going. I noted the narrow range of occupations in the employment of women and cultural minorities. I had been distressed by the town planning laws applied in such a European way in rural communities, requiring proof of the 'productive potential' of subdivided units. This stopped development of housing on rural Māori land, where the 'independent, productive unit' test was completely inappropriate. Waipā Council was working on changing its practice to enable settlement of whānau on their tribal land. I also reflected on comments Margaret Shields had made in her maiden speech, quoting Marilyn French on humanness. These were qualities Parliament might celebrate in a non-partisan manner. And I kept pushing on the issues of GDP and the national accounts.

I visited Arohata Prison twice in April to meet with staff, and to talk with the pre-release women. I made an appointment for an extraordinary constituent, farmer and environmentalist, Arthur Cowan, to meet with the Minister of Forests. There was a block of virgin forest on the market in the King Country which the Ministry wished to save, but all budget had been spent. Arthur mortgaged his property to make an offer and hold the land until government approved the purchase. In Waipā, I attended the Cambridge Forest Service Nursery open day and the agricultural field-days. I could just keep learning so much at these events, picking up material for speeches or questions in the House, and hearing lots of good as well as grave stories. I went to a dinner at Tūrangawaewae hosted by Dame Te Atairangikaahu. I enjoyed some hours in my garden.

The early-morning news bulletin on 5 May led with the Argentine invasion of the Falkland Islands. On arrival at work there was a message for an urgent caucus. I linked the two immediately. I went to my filing drawer where I kept a copy of key interviews in which I had made statements about what I would and would not be part of. I checked. I found the *Ms.* magazine interview from 1981. I would walk out and quit rather than be part of a declaration of war, I had said. I pulled the clipping from the file and put it in my pocket.

Then I called a friend, a very senior and experienced diplomat, who was at that time driving the UK desk in the Ministry of Foreign Affairs. There was very little she could tell me. 'We had to look the Falkland Islands up on a map,' she said. 'We certainly don't have a file on them. I have no idea what will be said at the caucus meeting.'

In I went. Muldoon outlined the little he knew of what was happening in the Southern Atlantic. I waited. He went on: 'We are expecting at any moment that Britain will declare war on Argentina. We will not declare war on Argentina.' Because of the requirements of the British naval strategy, New Zealand had been asked to send one of our frigates to the Indian Ocean to continue patrols to free a British vessel. That was the sum total of what we were doing. I was still an MP.

The regular weekly caucus on 6 May offered some good news. The Waihaha forests beside Lake Taupō would be preserved for all time. The virgin stands in the Pureora Native Forest, at the southern end of Waipā, would also become ecological reserves.

That meeting also had to deal with the new provisions on dog control, a long Bill setting out the statutory duties of dog owners. Ian McLean wanted to know: 'What is this about dog rights? The right to exercise?' Under-secretary Geoff Thompson was handling the Bill. 'We must have safeguards for dogs' protection: shelter and exercise,' he responded. What a kerfuffle, then, about making owners responsible for a dog's shelter and exercise. 'We apply legislation to the safe management of cows,' Geoff battled, 'and we can deprive owners of cows.' Caucus resolved that the Bill would go in with the provision that the dog received adequate exercise.

Bill Birch had an amendment to the Quarries Act 1944, but Clause 32 still restricted the employment of women. Caucus directed him to discuss this with Ruth and me before introduction. It was remarkable what could be held up with a majority of one, and with two women in the mix.

In early May I spoke on the Maori Affairs Amendment Bill introduced by Labour MP for Eastern Māori, and former GP, Bruce Gregory. The Bill suggested some possibilities for the recognition of traditional Māori healing practices and medicines. I acknowledged 'the racial bias implicit in colonisation that presumed the superiority of Western medicine'. I knew the Bill would not progress, but I hoped 'its introduction will ensure that someone finds the wit and the wisdom to do what the Bill seeks'.[6]

Although the government MPs were reduced in number, there was no great pressure to speak to fill in time in the House. Mike Minogue and I joined five other MPs elected in 1975 and still on the backbenches. I had moved up the government speaking order, as that was determined in the backbenches by how long you had been there, and then alphabetically. So

I had speaking rights before 1978 or 1981 MPs, some of whom were skilled researchers and debaters, and active in caucus, but any one of the other six 1975 backbenchers had priority over me.

From our April opening of Parliament I was active asking questions in the House: on the Maternity Services Committee, for example, and the ILO Convention 156 on equal-opportunity treatment for men and women workers and workers with family responsibilities. Following the Penal Policy Review Committee's report, what consultation was there to be with prison officers? When was New Zealand going to ratify the UN Convention on the Elimination of All Forms of Discrimination Against Women (CEDAW)?

As I expected, the Social Credit MP Garry Knapp had written to the PM asking for Social Credit representation on the proposed nuclear disarmament sub-committee. The committee would then be enlarged, with one extra government and one Social Credit member, and become a full select committee in its own right. Excellent news. Minister of Defence David Thomson explained that 'if the Opposition had extra information they would realise the nonsense of nuclear-free zones when they are not verifiable'. There were two international nuclear-free zones already, and New Zealand had been party to the first, the Antarctic Treaty.[7] I thought the 'extra information' might have quite another effect, but it would all take time. I was prepared to be very patient.

The government introduced the notice of motion to establish the Disarmament and Arms Control Select Committee on 11 May. Richard Prebble moved an amendment to narrow its terms of reference. I opposed this:

> The amendment moved by the member for Auckland Central seeks to proscribe the work of the committee. Under the terms of reference, the committee has two opportunities to discuss a nuclear-free zone in the South Pacific. The first opportunity is through the background note 'disarmament and arms control' produced by the Ministry of Foreign Affairs, and the second opportunity is through the United Nations Disarmament Conference texts, which members expect to receive. It is very important that the four terms of reference in the motion are adhered to.

> As recently as 1978 Governments vowed unanimously at a special United Nations session to work for complete disarmament, but after that moving experience, the Presidents and the Prime Ministers went home to order new battle tanks and submarines. They say that nuclear tests have been limited, yet 49 took place in 1980 – 20 by the Soviet Union, 14 by the United States, 11 by France, three by Britain, and one by China.
>
> Consider Pakistan and the assistance offered to it by numerous signatories to the Non-Proliferation Treaty. The technical co-operation that will enable the Pakistanis to have nuclear capacity is given by Canada, France, the United Kingdom, China, Niger and West Germany. The training and financial assistance to make it possible for that country to have a nuclear capacity are given by the United Kingdom, the United States, West Germany, Canada, possibly by Saudi Arabia and by Libya.
>
> The terms of reference must go further than defence pacts and consider the range of nuclear accidents. The world has a history of arms accidents. Through the nuclear arms race, there is a grave risk to the globe, and there should be no proscription from any member as to the terms of reference of this most important select committee.[8]

Muldoon responded to the committee by inviting another ship visit; the USS *Truxtun*'s arrival coincided with the Labour Party conference. Rowling announced: 'Nuclear weapons will not be allowed in New Zealand ports under a Labour government and that's the message.' At the Foreign Ministers' ANZUS Council meeting in June, Australia and New Zealand advised they accepted the 'neither confirm nor deny' policy concerning nuclear weapons. The Disarmament and Arms Control Select Committee called for public submissions.

On 13 May, the Domestic Violence Bill, the country's first, was reported back after hearing submissions.[9] At the beginning of my speech, I paid tribute to Mary Batchelor for her persistence over many years in introducing private member's bills on the issue. Her strategy caused the government to act. I recognised the work of Rape Crisis and refuge centres on the front line. They had finally made the issue too big to allow Parliament to run away. I advised that they needed resource support but were very wary of being dependent and of having interference from government departments. They had to keep women and children safe, including from agencies.

May was very busy with all my select committees. In an interview that month I described the way select committee work changed.[10] I had had three years with Ann Hercus on the PEC, and that continued. Now Margaret Shields had joined the Health and Welfare Committee, and Helen Clark was on Foreign Affairs, and Disarmament and Arms Control. I explained that 'some of the most constructive work that's accomplished in this institution – constructive because of its non-partisan nature – happens in Select Committees. There's a very real sense in which women members can play to each other, and assist each other across the select committee table.' I enjoyed working with Margaret to find a solution to proposed changes to the Board of Health which would affect the representation of women and children. In both committees I shared with Helen, I said, 'I can't ever envisage a situation where we'd be playing political games with each other. Women MPs generally despise the men who do that.'

'But what are the boys' games?' the reporter asked.

'Aggressive political expediency, point scoring as an end in itself, seeking of personal promotion. I think for women here there's too much at stake to play those kinds of games,' I replied. 'Women MPs tend to have much better-constructed arguments, whether Opposition or Government members.'

Aussie Malcolm, now Minister of Health, advised he intended to 'review the work of Family Planning Clinics'. In the political environment, this was usually read as signalling an impending cut, although it could also signal the opposite: assistance in pushing back against Cabinet pressure. I received a letter from the guidance counsellor and teachers of Ngā Tupuwae College, Māngere:

> [We have] found the work of doctors in the Family Planning Service invaluable in helping many school pupils who would otherwise have struggled on in ignorance rather than seek help. Our large number of Polynesian pupils are very modest and shy and find male, European doctors unapproachable. A number of our girls over the seven years the

> school has been open have been greatly helped by the Family Planning Service, and personal tragedies have been avoided. Family Planning provides an essential service for us.

The mobilisation of so many people on the CS&A legislation and in the women's movement meant there were many more, and diverse, submissions coming in across issues; Aussie had felt certain that support for the clinics would be mobilised and would assist him to push back against pressure for cuts in his budget.

There was a growing demand for fundamental changes in the law governing rape, and women's organisations were mobilising. The Rape Crisis Group in Whāngārei nailed the key changes needed:

- Rape should be included as one form of sexual assault [rape had been limited to vaginal penetration by a penis].
- There should be automatic suppression of the complainant's name.
- The judge should be obliged to instruct the jury that a late complaint is not necessarily a false complaint.
- Rape in marriage needed to be recognised as a crime.
- The 'mistaken belief that the victim had consented' should not be allowed as a defence.
- Policewomen needed to be available and specially trained in the support and humane treatment of rape victims.
- Police doctors conducting medical examinations should be empathetic women.
- Accident compensation should be available to aid the physical and psychological recovery from the trauma.[11]

I was nagging Jim McLay about new legislation, but he was finding some recalcitrant resistance in Cabinet. There was, however, about to be Cabinet fallout in a big way in the following days.

Derek Quigley was one of the 1975 intake promoted to Cabinet in 1978, becoming Minister of Housing and Associate Minister of Finance. In 1981, after he unsuccessfully challenged Duncan MacIntyre for the deputy leadership, Muldoon removed him from the Associate Finance post. In the 1982 Cabinet, Derek was Minister of Works and Development, and of Tourism. He had been somewhat muzzled at first by Cabinet collective responsibility protocols. I think he hoped he could affect some change on the inside. This didn't happen. New members of the caucus and significant numbers of National supporters were agitating for change, and Derek echoed this in an address to the Young Nationals Conference in early June.

Derek told them the government did not have sufficient information for an informed debate on the viability of each energy project in the Think Big programme. He spoke about the levels of borrowing to fund energy projects 'which provide little additional employment and would earn or save only limited overseas funds. Then when it is all over, we will be no better off.' He wanted a government commitment to lower inflation, and less regulation and licensing. Private enterprise needed space, he argued, and there should be less government intervention in the economy.

There was a refreshing release of pressure and good feedback in Waipā when the media covered the speech. But not for long. Bill Birch complained to the Prime Minister that he felt his management of the Think Big projects had been publicly criticised by a ministerial colleague, and he demanded an apology. Muldoon gave Derek a choice: apologise and stick to Cabinet collective responsibility, or criticise from the backbenches. Derek chose the backbench.

At caucus on 10 June the PM was at his favourite game: playing the room, taking time, provoking or taunting or cajoling whenever most of caucus had something to say or another opinion. And the subject matter, indirect tax, was also masterful, given the vocal group who wanted tax at one rate across the board. Muldoon led off: 'If we put 10 per cent on foodstuffs we would collect $193 million, and with 10 per cent on clothing an extra $69 million can be collected. To get to the $600 million that we need to collect, you need to tax foodstuffs and clothing.'

Simon Upton suggested we should reduce the tax on other items – records, boats, computers and so on – when we imposed taxes in new areas. Muldoon responded that we would have to keep taxes on these items; we couldn't reduce those and put it on food. Michael Cox said the Tax Task Force reported that food was not a major extra cost if taxed. He contended: 'We could put five per cent tax on most food and clothes and services and we can give valid tax reductions.'

Venn Young, Minister of Social Welfare, was called next: 'We must protect the economics of the family unit. People on lower incomes with children will not get an increased social welfare benefit, so we must look at increasing family benefit.' Muldoon agreed: 'One way of compensating is increasing the family benefit, especially as it is paid to the mother.' Geoff Thompson liked that idea: switch to a wholesale tax and give tax relief to low-income people. Dale Jones scoffed: 'People on low incomes don't support us.' 'That's not right,' Muldoon reacted. 'Some do support us.' Tony Friedlander tried: 'A tax on advertising will put the media against us.'

'They won't be any worse to us than they are at the moment,' said the PM. He stretched and relaxed. 'A retail tax can't be done in time.' He smiled. You just knew he had something else going on.

Ian McLean asked about the PEC Forest Service review which had recommended changing the commercial sector of the Forest Service into a trading company. The PM intervened quickly: Cabinet had looked at it but held it over while considering the possibility of amalgamating Forestry and other departments. Muldoon would use any trick at all to stop any commercialisation of state trading functions.

The next agenda item was on charging in the health services from Minister Aussie Malcolm. He circulated a detailed paper showing how we could charge for services. He spoke to each item and then said: 'In the long term it changes our system of health and I'm against it.' Merv Wellington, Minister of Education, spoke rarely in caucus, but here he was: 'You don't do it with a majority of one. You don't have the "user pay" principle in health.' Former Minister George Gair was against all the suggestions, except perhaps a type of charge for some pharmaceuticals. Then Venn Young (all these ministers!) said he was 'initially attracted to these charges but I have now changed my mind'. Geoff Thompson was exasperated: 'We must find savings for tax relief.'

John Falloon was Associate Finance Minister. Inland Revenue officials had told him there was massive tax avoidance by wealthy investors writing off their incomes by making six-figure investments in tax shelters in rural land. The investments also returned tax-free capital gains. I could see it happening in horticultural investment in Waipā, and colleagues described its effect in kiwifruit developments. There were also huge tax shelters in film production. Many of these 'investors' were urban National Party supporters. Of course, government policies for the last six years had been to encourage investment, but the tax loopholes made Muldoon furious. The consequence, the Income Tax Amendment Act, was imposed retrospectively and operated as a capital gains tax. No one would be permitted to offset more than $10,000 per annum of investment and development expenditure. This decision enlarged the gaping chasm of disagreement in the caucus, and infuriated Party supporters across the country. The tax deductibility of forestry establishment and maintenance expenditure available to companies would cease. The tax treatment of leasing would be tightened to close off this avenue for tax avoidance. There would be new legislation to prevent abuse of charitable companies in tax evasion and avoidance.

On 22 June Muldoon announced that inflation was our number one enemy, and that a wage and price freeze for 12 months would begin at midnight. This was the first item on the caucus agenda on 24 June. The PM explained:

> The Wage/Price Freeze Regulations arose from the FOL Conference decisions to toss out the wage–tax trade-off.[12] We have a commitment to move on taxation. The Budget will have some increase in indirect tax and reasonable tax reductions from 1 October. Unemployment is at 9 percent. Inflation remains too high. Most of the budget expenditure work is now completed, but what we have in the budget is not enough to deal with inflation. Every message I have received has been in favour of a wage/price freeze. You can always have a General Wage Order while a wage/price freeze is on. Caucus knew nothing of it and nor did Cabinet until Monday. The Cabinet Economic Committee had done all the work on it over the last four weeks.

I noted quietly that this period included the Quigley speech and time-wasting caucus taxation discussions.

Ian McLean accepted that action was necessary but foresaw problems: 'Some businesses won't be able to put up prices. It will just delay inflation for 12 months. Our voters will say "if we wanted socialism, we would have voted Labour."' He urged the PM to take the other ancillary measures that were necessary and review the situation in three months. 'There is little evidence these freezes work unless other measures are taken,' Ian continued. 'We need to increase state charges to make the state sector efficient, for example with the Post Office and Railways. The private sector should be able to compete where there is a monopoly.' Michael Cox added that as an accountant he knew many ways around the previous wage/price freezes, and he was sure there would be the same available this time. Dale Jones wanted to know about rates increases, and was told that local bodies had the power to reassess their rates.

Muldoon moved to indirect tax: 'We are working through some of the items.' He listed agricultural machinery, steel, iron, road vehicles. 'What about a sales tax on power?' he asked. We could get $50 million. Ian McLean asked if power was too cheap at the moment. Bill Birch said he didn't want to destroy relativity between forms of energy. Michael Cox argued that this was the time to make these major structural changes.

With a majority of one, Muldoon enjoyed all this. He could say caucus was consulted; they couldn't agree; he had to make the bold decisions. He read the list of possible targets for indirect tax to the accompaniment of yeahs and noes: chicken and fish, footwear and clothing, cut flowers, wreaths, bouquets, trees. Derek Quigley interrupted: 'It is stupid to go through this exercise. We will lose credibility if we make all these artificial distinctions. It may be better to cut back on government expenditure than have more taxes like pottery and boat taxes.' Muldoon ignored him and continued: '... books, periodicals, advertising.'

Finally, we reached the agenda item, in Ruth's name, on the Quigley resignation. She spoke about the backlash from Party supporters and the loss of Derek's input from Cabinet. 'The New Zealand electorate want change in the direction of the leadership,' she said. Muldoon responded that the majority of Party contacts he had heard from 'support me'. Geoff Thompson reported that the Young Nationals were volatile. Norman Jones said Quigley's absence was a blow to the South Island: 'We feel discriminated against.'[13] Ben Couch spoke up: 'The feeling in the Party is for Derek.' Peter Wilkinson added that the only people smiling were the press and the Opposition. These were strong interventions from some staunch Muldoon supporters.

The Canterbury–Westland Divisional Executive of the National Party had met on 14 June. They had passed a resolution for caucus: 'The Division expresses its deep concern at the damage done to the National Party's image as a party supporting free speech and free enterprise caused by the Prime Minister's call for the resignation of Hon D.F. Quigley. The Division reaffirms its support for Mr. Quigley.' This had been sent to every National MP, and the request that it be read to caucus was followed. The matter went no further for now, but we would all hear a lot more on this from disgruntled Party supporters. In Waipā, the rural Monavale branch brought a remit to the Electorate Executive, deploring the present centralistic style of political leadership and urging the National Party caucus to make a change. I received similar correspondence from other electorates. But it would all be lost now under the wage/price freeze and the forthcoming Budget.

Media were still conducting 'in-depth' interviews with me. Jane Clifton wanted to know why I was knitting in the House.[14] I had been doing it for years. 'Why not? I can hear what's going on. Knitting does not interfere with my aural powers,' I said. 'It is a pity Parliament does not adopt a more humane attitude towards MPs and their lives. I don't really care whether [a Labour MP] and I want to pair each other off so that we can go to a chamber music concert. And I don't see that it matters if two others pair off and go to the races. That's the real world. It's not the real world in here,' I said, waving in the direction of the House. 'Other people aren't sitting in this suffocating circus carrying on the way we do.'

Jane asked about the Springbok tour vote in 1981. I said:

> I just ran out of fight. I was so tired. You can fight something to the starting block, but if you can't run from there, it's no good ... What happens in the weeks after? When your colleagues won't talk to you, and you get all the hate mail? When you do it, you've got to have the energy to go the distance.
>
> I'm a very hard taskmaster. I ride myself hard. I've always had this idea that I consider my options daily. And you're foolish if you don't. Every Government member should be saying every morning: 'If today is the day that I have to put my principles on the line, then what will I do?' And if they are not asking themselves that question, then where are their principles?

Early in the year, I had been nominated by caucus to join Labour MP Bob Tizard on trips to Kiribati and Solomon Islands for the regional Commonwealth Parliamentary Association. We were to work with MPs in both countries on how their parliaments could run.

En route to Kiribati we had to spend a night on Nauru, where a population of 8,000 lived on 2,100 hectares of bird droppings that were mined for phosphate. Reserves were forecast to be depleted within three years. If you owned an acre of the multinational phosphate swamp, you were paid AU$25,000 every quarter. The Nauru government took three-quarters for investment, and the returns on this ran the budget, so there were no taxes. Everything including water was imported. Expensive Range Rover vehicles fell to pieces within three years from the combined effects of the sea salt and phosphate. It took 20 minutes to drive around the island. It was a strange place and situation. Kiribati had gained independence for its 33 islands and an estimated population of 56,000 on 12 July 1979. We would be working with the first parliament after national elections. In one of the parliamentary Order Papers of the previous week was a notice of motion urging the President to have discussions with the Chief Justice to ensure a return to the traditional rights of inheritance that meant sons were entitled to more than daughters were.

We landed on a narrow strip on Tarawa, and the single road took us to the accommodation past a line-up of churches: Catholic, Seventh Day Adventist, Latter Day Saints, Congregationalists, Baha'i and Pentecostal.

The prohibition on overseas buyers acquiring land did not apply to churches. The Catholic Church was dominant, and Kiribati had some of the highest population density and birth rates on the planet. A new woman GP had arrived on the island. She told me she had complained about the variety and type of the only two brands of contraception available, and sought to order more and different pills. The Director-General of Health, a man, would not allow any alternative contraceptives into the country. As well, as in many Pacific islands, the availability of oral contraception was not reliable, with extreme weather events, freight costs and delayed shipments hindering supply.

I saw abject poverty and some malnutrition. I walked around the Agricultural Research Station. There had been rain off and on in the past week, but the tomatoes looked sad, and the silverbeet and Chinese cabbage wilted in the heat. There was so little soil cover that in a heavy storm the entire garden could float away. Clean water was a very scarce commodity. The introduction of wage labour, mostly of men on Pacific fishing vessels, meant the women left behind bought imported food to replace the fresh fish previously caught by these men. This affected nutrition. Teachers showed me by pointing to the lines of children waiting to go into class. Rickets and stunted growth were evident in the younger children, and this was consistent with the changes in diet and male wage labour. Schooling after the age of 12 was extremely rare. The week before our arrival, 60 pupils at the local primary school had been expelled because of non-payment of fees by parents.

We made our visit to Solomon Islands in September. It was quite different in topography – lush forests were the backdrop for intensive subsistence agriculture, mostly undertaken by women. Fish was plentiful; barter was the extensive means of exchange. A number of the men elected to Parliament had been part of a transitional appointed Legislative Council and had participated in the independence negotiations, so were familiar with parliamentary practices. A highlight for me was to catch up with two women with whom I had gone to school in Hamilton. They had been the last two to win scholarships before secondary schooling opened for girls in Solomon Islands. I had sent a message to our High Commission, and by word of mouth our diplomats had tracked them down and organised for them to be in Honiara for the week I was there.

Bob and I used Parliamentary Standing Orders as the key document when talking to local politicians. The approach was to say, let us tell you everything we know about questions to ministers, for example – who uses them, how they can be used, how different Parliaments deal with them – and you can make up your minds what would be appropriate. Relations with the constituency covered a wide spectrum of queries. How do you teach the constituents to use the system? What is the best way of staying in touch with constituents? How do you use the radio or other forms of communication so that people know what you are trying to do for them? Which parliamentary procedure is best used when making a particular point on behalf of the electorate? How do you present problems to ministers? How do you campaign? How do you cope when electors ask you for money? How do you solve the conflict-of-conscience situation, when you want one thing, and constituents want another? We answered queries on relationships between ministers and heads of government departments, salaries and salary-fixing procedures for MPs and the public service, and pressures in the domestic lives of MPs.

These two visits were significant learning curves. Apart from a tourist holiday on a Fiji island, I had not visited our Pacific neighbouring countries, and the vast difference between Nauru, Kiribati and Solomon Islands also taught me not to homogenise and generalise about a whole region.

Back in New Zealand, the Labour Whips had made a case to the Members' Services Select Committee about the costs for some MPs of hiring their own electorate support or research staff. My accountant had corresponded with the Clerk of the House on this, and been told 'the costs incurred by a member for these purposes are not tax deductible because it is not a condition of employment of a Member of Parliament that he/she must supply his own additional staff'. The options which could be considered were: to provide an allowance for the purpose; to provide the staff at departmental expense; and to amend the Income

Tax Act to make such payments tax deductible. I was on the committee, and since there was no secretariat to help, I wrote to all MPs asking who employed assistance. Fifteen Labour and seven National MPs independently employed staff. Traditionally, wives of MPs did the electorate work. Muldoon was not interested in the issue, as my figures showed a response would assist Labour more than National.

Muldoon's constant carping at and blame of the media began to get some traction with my electoral supporters. The gender mix in the press gallery hadn't improved much: there were 29 men and six women. But I invited a group of the Wellington-based journalists to Waipā for a weekend. We visited Waikeria Prison, an export abattoir, farms and beaches.[15] There were dinners and morning teas with constituents, and the locals enjoyed being able to eyeball the people who wrote the columns they read. I thought it did the journalists good to hear some different voices.

On 5 August the Prime Minister welcomed new National Party president Sue Wood to caucus. She had been coping with a large number of resolutions about Quigley, leadership and economic direction. She told us she had a responsibility to unify the Party organisation and needed breathing space to do this. A focus would be the relationship between the Party and caucus. She saw the separation as one of our strengths, but it was important that Party members felt part of the team. Finances and membership were of concern, and we needed a peaceful period to allow the present tensions to ease. It was also important that caucus members on the Dominion Executive and the Party's Dominion Council reported back objectively to caucus.

After Sue left, John Falloon complained about statements Mike Minogue had made about increasing regulation, because 'we all have to work harder to justify Government decisions because of a member's criticism'. Muldoon replied that as far as caucus was concerned, any member could say anything anywhere: 'They can vote against all except a vote of confidence.'

Ruth had an item on the agenda. She wanted to introduce a Private Member's Bill to hold a referendum on extending the term of Parliament to four years. Michael Cox supported her: 'Wouldn't we get better economic management with a four-year term?' The PM wasn't going to invite discussion on this. He had a long monologue on the reasons. These were what he called constitutional issues: New Zealand's extra-fast legislative process, the unicameral system with tight party discipline. 'In this situation, the only sanction is the short three-year term.' Then there was political perception. This was extra sensitive. 'We would likely lose the vote and take a hit. If we won, the public would see it as a cunning move for National to extend its term. They would expect difficult decisions being taken after an election. This is not good for politics.' He described Michael's position that better economic management might come from a longer term as 'antique nonsense. We are electioneering all the time in terms of economic management. I am very much against the Bill.'

On 6 August the Children and Young Persons Amendment Bill reported back to the House from the Health and Welfare Select Committee. I spoke about how MPs had felt when considering this Bill because of conflicts between principles and reality. I had talked with young women who had not wanted to be returned home after being in the care of the state. This Bill extended the power of authorities even though we had been assured that social workers respected the children's wishes. Frequently it didn't work like that. There were no simple solutions to some cases. The possibility of abuse in either state care or the family was never discussed.

We had a major issue with young people being held in custody over a weekend and whether they were advised of their rights of access to a solicitor. I hoped that social workers 'will be instructed to obtain legal assistance when it could assist the child or young person'. I spoke of problems around the availability of secure facilities in some regions. We had also been concerned by stories we'd heard of the trauma for children when police exercised a warrant in criminal searches. I queried, too, the Bill's use and definition of the word 'unruly'. 'Part of the definition could easily apply to young people making a natural response to being picked up by authorities, rather than some kind of "permanent unruliness",' I said.[16]

In August the High Court ruled against the Clyde High Dam proceeding without a water right. To keep the project running and to maintain the workforce, the government would have to change the law retrospectively. Mike Minogue had signalled early he would not support this. I watched Ruth and Simon agonise through this issue. While Muldoon had brought the Social Credit MPs on board to cover Mike crossing the floor, the success of the legislation depended on the votes of Ruth and Simon. It was a bitter time for them. I knew exactly how it felt. They voted with the government.

I went to see Ruth to commiserate. 'It is far worse than you described, Marilyn,' she said. I replied that I'd thought if I told her 'the truth about it, you wouldn't believe me. You would think the issue was me.'

This was turning into quite a frantic year of unexpected surprises. On 19 July, the Privy Council in London granted New Zealand citizenship to all Western Samoans born since 1924.[17] The court held that all Western Samoans born between 1924 and 1948 were British subjects, and in 1949 they had become New Zealand citizens. This could mean that about 120,000 of 150,000 Samoans had a right to New Zealand citizenship.

Ten days later the judgment was available. The Privy Council decision demonstrated that New Zealand law did not comply with basic principles and policies of international law and practice. Talks then began between the prime ministers of New Zealand and Samoa. Any resolution would mean an international treaty. And this agreed that all Samoans presently in New Zealand, with or without a current visa, would have the right to citizenship, including those who had overstayed their visas. It also quashed earlier overstaying convictions. Muldoon brought the treaty proposal agreed with the Samoan government to caucus. Minister of Immigration Aussie Malcolm advised there were 6,500 Samoans in New Zealand who weren't permanent residents, and with partners and children who could now join them the total could reach 18,000. There was a lot of caucus grumbling about this. But the legislation was introduced and sent to the Foreign Affairs Select Committee.

The committee was put under pressure to move the Bill quickly, and reported back on 8 September. We had heard 60 submissions.

Richard Prebble had constantly asked submitters whether what people wanted was citizenship or the right to come to New Zealand. Labour tried to send the Bill back for more submissions. I opposed this: more submissions wouldn't change the relevant international law and practice that governed the legislation. The key issues were the concept of a state having responsibility for a defined territory and a defined population. At the time of the independence of Samoa, neither the New Zealand nor the Western Samoan government believed there had been a 'citizenship merger'.[18]

The pressure to move the legislation through all stages stayed on. Any Samoan in New Zealand before the law passed could be a New Zealand citizen. The Act came into force on 15 September, so there was no time for hundreds to fly in to beat the deadline for citizenship.

The economic indicators up to August 1982 were ugly. The Food Price Index had increased by 13.7 per cent in the July year. Wages increased by 17.4 per cent (male 17.2 per cent, female 18.4 per cent) in the year-to-May-1982 employment survey. Registered unemployed on 30 July numbered 48,487, including 3,309 school leavers. Import prices increased 13.9 per cent between the March quarters of 1981 and 1982. Export prices for the same period increased 10 per cent. The average cost of a barrel of oil in 1982 was NZ$64.70 compared with an average of $49.84 for 1981. The 1982 Budget forecast a fiscal deficit of $1,879 million. The current account deficit was $1,480.6 million, compared with $724.5 million a year earlier.

I spoke in the Budget debate in early August. I said the New Zealand tax system had allowed widespread avoidance, especially in agricultural and horticultural land: 'As avoidance increases, taxes on wage earners go up.' There was no backlash in Waipā on the tax changes in the Budget. I said there had been 'two key issues in Waipa electorate meetings during the 1981 campaign: the need for personal income tax deductions, and a plea from farmers for a crackdown on tax evasion. The Budget deals with both of these.'[19] I then spent considerable time critiquing Social Credit's support for income splitting. With Social Credit polling second in Waipā, this was appropriate. This policy proposed that a single-income two-parent family could split the income between the two and attract a lower tax outcome. Kerrin Vautier, the only woman on the Tax Task Force, had written a dissenting opinion on this. It seemed to me to be a fundamental breach of human rights on the grounds of marital and family status, as single-parent households could not qualify.[20]

I advised caucus on 26 August that the Estimates showed that Internal Affairs had given money to the NZRFU. This would come up in the Estimates debate, and I would not support it. Warren Cooper thought 'most of us would support the grant to schoolboy rugby as long as it was tied to NZ and not announced until after Commonwealth Games'. Muldoon instructed Minister of Internal Affairs Allan Highet to give the rugby union the money through the Lottery funds. Highet protested. Muldoon responded: 'Mr Highet: caucus has instructed you to do this.' He was to see the amount was removed from the Estimates. This would remove the grant from public parliamentary scrutiny.

A year after the Springbok tour, New Zealand was still watched keenly with respect to its commitment to the Gleneagles Agreement. The Commonwealth Games were due in Brisbane in September 1982. Delegates called for an extraordinary meeting of the Commonwealth Games Federation. The New Zealand delegates were ostracised; Tanzania and Nigeria asked for a vote to expel New Zealand. We were extraordinarily lucky that the New Zealand delegate present was Roy Dutton, deputy chair of the New Zealand Games Federation. Dutton did not support apartheid sporting contacts and would have found the animosity disturbing. He understood that to safeguard the Brisbane Commonwealth Games, Australia would support the motion to expel us. New Zealander Chris Laidlaw, working at the Commonwealth Secretariat in London, quickly drafted a statement for Dutton to read 'word for word'.[21] The motion condemned apartheid and recommitted New Zealand to the Gleneagles Agreement. The statement meant the resolution did not go ahead, and full attendance in Brisbane was agreed.

I kept up a steady run of questions in the House on issues important to me. Israel had invaded southern Lebanon on 6 June, and what would be three years of war began. I had not forgiven or forgotten the direction we had received in Copenhagen to abstain from the final document because of the mention of Zionism. I lodged a series of questions on the issue through August. New Zealand, I learned, had made two $50,000 grants for the relief of Palestinian refugees. New Zealand did not support or accept Israel's actions in Lebanon. New Zealand's peacekeepers in the UN Sinai force would remain in position. On 16 December 1982 the UN General Assembly would condemn the three-day September massacres at the Shatila and Sabra camps, with rapes and dismemberment, and declare these an act of genocide. New Zealand joined 22 other nations, 17 of which were white and Western, in abstaining on the resolution.

Closer to home, I learned that public buildings had to comply with the Disabled Persons Community Welfare Act 1975, but commercial building permits were granted to developers without provision of disabled access.[22] The government was to fund three child abuse projects permanently.[23] There were 25 Te Kōhanga Reo centres for 387 children.[24] Fifteen more were to begin soon.[25] New Zealand was one of the first countries in the world to offer native trees for the John Lennon memorial, 'Strawberry Fields', in Central Park, New York City.[26] In mid-September I supported making it a condition of a benefit payment that the applicant had an account with the Post Office or a bank so that they could be directly credited with their payments. I had witnessed and heard about the threatening stand-over tactics used by some just after an individual had cashed their benefit cheque. I also supported minor changes in the superannuation scheme, but more would need to be done given expected costs over the next 20 to 30 years. Payment of two fortnightly instalments (as opposed to payments over a period of 13 weeks) would be made after the death of a married superannuitant, with a means-tested lump sum for the surviving partner, a provision previously restricted to women.

Battling the boys' system was exhausting. The government's Advisory Committee on Women's Affairs (ACWA) did not receive a sitting fee and allowance comparable with those for other statutory bodies. The chair, Colleen Dewe, received an honorarium.[27] ACWA was definitely working hard. They made an excellent submission on the Accident Compensation

Amendment Bill, raising key issues. The definition of spouse had to change 'to ensure that the Commission does exercise its discretion to cover de facto spouses who are dependent, fully or partially'. They argued that the failure to compensate for non-economic loss might severally disadvantage women, especially those who didn't qualify for earnings-related compensation. For example, compensation for pain and mental suffering and loss of enjoyment of life should be available to victims of rape or sexual assault: 'It would be unjust for a rape victim to have to sustain physical injury before compensation is payable. Proof of physical injury is not required to secure a conviction for rape.' Another example was where, as a result of medical misadventure, a woman became unable to bear a child. ACWA also regretted the lost opportunity to improve compensation to non-earners: 'It is not sufficient that the earning spouse is compensated if he must employ someone to replace her services. There is also the question of compensation for loss of future earnings, for those who are temporary non-earners because they have the care and responsibility of dependants, e.g. young children.'

On 2 September Aussie Malcolm asked caucus for a decision on new venereal disease regulations. The options were: Draft A: the doctor may notify the parent, guardian, or other person in charge of the child if in his opinion it is desirable to do so in the interest of the health or wellbeing of the child; or Draft B: the doctor shall notify the parent, guardian, or another person in charge of the child, unless, in his opinion, it is undesirable to do so in the interest of the health or wellbeing of the child, or in the wider interests of public health.

Norman Jones said as a parent he would expect the doctor to tell him. Michael Cox, Ian McLean, Jim McLay and I all thought the top priority was to get children to seek treatment, and supported Draft A. Derek Quigley thought it should be left to the doctors. Caucus voted for Draft B.

There were hundreds of active feminist organisations throughout the country, and I continued to receive their remits and resolutions. They were extensive. The New Zealand Women's Health Network, for example, sent their list from their final session on 19 September. These included asking for extensive support to the home-birth movement; supporting the establishment of health centres for Māori and Pacific Island people throughout the country; and a demand that the Māori language be taught in all schools. They opposed the dumping of nuclear waste and the testing of nuclear weapons in the South Pacific and elsewhere, and supported the independence struggles of the indigenous peoples of the South Pacific. The list triggered a memory of Muldoon introducing me to HRH Princess Anne at a parliamentary reception. 'This is Marilyn Waring, and she's interested in women's issues,' he said. She looked down at him and said royally: 'Really, Prime Minister, all issues are women's issues.'

On 26 October the National Council of Women's list was sent to all parliamentarians. As an umbrella 'representative' group with more than 160 affiliate organisations, they eschewed the label 'feminist', but they did pretty well. The policy changes they sought included the provision of an adult guardian appointed for each child 'in care', and the labelling of all alcohol so the public was advised of its health hazards. They opposed the income-splitting tax proposal. They sought curricula changes in schools to teach Māori language and culture, and the culture of minority and migrant groups. NCW called on the government to fully implement professional counselling for all women considering an abortion, to increase the funding for registered childcare centres, and to lower the lead content in petrol. They wanted an emergency benefit to be available for children under 16 who had no other means of support, and called for an urgent, nationwide programme of immunisation that was compulsory for all children unless exempted by their doctor.

Oh well, I used to think, that little list should keep me busy for a while. Meanwhile, Ruth had her sleeves rolled up in the Statutes Revision Select Committee after all submissions had been heard on the Domestic Protection Bill. The committee was beginning deliberations. Ruth brought issues to caucus on 26 August. If, she asked, we give an occupation order to a spouse, should we also give possession of chattels? Dale Jones argued it had never been our policy to extend to chattels, and there was only one submission on it. He said it was a back-door way of extending the matrimonial property to de facto relationships. Mike

Minogue thought there were some practical problems. Did it include motor cars? Ruth replied that the term 'chattels' could be defined to exclude this. Muldoon concluded that 'caucus did not support Ruth Richardson, but it was confusing, so we would go back to the caucus committee'.

On 28 October she tried again. Should de facto partners have home and protection orders? Jim McLay said the courts could make an order giving use of household effects for the time of an occupation order. Ian McLean argued that we intended to protect women with children, so that meant de factos, but the order should be temporary. 'Why not confine it to women with children and make it temporary?' the PM asked. Ruth was ready: 'Because under the Matrimonial Property Act a person without children can get an order.'

Ruth and I worked together on a list of women nominees for the Human Rights Commission. None was successful. We made some progress advocating for some recreational facilities at Christchurch Women's Prison – there were none. Other issues kept arising, whatever the context. The legislation governing the Department of Health stated that the Director-General of Health must be a medical practitioner. The outcome of this was it was unlikely a woman could get the job. Margaret Bazley was Chief Nurse in the department, in charge of the largest national workforce, and I couldn't see why she shouldn't be considered for such a position. In the Health Estimates I asked for this to change 'so another medical professional could be appointed, e.g., a nurse'. I congratulated the Family Planning Association in Auckland for their work on menopause. I asked if adult women who lost their hair through chemotherapy could be granted a subsidy for more than one wig. I also wanted New Zealand-trained GPs to be taught more about Māori health, especially Māori women's health.[28]

The electorate was busy all year, but from June onwards I was besieged with requests for exemptions from the price freeze from local councils and trucking companies, for example. I was battling rural lending institutions where, when farms were owned in partnerships, replies regarding loan applications only ever dealt with the male partner's experience. Gwyneth Wright's research on rural women was proving extremely useful. People were not getting war disability reviews, and the income threshold for receiving benefits had not been changed for many years. I worked to get home help for those with a disability.

Every year at the end of June there were issues with primary schools somewhere in the electorate. The new contract year for sharemilkers was 30 June, and this family mobility could affect rolls, staffing ratios, teacher housing and maintenance, and school-bus transport budgets, all determined in February. Every year I had the same battles. There had also been an outbreak of brucellosis, and there were issues of compensation for herds destroyed and movement quarantines. There were always immigration cases, too. Many of them were for family reunification, and most were denied. I was a target for gay couples with immigration requests, and Aussie Malcolm was a sympathetic Minister on some of these.

I felt overwhelmed by demands at times, so I was grateful for thanks. On 20 December Robert Rasmussen wrote from Pirongia: 'We are all grateful for the support and concern you have shown us. I hope you will believe my sincerity in the observation that while there is always plenty of debate around this part of the Waikato as to who should govern or lead the parties, there is never any doubt expressed as to who should be representing the Waipa electorate.'

Hundreds of New Zealanders had responded to the call for submissions to the Disarmament and Arms Control Committee. I sent more of my information requests to the General Assembly Library to avoid the Party unit being apprised of what I was looking at. Among the horror stories I recorded for the year was a US recommendation for the manufacture of nerve-gas munitions. New Zealand refused to declare its opposition because the Geneva Protocol of 1925 prohibited their use, but not their development or production.

Parliament restricted the introduction of private members' bills to only one on a particular issue per session. I expected someone would try again on a Nuclear Free Bill in 1983, and we would have a select committee to refer it to. There was an interminable heaviness about being part of this government, but this, at least, was one issue that was progressing. Every day I had to anchor any anticipation of getting out of the institution and deal with the day. Perceptive Michael Young from Hamilton wrote: 'Forgive me for saying this, but you are not the entity you once were.'

Well, of course not, that would be obvious, I thought, but I wonder who you think I was?

1983

Summer helped alleviate my wretched despondency and the knowledge I had to last another two years. Being warm, bodysurfing, playing tennis, gardening all helped. I had dreams about a little country farm I might have. I took an inordinate interest in tree crops such as olives or macadamia nuts. I looked at the leucadendron and blueberry markets. I read about beehives. There would be hens. Beautiful Black Orpingtons would look great. There'd also be an orchard and a big garden. I spent time visiting the Lands and Survey goat farm at Waitangi. I liked the goats. They were sensual and wickedly clever. I read all the agricultural magazines that were sent to MPs with a new fervour. I found books aimed at women living rurally. My secret fantasy farm sustained me.

The round of Waipā meetings began in early February. The logistics of fitting them all in on Monday or Friday nights, with three full days of select committee sittings in Wellington every week, were tiring. Branch members in Puahue, Te Kawa, Oparau, Monavale, Kihikihi, Pāterangi, Pirongia, Wharepūhunga, Kāwhia, Mangakino, Ōhaupō, Arohena, Cambridge, Ōtorohanga and Te Awamutu, three Women's Sections and the Young Nationals were all grumpy and fed up with Muldoon. They expected me to 'take the message to caucus'. They had no idea of the weekly cost of conveying their sentiments. Electorate surgery sessions were full, reflecting the host of economic pressures from the wage/price freeze. I was fortunate that the Waipā Council's PEP scheme soaked up so many unemployed, or it would have been much worse.

The government rules did not make it easy for Waipā Council to manage the PEP scheme. The council's office in Te Awamutu soaked up the additional management and supervision requirements. They did it because they were totally committed to playing their part. During

February and March eight schemes would be finishing and restarting, meaning 350 terminations and the same number of engagements. These involved interviews at the Labour Department for new employees, final pay for ex-employees, Social Welfare forms for ex-employees, tax certificates for all employees, special returns to the Labour Department for all employees, and training of new employees. Of the workers taken on, 75 to 80 per cent returned in subsequent schemes or were employed by other authorities. The PEP employees knew they had only six months' work, and towards the end of this period work output reduced and discipline was difficult. The constant round of terminations and re-employment made the workers feel like second-rate citizens. There just weren't permanent jobs available. To make it worse, the government increased the stand-down period for PEP employees going on to a benefit from four to eight weeks.

This was all too much trouble for some local authorities, but Waipā Council just kept at it. They thought they had a role in employment creation and that one per cent of rates was a reasonable investment in this. Most of the councillors belonged to the National Party and several chaired Party branches. They had a collective will to make a difference.

A significant moment on 28 March arrived with little fanfare. The Closer Economic Relations (CER) comprehensive bilateral trade agreement between New Zealand and Australia was signed. Prime Ministers Muldoon and Fraser had agreed in 1980 to work on the new agreement, which meant free trade in goods and nearly all services by 1990. Much of the work was done by Brian Talboys and then Hugh Templeton, because Muldoon's antipathy for Malcolm Fraser meant he had to be kept out of the way of the initiative as much as possible.

At the end of March, too, Jane Wilson left parliamentary employment and Mary McGuiness became my assistant. Backbench MPs' staff were selected and appointed by the Whips' Office. Our first conversation was simple: 'Mary, before we get down to work, could you please tell me honestly where you stand on the issue of abortion?' If she had an anti-abortion stance, I would have to keep some correspondence and information flows out of her hands. 'It's a woman's choice,' she said. I could relax on that score.

Parliament began again on 7 April. I gave my Address in Reply speech on 19 April.[1] The first job-sharing appointments had been made at universities. Some employers were introducing 'glide time': as long as they worked their hours, employees could arrive between seven and nine and leave between three and five. I thought there was probably a range of other possibilities, so that more people were employed and plant and machinery was used more efficiently. I told the House: 'We hear the same old rhetoric every day from the majority culture, the comfortable, white, middle-aged males; that cultural cohesion that heads the Federation of Labour, political parties, their friends in the chambers of commerce, economists, bankers, editors, and heads of government departments. The 40-hour week was needed in the 1890s but it was an instrument of the 1890s.' Young people were talking about job sharing, shorter working days, and shorter working weeks, shorter working years and flexible working hours.[2]

A change in our approach to unemployment was needed, including looking at cultural initiatives such as Kōkiri Centres promoting and advocating work-skills development for young people, or cooperatives which could tender for agricultural work if farmers paid horticultural workers award wages instead of hiring casual labour. I suggested Rural Bank loans should be linked to employment creation rather than capital gains.

Then I spoke again about Waipā's PEP scheme, which now employed 600, the largest number of workers of any local authority, on 14 diverse schemes. In a new environmental and training initiative the council bought 40,000 trees at five cents each and had a nursery, rather than paying $5 each for larger trees. Residents reported nuisance trees (for example, on blind corners) to be cut down and chopped for firewood for poorer households. I said there was too much talk from other agencies about the need to change schemes – 'the need is to make use of existing ones. [Council] Clerks and engineers should have development of PEP schemes as part of their annual assessments. Local authorities should employ a lot more people.'

In late April I told a journalist that it was noticeable that constituents were coming to my surgery sessions with documentation on issues for immediate family members who lived elsewhere. I had always seen and responded to women from outside Waipā, but this new phenomenon was increasing. I also told her that I would 'not leave now, because Governments should fall at the will of the people, not at the will of an individual'.[3]

The leaving comment was not true. I had applied for a senior position in a New Zealand company. A management consultant had conducted the interview as well as a psychological or personality test. This had been amusing. I was left alone with a good length of time to complete it. I had spent the last seven years being sorely tested. I didn't need any time to think about what my responses would be in the hypotheticals: I felt as if I had been living them. I knocked on his door to say I was finished. Didn't I want longer to go over my responses? No, I didn't. So off he went to convert me into a radar diagram. When he returned he was bothered. My profile was nicely balanced except for one sector. 'This is very puzzling,' he said. 'It suggests that you don't have any personal ambition.' I laughed. 'I thought that was perfectly obvious,' I told him. 'I am ambitious for ideas, and I can be very ambitious for this company. I just don't want to be the Chief Executive.' I made it to the shortlist of two, and was advised on 10 May I had not been successful. 'The Board thought you were too hot to handle,' the consultant said. So it would have to be back to farm dreaming to get me through.

I was accepting many fewer speaking invitations, but Waipā still had Rotary, BPW, Plunket and Federated Farmers meetings I needed to go to. In May I was able to send a telegram to Sonja Davies, elected as vice-president of the Federation of Labour Executive. The Apostolic Church in Invercargill wanted my photo for their prayer board. I went to a two-day women's self-defence course in Cambridge led by Sue Lytollis, who had been supported for this nationwide initiative by Allan Highet, Minister of Internal Affairs. I nominated members of Split Enz for a New Year's honour: both Neil and Tim Finn had been born in Waipā and their parents still lived there. The YWCA, led by Elizabeth Sewell, held a national conference on sexual violence against women and children, and I attended that too.

Persecution of women on the DPB was still going on. I was battling for a constituent whose benefit was stopped after she was accused of having a de facto relationship with the father of her two children. There was certainly no de facto relationship and she was not receiving maintenance. Once this was clarified with the department, her benefit was reinstated. Then the department advised her she should not see this man at all. I wrote to Social Welfare Minister Venn Young that I found it 'totally unreasonable that her children should be denied access to their father. I recognize that there are difficulties of administration in this area of the Domestic Purposes Benefit, but to compel a mother to keep her children from their father is really taking paranoia too far.'

I was also battling the Department of Social Welfare's proposal to reduce the maximum rate of the childcare subsidy for individual families from $18 to $15.50 a week. In the end, they 're-examined the proposals and decided to retain the $18 a week rate for low income families'.

Members of the Select Committee on Disarmament and Arms Control were overwhelmed with material supplied to us by the embassy of the USSR. The USA invited the committee to their embassy for a video link-up with Eugene Rostow, director of the US Arms Control and Disarmament Agency. On another evening the government members of the committee were invited to a dinner at the US ambassador's residence to meet a State Department official. There I took the line that my caucus was being told we had to remain in ANZUS because of our trade interests but frankly I couldn't see that we had ever been advantaged because of this. Some staff at our Ministry of Foreign Affairs pushed the same line. Much to the ambassador's embarrassment, the State Department official said it was the first time he had heard this argument.

On the select committee I asked that we seek written material from each of the nuclear powers that had an embassy in Wellington. At least we should have copies of their addresses to the United Nations Session on Disarmament. And while we couldn't summon another nation to our select committee, we could ask the Australians if they would like to talk to us. The new Labor government in Australia had a long policy commitment on disarmament and arms control in its election manifesto.

The Waipā National Party Executive were getting ready to take their remits to the Waikato divisional meeting of the Party. They were very consultative in the community in this work. It was not something I organised or managed: this was their space, and my part was just to supply more detail and background if it was available. I always felt proud of their standards of presentation and debate, even when I did not agree with them. I remained silent about my disagreement with their support for voluntary unionism. Valerie Forbes was an active campaigner on this, and most of my Executive were under the illusion that such a change would affect the meatworkers, ports and dairy-sector unions. My view was that these would remain a closed shop, whatever change was made.

In the 1983–84 Budget estimates, the provision for National Superannuation was the largest line item at $2,521,876,000. Ruth and I were asking questions about raising the age for receipt, but new data was demonstrating that any increase would have a gendered effect. At age 60, 75 per cent of all men and 25 per cent of all women had other income greater than the superannuation payment. By age 64, those proportions fell to just under 50 per cent of all men and 11 per cent of all women. We would have to raise the age at some point, but the data showed women would take the major impact.

On 7 June Minister of Defence David Thomson gave a speech in Christchurch on peace and disarmament. He described those of us who supported a nuclear-free New Zealand as 'sucker tucker'. I wrote to him that the term 'might more adequately be an expression levelled at those who continue to support the production of arms when there is quite enough to blow up every city on the earth twelve times over. It was a highly offensive remark and quite uncalled for.'

I was fed up with these games. I had been working in the library in the evenings and I had read every ANZUS communiqué since 1953. These were all published in the Foreign Affairs Review. It was patently obvious what the ANZUS Treaty did and did not commit to. I wrote to the American ambassador on 18 July. I knew it would have no effect but it would make me feel better. It was also timed to coincide with the ANZUS summit in Australia, and I released the letter to the media during that meeting.

> Dear Mr Ambassador
>
> I write in respect of the forthcoming visit to New Zealand of the U.S.S. Texas. I am aware of the policy of your government of refusing to disclose whether or not any vessels in your navy are carrying nuclear weapons. It is not my job to defend the policy of your government in New Zealand; it is my job to see that the policy of successive New Zealand governments is maintained. New Zealand refuses to manufacture, to possess or to permit to be stored, any form of nuclear weapon in this country, and New Zealanders would expect that policy to extend to any vessel of the New Zealand navy tied up at any wharf or anchored in any harbour in this country.
>
> It is an abhorrent breach of faith in our stated policy to face the possibility that a vessel of another country, whether conventionally or nuclear powered, may carry nuclear weapons in circumstances in which New Zealanders believe themselves free from that presence.
>
> New Zealand could not be defended by the use of nuclear weapons; New Zealanders do not wish to see themselves defended by the use of nuclear weapons.
>
> New Zealanders have the right for an assurance that our desired policy will be honoured by treaty partners. I do not have to tell you that a continued failure to provide that assurance will leave the New Zealand public pressing to sever alliance ties totally. I trust that the United States will recognize the sincere desire and stated policy of this country to remain free from the presence of nuclear weapons at all times.

I wrote another letter on 18 July, to a world leader who was incarcerated. It was Nelson Mandela's birthday.

At the first press conference on the first day of the ANZUS meeting in Australia, US Secretary of State George Shultz said that all ANZUS guaranteed in the event of a threat against, or an attack on, a member country was a 'response' from the other members. The response would not necessarily be military and there was a range of alternatives. Shultz also emphasised that any response would be in accordance with the constitutional processes of member states.

Australian Foreign Minister Bill Hayden told his Cabinet that America's limited commitment was clear in the wording of the 1952 treaty. Overnight, Hayden's memo continued, Muldoon tried to persuade the US to mislead New Zealanders on the extent of any US commitment to defend the country under the ANZUS alliance. Muldoon did not want New Zealanders to understand the limits Washington had placed on military support. The US and New Zealand tried to fudge the reality of America's position in the communiqué issued by the ANZUS Council:

> There is no doubt that the New Zealanders' attitude was very much conditioned by domestic political considerations. It is quite obvious that they are hoping to get the New Zealand Labour Opposition wrong-footed by presenting ANZUS as a firm and unwavering guarantee of military commitment by other members in all threat/attack circumstances. ANZUS is not such a guarantee.
>
> As a consequence of this New Zealand sensitivity, both the US and New Zealand were reluctant to spell out in detail in the communique that there could be a range of responses other than direct military support in the event of an attack or threat. Australia and New Zealand could expect the US to 'assist' in circumstances of a great power conflict, but that this could not be taken for granted in a lesser contingency involving the use of force. Treaty members were expected to maintain a decent level of defence capacity able to operate on its own in small-scale emergencies.[4]

The National Party annual conference was held in Dunedin from 29 July. I had never been given a slot to speak to the whole conference. In 1983, the Young Nationals asked me to be their keynote speaker at the same time as the conference church service was held. I would speak on disarmament and arms control, and I worked very hard on the address, reading well beyond the mountains of submissions the select committee had received.

To my surprise and pleasure, Sue Wood put the issue on the table in her president's address to the conference on Saturday morning. Sue was just back from a meeting in Europe of the International Democratic Union and had been 'struck by the sheer scale of the anti-nuclear rallies'. She highlighted this as an issue the Party should be focused on. Muldoon, who had been sitting next to her at the Party conference, was not pleased. Raising the issue was a mistake. 'New Zealanders don't vote on foreign policy.'[5]

On Sunday morning the Waipā delegation joined the Young Nats, a crowd of other delegates and a couple of my colleagues, as well as media and representatives from diplomatic missions who had received invitations to the conference. I began:

> 'One of the things that history demonstrates is that the desire of ordinary people to be freed from the burden and danger of armaments is not strongly or consistently reflected in the policies of Governments. Everywhere, in fact, the people of the world have made manifest their determination that the ceaseless escalation of armaments must end, now they are demanding action. We risk the bitter condemnation of future generations – or worse the very denial of their future'. Strong words, and words with which I am happy to be associated, for they were part of the New Zealand Government's official statement to the UN Disarmament Conference in 1982.

I reminded the audience that on Friday 13 July 1951 Prime Minister Sid Holland announced the formation of ANZUS to the New Zealand Parliament, and said: 'This agreement expresses nothing new in the relationships of the three [signatory] countries.' New Zealand's primary concern was to guard against the resurgence of Japanese militarism, and New Zealand's and Australia's unease that Britain might think they were deserting the Empire was obvious in their statements when the ANZUS Treaty was signed in September 1951. The Treaty purpose was 'to strengthen the fabric of peace in the Pacific area'. The New Zealand representative, Sir Carl Berendsen, had reflected at the signing: 'Finally the Treaty has no effect unless and until one of its parties is attacked.' This was still precisely the interpretation of the Treaty endorsed by George Shultz earlier this month, I reminded the crowd – and called the Treaty 'a very nebulous document'.

Then I analysed the National Party policy statements on foreign affairs and defence published in election manifestos in 1975, 1978 and 1981. The 1975 and 1978 policy statement on foreign affairs read:

'New Zealand has interests and responsibilities as an independent, outward looking member of the world community and will promote (amongst other things) the elimination of nuclear testing and Nuclear weapons proliferation.' In 1978 an additional paragraph appeared on disarmament. It read:

> National considers that general and complete disarmament under effective international control should be the ultimate goal of disarmament negotiations. A National Government will continue active support in the United Nations for a realistic programme of action including the prohibition of nuclear testing in all environments, and more effective measures to ensure against the proliferation of nuclear and conventional weapon stocks.

I pointed out differences in the 1981 policy statements with a focus on the security and stability of the Pacific region, and our defence relationship with the United States and Australia, as well as with our Pacific Island partners and the ASEAN nations. I quoted from other statements, the Declaration of the South Pacific Forum in Rotorua in 1976 and the Prime Minister's speeches at the UN General Assembly in 1978 and 1980, as well as New Zealand's 1982 official statement at the UN that had been approved by the Minister of Foreign Affairs, by a parliamentary select committee with a government majority, and presumably by the Prime Minister. A key paragraph was that on nuclear weapons-free zones:

> New Zealand supports the principle and objective of nuclear weapon free zones. We should like to see the whole world free of nuclear weapons and nowhere more than our part of the world, the South Pacific. NZ would favour the establishment of a verifiable nuclear weapon free zone in the South Pacific compatible with the relevant rules of international law and the security arrangements to which New Zealand is a party.

Then I examined the ANZUS communiqué released on 21 July 1983:

> After indicating support for the principle of a nuclear free zone in the South Pacific the communiqué said: 'In this connection [the parties] stressed the importance of upholding the principles of freedom of

> navigation and over flight as provided in international law. They also noted the importance to the alliance and the region of security considerations including access by allied aircraft and ships to airfields and ports in accordance with the sovereign right of states to receive such visits.'

I pointed out that in the pedantry of diplomatic statements 'stressing' is far more important than 'noting'. I described an apparent confusion about how the vessels come to be here. The PM denied that we 'invite' such visits. The Minister of Defence was reported as saying that 'there is a standing invitation for visits'.[6] My understanding was that the New Zealand government received a list of vessels that might call and dates on which they might call. It then indicated whether it would receive such a visit.

> It would be generally known whether or not a particular vessel is likely to carry nuclear weapons. At that point and in that context, New Zealand already has the opportunity to ensure that it is nuclear weapons free at all times.
>
> Prime Minister Muldoon says that 'New Zealand continues to attach primacy to the NPT and to adherence to it'. If you interpret the Treaty pedantically, it will be agreed that weapons on board vessels such as the USS *Texas* are in transit and are not being stored. But what is the intent of a signatory to the NPT? It is a desire to be free from the presence of nuclear weapons at all times.
>
> Then there is the question of sovereign territory. Picture the Overseas Terminal in Wellington where it is prohibited to store nuclear weapons. Yet on the USS *Texas*, pulled alongside the terminal, such weaponry can be 'legitimately' carried. That makes no sense to me, and is not what I envisage as 'territorial sovereignty'.
>
> Why is the USS *Texas* coming and what is it doing here? Let's be quite clear: there is nothing in the ANZUS Treaty which suggests or compels its visit, quite the opposite, for ANZUS is not activated 'unless and until one of its parties is attacked'. So the crew is coming for rest and recreation, necessary for good will. The ANZUS Treaty does not require the provision of rest and recreation stops.
>
> It cannot be argued that the USS *Texas* is here in response to a threat. The USS *Texas* is not here to protect us. If it is, by whom are we

> threatened? New Zealand cannot be protected through the use of a nuclear weapon. New Zealand has declared itself through successive governments' statements to be opposed to the use of nuclear weapons.

Social Credit leader Bruce Beetham's Private Member's Bill, the Prohibition of Nuclear Vessels and Weapons, had been publicly announced. I advised I would support the introduction of the Bill and its referral to a select committee 'because this is not incompatible with Government policy. It may seem to be a different position from that practised by Government, but it is a position permitted and endorsed by Government rhetoric. I now adopt it as my minimal position: that there should be no nuclear weapons inside our sovereign territory.'

In conclusion, I recalled the words of Brian Talboys addressing the United Nations Disarmament Conference in 1978:

> 'The world will not long sustain a situation where peace turns on the avoidance of nuclear war simply because nuclear war is unthinkable. If it is unthinkable, it must be made impossible. That is our task. We look forward to the day when general and complete disarmament is a realistic objective and security alliances are no longer required. Without a substantial record of achievement,' he said, 'we have failed our nations and humanity as a whole.'

I am concerned not to fail myself.

Bruce Beetham's Bill was introduced on 3 August and referred to the Select Committee on Disarmament and Arms Control.

Colin James, writing in the *National Business Review*, castigated himself and other media for missing the difference between 'stressing' and 'noting' in the ANZUS communiqué. He observed that I had done the kind of investigative journalism on the history of ANZUS and the National Party commitments that a good journalist should have researched. Interviewing me for the article, he asked if I had a long-term goal in respect of the whole nuclear issue. Yes, I replied. But, tactically, I wasn't telling anyone. He wanted to know if my nuclear stance might 'further harm' my political future. I laughed. 'I don't even think about it. It's quite inconsequential to me. I feel as powerless as anybody else in these situations. At each point it was "What are you going to do now? How can you use yourself most constructively?"'

He asked about my being 'different'. I replied: 'I'd go bananas if I spent my whole life wondering what people were thinking about me. I've got a job to do and I get on with it.' He wondered why I didn't join the Peace Squadron, the New Zealanders who took to the water to protest the ship visits. 'The group whose feelings I do strongly consider are my party people in Waipa. They're the people who give up hours of their free time to support me and keep me going. I know they don't want me bobbing around in a boat. I respect that.' Would I stand again in 1984? 'I've always said I'm here from day to day and I haven't changed my story. I mean we must all have principles – a point which you would have no option but to walk out.'

Jenny Wheeler interviewed me for the *New Zealand Woman's Weekly*.[7] I told her I was quiet – 'thinking and reading and asking questions, just satisfying myself as to exactly what I wanted to do'. She asked about getting Bruce Beetham's Bill to a select committee. 'As a measure of progress over eight years it might seem pathetically small to people out there,' I said. But in terms of the way Parliament moves 'it's big. You've got to have a lot of patience in this business.'

Jenny described me as 'a careful thinker, devastating debater and committed feminist'. She said I had 'a new vigour'. My response was: 'I've got more energy. I just have more time out for myself. I have the confidence to work alone now. I'm not collaborating with anyone. I'm not consulting. I know what I think. I know what I'm trying to do and I'm very happy to get on with it and not have other people try to compromise me or score petty political points. If I work on my own I can just stick with the issue. I don't have to play games.'

But in truth I was wrung out. The effort to heave my body into motion each morning was accomplished by moving immediately the alarm woke me: swing my legs off the bed; get into my tracksuit, out the door and immediately running. Running gave me the one up, endorphin-driven moment of the day. Running in all weathers. Running to the place of work. Running to despair. Running through the bottom door of the old building directly to the bathroom to be sick. Every day the same, and no way to control it. Every day my body saying, 'I can't stomach this any more.'

I had also given myself a fright in Waipā. I was driving to Mangakino, coming past Wharepūhunga. It might have been the lyrics of Gerry Rafferty's 'Baker Street' or Joni Mitchell's 'Amelia' on the tape deck in the car that triggered me. I heard myself say out loud, 'I hope she's still there when you get out.' I pulled to the side of the road and took a little walk, accompanied by the sound of spring lambs and their mothers. Politicians did speak about themselves in the second person. I had noticed Helen Clark do this. But in the third as well? And in one sentence? I was doing my best to keep myself together. I couldn't unravel now.

Work grounded me. In Mangakino I found that the Work Skills Programme operating at the Pouakani Marae was going to collapse. The Labour Department was withdrawing the subsidies for the backbone of the whole scheme – two teachers and administrators. Both were over 60 and receiving National Superannuation, so 'no longer qualified' for subsidies because the teachers and administrators had to be unemployed. The cultural mana attached to age and the leadership such elders could provide on marae schemes was of no consequence. Mangakino had so little. Everything was a challenge. And now we were going to close one bright future-focused scheme that had a strong cultural input and high attendance. Dealing with issues like this kept me focused.

But my fragility would begin to leak out, especially when I was tired. I told journalist Helen Paske in early September: 'The best days for me are when I go home and feel all right about myself. When I go home and feel satisfied. Not that I've done all that could be done. Not that I've done all that should be done. But that I've worked myself to my limits. The most important thing you do here is stop things happening and no-one knows about it. I know that if I never slept I couldn't stop everything. It is a physical, intellectual and emotional impossibility.' What about criticism that you are capitulating to the system, she asked. 'You learn patience here. I've been waiting for eight years, and finally refuges have got something in the budget.'

'What have you sacrificed to be in here?' Helen asked. 'Life.' She reported there was a long silence. What would you do if you weren't here? 'Farm.' What has kept you here? 'The desire to go on my own terms. As long as I was subject to challenge I was going to fight it.' The worst thing? 'It's the inability to be anonymous. I cannot run along a beach, have dinner in a restaurant, go to the movies, sit on an aeroplane, and do anything without being interrogated, being stared at, talked to, talked at.'

And were there rewards? Helen asked. 'People are the good side. There are real rewards in the constituency work. The personal rewards are the opportunities I've had, like Harvard. But I take pleasure in little things, when people who you haven't seen for years remember you used to be a musician and you're really starved for music and they do something about it, send you a tape or invite you to a soiree. When some people remember that there's still a person in there.'[8]

I had been talking with my friends in the Ministry of Foreign Affairs about the Optional Protocol to the International Covenant on Civil and Political Rights, and was becoming exasperated. Under questioning the Minister told me there were 'no immediate plans to sign the Optional Protocol'. My supplementary question was quite clear. 'If New Zealand, as the Prime Minister has stated on a number of occasions, in both comparative and legal terms, has nothing whatever to fear from review of its civil or political rights, why has the signature been subject to three postponements?'[9] I suspected some in Cabinet were afraid that their intentions regarding the Industrial Law Reform Bill might be challenged by use of the Optional Protocol. Or else Muldoon was kowtowing yet again to the isolationist right wing who thought the UN was a bunch of communists who shouldn't be telling New Zealand what to do.

The National Party had campaigned on a policy of changing the law so that union membership would become voluntary. Minister of Labour Jim Bolger had brought the issue to caucus on 7 July. He had more on his agenda for this legislation. He also wanted to introduce universal youth rates into awards which didn't have them. Emerging from the wage/price freeze he wanted to legislate for industry grouping and plant bargaining to prevent plant stoppages when just one union was on strike. Under questioning from Derek Quigley, Muldoon admitted, 'It is a fact that some, for example the abattoirs, will refuse to work with non-union labour.' But he asked caucus to agree to the drafting of the legislation.

The Industrial Law Reform Bill was brought back to caucus on 16 September for approval. It would implement a system of voluntary union membership, and permit the payment of wages to young people under 18 at rates lower than adult rates. There would be secret ballots for all decisions on strikes and lockouts. Provisions giving rights of entry to union officials or representatives would be repealed. The Bill would be sent to the select committee for hearing submissions. Muldoon wanted the legislation passed before the end of the year.

On 19 September 1983 we marked 90 years since all New Zealand women had the right to vote. The women MPs managed to persuade the Speaker to have the Women's Suffrage Petition of 1893, which was kept in the records of the Legislative Department but not on public display anywhere, brought to the main lobby of Parliament Buildings. It should have served as a reminder of how far we had to go. By 1983 there had been only 20 women elected to Parliament over that period.

I spoke in the Education Estimates in September. After years of battle for one child at a time, bursaries were to be granted to children with learning difficulties to go to schools where their needs were supported. Thanks to work by my constituents, Katherine and other parents, the University Examination Board made reader-writers available for the University Entrance exam. I asked what curricula revisions were being undertaken so that History was not about Europe but perhaps about the colonisation of the Pacific, or Geography studies were focused not on North America but on the Pacific Islands? What ability was there for Tongan and Samoan children to attain School Certificate or University Entrance in their own language, as Pākehā and Māori children could?[10]

Soon after this I was invited by the Prime Minister to accept one of the two seats available every December on a Hercules flight to the Antarctic. These were highly sought after, and so not offered to Opposition MPs. I had always been excluded because the two travellers had to share a bunkroom when on the ice. The PM told me his wife Thea was keen to go, and so would I like to join her? I knew that Ruth Richardson, National's other woman MP, was now nursing her daughter Lucy, so was unavailable. For me it was a lucky break. I got on well with Thea Muldoon. She would tell me how 'important it was for young women to have careers' – and how 'Bob just didn't understand some things'.

In the early evening of 12 October Ann Hercus indicated she wanted to see me urgently. She handed me a copy of a Private Member's Bill entitled the Status of Unborn Children Bill, in the name of Doug Kidd. It would be brought to the National caucus in the morning for introduction that afternoon.

'Obviously someone else has to introduce an opposing Bill. Who would do that in your caucus?' I asked her.

'No one from either side in our caucus is allowed to touch the issue,' she replied.

I didn't need any more stress, but told Ann I would do it. If we didn't push back, there was a possibility Kidd's Bill would get in. We knew our colleagues were so predictable that if there were two Bills up they would vote both out, so consulting wasn't an issue. It would all be over quickly. I went straight to the Clerk's office and asked if someone could draft a Bill for me. It should just make the decision on termination of pregnancy an issue between a woman and her doctor. I would need to lodge it before midnight for introduction the following day.

At caucus on 13 October Kidd told us he had decided to accept the task of bringing in the 56-clause Status of Unborn Children Bill. It proposed a legal code for the rights of unborn children. Abortion was allowed if the mother's life was imperilled. If there was a risk of serious permanent injury to the mental health of the mother, abortion may be permitted. Muldoon knew all about it: 'This one issue is most fraught with danger to the Party. The Bill will come in anyway.' The hubbub in caucus began: 'I could lose my seat on this. Who put Doug up to it?'

I asked that the Bill be withdrawn. Muldoon said no.

'Well, there will be two Bills then. Mine will be a liberal one. And since I have seniority over Doug in the House, mine will be first.'[11]

'But Miss Waring,' the PM said as if patronising an infant, 'you do not have a Bill.'

'It was lodged with the Clerk's office before midnight. I have a Bill.'

I do believe there was even a moment of surprised respect from Muldoon. 'Then there'll be two Bills,' he said.

Oh, what relief to the garrulous caucus bunch, all chirping that now they could throw out both Bills.

When I gave notice in the House that I would introduce a Bill, dear Geoffrey Palmer came up to me and said, 'Marilyn, this Bill gets rid of everything. It needs some amendments.' These could be done before the formal introduction in the House. 'Geoffrey, thank you,' I said. 'Amend it in any way you like to be comfortable with it. It is only a device and it will be thrown out, but I will be grateful for your help.'

My Bill got 17 votes for introduction. All women MPs supported it.[12] Both Bills were thrown out.

Barrie Leay, general director of the National Party, came to my office afterwards. 'Please give me a copy of your Bill. I want to put it in my top drawer at headquarters in case anyone else tries that mad stunt again,' he said. 'Thank you.'

In October I met with a Japanese parliamentary delegation, attended a cocktail party with the ASEAN heads of diplomatic missions, and listened to delegations from the Clerical Workers Union, the Trades Council, the PSA, the Film Commission and the Human Rights Commission. I managed to get to the Paul Klee exhibition at the Wellington Art Gallery. In the Social Welfare Estimates debate on 20 October I noted the $60 million outstanding maintenance debt from non-paying fathers. I also wanted to know if the Ministry's director-general was responsible for the human-relationships development and education of all children in residential care. How did he go about fulfilling those responsibilities?

The Industrial Law Reform Bill Select Committee had reached the deliberation stages. The committee chair was bringing tricky issues to caucus on 17 November. Committee members thought that there should be an additional clause attached to youth rates that prevented the dismissal of any worker when they reached 18 and adult-rate entitlement. Muldoon shot it down quickly: 'There will be problems with enforcement. Also, it will discourage employees taking on young people.' Caucus agreed. I didn't. I wanted to know: 'What about rights of appeal for people who are dismissed to make way for youth-rate workers?' Ruth chimed in: 'What if I am dismissed because I am female? The onus is on the employer to prove that wasn't the reason. It should be the same for age – if a person is dismissed to make way for youth.' Mike Minogue suggested youth rates were a hot issue among working women in marginal seats. Jim Bolger was dismissive: 'These women are totally unaffected by the Bill, as almost all of their awards have youth rates.'

A week later the issue was the State Services Conditions of Employment Amendment Bill. On 24 November Deputy Prime Minister Duncan MacIntyre was in the chair, with Muldoon overseas. He told the meeting Minogue and Waring would vote against clauses 14, 15 and 16 of the Bill. We were also 'against the Industrial Law Reform Bill. If both of these don't proceed we may well have to go to the country.' The clauses at issue were a vindictive move by Muldoon to label electricity workers part of 'essential services' who could not go on strike. Mike responded that clauses 14 to 16 of the State Services Bill were a stupid provocation. The PSA had written to show they would negotiate seriously on electricity supply. Simon Upton thought the clauses were 'a political liability'. Ruth thought 'we should look at the whole field of essential services'. Dale Jones described the approach as 'small minded and petty. I feel strongly clauses 14–16 should not be in the Bill. If any member crossed the floor I would too.' I advised that in the committee stages I would move that those clauses go back for recess study to consider the question of the right to strike in the provision of essential services.

Parliament sat from 2.30 p.m. Thursday for 19 hours, with two hours for dinner on Thursday and one hour for lunch Friday. In the House my amendment was lost by 44 votes to 43. The Minister made some amendments which modified the anti-strike clauses, and this satisfied others. Mike did not support my amendment and I didn't mind. He described 'the atmosphere here, the lunacy of last night, bell clanging, idiocy, trying to find some quiet, journalists demanding an explanation for this or that. It's a madhouse literally.'

A special 5.30 p.m. caucus was called on Thursday 1 December. The PM advised that the report back of the Finance Bill did not have full support. The PM had the power to regulate to impose the wage/price freeze, but he could not freeze interest rates, and this legislation gave him this authority. It was not a confidence vote, so MPs 'can't be required to vote for it', he said. Dale Jones advised he would be against the second reading. Derek Quigley had no objection to tidying up regulations relating to new mortgages but did object to the fact we were interfering with existing contracts. Ruth argued that interest rates would come down with market pressures. The PM said he couldn't see why they were objecting: 'The issue is not big enough. It will damage the credibility of the government's economic policy. We can't go through the session next year like this.' Government Whips ensured the Social Credit and Independent MPs voted with the government, and the Bill passed.

Earlier at the regular morning caucus MacIntyre had been in the chair. I advised I would support the vote to report back the Industrial Relations Bill so long as I could speak to it in the House. I opposed the Bill, but I could now see that the government would wait to hold the debate until I went to Antarctica the following week. Knowing this, MacIntyre and David Thomson supported my speaking. I was relieved. I had done a lot of work on the issues, without being on the select committee.

When Mike told this same meeting that he would support voluntary unionism, but not youth rates, MacIntyre hit his repeat button: 'In my opinion we would have to think about going to the country if we are defeated.' Mike replied that he would support the government on a confidence motion, 'but if I am threatened that this Bill will precipitate an election then that won't make me change to vote for it'.

I gave my speech in the evening of 1 December. I referred to the 1975 policy that said the National government would provide for secret ballots to give workers a choice of compulsory or voluntary unionism. Then I described sitting in a caucus that purposely picked soft and female-dominated unions for ballots, which, without exception, returned a majority for retention of the present system. I noted that numerous National Party conferences had endorsed the principles of voluntary unionism, nowhere more so than in the Waipā electorate. They did this because they believed that disputes in industries such as freezing, pulp and paper, transport and dairy, and on the wharves or at the oil refinery, might be contained.

> They supported it in spite of the comments of the Minister of Labour in 1982 when he said, 'As long as I am Minister of Labour I will ensure that rank and file workers have the opportunity in the legislation under my jurisdiction democratically to exercise a choice of compulsory unionism.' I wish they had heard the submissions to the select committee which stated that there is no prospect of union members working alongside non-union members in the unions that concern them. The New Zealand Freezing Companies Association, Waitaki NZR and the waterfront employers said that. The industries that concern my constituents will operate closed shops; strong unions will be stronger; and militants will be reinforced. The effect of the Bill will fall on weaker unions seldom involved in disruption – shop employees, clerical workers, cleaners and caterers.

I gave some specific details of how this would happen. Section 101, clause 7 states: 'Discrimination – it shall be unlawful for an employer – (a) to refuse or omit to employ any person by reason of that person's membership or non-membership of a union.' The submissions to the committee by clerical workers proved that this happened already. The penalty of $500 was (just) a licence fee. The penalty needed to ensure that the question of intention of union membership could not be raised in a job interview. There were 50,000 clerical workers, predominantly women, in 20,000 workplaces. Eighty per cent of the membership were low-income earners, and there was a high turnover in the jobs. Details of intimidation in the past year, given to the select committee, showed there had been a $1.3 million recovery for underpayment and failure to meet award provisions.

> Women are particularly vulnerable in areas I know best – in the small workplaces in provincial towns. A woman with the dollars, the legal

> expertise, and the courage to mount a personal grievance procedure will be a stirrer, and in the towns I know she would not find another job, so she will put up and shut up to keep the job. The question of undue influence in the proposed new section 103 in clause 7 is relevant, but the amendment is inadequate. Will a spoken comment in a job interview – seldom witnessed – to a prospective employee about the wisdom or otherwise of joining a union be constructed as undue influence? Will the distribution of pamphlets encouraging women to join unions and pointing out the advantages of doing so be constructed as undue influence? Even if it is proven, will anybody want to wait seven months before they hear a case in the Arbitration Court?
>
> Unions whose workers are scattered among small work places will suffer. They will not have the resources to recruit their members and maintain a membership service at the same time. As the member for Wellington Central said, the Bill's effect on working women can be noted in an examination of the present experience of the Early Childhood Workers Union. Inhibited by the lack of award because of the wage freeze, the union – 98 percent female – depends on 1 paid part time and 10 voluntary officials, who are working 40–70 hours a week visiting workers, keeping membership records, organising meetings, consulting with departments, and writing newsletters. They have neither time nor resources to work effectively in health, safety and welfare, be alert to technology affecting workers' jobs, and representing workers in negotiations with management in a skilled and informed way. This will not be the expectation for closed shop, economically pivotal, male-dominated unions.
>
> The burden of the Bill's effect will fall nationally on scattered workers, particularly females.

Then I examined the proposal to introduce youth rates. The 1983 conference of the ILO chaired by the Minister of Labour unanimously passed a resolution inviting members to apply fully to young people the principle of equal remuneration for work of equal value. This was endorsed by the whole New Zealand delegation: the government, and representatives of employers and workers.

The 'costs' of youth rates were born by women. I pointed out that during the hearings of the 1983 Labour Department Estimates in the PEC, the department had been asked what it believed would be the effects of youth rates on working people. It had responded with an Australian example. The implications included a possible uneven spread of effects so the most disadvantaged did not benefit. The most disadvantaged in youth unemployment are female. Gains in youth employment are likely to be at the expense of adults, especially females.

> Who are those women? One of the major unions without a youth rate is the cleaners' union. The Wellington union has 4500 members, and 75 per cent of them work an average of 17 hours per week. Working mothers are the largest group. It is low pay and is a supplementary income for many families in marginal positions. The Minister of Labour has told me that that is the only major union affected with a large female membership because other union awards have youth rates. Other union awards do have youth rates, but that reassurance is patently untrue, because the Bill proscribes all other instruments in relation to youth rates, and that means all other awards. One can take the example of the Wellington District Hotel, Hospital, Restaurant and related Trades Employees Union with 13,000 members, 72 per cent of them working women. Many of them have employers who, by legislation compulsion, are members of the Hotel Association of New Zealand.
>
> About 6,800 casual or part time women workers earn between $50 and $100 a week, the difference between meeting the family mortgage commitment and losing the mortgage. They do have a youth rate, but clause 13 of the award states that the youth rate is payable only for a 40-hour week where two people are employed on a youth rate in a ratio to one adult worker. Under clause 18, a part timer who might otherwise jeopardise those women's jobs if the youth rate were to apply, must be paid the adult hourly rate. Those workers, particularly part time women workers, are vulnerable because the protection offered by the award against offloading in favour of cheaper workers is overthrown by clause 20 of the Bill. The Workers Union clause of equal pay for work of equal value – a protection against the exploitation of young workers – is another demonstration in that area.
>
> For these, and many other reasons, I notified the Government Whip and the Acting Prime Minister more than a week ago that I would oppose the Bill. I undertook at that time to allow the Bill to be reported back to the House, but I shall vote against the second reading and every subsequent stage.

The galleries of the House were full and there was sustained applause. I was spent. This time I knew I would have upset many close supporters in Waipā.

I was back in my office when Ann called in. 'I have to bring you the news,' she said. 'The Labour Whips have refused your leave to go to the Antarctic. We all know they will put the Bill up then, so we need you here to vote.' A handwritten note arrived from a staff member in Muldoon's inner office: 'Please don't go to the Antarctic. It will still be there, but we need you now.'

Muldoon had shown just how out of touch he was in an interview with Sharon Crosbie on Radio New Zealand. Youth rates – is that really going to create more jobs? she asked. 'Yes unquestionably,' he replied. Sharon tried again: 'At the expense of women in work, women in part-time employment? I feel concerned that older women in the workforce that need that income for their families will be pushed aside because it will be cheaper to take on young.' The PM cut across her:

> Yes I've heard that argument. Indeed one of my members argues that way, but we're talking about a job for a young woman and we have to weigh up the desirability of having a young woman in the work force rather than coming out of school and going on the dole for an indefinite period. A second income in a family of a married woman whose husband is in employment – because when you talk of a family you are really talking in most cases of a married woman whose husband is in work – if you're talking of a woman with a family who has no husband, that's normally a social welfare situation, say a solo parent.[13]

I stayed in Wellington and voted against every provision of the Act at all stages, crossing the floor 18 times. On the Friday night the government suffered an historic defeat when it lost the vote on the youth-rates provision, with Labour, Independents, Social Credit, and Mike and I voting against. The government won all the other provisions, including on voluntary unionism, with the help of the Independents. I was shut out of the whole debate by government speakers, though I got two minutes of time ceded to me by a Labour frontbencher. It was deeply ironic to be legislating about lockouts and compulsory unionism when I was locked out, and in a place where every year I had to join the Inter-Parliamentary Union and the Commonwealth Parliamentary Association.

The telegrams and letters on the Bill and my vote were heavy. Waipā National supporters were disappointed with me. There seemed to be an organised National Party response from Tāmaki, Pakuranga and Albany electorates. Ken Kelly wrote from Te Awamutu: 'Have you ever thought about the farmer who slogs away milking his cows only to see the milk dumped at the factory or worse still left on his hands to be disposed of at home, and about his consequent loss of income?' Yes, I had, and this Bill would not change a thing for that farmer. People were quite worked up. 'The unions are now controlled completely by communist sympathisers and labour party lobbyists. Why on earth did you act so stupidly? You are fortunate to belong to the National Party. We are not so fortunate to have to put up with your naive and irresponsible attitudes,' wrote Linda Cairns. Harriett Lowry-Bedingham QSM of Kohimarama telegrammed: 'Grow up. Much too old to behave like a backward child still. You are here to represent the people not grind your own little axe.' Her sentiments were shared by Betty Hayward-Ryan, a 40-year member of the National Party: 'Your latest bout of exhibitionism is your worst. You are infantile.' At least they bothered to give me their full names, unlike others: 'I think you are a rotten bugger and not fit to even sit in Parliament near Mr Muldoon. True Nationalist.' Perhaps the tenor of such responses was why my colleagues seemed to think it was me who was out of touch, courting publicity, being influenced by all the wrong sorts of people. They could not have been more wrong.

I was deluged with supportive messages. Many began, 'I have meant to write to you many times and on many issues' or 'This is the first time I have bothered to write to parliament.' One of the first letters was from Peter Blomfield, executive director of the New Zealand Freezing Companies Association. 'I thought the speech in the House on Thursday night was excellent,' he wrote. 'It is a pity that more of our members are not prepared to stand up and speak with such honesty and sincerity.' John L. Marshall from Buddle Findlay law practice wrote that 'it appears to me that the Bill is being rushed through for narrow party-political advantages, without concern for the probable consequences, at a time when Government should be seeking to heal the divisions which already exist within our society – not add to them. Thank you for the stand you are taking.' Peter Waugh from Federated Farmers in Hamilton congratulated me 'on your present stand. It must be very lonely being an outsider but please keep up your strength.' Barbara Mabbett, who chaired the National Advisory Council on the Employment of Women, wrote: 'Your analysis of the likely effects of the legislation on women workers is, unhappily, correct. The defeat of the youth rates section is the one bright spot in last week's tensions, and your courage and principles are an example to all people making decisions.' The National Executive of the New Zealand Federation of Business and Professional Women's Clubs commended me 'for the stand you made when the issue of special Youth Rates was debated in the House. It was a courageous decision for which New Zealand women, especially those in employment, must be grateful.' I particularly treasured a letter from Gordon Stephenson, who was Dairy Section chair of Federated Farmers. We'd met many times over the years. 'When I saw you at Hamilton Airport last Saturday [we were on the same aircraft] I wanted to shake your hand and thank you for your courage, but you left too quickly for me. What matters in a democracy is whether we can say – and vote – without fear or favour, according to the dictates of our conscience. I take my hat off to you. Please don't lose heart, we all need the likes of you.'

Back in caucus I laughed as compulsory membership had to be removed from the Surveyors Bill. The Bill for registering veterinarians was not proceeding for the same reason.

Jim McLay brought proposals for the Rape Law Reform Bill to Caucus on 8 December. It changed both the definition of rape and the provisions about consent. Muldoon argued: 'From a practical point of view don't you put the offender at risk with these consent changes? He would have other things on his mind.' Two lawyer colleagues didn't like the consent changes. Ruth rebutted them: the offender can't take refuge by arguing he believed he had consent. Jim gave further details. The penalty on conviction would be changed. The offender must be imprisoned unless there are special circumstances. The court will be cleared for the trial and preliminary hearing when a complainant gives evidence. At the preliminary hearing, evidence can be in writing. The Bill would also abolish the need for a judge to direct the jury that there must be corroboration of the offence. The Bill was approved for introduction.

I had to stay alert for one more possible trick from Muldoon. The Disarmament and Arms Control Select Committee had prepared an interim report for the House. I was quite happy about it. It explained what had been going on and what point we were at. I told the House that in 18 months we had been fully briefed by Defence, Foreign Affairs and the external intelligence agencies. We accepted submissions from concerned New Zealanders on the subject of disarmament and arms control. The committee was consulted and had an input into the New Zealand statement at the UN Disarmament Conference. There could be no argument about government or Parliament's support for the non-proliferation treaty or test ban treaty and the principles for a nuclear weapons-free South Pacific. The Private Member's Bill introduced by Mr Beetham focused the committee on the specific question of a nuclear weapons-free New Zealand and the visit of nuclear-powered vessels to our shores. Many New Zealanders wished to make further submissions. We heard those. The interim report was 'no more than a brief record of the major points made by those who made submissions to the committee. No consideration has been given by the committee to the merits of those arguments.' That lay ahead for 1984.

At the end of each year the Leader of the House would move a motion that only some of the work before select committees would be carried over for recess study and be 'alive' for the following year. Opposition Private Member's Bills could get this treatment. I thought it was a fair bet that Muldoon would try to kill not only the Beetham Bill but also the whole committee. In our final meeting before the interim report, I asked the chair, Doug Kidd, if we could have it on record that the committee and the Bill would be carried over. He gave us that assurance.

On the final day of sitting, Chief Whip Don McKinnon sat down beside me. 'The boss wants to kill the Disarmament and Arms Control Committee in the final motion,' he said.

'I'll have to have a point of order then,' I told him. 'Kidd assured us this wouldn't happen. I would have to say the chair misled the committee.'

Don went back and told Muldoon. The work of the committee would continue.

1984

David Lange became leader of the Labour Opposition in February 1983. He had a sharp mind, was the best orator in Parliament and made us laugh. What a relief. He had such witty repartee and resonating delivery. Mike Minogue and I didn't bother to contain our enjoyment of his performances, and other National MPs could see Muldoon had already lost control of this space. The Prime Minister became Sir Robert Muldoon in the New Year's Honours List. Lange remarked that after a very long year we had a very short knight.[1]

In early 1984 the wage/price freeze was still in place. Muldoon had introduced the regulations to control mortgage interest rates. One outcome was that finance houses lifted their interest rates to over 20 per cent as investments sought the non-mortgage market. Muldoon was now blaming merchant banks and finance houses for the outcomes of his policies. International credit rating agency Standard & Poors dropped the country's credit rating from AAA to AA+ because of the size of the government deficit. There was a significant trade deficit as well, but the PM would not devalue the currency. Each year in late January, Muldoon made an address at the Ōrewa Rotary Club, north of Auckland, usually about New Zealand's economic situation. In 1984 he ignored this and gave the speech we usually heard in caucus when he came back from international travel, all about the need for reform of the international monetary system.

In January I was having a holiday. With retirement looming, I was beginning to prepare for 'afterwards'. I had no idea where I would go, but I would need to leave Waipā. I propagated roses – many from electorate chair Eon Fraser and his wife Maureen's garden – along with azaleas and hydrangeas. I was collecting seeds from aquilegias and cornflowers. I made Elizabeth David's green tomato chutney, and dolmades with my grapevine leaves. I fed my great compost: it was always easy to collect dry cowpats from the roadside in a dairy-farming electorate. I listened to more music. The soundtracks of home ranged from Leonard Cohen to Miriam Makeba, from any LP featuring contralto Janet Baker to Messiaen's *Quartet for the End of Time*.

I would announce I was retiring at the February Waipā National Party Executive meeting. I'd already advised Eon Fraser, so that he was prepared to move straight into the selection process. I had also told Katherine O'Regan in 1983, so that if she wanted to run she would be able to strategise quietly for this. While it was obvious National would lose the election in 1984, Waipā was a safe seat, and there would be a range of contenders. In addition, with a new candidate selection process, the electorate Party membership would increase as branches sought to maximise the number of voting delegates they would have. There were quite a few apartheid rugby and anti-abortion advocates who had left the Party because of me to come back to the fold. I told Muldoon on 9 February I was retiring, as he was heading off on an overseas trip.

On Monday 13 February I advised the Waipā National Party Executive that I would not be standing again. Eon Fraser told media my departure was a sad day for the National Party and the Waipā electorate. I am sure there were a good number in caucus who had quite the opposite sentiment.

The electorate would advertise for candidates the next day and hold nominations open for a month. The selection meeting date would be 5 April. Branch meetings began. I attended them all, writing notes for Katherine about who was selected as voting delegates, what the remits were and who was advocating for these. I spent whole days in different centres, visiting schools and businesses, and picking up news to pass along. Katherine had Waipā County Council covered, so I went to Cambridge and Te Awamutu Borough and Ōtorohanga District Council meetings to pick up their minutes and agendas and hand them on.

The media commentary on my retirement decision was kind. Alan Simpson, a political scientist at the University of Waikato, called my departure a 'serious loss' of a 'conscientious and competent' MP.

Alongside other commentators Alan was concerned at 'the increasing centralisation of Government around the Prime Minister. Cabinet threatens the place of Parliament and the job of the individual MP. Marilyn Waring has understood and asserted the role of the individual backbench MP, first, in the party caucus and secondly, in the House of Representatives. It is the role of Caucus to challenge Prime Ministers to think again. There is no other body to provide such a check on the political executive. Marilyn Waring understood this and acted on it.'

During my period chairing the PEC, Alan had been making a video for students on parliamentary procedures. We permitted him to film the committee in informal discussions, and he also spoke with staff assisting us. Alan wrote:

> In her all too short spell chairing the PEC, Marilyn Waring constantly sought to ensure its effectiveness. Under her guidance, its members worked in a bipartisan way to frustrate the efforts of departments to obfuscate matters regarding policy and expenditure. She sought better resources to do the job. No department, no public servant, could take her committee for granted. Marilyn Waring took the view that the loyalty of public servants was not just to ministers and the Government of the day. They had a clear loyalty to the taxpayer to be a responsible trustee.[2]

In the following Saturday's *New Zealand Herald*, press gallery journalist Greg Shand wrote that I had done 'the unthinkable':

> [S]he decided voluntarily to quit a job most must be wrenched from. That she did not fall victim to the disease of power and influence that keeps most politicians in Parliament until either age or electoral disaster overtakes them speaks volumes for her relatively brief but controversial career. Her voluntary retirement at 31 is thought to be unprecedented. To her friends and admirers, Marilyn Waring's success is better measured by her rare and refreshing firebrand independence, a commitment to integrity not always in harmony with the unity decreed by the party system. For all the headaches she caused, few in the National Party would appear to hold any real grudges. One official said last week 'Marilyn was as politically honest as you can get: I mean she was so unshakeable. She will be sorely missed.'

Shand contended that 1983 had been a particularly difficult year, with the voluntary unionism legislation, the defeat of youth rates, the National Party conference speech on nuclear ship visits, and the rearguard action to defeat the Kidd anti-abortion Bill.

> Marilyn Waring did not seek status as an MP, just a platform to promote greater awareness of social concerns. She is enormously popular in her electorate. To many her representation of a conservative rural electorate has seemed a bit of a paradox. But political journalists who toured Waipa soon found the answer. Though some did not share her views, they all admired her courage and independence. They all said she was second to none as a hardworking MP for her electorate.[3]

I told the *Evening Post*: 'I have been interested in being able to use whatever talent I have constructively. Parliament is particularly difficult for a woman. You are always on the defensive; there is no time to be innovative. That has been frustrating.'[4]

Despite doubling the numbers of women MPs and mayors since 1975, women were still left grasping for traction. In 1984 we were eight of 92 members of Parliament. Twelve of the 26 major cities had women mayors. The ministerial private-secretary count had increased to 12 of 55. Seven of the 26 members of the parliamentary press gallery were women. There was one head of a government department, one magistrate, and no women Cabinet ministers, judges or editors of metropolitan daily newspapers. There had been some significant legislative changes in the past eight years, but I couldn't relax when it came to what this leader or caucus might try, or renege on, before the election.

An intended retirement did not mean a leisurely few months. I attended the opening of the Pasifika Women's Conference. I had a host of electorate delegations making visits to ministers: Justice on the closure of the Cambridge courthouse; Transport on road-user tax charges; Agriculture on abattoir regulations; Internal Affairs on grants for schools, local government, refuges or women's self-defence training. I had various special cases from the Waikato: urgent housing needs; a pregnant prisoner; and reappraisals of rural bank loan applications.

However, it was a great relief to think I didn't have to be on the hustings defending the management of the economy. My colleagues would have to do this. Early every year at caucus Michael Cox wanted to know what the plans were for deregulating the economy. In 1984 he wanted to know what the programme for privatisation would be. Muldoon advised him he hadn't seen 'how it will fit into the budget. Air New Zealand is not ready for it.' That was a red herring. He would never have got support to privatise our national carrier through this caucus. Muldoon suggested that the petrochemical and methanol plants were ready, and would probably be the first two we would look to privatise. Bill Birch thought the Natural Gas Corporation could be added to the list and this would be good in the 1984 Budget. This was crazy talk. Budget decisions for June should have been close to finalised. Selling government corporations wasn't like selling a house. Unless Treasury had been asked to begin preparing for such initiatives (and they hadn't), all the Budget could announce was an intention.

I had a quiet game plan for the Disarmament and Arms Control Committee. The text of our report was coming along nicely as far as I was concerned. There would be another Private Member's Bill for a nuclear-free New Zealand introduced by someone during the session, and Bruce Beetham's Bill was still alive in front of the committee. By now nuclear-free zones had been declared in local-government areas covering more than 60 per cent of the population. I would bide my time and see how and when different players moved. I expected that Muldoon would be more preoccupied with how to appease a number of my colleagues in his Budget decisions than looking in my direction.

I had a long interview on 23 February with Sharon Crosbie on Radio New Zealand. I told her I was not blindly loyal to the Party. 'It was unfortunate that I was sent to Parliament with a mind, and I am going to use it, but it doesn't make people happy. As a National Party MP, the political hierarchy can't interfere in the electorate. They can't stop you being a candidate. They can't stop people voting for you. They can't threaten not to give sums of money to your campaign. What's left is to try to break your spirit, to wear you down.'

Sharon asked what advice I would give to women going into politics. 'There were the usual clichés,' I told her. 'You've got to be twice as good, you've got to over-prove yourself, you've got to be extraordinarily honest with yourself. You are going into a totally male environment. There is no free flow of energy in there. You will be sucked dry in every kind of way. You have to structure places where you can go to get your batteries recharged with women; you have to structure privacy. It took me six years to learn that part.'

Sharon reminded me of another radio programme in which I had said I now recognised how people became Nazis, looking for simple clichés and someone to blame. I explained that as a student I had never understood that ideology and history. I couldn't understand at all how people could respond in such a way in a political environment. 'It's been quite a tragedy to me in the last nine years that I have seen enough political behaviour across wide spectrums of the New Zealand public to demonstrate to me how this can happen. It's a problem with patriarchy that we are taught that things are male–female, black or white or right or wrong. In politics the main colour is grey. It takes most politicians a lot of courage to admit that. They like to work in clichés.'

Sharon noted I had 'been criticised of course for displaying emotion in the House. How did you cope with it time and again?'

'I can't control it,' I said. 'It just happens. Tears are an emotion. Apparently, anger and bullying and throwing legislation across the House, which is what boys do, isn't an emotion. I've heard the boys' voices crack and weep in the House, but it's never a headline. Weeping is honest. Isn't it amazing how threatening it is to be that honest?'

This criticism of me had backfired, she suggested: 'Other women were moved by your feelings and that ... was a very positive thing ... Is Parliament as awful as you've implied?'

My views were clear: 'I have not had a great deal of enjoyment of Parliament, I loved the electorate passionately, loved the environment, and I loved working overseas, but I've hated getting on the plane to come to Wellington. Parliament can be extremely boring and very unidimensional, very tedious and repetitive, full of games, full of scoring and winning and chalking up the little victory regarding the standing orders procedure. I find that pretty pathetic.'

What about caucus? Sharon wanted to know. I told her: 'Nothing you have ever done prepares you for the government caucus.'

'Is it a bun fight then, is it not orderly?'

'Oh, it can be extremely orderly; sometimes you don't dare breathe,' I replied.

'Is caucus like mental wrist wrestling then?'

'No nothing that intelligent,' I laughed.

Sharon asked if being a feminist made it easier or harder.

'It is what gave me my strength and energy every day. It gave me my political commitment to get up every day, yet it's a foreign culture in Parliament. No one knows what you are talking about, so you hammer until they listen, which is a tremendous advance, and still nothing gets done.'

'What would you like to see change? Are you with Geoffrey Palmer that it's time the entire way it is organised was updated?' Sharon was reflecting growing public opinion that there needed to be consideration of a new voting system.

'It's a patriarchal institution. It's a system where we only elect white middle-class, middle-aged men en masse. That's what's got to be changed,' I replied.

I told Sharon I thought it was impossible for me to assess what one person might accomplish in Parliament, 'especially when you are the only woman in the Government caucus ... There are eight enormous issues coming at you, and there is only one little body so there is only one bulldozer you can throw yourself in front of. You've got to choose which one and tomorrow you've got to choose another one, and I don't find it a terribly constructive way to live.'

'Marilyn Waring, thank you,' Sharon concluded. 'We will miss you.'

In all of these 'exit interviews' I was asked what I thought had been my achievements. I cited the letters I'd been receiving from women that simply said, 'You've given me a political consciousness.' As I had told Greg Shand: 'My electorate people say they have never been asked so much for their views, they have never thought themselves as politically aware as they see themselves now. That was the best accolade a retiring MP could wish for.'

Once a month from January to April, caucus met for two full days at a time. My select committees – especially Health and Welfare, Disarmament and Arms Control, and Public Expenditure – were working long days, but caucus committees were trying to draft election policy somewhere down a dark tunnel. Every proposal was met with: It depends on the budget, or it depends on the PM. I had no useful purpose in these debates, and I could ease out of them. At the caucus meeting on 14 March, there was a bizarre debate about allowing advertising on radio and television on Sundays. Radio and television were state corporations; there were no advertisements on Wednesdays or Sundays. In the nightmare of the economic indicators and budget decisions, this was a morsel for caucus. 'Why couldn't the non-advertising day be Sunday?' There were revenue advantages to lifting the Sunday ban. 'Is it extra revenue?' Yes, $8 million. 'My electorate's against Sunday advertising.' Would they rather have an increase in the licence fee, then? Caucus made no progress on advertising on TV on Sunday and left the Broadcasting Tribunal to decide on radio.

In the afternoon caucus session of 15 March, environmental protection and enhancement procedures were on the agenda. Environment Minister Ian Shearer reported that all ministries had assessed these, but Works and Development still had reservations about the inclusion of 'social and cultural' impacts. Warren Cooper thought this inclusion would be a barrier to development. 'The Commissioner of the Environment may become unmanageable,' he warned. 'There will be a proliferation of staff. The environment does not feature as a political concern.' Don McKinnon argued that the environment had physical characteristics and you could separate this from the impact on people. Bill Birch said the definition was too wide; the commissioner would be empowered to do things outside the control of the Minister. Norman Jones suggested they 'will poke their nose into every subdivision change and planning'.

Shearer responded that he did not accept that environmentalists impeded development or stopped job creation. The commissioner would not have any additional powers but could not ignore the social impact of big projects. I argued that we couldn't separate the physical environment from people. 'We live in the environment. It is unrealistic to divorce social and cultural impacts from public discussion: think of noise as an example of social impacts; the sites of urupā are a cultural environment issue,' I said. Ruth argued we should look at the Commissioner for the Environment as a good insurance policy, not a handicap. Assessing social and cultural impacts needed a statutory base. George supported her.

Muldoon said he disagreed with the politics of the issue. It was thoroughly bad in an election year. If the Bill was introduced, it would be dragged out and dominate the session. It was agreed, however, that it would be introduced late in the session for recess study.

In late February Duncan MacIntyre had announced he would retire from Parliament and step down as Deputy Prime Minister. At caucus on 15 March the PM nominated Bill Birch to replace him. Both Jim McLay and Jim Bolger were also nominated. I supported Jim McLay, and he became Deputy Prime Minister.

In Wellington, I was working with Amnesty International (AI) and their campaign 'Parliamentarians for the Abolition of Torture'. We had 21 members in a cross-party branch of AI in Parliament, and like many women around the world I was lobbying AI to recognise imprisoned feminist activists as political prisoners. I met with international representatives from the UN Economic and Social Commission for Asia and the Pacific, and the All-China Women's Federation; I also met with representatives from the Africa Information Centre, and gave a lecture for the Women's Studies course at Victoria University. Brenda Cutress and Barbara Goodman came to discuss election preparation on the reproductive freedom issues, and Denis O'Reilly came to discuss PEP. In Waipā, alongside Party branch meetings, there was lunch in Cambridge with the Governor-General, a speaking engagement at the Cambridge Parents Centre AGM, and meetings with Eva Rickard and Moana Wikaire. On 5 April Katherine O'Regan won the Waipā selection ballot to replace me as the MP at the general election. I was very happy that the electorate had Katherine. She would be there for them. Both were in safe hands.

The Statutes Revision Select Committee hearings on the Rape Law Reform Bill had concluded, and at the caucus meeting on 11 April Dale Jones advised that the evidence before the committee called for rape within marriage to be a criminal offence. The Caucus Justice Committee agreed. Paul East thought it should be a conscience issue, and met strong disagreement from Venn Young and me. David Thomson and Pat Hunt wanted to know who wanted this law change and where the demand had come from. Simon Upton replied that the submissions set out the evidence and support for change. Ruth wanted to know where the logic lay that allowed a charge of assault but not rape. Caucus resolved to change the law to make rape a crime within marriage, but I was not at all confident they would follow through.

Another item in this two-day caucus was nuclear disarmament. John Banks reported that support for nuclear disarmament was growing in Northland. Norman Jones agreed with the growth in support: 'We can just say we are against nuclear weapons.'

'But you can't un-invent nuclear weapons,' responded Jim McLay. 'We want to reduce the stockpile but still have a deterrent.' Foreign Minister Warren Cooper said we were 'sympathetic to the mainstream of the peace movement. We don't want to fight with the peace movement on this.' The PM intervened. 'Labor in Australia were anti-ANZUS, and in government they have changed right around.'

I disagreed. 'Australia is far more locked into ANZUS with its bases. ANZUS is interpreted as being consultative. ANZUS doesn't need us to have nuclear ships in New Zealand. The nuclear stockpile is way past deterrence levels. If you are opposed to nuclear weapons, why have ships here?'

'They are points of view that can be argued,' he replied. 'ANZUS is evolving all the time, supplemented by discussions. One issue is whether we require disclosure of nuclear weapons on board US naval vessels. We are opposed to the use of nuclear weapons but do we want the US as an ally or not? It has nuclear weapons. We have options. We can get out of ANZUS.'

In late April Muldoon had told a radio talkback caller that New Zealand would not ratify the Convention on all Forms of Discrimination Against Women (CEDAW). I raised this at the 3 May caucus. Jim McLay (Justice) and Warren Cooper (Foreign Affairs) had been handling this. Our research unit had produced a paper setting out why we should support CEDAW, and it had gone out to candidates. The PM replied he had given his personal opinion against the convention. It was not widely ratified and 'certainly not by the third world. We are already carrying out what is needed. And we face nonsense with the Human Rights Commission. Thinking politically I'm not keen to move further.' Ruth argued. Politics requires action, she said; we only lose ground after doing so much.

Ian Shearer noted that the Labour Party's position on CEDAW was clear. What was the National Party position for the election? Mike Minogue cut in: 'Officially the Government has not taken a position. Cooper's document undertook to canvass women's views. You have misled us.'

I stood up again: 'Prime Minister your words were: "My Government has no intention of adopting CEDAW." Cooper gave assurances in the House on consultation. A retraction is needed.' None was forthcoming.

On 17 May CEDAW came up again. Muldoon was overseas; McLay was in the chair. He told us the PM had a right to declare this a conscience issue. Good grief. Fundamental human rights were a conscience issue? I had relied on Jim to hold to some basic lines, but so much was falling apart.

I had been mulling over prospective amendments to the Human Rights Commission Act for a Private Member's Bill, and raised this at the same meeting. The issues addressed would be the Bill's sexual harassment provisions, removing restrictions on the membership of some clubs, and provisions on inciting racial hatred. I was getting some help in having a draft Bill for introduction, and I hoped this would be sent to a select committee for recess study. I'd argue that there was a strong liberal membership in the Party who would be grateful to see it. Paul East was drafting a Bill on the expungement of criminal convictions. Ruth was also considering a Private Member's Bill.

After the initial February flurry of media attention on my retirement, there was a lull, but interest returned with the impending parliamentary session. Neale McMillan wanted to know if I would be changing my behaviour. 'I will behave no differently this year from in the past,' I told him. 'I exercise my judgements with a great deal of seriousness and with a clear comprehension of the magnitude of some of the decisions I have made. I have done it with all sincerity, and I don't intend to change that.' On rape law reform we were 'confronting the issue of the kind of society that breeds a group of people who either don't understand what violation they are perpetrating against other people, or don't care', and I was reserving my right to vote against the government on this issue.

Asked to define myself, I said: 'I think about myself quite simply and in quite uncomplicated terms. I am not a person who likes institutions ... I like to be outside, farming or gardening. I certainly understand the spiritual connection of a culture with the land. But I have little tolerance for institutionalised religion.'

I explained my role for the past eight years:

> I am better at asking questions than providing answers. I try to push my own knowledge and theoretical perceptions: to push out the lateral boundaries in my head. I don't like to get too inflexible about anything. I didn't set out to come here at all – but I have learned a lot about myself and about people. I have never perceived myself as a spokeswoman or leader because I don't like those ways of working very much. I have just been part of lots of movements because the office and status of an MP give you a chance to articulate on behalf of other people and this has to be used.[5]

In April the *New Zealand Listener* had asked me to write 'a frank personal account of what it is really like to be an MP in the NZ parliament, especially from the point of view of a young woman'. I wrote this as a letter to 'My Dear Sisters', unapologetically addressing women whose 'oppressions far exceed any succinct numberings of our absence;

they run deeper than our ability to count, and too frequently beyond our ability to express them'.[6]

There were particular paragraphs addressing the games inside the National Party caucus, where 'national two channel coverage for television could be a safe bet for an inclusive and wasted hour when there was major electoral discontent that should have been aired'.[7] I wrote of the 'good old pre-budget kite flyers, to make the backbenchers feel they have just been consulted: prescription charges, indirect taxes. When just enough new members enter every three years, and just enough older members think they might jeopardise promotion chances by getting involved, and just enough don't want to get involved, and just enough think it's a pointless waste of energy anyway, old dogs don't need new tricks.'

I had noted down a comment novelist Salman Rushdie had made in an interview, and introduced it to my letter: 'We live in an age in which the people who control history, who control reality, are increasingly telling lies about it. Politicians have understood it. In order to control the future, it is necessary to control the past. And it is the people who control the memories of nations that control its destiny.'

I also addressed how I had managed to get through: 'There have always been moments of comfort – supportive words on the street, kind letters, people who work in Parliament Buildings and having no games to play become touchstones for sanity – librarians, messengers, secretary typists, catering staff. There are those who bring flowers and those who are unasked for and so welcome, at my door when I need them. There have been too, colleagues who would bring me water when my voice broke, handkerchiefs when I wept, who would shift from their allocated seats in the House to sit close to me and quietly talk me through the speeches I found most difficult to deliver, whose quiet simple notes and reassuring phone calls I have cared for and needed.'

The 'Letter' became the cover story. One caucus colleague told me it was a very bitter piece. I was surprised any of them bothered to read it.

In May the Disarmament and Arms Control Select Committee heard the US was planning to deploy Tomahawk cruise missiles with conventional or nuclear warheads on their vessels in the Pacific. We asked for clarification. The US confirmed this would begin in June and many missiles would be nuclear armed.

Muldoon was away a lot in May, travelling to the US, France, Britain, Canada and Australia. This meant there was little caucus discussion on the forthcoming Budget. It looked a nightmare to lift the wage/price freeze and interest regulations, continue to lift import controls and remove tariffs, and stop supplementary minimum prices for farmers. There was complete inertia in developing policies for the election. Everyone was waiting for some indications from Muldoon as to what would be in the Budget. George had given up and tried another route. He took his plans for deregulation in the transport industry to the Dominion Executive of the National Party. Their endorsement would give him backing in caucus.

The Prime Minister was back for the 7 June caucus meeting. Another backbencher put CEDAW on the agenda and argued that it should be a conscience, not a policy, issue. Muldoon changed his earlier position: 'I would rather not formally say it is a conscience issue. I would prefer nothing on it this year. It's best to let the matter drop.' Then came one of those complete fictions Muldoon delivered as an art form. 'Ratification would give us problems with our trading relationships in places like Iran and Saudi Arabia.'

Doug Kidd led the next item on the Disarmament Select Committee. He gave caucus an outline of what the committee's final report to Parliament might look like. Dale Jones noted that our support of an earlier nuclear-free zone, in the Antarctic, was included in the report. Muldoon led with his constantly reiterated lie: 'It is a Government policy we remain in ANZUS *and ANZUS as we know it requires nuclear-propelled ships to come here.* If we are defeated in the House, we will have to go to the country.'[8] He added that the report seemed okay.

Richard Prebble had given notice that he would introduce another Nuclear Free New Zealand Bill. Paul East wanted to know what we should do with Prebble's Bill. I had indicated I would cross the floor in support of it. Chief Whip Don McKinnon advised: 'We have to let it go to the select committee as we haven't got the numbers to defeat it on the first reading.'

That evening I was working in my room when Leader of the House David Thomson came to see me. He was there to persuade me of the errors in my thinking. He began patronisingly, telling me he had been idealistic in his youth too: 'We all want peace.' He told me I didn't understand the commitments in the ANZUS alliance, and I told him precisely what they were. He argued the US was there to protect us and was necessary for New Zealand's defence, and I argued we were only a target when the Americans visited, and all ANZUS required was 'consultation', not defence.

He changed tack: 'The government would have to go to the country if we lost the vote.' This was getting to be a broken record from the old men in caucus. Prebble's Bill had not been declared a confidence vote on a matter of national security precisely because the ANZUS Treaty would not stand scrutiny on that count. 'An early election would compromise your future. You are only months away from qualifying for your parliamentary superannuation, and you could lose it all,' Thomson noted. That didn't get any traction either. He played his last card: 'Even if a majority of Parliament were to vote to support the legislation, the Cabinet would withhold the legislation from going to the Executive Council for the Governor General's signature.'

'David, I can't believe you threatened that,' I said, rising. 'You had better leave before this gets any worse. How dare you suggest this? It totally undermines democracy and the essence of what the National Party stands for. And I suggest you keep that threat to yourself and don't repeat it anywhere.' I showed him out the door.

Tuesday 12 June we were waiting in Parliament for Prebble's Bill. As the Clerk called this item, the Speaker rose and intervened. He drew the attention of the House to Speaker's Ruling 15/5: '"It is not competent for the House, even by unanimous consent, to pass without the recommendation of the Crown, a Bill affecting the rights of the Crown."[9] The Bill does not involve an appropriation of public money and can therefore proceed. However, I point out in accordance with Speaker's ruling 15/5 it is not competent for the House to pass the Bill into law unless at some stage in its passage it is recommended to the House by a message from the Governor-General.'[10]

I couldn't believe it. 'Thomson pulled that one on me last week,' I gasped to Mike Minogue as we both reached for our desk copies of Standing Orders.

'The lunatics have taken over the asylum,' Mike muttered.

Richard Prebble raised a point of order. 'This is my third such Bill and the member for Rangitikei has also introduced a similar Bill. Previous Bills have been allowed to be introduced in the House without such a ruling.'

Here was David Thomson, spieling forth again: 'The present Bill cannot be passed without the Governor-General's message, and that will not be available, and it should not have been available for the Bill introduced by the member for Rangitikei. That Bill was referred to a select committee and has not proceeded any further. It will not be passed because the Government will not recommend to the Governor-General that he give the Royal assent.'

Richard fought back: 'It would be a grave step backwards to introduce limitations on the powers and rights of the House.'

But he was sat down by the Speaker again: 'Ruling 15/5 states that a Bill affecting the rights of the Crown cannot be passed without the recommendations of the Crown.' The Speaker was not prepared to hear any further argument on the matter.

It was obvious from the outset that Richard's Bill would be voted down. I also knew National would ensure I never got the call for this debate in Parliament. But it was all over for me now. I had finally hit the point of no return, and it had come with such simple clarity. The government had threatened that the essence of democracy – a vote of the majority of MPs in Parliament – could be suspended. I would get through this Bill and assess what to do after that.

The Nuclear Free New Zealand Bill would prohibit nuclear power stations, nuclear-powered vessels and the dumping of nuclear waste. It would make New Zealand the first sovereign nation to be completely nuclear free by law. David Thomson called the Bill a 'cruel and heartless fabrication, a hoax without humour, to seek to make political profit from the genuine concerns, fears and hopes of many thousands of New Zealanders – those who are inadequately informed about the realities of the nuclear age.'[11]

Helen Clark replied that 'the cruel and heartless hoax is to say that New Zealand always has been nuclear-free, when the Government willingly permits visits of warships to New Zealand without inquiring whether they are nuclear armed, and in the knowledge that they probably are. New Zealanders do not want the defence provided by nuclear weapons. They know that if those weapons were ever called up to our defence, we would be history.'[12]

Muldoon continued to argue that ANZUS could not survive if the Bill was passed. Bill Birch claimed 'the Bill is the worst example of fear politics, of claptrap and emotion'.[13]

Former Labour leader Sir Wallace Rowling told the House he could not 'recall another occasion when a private member's Bill has produced a Prime Minister, a Deputy Prime Minister and a Leader of the House as the first three Government speakers. I know they are concerned about the position in which they find themselves, and I suspect they are equally concerned that the member for Waipa might get a turn in the debate if some of the fellows on the front bench do not get up. I detect a great deal of determination on the part of the Government to keep her out of the debate if at all possible.'[14]

I played the game, standing to take the call after every speaker, but I knew I would be cut out. In the last moments of the two-hour debate, Jonathan Hunt tried to give me his call, but those minutes were lost as National MPs took points of order to shut me out in the afternoon session.

In the evening Standing Orders were suspended to interrupt ordinary business so that the Whangarei Refinery Expansion Project Disputes Bill could be introduced and pass through all stages to become an Act that evening. The oil refinery expansion was one of the Think Big projects. Work had come to a standstill. The legislation said the employers could not lock the workers out, and forced any worker employed to return to work or be treated as voluntarily unemployed. Muldoon went looking for industrial disputes. He believed this helped shore up support for his party and government. While he was never the Minister of Labour, he called the shots during disputes. I also thought he was looking for a reason for an early election, and clashes with unions were his tried-and-true territory.

The debate on the Nuclear Free New Zealand Bill resumed on 12 June with Prebble's right of reply. I was pleased he was able to get something clear and on the record about ship visits. The select committee had asked US State Department officials, 'Why do you send nuclear-powered warships to New Zealand?' The House needed to know that their reply was: 'We never, never requested that a nuclear-powered ship visit New Zealand. Every single visit has been in response to a particular request from the National Government.'[15]

The Bill lost by one vote on introduction. Mike was still seething from the Speaker's ruling, and voted with me, the two Social Credit members and the Labour caucus. The two old Labour Independents voted with National. Now I had some hard thinking to do.

I went home to the apartment and spent some hours mind-mapping alternatives and likely consequences. I could resign from the National Party. I didn't see why that should happen. I thought my National supporters in Waipā – in fact, Party supporters across New Zealand – would be outraged if the significance of Thomson's threat was explained to them. There was a loyalty partnership in Waipā developed over eight years, and my supporters did not deserve the rejection of all they stood for if I resigned from the Party. Sue Wood and Barrie Leay did not deserve this either. And I did not want to impact on Katherine's election campaign.

I could resign from Parliament. That would leave the government without a reliable majority and Muldoon would ensure I became an election issue. I did not want any more vitriol and savagery, and I was tired. The reason for my resignation – an issue which I regarded as a constitutional crisis – would likely be lost in the maelstrom. And resigning from Parliament could affect other women candidates in 1984 and the future.

I had to do something so I could live with myself. Doing nothing was not an option. There must, I thought, be a strategic route through all of this, whereby the outcome would be an election but I could try to protect myself from being the scourge of the Prime Minister.

How much line would he need to take the bait and to call the election himself, blaming me? It was the National Party caucus that I needed to abandon – a caucus that sat while New Zealand burned and this leader bullied onwards, a caucus with the tide going out on their re-election chances. I remembered what Alan Simpson had written: that it was caucus members who had to act as a check on the Executive. Except for the handful of colleagues who did continue to try to push back, I had lost patience with the rest. What would be the effect if I withdrew from caucus and all select committees? My other options would remain open. It would make the Whips' work extremely difficult to replace me every week on three committees. It didn't matter if I didn't go to caucus – the bully would prevail anyway. If he decided to limp along like that, I would have two or three mornings each week to be human. There would be no effect on Katherine. On the other hand, if he did take the bait, he would blame me. That would be easier than my actually triggering the election. I thought the PM was so out of control, he wouldn't need too much assistance to do that himself.

I sat up a lot of the night, adding reasons and outcomes for each possibility. On 14 June, Thursday morning, I went to ask Charles Littlejohn, the Clerk of the House, if there were any standing orders, Speaker's rulings or any constitutional provisions that would cover my withdrawal from caucus, but not from the Party or the Parliament, where I would also give the government an assurance of my vote on confidence and supply. Charles advised me that none of these documents said anything that might pertain to such a situation. I then wrote a letter to Government Whip Don McKinnon advising that I would not be at the caucus meeting and was taking the morning off. With Gair, Cooper, Highet, Friedlander, Bolger, Templeton and three other backbenchers away, I was not missed.

Caucus discussed Ruth's Private Member's Bill to make it compulsory to fence swimming pools. The Prime Minister was worried about the political impact: 'Local authorities don't want to make the decisions and are passing the buck.' MPs claimed that they would be hurt electorally. 'A lot of people have electorates with pools. The time for this is after the election.' In the context of all this government had done to reach its current unpopularity, the claims against Ruth were bizarre: 'This may put some of our members out of office.' 'We'll just get the flak for this idea.' When Ruth argued that the issue should be before Parliament, she was told she was undermining her colleagues. Muldoon asked for a vote. Ruth was the only caucus member in support.

The only Budget item discussed seemed to be the question of how long those in receipt of National Superannuation could be absent from New Zealand 'on the trip of a lifetime', and still be paid superannuation in their absence.

There was a report back to caucus from the Party Dominion Executive meeting the previous day. Sue Wood told me: 'At that meeting, we evaluated the membership figures and the general state of the organisation for each of the marginal seats. It was a grim picture, to say the least, dire.'[16] Sue had opened the meeting by saying that the government was 'fighting for its political life'. Membership and finances were low; the Party organisation was poor in some crucial electorates. Barrie Leay reported a list of the marginal seats likely to be lost.

Muldoon tried to play down Leay's forecasts, but caucus was growing anxious. MPs reported: the Labour Party had a good system working in the Eden electorate on a telephone survey. They 'had funds'. Labour was 'sharpening up on what they learned last time. They had enrolled an additional 2000 people on the roll in Hunua.' They were 'better organised with their dot system', especially on election day.[17]

Meanwhile, I called a friend, and we went to a violin master class at Victoria University – good for some reflective thinking – then on to lunch. I was back in the House for the afternoon's sitting. I wrote a memo to Don McKinnon advising him I would no longer attend caucus or be available to sit on select committees. I thought that Muldoon might be clever enough just to ignore it and leave me having to explain publicly what I had done. Earlier in the year, Brenda Cutress had spoken with me about the issue of abortion for the 1984 election and beyond. We were tired of always being on the back foot, responding, and not taking any initiatives to improve the laws. We wanted to discuss this further, and safely. Brenda was in touch with Dame Barbara Goodman, Lady Beverley Scott and (later Dame) Honor Bonisch, and that Thursday they had all arrived in Wellington so we might have dinner together. We planned to spend the rest of the evening mapping out possible strategies. By the time I left for the restaurant at 5.30 p.m., I had not had any response to my memo.

Sue Wood had gone back to Auckland around midday. She recalled that 'in the late afternoon I received a phone call from the leader. He said: "I am calling to inform you that Marilyn Waring has withdrawn from caucus and select committees." I asked: "Do you want me to talk to her?" He replied: "No, I am informing you as President" and hung up.'[18] Sue decided to fly back to Wellington that evening. She called Don McKinnon and said, 'I will be at Parliament around 9 p.m. and I want to meet with Marilyn in your office.' Sue stressed this was strictly confidential.

After dinner, when I returned with my friends to my office, I knew the memo was open. There were notes from messengers on my desk that I should call Sue Wood and Barrie Leay. I called Sue's home and was told she 'was on her way to Wellington to see you'. I had the same answer from Barrie's home in Wellington. I began to take the notes for our meeting. A little later came a call from the Whip's office, advising me that Sue wanted to talk to me.

When Sue arrived at the Whip's office, Rob Muldoon was waiting. Barrie Leay and Don McKinnon were there too. Sue recalls: 'He said: "what are you doing here?" At the same time, you arrived as I had arranged. You were "ambushed."'

'Just what do you think you are up to now, you perverted little liar?' was the PM's opening line as I walked in. So much flashed through my mind: I could hear both Barrie and Sue, who looked stunned, reprimanding him for this language. So – he had taken the bait. With that opener, he would not back down. The next few hours would be vicious. Okay, I would give as good as I got. 'If you say that again outside this room I will sue the shit out of you,' I replied.

Sue was furious with Muldoon. 'Rob, I came to have a conversation with Marilyn,' she said, 'and we will do that.'

We left to meet in the room next door. 'Now tell me what this is all about?' Sue asked. I relaxed and told her about the threats made in the House, and to me, to circumvent democracy. I told her I wasn't in a fit of pique because we lost the vote on nuclear-free New Zealand, or because I was shut out of the debate. 'That's the way this place works, and that was the outcome,' I explained. 'But I am not here to be passive when such a basic threat is made on such a fundamental principle of democracy.'

In all the events of the evening, Sue and Barrie were the only people who asked what my decision was about, and neither of them attempted to contest it.

I told Sue I had no intention of making a big deal about my withdrawal, and I didn't want to hurt Katherine. I would reserve my position on changes to the rape law, and on disarmament issues – exactly the assurance I had given her late in 1983. I would support the government in a confidence vote on the Budget because that was what Waipā had elected me to do. But I could not sit in a caucus so devoid of integrity that they thought Thomson's threat and the Speaker's ruling were okay. That was it. I had hit my limit.

We returned to Don's office. Sue said, 'I have Marilyn's word that she will not bring the government down. I accept her word.'

'She is a liar,' Muldoon interrupted, and with another brandy and ginger poured by McKinnon, he was off again. 'She can't be trusted. She's just after headlines to please her lefty feminist friends,' he said. 'Always loving the headlines. She won't be quiet.' He swung around to Don and began rehashing some of the lines I had written for the *Listener piece 'On Leaving Parliament'*. I was very surprised. He certainly knew all the parts most critical of him. He kept yelling his poisonous rant at me, then saying, 'We don't behave like that do we, Don?' And all evening Don just agreed: 'Yes Prime Minister' or 'No Prime Minister.'

Barrie asked to speak with me, and off we went. 'He's just using you, Marilyn,' he said. 'He hasn't got a clue how to put a Budget together.'

'Well, Barrie, that's another reason why he should go to the country if that's what he wants,' I said.

'Membership is dreadful; we don't have enough money to go to an election,' he went on. Well, that wasn't my fault. 'The polling is dreadful. We will lose some really good people.' He reeled off a list of names.

'Look, Barrie, I have done my best here to fight back against him, but they weren't standing beside me then. They only have themselves to blame.'

Back again to Don's office, and the next round was on how Muldoon couldn't trust my vote on his next Budget. I told him he had a lot more of his caucus to worry about on that score. In the meantime, Don had sent Paul East around all the MPs in the House to ask them if they would be prepared for a snap election. The tide was going out so fast, they were overwhelming in their 'yes' response. McKinnon poured the PM another drink, and Muldoon recommenced his abuse, now baiting me on what I would do in the election campaign to stay in the headlines.

I laughed. 'No, Prime Minister, I won't be doing that,' I told him. I didn't add – 'you taught me that in 1976'. I just thought to myself: I will just disappear so you can't make me an issue, and you will have to fight on your lousy leadership, poor economic management and abusive personality. I had taken an apple with me. I munched it as his tirade continued and got steadily worse. Barrie Leay called the performance 'drunken megalomania'.[19]

But I did not have to fight any more. I was exhausted to the bone, and the tears came.

The others had to move to election preparation. Eventually I extracted myself and went back to my office. There the meeting on abortion strategy was still going on. I picked up the pad to keep taking notes. Shortly after 10.30 p.m. came the sound of MPs shuffling into the government caucus room right beside my office. I went and snibbed the locks on my door.

'What's going on?' Brenda asked.

'There's going to be a snap election,' I replied. My friends leapt up and gave muffled cheers. 'There's a caucus meeting on now. I will be blamed for this.'

In the next room, Muldoon told caucus that he couldn't guarantee a majority through till the election:

> Marilyn Waring is the problem. Mr. Minogue is part of the problem with his vote this week. We can't go through election year not knowing if we have a majority. Discussions have been going on with Marilyn and Sue Wood. Marilyn has said she would not be a member of a select committee. She will vote for the Government other than on rape, defence, and nuclear issues. She will not attend the caucus. The problem is this will become public. She will inevitably become independent. I propose to go to the Governor-General tonight and say I don't have a majority in the House and to call an election. Does any member of this caucus counsel against that decision?

No one did. From my room, we heard a brief and unenthused round of clapping.

The press would be straight to my door, so I crawled under my desk to hide. The knocks came, but then there was a very funny moment. My friends could not work the snib locks. The door was tall with an old lever window into the corridor. I watched them push a table under the window. Brenda climbed on top of it and poked her head out. 'I'm so sorry,' she said. 'We are having trouble unlocking the door.' 'Where's Marilyn?' they demanded. 'We don't know,' she replied, 'she went off to a meeting and hasn't come back.' I crawled out, quickly undid the locks and retreated under the desk. 'Just a minute,' Brenda said. 'One of us has just managed to unlock the door.' It opened, and the gallery journalists looked in.

'What's going on?' Brenda asked them.

'There's a snap election,' they told her. 'Marilyn has been blamed.'

'Oh dear,' Brenda said. 'I hope she's okay. But we don't know where she is.' And the journalists left.

I dictated a short press statement, which Brenda typed in my secretary's office and then delivered to the press gallery, telling them I had phoned it in. It said:

> This afternoon I advised the chief government whip that I would no longer be available to attend meetings of the Government Caucus or parliamentary select committees.
>
> This evening in a meeting with the Prime Minister, the party president, the general director of the National Party and the Chief Government Whip I repeated an assurance that I had given Mrs. Wood and Mr. Leay in a visit to me late last year; that I would vote on all procedural motions and on all matters of substance for the Government for the 1984 parliamentary year with my position reserved on disarmament matters and the rape legislation.
>
> I have nothing further to say on this matter.

We knew the news of the election was out as soon the first telegrams began to arrive for me from Parliament's post office. Straight after the caucus meeting Muldoon had left for Government House to advise the Governor-General to call an election. Jim McLay was there at a media dinner, and this was how he and many journalists knew the election had been called. *Listener* editor David Beatson was drafted in to type the proclamation. Muldoon had another drink before returning to Parliament to give the infamous drunken press conference announcing the election.

My office was on the third floor of Parliament Buildings in the furthest corner from the one door open at midnight. The parliamentary press gallery offices lay to both the left and right of my door. There was an internal staircase across the corridor from my room, but that would still leave me two long ground-floor corridors to navigate without running into anyone. Several times Barbara wandered along to the gallery offices to see if journalists were about. My friends had determined they were taking me back to Brenda's home for what remained of the morning. Shortly after 1 a.m., escorted by Barbara, and with the messengers giving us stop and go hand signals if anyone else was about, we made it out the bottom door.

I was free. It was over.

In the election on 14 July 1984, the David Lange-led Labour Party won 56 seats to National's 37. On 8 June 1987, the New Zealand Nuclear Free Zone, Disarmament and Arms Control Act was passed into law, establishing the country as a nuclear- and biological-weapons-free zone.

References

Clark, M. (ed.). (2004). *Muldoon Revisited*. Palmerston North, New Zealand: Dunmore Press.

Garnier, T. & Levine, S. (1981). *Election '81: An End to Muldoonism*. Auckland, New Zealand: Methuen.

Gustafson, B. (2000). *His Way: A Biography of Robert Muldoon*. Auckland, New Zealand: Auckland University Press.

Johansson, J. (2005). *Two Titans: Muldoon, Lange and Leadership*. Wellington, New Zealand: Dunmore Publishing.

McCallum, J. (1993). *Women in the House: Members of Parliament in New Zealand*. Picton, New Zealand: Cape Catley.

Templeton, H. (1995). *All Honourable Men: Inside the Muldoon Cabinet, 1975–1984*. Auckland, New Zealand: Auckland University Press.

Templeton, M. (1998). *Human Rights and Sporting Contacts: New Zealand Attitudes to Race Relations in South Africa, 1921–94*. Auckland, New Zealand: Auckland University Press.

Templeton, M. (2006). *Standing Upright Here: New Zealand in the Nuclear Age, 1945–1990*. Wellington, New Zealand: Victoria University Press.

Notes

Preface

1 *The Author's Dimension: Selected Essays / Christa Wolf*, introduction by Grace Paley, edited by Alexander Stephan, translated by Jan van Heurck, Farrar, Straus & Giroux, New York, 1993, p.xi.

1975

1 Private Member's Bill: a proposed law change introduced by an MP who is not a Cabinet minister.

2 Committees made up of a small number of MPs from different parties, usually specialising in a sector, to deal with particular issues, proposed laws or special inquiries.

3 The caucus is the regular meeting of all the MPs of a particular party.

4 Branches of the Party were entitled to one voting delegate for every 20 Party members.

5 Price stabilisation: a scheme to reduce variability in income and prices for agricultural products.

6 I did not know until later that week that this adjudicator, E.B. Allison, was in the hall, and a buzz went around when he confirmed the story to those close by. Dame Hilda Ross had been an MP for Hamilton from 1949 to 1959, and was the only woman to be a Cabinet minister for the National Party.

7 The Kīngitanga was a movement among Māori tribes in the 1850s to establish a role equal to that of a monarch to stop colonists taking Māori land. The strongest support came from the Tainui people. The Crown refers to Queen Victoria's representatives in New Zealand.

8 Inscription on the memorial at the battle site. But the back story is much worse. See Vincent O'Malley, *The Great War for New Zealand: Waikato 1800–2000*, Bridget Williams Books, Wellington, 2016.

9 Sharemilkers run another person's dairy farm for a percentage of the profits, sometimes owning some of the herd.

10 Straddle carriers are vehicles used to stack and move containers at ports.

11 Te Awamutu had a population of 7,619.

12 Deficit before borrowing: the difference between revenue and expenditure.

13 Fixed investments: physical assets in buildings, machinery, vehicles, technology, etc.

14 *Dominion*, 31 July 1975.

15 *Dominion*, 2 August 1975.

16 Judy Zavos, *Thursday*, 24 July 1975.

17 Social Credit took 7.43 per cent of the votes cast, and the Values Party 5.19 per cent. In the 1975 election, these parties did not win seats and were not represented in Parliament.

18 A decision had been made to build the country's largest thermal power station in this town in 1973. Gas would be piped from the gas fields in Taranaki, and coal

would be mined in Huntly and surrounding districts to fuel the plant to provide for a generating capacity of 1000 MW. There were 50 million tons of steam coal underground to the west of Huntly, and the Rotorua field nearby contained 10 million tons.

19 Whips are responsible for managing logistics (leave, etc.) and parliamentary party discipline.

20 The value of imports far exceeded the value of exports.

21 The total of all caucus MPs with parliamentary experience.

22 New Zealand has only one House of Parliament. There is no upper chamber, such as a Senate.

23 New Zealand was the first country in the world to achieve universal suffrage, including women, and both women and men of the indigenous Māori people.

1976

1 *The War Game* won the Oscar for best documentary in 1965.

2 ANZUS was a 1951 treaty between Australia and New Zealand and the USA with respect to security matters in the South Pacific.

3 The PEC was seen as a high-status select committee, especially for a new backbencher. It examined the Public Accounts, and the public expenditure of 45 ministries, departments and state trading organisations.

4 For the Privileges Select Committee, see 'Privileges', New Zealand Parliament, www.parliament.nz/en/pb/sc/scl/privileges (accessed 25 February 2019).

5 Under the First Past the Post system, the candidate with the most votes in a particular electorate won the seat.

6 Green would become notorious as the leader of an unethical experiment under-treating women with cervical cancer without their consent or prior approval. His superior was found to have engaged in disgraceful conduct. Green was deemed too frail to be charged. Nineteen women received compensation in an out-of-court settlement.

7 MPs are not subject to party control and cast their votes as individuals.

8 *Sunday Times*, 18 January 1976.

9 'The Real Marilyn behind the MP for Raglan', *New Zealand Woman's Weekly*, 8 March 1976.

10 The author, speaking in 'Take a Girl Like You', directed by George Andrews, *Encounter*, 1976.

11 *New Zealand Parliamentary Debates* (*NZPD*), 2 July 1976, vol.403, p.251, Address in Reply debate (Waring).

12 The Supplementary Order Paper contained all the notices of motion and questions from the previous week.

13 The Appropriations Bill authorises each agency budget for specific spending in the forthcoming year. It is also referred to as the Estimates debate.

14 Until this Act, women lost the right to independent domicile on marriage.

15 The Commonwealth is the organisation of nation states which includes most former British colonies.

16 *NZPD*, 18 August 1976, vol.404, p.1756, Evidence Amendment Bill, First Reading (Waring).

17 In November Dick Heron sent me an invoice of $62.62 for disbursements in the

case. Neither he nor Julian made any charge for professional services, which were considerable.

18 When Beattie was New Zealand's Governor-General (1980–85) he advised me that it was something he had been very happy to do, both as a judge and as a New Zealander. 'It was gutter tactics, we don't need that,' he said.

19 Seven of these Cabinet members had opposed, and seven had supported, Venn Young's 1974 Bill attempting to repeal the law making homosexual acts a crime.

20 Don't let the bastards grind you down.

21 *Waikato Times*, 24 August 1976.

22 Redmer Yska, author of *Truth: The Rise and Fall of the People's Paper*, Craig Potton Publishing, Nelson, 2010, claims publishing this story was a grave miscalculation, creating shockwaves and bringing a massive backlash against the newspaper, which was eventually closed.

23 Waring Story Rouses Anger', *Waikato Times*, 31 August 1976.

24 *Sunday Times*, 5 September 1976.

25 *NZPD*, 1 September 1976, vol.405, p.2214, 1976 Health Amendment Bill, Second Reading (Waring).

26 Cartwright has subsequently had a significant career as a judge; as chair of the commission which found Herbert Green's research unethical; as New Zealand Governor-General; and as a member of the Cambodian War Crimes Tribunal. See 'Silvia Cartwright', Wikipedia, https://en.wikipedia.org/wiki/Silvia_Cartwright (accessed 25 February 2019).

27 People from Samoa, Tonga, Niue, the Cook Islands and other Pacific nations had migrated to New Zealand.

28 The Court of Appeal was then the highest appeal court in New Zealand. Until 2003, the Privy Council in London remained a remnant of colonial systems in New Zealand, and was the final Court of Appeal.

29 Supplementary Estimates contain the additional expenses and capital expenditure needed by the government to finance activities until the end of the financial year.

30 Convened five-yearly, and consisting of independent civil servants (e.g. the surveyor general or government statistician), the commission follows prescribed population quotas to redraw electoral (constituency) boundaries.

1977

1 All MPs belonged to the IPU and the CPA.

2 Bridging finance was a short-term loan, typically to purchase a new home before the existing home was sold.

3 From 1954 to 1991 the KGB was the internal security agency of the Soviet Union.

4 Ngāti Mahuta is a hapū (sub-tribe) of the Tainui iwi.

5 Robert Mahuta was a Tainui tribal leader and Director of Māori Studies at Waikato University.

6 *Christchurch Star*, 19 March 1977.

7 J.A. Burnet, *New Zealand Herald*, 23 March 1977.

8 Australia and New Zealand hold services on 25 April, across both countries, to commemorate those who died in war, and to wish for peace.

9 245T is also known as Agent Orange.
10 *Waikato Times*, 15 June 1977.
11 *New Zealand Herald*, 4 July 1977.
12 *New Zealand Herald*, 15 July 1977.
13 *New Zealand Parliamentary Debates* (*NZPD*), 1 June 1977, vol.410, p.296, Address in Reply (Waring).
14 *NZPD*, 5 July 1977, vol.411, p.1202, Evidence Amendment Bill, Second Reading (Waring).
15 In the 20th century the minister in charge of the SIS was always the prime minister.
16 *NZPD*, 16 August 1977, vol.412, p.2193, Appropriations Bill (Waring).
17 Hansen had held the Littauer Chair in Political Economy at Harvard.
18 In the 1978–79 racing season, Linda tied for second in the New Zealand jockey premiership.
19 On 21 March 1960 in Sharpeville, South Africa, police fired on demonstrators, killing 69 people. Many of them were shot in the back.
20 *NZPD*, 11 October 1977, vol.414, p.3580, Contraception, Sterilisation and Abortion Bill, Second Reading (Waring).
21 If an MP died or resigned in office, an election in that constituency had to be held to elect a new MP.

1978

1 *New Zealand Herald*, 6 January 1978.
2 *New Zealand Herald*, 12 January 1978.
3 This is the term used to describe what a petition seeks from Parliament.
4 Tony Friedlander, personal communication, 19 September 2016.
5 *New Zealand Herald*, 7 March 1978.
6 Suzanne Upton, *Press*, 8 May 1978.
7 The protest was to last 506 days. In 1952 the people had been evicted from their land, and their whare destroyed, as in Raglan. The local Ngāti Whātua had seen their land reduced by government acquisition. In 1977, the government had proposed housing development on Bastion Point.
8 'Egmont' was the name given to the mountain by British colonisers. 'Taranaki' is the Māori name of the mountain.
9 In 1887 Ngāti Tūwharetoa gifted the mountains in the central North Island to the government for a national park – Tongariro National Park.
10 A 1987 Waitangi Tribunal Report adopted by the Labour government recommended the return of the land to the local iwi. Much of it would remain as public reserve. A $3 million payment was also made for marae and iwi development.
11 I was constantly updated on these numbers by doctors and activists.
12 *New Zealand Parliamentary Debates* (*NZPD*), 31 May 1978, vol.417, p.490, Contraception, Sterilisation and Abortion Bill, Second Reading (Waring).
13 *NZPD*, 30 May 1977, vol.417, p.413, Address in Reply (Waring).

14 *NZPD*, 11 July 1977, vol.418, p.1681, Social Security Amendment Bill, Second Reading (Waring).

15 Usually 14–16 years old.

16 In later years, a number of undercover officers made successful claims to the ACC. They claimed they had become drug-addicted in the course of their employment as a result of this legislation.

17 A native wattlebird, with extraordinary song, the kōkako is a poor flyer, and has been decimated by introduced mammals.

18 A national campaign to prevent a lake rise of 30 metres as part of the plans for the Manapōuri Dam.

19 Barry Brill, letter to the Minister of Social Welfare, 15 August 1978.

20 In the September/October 1978 edition of *Nathena*, the National Party women's publication, I wrote about the Select Committee on Violent Offending: 'Domestic violence, and particularly rape and wife beating, have been veiled under a conspiracy of silence. Many of my male colleagues either deny its existence or insist they are only occasioned by provocation. Some of the most frightening and harmful violence in western society takes place inside the family, affecting wives, children, and grandparents.' Marilyn Waring, *Nathena*, September/October 1978.

21 *New Zealand Herald*, 23 August 1978.

22 Rex held the seat of Awarua and was one of the two Māori in National's caucus who had won general seats.

23 Judy Addinell, *New Zealand Herald*, 5 August 1978. Addinell was one of only four women in the 38-member parliamentary press gallery in 1978, and senior writer for the *Herald*.

24 Ian Templeton, *Auckland Star*, 5 August 1978.

25 He had been a Labour MP, 1972–75, for Hamilton East.

26 Ian Templeton, *Auckland Star*, 1 December 1978.

1979

1 *Auckland Star*, 4 January 1979.

2 *Auckland Star*, 17 January 1979.

3 The Beatles' 1969 album was *Yellow Submarine*.

4 *Press*, 27 February 1979,.

5 Ray Dykes, 'PM Tosses "Bombshell" Among Bureaucracy', *New Zealand Herald*, 27 February 1979.

6 A handful of other MPs paid electorate assistants.

7 A little dig: Ian had written a publication in 1978 for the NZ Planning Council on the future of New Zealand agriculture.

8 Patricia Webb, *Justice Department Review of the Law on Adoption*, Justice Department, Wellington, 1979.

9 *New Zealand Herald*, 28 April 1979.

10 Ann Munz, Wellington Abortion Trust, personal communication, 22 May 1979.

11 In New Zealand, car owners selected a day of the week on which they would not use their car, and this was displayed on a sticker on the windscreen.

12 John A. Lee was a Labour MP in 1922–28 and 1931–40. He was expelled from the Labour Party in 1940 for his criticism of their failure to implement socialist

policies. He remained an MP until 1943.

13 *New Zealand Parliamentary Debates* (*NZPD*), 23 May 1979, vol.422, p.88, Discussion of Motions (Batchelor).

14 The Speech from the Throne outlines the government's policy and legislative priorities, and is read by the Governor-General on the second day of each new parliamentary year.

15 When she became an MP, Katherine O'Regan introduced a Private Member's Bill to amend the Education Act to include children with learning difficulties, but this was opposed by teachers' unions and was never enacted.

16 *NZPD*, 23 May 1979, vol.422, p.245, Address in Reply Debate (Waring).

17 When there are any irregularities in an electorate poll, or where the result is particularly close, this might result in a recount presided over by a magistrate.

18 Muldoon had been extremely rude to US President Jimmy Carter, had had an invitation to meet him in the USA withdrawn, and had to use the goodwill built up by New Zealand diplomatic staff to get another invitation.

19 *NZPD*, 10 August 1979, vol.424, p.2238, Criminal Justice Amendment Bill (Waring).

20 Textiles, packaged goods, plastics and wines, radio and television, footwear, glassware, rubber products, motor vehicles, starch and margarine.

21 *The Republican* was published by Jesson from 1974 to 1995, covering republican and left-wing issues.

22 Coney was co-editor of the feminist magazine *Broadsheet*. In later years she was elected to the Auckland Regional Council and the Waitematā District Health Board.

23 Christine Dann was national organiser for the Values Party, and later a Green Party activist and organiser.

24 *NZPD*, 28 August 1979, vol.425, p.2553, Appropriation Bill – Estimates – Department of Justice (Waring).

25 *NZPD*, 11 September 1979, vol.425, p.2850, Appropriation Bill – Estimates – Department of Health (Waring).

26 Plunket is a nationwide health service for mothers and babies.

27 *Press*, 24–25 September 1979.

28 *NZPD*, 30 October 1979, vol.427, p.3862, VD Tests on Children (Gair).

29 *New Zealand Woman's Weekly*, 22 October 1979.

30 *Australian Women's Weekly*, 31 October 1979.

31 *Auckland Star*, 2 November 1979.

32 A Commission of Inquiry into Police Conduct, and especially sexual assault, was carried out in 2006–7 by Dame Margaret Bazley, beginning with 1979. The first paragraph of the Commissioner's overview read: 'I saw evidence of disgraceful conduct by police officers and associates over the period since 1979, involving the exploitation of vulnerable people. There was also evidence of officers trying to protect alleged perpetrators. These incidents, which occurred mainly in the 1980s, include evidence of officers condoning or turning a blind eye to sexual activity of an inappropriate nature; a wall of silence from colleagues protecting those officers complained about; negative stereotyped views of complainants; and a culture of scepticism in dealing with complaints of sexual assault.' *Report of the Commission of Inquiry into Police Conduct*, Commission of Inquiry into Police Conduct, Wellington, March 2007, www.parliament.nz/resource/0000055162 (accessed 26 February 2019).

33 *New Zealand Herald*, 10 November 1979.

34 *Dominion*, 12 November 1979.

35 *Waikato Times*, 12 November 1979.

36 The two New Zealanders at the mission in Teheran, Chris Beeby and Richard Sewell, were working with British and Canadian diplomats in the successful plan to smuggle six US embassy staff out of Iran after the revolution.

37 Rod Alley (ed.), *The State Services in the 1980s*, New Zealand Institute of Public Administration, 1980; Steve Hoadley (ed.), *New Zealand's Democracy: Choices for the 80s*, New Zealand Foundation for Peace Studies, 1979.

38 I wrote that:

- while individual ministers could play a part, the usual system for resource distribution was incremental on top of the previous year's expenditure, with some account taken for inflation
- private-sector forces selected by competitive tendering should be used rather than expanding government's capacity
- Acts and regulations could be left substantially intact by successive administrators for 30 years for the perpetuation of staff positions and departmental functions, regardless of the real need for them
- old policies are compared with each other, and new policies are compared with each other, but new policies are never contrasted directly with old policies. We must look to a system of limited tenure in all positions in the higher echelons of the public service, employing people on contract.

39 A revolving fund is a financing arrangement whereby the receipts of an operation are permitted to be expended on continuing that operation.

1980

1 The Speaker attended caucus meetings when the House was not sitting.

2 In time this hotel and Summit Trekking would employ over 300 people, with the hotel purchased by Nepali people in 2010.

3 She was re-elected in 1981 and 1985. She died in 1986.

4 *Te Awamutu Courier*, 10 April 1980.

5 'Women's Role Stereotyped', *Waikato Times*, 8 April 1980, p.10.

6 Bartlett was a former nun, who began the Society for Promotion of Community Standards and was a leading Society for the Protection of the Unborn Child (SPUC) campaigner.

7 *North–South, A Programme For Survival*, Report of the Independent Commission on International Development Issues, Pan Books, London, 1980. The chair of the commission, Willy Brandt, was the Chancellor of the Federal Republic of Germany from 1969–74.

8 Carol held this position until 1985. From 1995 to 2005 she was executive director of UNICEF.

9 A former British Labour MP (from 1964) and Cabinet minister, Williams helped found the Liberal Democrat Party in 1981. She was a professor in the Kennedy School, and subsequently served as a member of the House of Lords in the UK Parliament. Lee Kuan Yew was prime minister of Singapore from 1959 to 1990.

10 *New Zealand Parliamentary Debates* (*NZPD*), 5 June 1980, vol.429, pp.545–48, Address in Reply (Waring).

11 Helen Brown, 'Facing the Truth, the Waring Way', *Otago Daily Times*, 12 July 1980, p.19.

12 Janet Watts, *Observer*, 27 July 1980.

13 *NZPD*, 5 August 1980, vol.432, p.2400, Appropriation Bill Financial Statement (Waring).

14 *NZPD*, 20 August 1980, vol.432, p.2862, Debate, Public Expenditure Committee Report (Waring).

15 The committee spoke with representatives of the NZPPTA (Post Primary Teachers' Association), NZEI (primary teachers), NZSBA (Secondary School Boards Association), NZKTA (Kindergarten Teachers Association) and NZEBA (Education Boards Association), as well as the Department of Education.

16 *NZPD*, 21 August 1980, vol.432, p.2885, Debate, Appropriation Bill – Estimates – Economic Stabilisation (Waring).

17 *NZPD*, 26 August 1980, vol.432, p.2942, Debate, Appropriation Bill – Estimates – Dept of Trade and Industry (Waring).

18 Ibid., p.2954, Debate, Appropriation Bill – Estimates – Customs Department (Waring).

19 *NZPD*, 23 September 1980, vol.433, p.3599 (Highet).

20 *NZPD*, 11 September 1980, vol.433, p.3350, Debate, Appropriation Bill – Estimates – Ministry of Foreign Affairs (Waring).

21 Ibid., p.3357, Debate, Appropriation Bill – Estimates – Housing Corporation of New Zealand (Waring).

22 *NZPD*, 7 October 1980, vol.434, p.3951, Debate, Appropriations Bill – Estimates – Health (Waring).

23 Muldoon did not consult with or inform National Party leaders about Gill's appointment and the possible readiness for the by-election.

24 Muldoon had attacked the protests against the visit of the USS *Truxtun* to Wellington Harbour in early September.

25 *NZPD*, 22 October 1980, p.4332, Debate, Discussion of Ministers' Replies to Questions (Waring).

26 *New Zealand Engineering*, 1 November 1980.

27 *NZPD*, 4 November 1980, p.4705, Shop Trading Hours Amendment Bill, Second Reading (Waring).

1981

1 McGovern was Democratic Senator for South Dakota for 18 years; Constanza an activist for women's rights and gay rights; Lindsay front man for ABC's *Good Morning America*, as well as a representative of Manhattan in Congress and Mayor of New York City; Suzman had been an MP in South Africa since 1953, and sole anti-apartheid parliamentarian from 1961–74; and Rather was a journalist with *CBS Evening News* and *60 Minutes*.

2 Ellen Malos, *The Politics of Housework*, Allison & Busby/Schoken Books, New York, 1980; Janet Radcliffe Richards, *The Sceptical Feminist: A Philosophical Inquiry*, Penguin, London, 1980; Kathleen Barry, *Female Sexual Slavery*, New York University Press, New York, 1979; Florence Rush, *The Best Kept Secret: The Sexual Abuse of Children*, Prentice Hall, New York, 1980.

3 To beat someone with birch sticks.

4 Victoria Irwin, *Christian Science Monitor*, 13 May 1981.

5 *Evening Post*, 6 May 1981.
6 David Barber, *Evening Post*, 28 May 1981.
7 *Auckland Star*, 29 May 1981.
8 Milton Friedman and the Chicago School theorists promoted economic liberalism and free markets.
9 Because Jamaica was a member of the Commonwealth, and we did not have a mission in Jamaica, the closest mission in another Commonwealth country, in this case Canada, looked after bilateral relations.
10 *New Zealand Parliamentary Debates* (*NZPD*), 17 June 1981, vol.437, pp.529–31 (Waring).
11 Yes, the firm with discriminatory practices in the cutting room. While I was at Harvard the Human Rights Commission had written to say the issues around discrimination in tasks had been resolved, and men and women now did all roles.
12 David Beattie was the judge who had intervened on a Saturday night to stay the publication of the *Truth* story in 1976.
13 In fact, Alison Quentin Baxter retained her seat, based on her individual credentials and experience. In the election for a seat on the UN Security Council, New Zealand lost by a significant margin to Malta.
14 Tony Garnier and Stephen Levine, *Election '81: An End to Muldoonism?*, Methuen, Auckland, 1981, p.153.
15 Twenty-eight years later, we still remember who took what side. It is ingrained in the memories of several generations of Kiwis.
16 *NZPD*, 3 September 1981, vol.440, p.3205, Appropriation Bill (Waring).
17 *NZPD*, 1 October 1981, vol.441, p.3800, Appropriation Bill (Waring).

1982

1 *New Zealand Parliamentary Debates* (*NZPD*), 20 April 1982, vol.443, p.280 (Wilde).
2 *NZPD*, 20 April 1982, vol.443, p.266 (Waring).
3 Ibid., p.267 (Waring).
4 UN General Assembly Special Session on Disarmament.
5 *NZPD*, 29 April 1982, vol.443, pp.698–701, Address in Reply Debate (Waring).
6 *NZPD*, 6 May 1982, vol.444, p.881, Maori Affairs Amendment Bill (Waring).
7 The Treaty of Tlatelolco 1967, for the Prohibition of Nuclear Weapons in Latin America and the Caribbean, was the second.
8 *NZPD*, 11 May 1982, vol.444, pp.1031–32, Select Committee on Disarmament and Arms Control (Waring).
9 In the committee stages, this would be recast as the Domestic Protection Bill.
10 *Evening Post*, 31 May 1982.
11 *Whangarei Rape Crisis Newsletter*, 4 June 1982.
12 Muldoon had offered tax deductions with wage increases as opposed to a gross wage increase.
13 Quigley was one of the few in Cabinet from the South Island.
14 Jane Clifton, *New Zealand Times*, 20 June 1982, p.6.
15 Waikeria Borstal became a prison in 1981.

16 *NZPD*, 6 August 1982, vol.445, p.1839, Children and Young Persons Amendment Bill (Waring).

17 Officially the Judicial Committee of the Privy Council, an English court, this was New Zealand's highest court until 2004. Judges from other Commonwealth countries heard appeals from New Zealand courts in London.

18 Samoa gained independence on 1 January 1962; *NZPD*, 8 September 1982, vol.446, p.3124, Citizenship (Western Samoa) Bill, Second Reading (Waring).

19 *NZPD*, 11 August 1982, vol.445, p.2110, Appropriations Bill, Second Reading (Waring).

20 Ibid., p.2111 (Waring).

21 A former All Black and Rhodes scholar, Laidlaw was well respected by Dutton.

22 *NZPD*, 8 September 1982, vol.446, p.3034, Response to Question to Minister of Local Government.

23 *NZPD*, 14 September 1982, vol.446, p.3164, Response to Question to Minister of Social Welfare.

24 Pre-school centres for Māori-language immersion.

25 *NZPD*, 2 September 1982, vol.446, p.2821, Question on behalf of Waring to Minister of Māori Affairs.

26 *NZPD*, 1 October 1982, vol.447, p.3759, Response to Question for Written Answer to Minister for the Environment.

27 *NZPD*, 19 August 1982, vol.445, p.2330, Response to Question to Minister of State Services.

28 *NZPD*, 9 November 1982, vol.448, p.4562, Debate, Appropriation Bill – Estimates – Department of Health (Waring).

1983

1 *New Zealand Parliamentary Debates* (*NZPD*), 19 April 1983, vol.450, p.263, Address in Reply (Waring).

2 Hugh Templeton wrote of my advocacy on these issues: 'Muldoon's reaction when Marilyn Waring suggested we should trial a three by 12-hour six day working week was simply one of horror. To give more emphasis to employment she wanted to split the Labour portfolio in two, one for industrial relations and the other for employment. These were the sort of innovative proposals that might have given flexibility to the labour market and to its managers. But Muldoon turned them down. Neither he nor his Minister of Labour was prepared to accept the ideas of a far too radical young woman.' Hugh Templeton, *All Honourable Men: Inside the Muldoon Cabinet, 1975–1984*, Auckland University Press, Auckland, 1995, p.204.

3 Briar Whitehead, *Press*, 28 April 1983, p.21.

4 Submission of a report on the ANZUS meeting from Bill Hayden to his Australian Cabinet colleagues following the 1983 ANZUS summit. *New Zealand Herald*, 2 January 2012.

5 Sue Wood, personal communication, 19 October 2018.

6 *New Zealand Herald*, 1 July 1983.

7 Jenny Wheeler, *New Zealand Woman's Weekly*, 29 August 1983.

8 Helen Paske, *Listener*, 9 September 1983.

9 *NZPD*, 30 August 1983, vol.452, p.1896, Optional Protocol on the ICCPR Question (Waring).

10 *NZPD*, 22 September 1983, vol.453, p.2615, Education Estimates (Waring).

11 Doug had entered Parliament in 1978.

12 Whetu Tirikatene-Sullivan was on leave.

13 Prime Minister Robert Muldoon interviewed by Sharon Crosbie, Radio New Zealand, 7 December 1983, Ngā Taonga Sound & Vision, Sound Collection, Reference Number 27281.

1984

1 Muldoon was about 155 cm tall.

2 Alan Simpson, *New Zealand Herald*, 15 February 1984, p.6.

3 Greg Shand, 18 February 1984, p.12.

4 *Evening Post*, 14 February 1984, p.3.

5 Neale McMillan, *Otago Daily Times*, 19 May 1984.

6 Marilyn Waring, *New Zealand Listener*, 26 May 1984.

7 Many provinces could access only one channel.

8 These are my italics.

9 *New Zealand Parliamentary Debates* (*NZPD*), 1934, vol.240, p.107 (Statham). After the Speaker's ruling on the Mortgages and Tenants Relief Amendment Bill in 1934, the House permitted the referral of the Bill in the next stage to the Statutes Revision Select Committee for submissions. The ruling remains in New Zealand Speaker's Rulings, now under Crown Consent. I have found no instance of its use after 1984.

10 *NZPD*, 12 June 1984, vol.456, p.254 (Harrison).

11 *NZPD*, 11 June 1984, vol.456, p.257, Nuclear Free New Zealand Bill, Introduction (Thomson).

12 Ibid., p.264 (Clark).

13 Ibid., p.271 (Birch).

14 Ibid., p.269 (Rowling).

15 *NZPD*, 12 June 1984, vol.456, Nuclear Free New Zealand Bill, Introduction, p.317 (Prebble).

16 Sue Wood, personal communication, 19 October 2018.

17 Both parties used dots on their electoral rolls to highlight supporters, and to ensure these people all got to the poll.

18 Sue Wood, personal communication.

19 Barry Gustafson, *His Way: A Biography of Robert Muldoon*, Auckland University Press, Auckland, 2000, p.375.

Acronyms and Abbreviations

$	Unless otherwise specified, these are New Zealand dollars.
ACC	Accident Compensation Corporation
AGM	Annual General Meeting
AI	Amnesty International
ALRANZ	Abortion Law Association of New Zealand
ANZAC	Australian and New Zealand Army Corps. Anzac Day in New Zealand is the major remembrance day for servicemen and women who have died in active service
ANZUS	Australia, New Zealand and United States Security Treaty (1951)
ASC	Abortion Supervisory Committee
BPW	Business and Professional Women
CAG	Controller and Auditor General
CEC	Caucus Economic Committee
CER	NZ–Australia Closer Economic Relations
CHOGM	Commonwealth Heads of Government Meeting
CIB	Criminal Investigation Branch of the New Zealand Police
COW	Committee on Women
CPA	Commonwealth Parliamentary Association
CPI	Consumer Price Index
CS&A	Contraception, Sterilisation and Abortion
CSSO	Combined State Services Organisation
DOL	Department of Labour
DPB	Domestic Purposes Benefit
DSW	Department of Social Welfare
EEC	European Economic Community
EEZ	Exclusive Economic Zone
FOL	Federation of Labour
FPP	First Past the Post voting system based on seats won in an election
GDP	Gross Domestic Product
GNP	Gross National Product
GP	General Practitioner: doctor who provides primary health care
GST	Goods and Services Tax: added-value tax in New Zealand

HART	Halt All Racist Tours
HRC	Human Rights Commission
ICW	International Council of Women
ILO	International Labour Organisation
IMF	International Monetary Fund
IOP	Institute of Politics, Harvard University
IPU	Inter-Parliamentary Union
IWY	International Women's Year
IYC	International Year of the Child
IYDP	International Year of Disabled Persons
JP	Justice of the Peace
MP	Member of Parliament
MWD	Ministry of Works and Development
MWWL	Māori Women's Welfare League
NACEW	National Advisory Council on the Employment of Women
NCW	National Council of Women
NFZ	Nuclear Free Zone
NGO	Non-Government Organisation
NOW	National Organisation of Women
NPT	Non-Proliferation of Nuclear Weapons Treaty
NZOCGA	New Zealand Olympic and Commonwealth Association
NZAEA	New Zealand Atomic Energy Agency
NZRFU	New Zealand Rugby Football Union
OECD	Organisation for Economic Co-operation and Development
OPEC	Organisation of the Petroleum Exporting Countries
PEC	Public Expenditure Committee
PM	Prime Minister
RBNZ	Reserve Bank of New Zealand
RNZAF	Royal New Zealand Airforce
SIS	Security Intelligence Service
SOS	Sisters Overseas Service
SPELD	Specific Learning Difficulties New Zealand
SPNFZ	South Pacific Nuclear Free Zone

SPUC	Society for the Protection of the Unborn Child
SROW	Society for Research on Women
UN	United Nations
UNSNA	United Nations System of National Accounts
USSR	Union of Soviet Socialist Republics
VAT	Value Added Tax
WEA	Workers' Educational Association
WEL	Women's Electoral Lobby
WONAAC	Women's National Abortion Action Campaign
YWCA	Young Women's Christian Association

New Zealand's Political Structure, 1975–1984

FPP Electoral System

New Zealand has a single House of Parliament, situated in Wellington. From 1975–1984 a Member of Parliament (MP) contested a First Past the Post (FPP) General Election.

Political candidates stood for constituencies (also called electorates, or seats in Parliament).

An independent Electoral Boundaries Commission was convened every five years. The permanent members were independent public servants (e.g. the Surveyor General or the Chief Government Statistician). The commission followed prescribed population quotas to redraw electoral (constituency) boundaries.

The person with the highest number of votes in each constituency became the MP. The political party with the highest number of seats become the government. The parties represented in Parliament between 1975 and 1984 were National, Labour and Social Credit.

National Party Organisation

The National Party was organised nationally, regionally (by 'divisions') and locally. In the Raglan and Waipā electorates, there were branches of the Party in most settlements. They canvassed for membership, researched and moved remits for consideration at regional and national level, fed back sentiments and concerns from the grass roots, and organised public meetings and appointments for me.

The branches belonged to the Party at electorate level. The electorate chose delegates for the divisional and national conference, representatives from the electorate belonged to the Divisional Executive, and in turn, the divisional conferences selected representatives for the Party's Dominion Council and Executive. There was a president of the Party elected by all delegates to the annual conference, and the Party organisation was led by the general director.

Parliamentary Structures

Caucus

The caucus is the regular meeting of all the MPs of a particular party. The government caucus chooses their leader, who is then the Prime Minister. There are caucus subject committees.

Parliament

Parliament is chaired by the Speaker, an MP appointed by Parliament. The Clerk is Parliament's chief executive, and advises the Speaker on parliamentary law and procedure, consisting of the Standing Orders of Parliament, and guided by previous Speaker's rulings.

Order Paper

The daily agenda for the work of Parliament was contained in an Order Paper. This advised the business for the day, including notices of motion, select committee reports, and the Bills for debate in an order prioritised by the government. It contained the questions for oral answer, and replies to written questions.

Governor-General

The Governor-General has what are called 'reserve powers' in the New Zealand constitutional structure. Governors-General appoint the Prime Minister who has a majority of support after an election. They can also dismiss a Prime Minister, or not comply with a Prime Minister's request for a new election. If they do agree to this, then they dissolve Parliament and call for new elections. No legislation can become law without the signed assent of the Governor-General.

Confidence and Supply

A government may remain in office provided they do not lose a vote on issues of 'confidence' or 'supply'. At the beginning of each parliamentary year, in the first debate, it was usual for the Leader of the Opposition to move a motion of no confidence in the government. 'Supply' is the word used for budgetary policies of the government, and a vote lost on 'supply' could cause an election.

Cabinet

MPs who are appointed as ministers of government agencies or business by the Prime Minister. They meet every Monday.

Executive Council

The Executive Council advises the Governor-General. All members of Cabinet are members of the Executive Council.

Bills

Proposed legislation is introduced into Parliament by government ministers. After an initial debate, it is sent to a select committee, who will usually call for public submissions on the issues. After hearing all submissions, the public are excluded, and the committee takes advice from legal counsel and departmental and legislative department advisers, and 'deliberates' on each section of the Bill, agreeing, by majority, any amendments on the original. The amended Bill is then reported back to Parliament, with amendments that must be moved during a 'committee' stage debate. Both the government and Opposition can move these amendments. The amended Bill then has a second and third reading, before it is sent to the Executive Council.

Private Member's Bill

This is a proposed law change introduced by an MP who is not a Cabinet minister. If an Opposition MP introduced such a Bill, Standing Orders provided it would not have government support in the the first reading, because its implementation would involve a budgetary appropriation –a usual tool for stopping all but 'conscience issue' Bills from the Opposition.

Conscience Votes

MPs are not subject to party control and cast their votes as individuals.

Maiden Speech

A maiden speech is the first speech an MP makes in the House in the Address in Reply debate, loosely based on the programme the government has laid out in the Speech from the Throne at the beginning of the parliamentary year.

Parliamentary Select Committees

These are made up of a small number of MPs from different parties, usually specialising in a sector, to deal with particular issues, proposed laws or special inquiries.

Glossary of Māori Words

hapū	kinship group, clan, tribe, sub-tribe
hīkoi	walk, march
iwi	extended kinship group, tribe, nation, people
Kīngitanga	King Movement which developed in the 1850s, with its strongest support coming from Tainui
kōkako	blue-wattled crow
kōkiri	promoting, advocating
kuia	elderly woman, female elder
Māori	indigenous people of New Zealand
mana	authority, prestige, honour
marae	central area of village and its buildings
pā	stockaded village
Pākehā	New Zealander of European descent
papakāinga	original home, village
poukai	King Movement gathering
tapu	to be sacred, prohibited, set apart
tangata whenua	local people, indigenous people
te kohanga reo	pre-school centres for Māori language immersion
te reo Māori	the Māori language
urupā	burial ground
waka	canoe
whare	residence
whenua	land; also afterbirth

Acknowledgements

I am grateful to the people who with their insights and precision have made these nine years of research and writing companionable. Katherine O'Regan and Sue Wood added to the electorate and National Party reflections with their suggestions. Sue Bradford pointed out where the old First Past the Post electoral system needed to be explained, and asked key questions. Leila Tayebi honed in on terms we all take for granted in the Commonwealth tradition of Parliament and elections. Grant Duncan, Liese Groot and Meena Shivas gave feedback and encouragement from the first draft of early chapters.

AUT University's Faculty Research fund supported some travel and accommodation in Wellington to visit the Alexander Turnbull Library, as well as a period of research leave to make progress. My students and colleagues at AUT have been supportive and encouraging across the years of research and writing.

I am deeply grateful to the team of librarians in the Reading Room of the Alexander Turnbull Library who did all possible to assist my steady progress through my archives. Special thanks to Katrina Hatherley on the National Library staff, who was there for coffee when I needed a break. My thanks to staff at the Parliamentary Library, especially Bessie Sutherland; and to the Auckland Harbour Board archivist and Hamilton Public library staff.

I had research assistance from Dr Sue Bradford and Josephine Stewart-TeWhiu. Gwen Ferguson assisted with hours of transcription. Jude Tewnion went through the Fairfax collection of photographs for me: a significant task, as the material had not been digitised. She used spreadsheets of the captions to track the photos. Geoff Minchin, Tony Friedlander, Don McKinnon, Hugh Templeton and Sue Wood kindly responded to my queries and added to what I knew. My friends Maggie Eyre and Jenny Tucker were there for the long haul.

My dear cousin Leslie and her husband Phil have offered their home to me for a week over several years. I was completely protected from interruptions, and on each visit made serious progress in my writing.

The early years of working on this book coincided with my father's diagnosis of brain cancer, and I spent 14 months helping to care for him before his death in 2014. Often my mother Audrey and I would pack a picnic, get Dad in the car, and go for a drive through the old Raglan and Waipā electorates. We would tell stories of earlier years as we went – my father's business with many farmers, my mother's sports participation, my electorate work, and the families in these areas 40 years ago.

I have had very particular support from my brother Gavin. He lives in Melbourne but has crossed the Tasman most months over these years to free me for a weekend to work on this book, and to help care for our parents.

I have known publisher Bridget Williams for more than 30 years, and I knew I could bring the book to her and work with her great team: Tom Rennie, Julia Wells, Madeleine Rashbrooke, Caren Wilton, Sarah Bennett, Tim Vaughan-Sanders, Tina Delceg and Nancy Swarbrick. My thanks to Jo Bailey for her cover and page designs. Editor Jane Parkin has been a joy to work with, and my students enjoyed seeing their professor's marked-up manuscript, recognising we all need help to reward the reader.

Special thanks are due to Gillian, Ed and Chris, who cared for my back, neck, shoulders and arms to keep them functioning through the years at the computer.

Index